TRAVELER'S GUIDE TO

MEXICAN CAMPING

Explore Mexico With Your RV Or Tent

Mike and Terri
Church

ROLLING HOMES PRESS

Published by
Rolling Homes Press
P.O. Box 2099
Kirkland, WA 98083-2099

Printed in the United States of America
First Printing 1997

Publisher's Cataloging in Publication

Church, Mike, 1951-
    Traveler's guide to Mexican camping : explore Mexico with your RV or tent / Mike and Terri Church
    p. cm.
    Includes index.
    Preassigned LCCN: 97-91646
    ISBN 0-9652968-1-4

    1. Mexico—Guidebooks. 2. Camping—Mexico—Guidebooks. I. Church, Terri. II. Title.

F1209.C48 1997   917.204/836—dc21

WARNING, DISCLOSURE, AND COMMUNICATION WITH THE AUTHORS AND PUBLISHER

Half the fun of travel is the unexpected, and self-guided camping travel can produce much in the way of unexpected pleasures, and alternately, complications and problems. This book is designed to increase the pleasures of Mexican camping and reduce the number of unexpected problems you may encounter. You can help ensure a smooth trip by doing additional advance research, planning ahead, and exercising caution when appropriate. There can be no guarantee that your trip will be trouble free.

Although the authors and publisher have done their best to ensure that the information presented in this book was correct at the time of publication they do not assume and hereby disclaim any liability to any party for any loss or damage caused by errors, omissions, or any other cause.

In a book like this it is inevitable that there will be omissions or mistakes, especially as things do change over time. If you find inaccuracies we would like to hear about them so that they can be corrected in future editions. We would also like to hear about your enjoyable experiences. If you come upon an outstanding campground or destination please let us know, those kinds of things may also find their way to future versions of the guide. You can reach us by mail at:

Rolling Homes Press
P.O. Box 2099
Kirkland, WA 98083-2099

TABLE OF CONTENTS

INTRODUCTION 9

CHAPTER 1
WHY CAMP MEXICO? 13
Some Possible Itineraries................................... 17

CHAPTER 2
DETAILS, DETAILS, DETAILS.. 31

CHAPTER 3
CROSSING THE BORDER 60

CHAPTER 4
HOW TO USE THE DESTINATION CHAPTERS............................ 75

CHAPTER 5
THE NORTHERN WEST COAST:
NOGALES TO TEACAPÁN 82
  Introduction..................................... 83
  Selected Cities and Their Campgrounds
    Álamos...................................... 87
    Bahía Kino 90
    Culiacán 95
    Guaymas and San Carlos 97
    Los Mochis Area........................ 101
      Las Glorias 102
      Los Mochis............................. 103
    Magdalena and Santa Ana 105
    Mazatlán.................................. 106
    Navojoa................................... 114
    Teacapán 115

CHAPTER 6
THE CENTRAL WEST COAST:
SAN BLAS TO ACAPULCO..118
  Introduction..................................... 119
  Selected Cities and Their Campgrounds
    Acapulco 123
    Ixtapa/Zihuatanejo 129
    Manzanillo and the Coast North 131
      Manzanillo 131
      Melaque/San Patricio 133

Boca Beach 134
Chamela 135
Pérula 136
Playa Azul........................ 137
Puerto Vallarta and the Coast North 138
Puerto Vallarta 142
Bucerías........................ 143
La Cruz........................ 145
Sayulita........................ 145
Lo de Marcos........................ 146
Rincón de Guayabitos 148
Peñita de Jaltemba........................ 153
Miramar........................ 153
Playa Amor........................ 154
San Blas........................ 155

CHAPTER 7

THE INTERIOR OF MEXICO **156**
Introduction........................ 157
Selected Cities and Their Campgrounds
Aguascalientes 163
Chihuahua Area 164
Chihuahua 165
Ciudad Camargo 165
Cuauhtemoc 166
Ciudad Valles........................ 166
Creel........................ 168
Cuernavaca........................ 171
Durango 178
Guadalajara 179
Guanajuato 186
Los Azufres 188
Matehuala........................ 190
Mexico City (Ciudad de México) 191
Monterrey........................ 201
Morelia........................ 204
Pachuca........................ 206
Pátzcuaro........................ 207
Puebla 210
Querétaro 211
Saltillo........................ 213
San Luis Potosí 214
San Miguel de Allende 216
Tepic 218
Tequisquiapan........................ 220
Tlaxcala........................ 222
Toluca 223
Torreón/Gómez Palacio 225
Uruapan........................ 226

Valle de Bravo 228
Zacatecas... 229

CHAPTER 8
THE EAST OR GULF COAST...**232**
Introduction... 233
Selected Cities and Their Campgrounds
Agua Dulce 237
Catemaco 237
Ciudad Victoria... 239
Emerald Coast/Nautla 242
Tampico 245
Veracruz.. 246
Villahermosa.. 248

CHAPTER 9
CHIAPAS AND OAXACA **252**
Introduction... 253
Selected Cities and Campgrounds
Arriaga 257
Oaxaca 257
The Oaxaca Coast... 261
Bahías de Huatulco 261
Puerto Angel 263
Puerto Escondido 265
Palenque.. 267
San Cristóbal de las Casas 271
Tamazulapan... 273
Tehuantepec 274
Tuxtla Gutiérrez... 276

CHAPTER 10
THE YUCATÁN PENINSULA...**278**
Introduction... 279
Selected Cities and Their Campgrounds
Campeche.. 283
Cancún 284
Chetumal... 286
Chichén Itzá 289
Isla Aguada 291
Mérida... 292
Quintana Roo Coast South of Cancún 296
Paa Mul 298
Puerto Morelos... 299
Akumal.. 300
Uxmal... 304

8

CHAPTER 11
THE NORTHERN GULF OF CALIFORNIA **308**
Introduction.. 309
Selected Cities and Their Campgrounds
Golfo de Santa Clara.. 313
Puerto Peñasco.. 315
San Felipe.. 322

CHAPTER 12
NORTHERN BAJA PENINSULA **332**
Introduction.. 333
Selected Cities and Their Campgrounds
Bahía de Los Ángeles 339
Cataviña 341
El Rosario 343
Ensenada 345
Estero Beach 349
Punta Banda 351
Rosarito.. 353
San Quintín Area 355
Colonia Vicente Guerrero 356
San Quintín 357
Santo Tomás 359
Tecate... 361

CHAPTER 13
SOUTHERN BAJA PENINSULA...**364**
Introduction 365
Selected Cities and Their Campgrounds
Bahía Concepción.. 369
Ciudad Constitución 374
Guerrero Negro 376
La Paz 379
Loreto... 384
Los Barriles Area 387
Los Barriles 388
La Ribera.. 389
San Antonio.. 389
Los Cabos 390
Mulegé 395
Puerto Escondido 397
San Ignacio 398
Santa Rosalía... 400
Todos Santos.. 402
Vizcaíno Junction 403

INDEX..**405**

INTRODUCTION

Some five years ago we decided to put careers on hold and spend some time exploring the world and ourselves. Work was fun, but it didn't give us much time for anything else. We thought that a year or two traveling, relaxing, and getting in shape certainly wouldn't be wasted time.

We bought an RV and explored the U.S. and parts of nearby Canada. During our travels we pursued interests ranging from running marathons, to visiting all of the National Parks, fishing, hiking, studying languages, and lots of reading. We visited almost everyone we knew around the country. After a time, however, we began to feel that the U.S. was beginning to pale. The cities, highways, countryside and culture were all becoming somewhat over-familiar.

The obvious answer was some foreign travel. After very little research the destination was equally obvious - Mexico. Mexico offered a wonderful winter climate and a fascinating and very different culture. Best of all, we could visit Mexico in our own RV and spend even less than we were spending in the U.S.

As is our habit we began to research our new destination. We found lots of information aimed at the airplane-riding tourist. A multitude of guidebooks told us about sights, restaurants, and hotels. Camping information, however, was scarce.

We found two kinds of camping guidebooks. The first gave campground basics. City by city they would give a short listing of available campgrounds, scanty details about services offered, a short description of the campground location (something like "SW of the City"). Often there would be a short notation (Not Visited). The other kind of guide was short on details but long on anecdotes. These guides didn't tell us much about what to expect but they sure made it sound interesting. Unfortunately, they were all over five years old.

Armed with our guidebooks we headed south for Mexico. It seemed like an excellent idea to spend a few days at a campground near the border to pick up some invaluable first-hand advice. Where was the best place to buy insurance, what are the popular destinations, how are the roads? We found a nice place just minutes from a popular border crossing and began to ask around.

Even with the help of the entertainment director of the campground we could find no one in that 300 space campground with much Mexico experience. We did get a lot of advice however. We heard that the roads were terrible, the tolls outrageous, the gas hard to find, and the bandidos active. The overwhelming opinion of people in that campground was that it just didn't make any sense to travel any farther south. Why not just settle down for the winter right where we were.

Armed with what little information and advice we could scare up we plunged across the border and into Mexico. The border area was intimidating. There were lots of people, lots of trash, terrible traffic, and friendly but still slightly scary Mexican border officials. As we headed south away from the border things became somewhat calmer. The traffic thinned considerably, the roads were fine, there was much less trash. We began to have a chance to look around us and enjoy the unfolding countryside.

There was some problem finding the campground that first night. All of our guidebooks agreed that there was one. Some of the directions for finding it were even somewhat similar. The town had obviously grown a lot since our guidebooks were written. Stops at several gas stations yielded few people who even knew what a trailer park was, let alone that there was one in their own town. We finally unhooked our tow car and did a street-by-street search.

That first campground was like many we've visited since. It was a calm haven and a fantastic source of information. It was full of people who were more than happy to tell us where to shop, what to see, and even how to find the next campground on the way south. Their enthusiasm and love of what they were doing was in direct contrast to the people we'd met north of the border.

For the next four months, and for four months each year since that time we've continued to explore Mexico. We've driven most of the major routes, visited every region, and met hundreds of people who return year after year.

The decision to write a decent guidebook to Mexico's campgrounds came during that first trip. One day we had mechanical trouble on the road. Getting the rig fixed was easy, but it delayed us. We found ourselves approaching a large unfamiliar coastal city long after dark. Our out-of-date guidebooks showed two campgrounds. We searched for them for three hours. After talking with at least a dozen people we became almost certain that we had located the campground sites, unfortunately both were occupied by almost-new apartment complexes. Finally, in desperation, we decided to pull into a side street and inconspicuously (not easy in a big motor home) wait out the night. When we stepped out to scout the immediate neighborhood we were amazed to find that we had, entirely by luck, parked just outside the gates of the only campground in town. It was not even listed in the guidebooks we carried. We didn't need any more proof that a new camping guidebook would find an enthusiastic following.

Traveler's Guide to Mexican Camping is our second camping guidebook. The first was the very similar *Traveler's Guide to European Camping*. We actually started writing the Mexico book long before beginning the Europe book and we've spent a much longer time on the road researching it. Research always seemed like more fun than writing so we have put off publishing for several years. We've visited each of the campgrounds listed here, we've spend the night at the majority of them, and we've lived several months at more than one. We love Mexico and camping there. So here's the best guide we can write about camping in Mexico, you can be sure that this won't be the last edition.

CHAPTER 1

WHY CAMP MEXICO?

The U.S. - Mexico border is like no other border on earth. Between the two countries there are huge contrasts in culture, language, wealth, lifestyle, political systems, topography, and climate. All of this means that Mexico is a fascinating place to visit. We think that driving your own rig and staying in campgrounds is the best way to do it. We hope that with this book in hand you will think so too.

MEXICO IS A LAND OF AMAZING VARIETY

Most people who visit Mexico probably climb on a jet and spend a week or two at one of five or six Mexican beach resorts. These places are world-renown – we've all heard of Cancún, Acapulco, Puerto Vallarta, Ixtapa/Zihuatanejo, and Cabo San Lucas. These are great places to visit and the best way to do so is in your own vehicle. They all offer good campgrounds and have their own sections in this book. But there are lots of other attractions in this fascinating country. The vacation traveler who only visits the tourist cities misses almost all of the best Mexico has to offer. Here's a very incomplete listing of some of the things to see and do in Mexico.

The beach resorts are on the coast, of course. But there is lots more coastline in Mexico, the country has a huge coastline. Mexico's beaches are beautiful, mostly empty, and generally sport truly superior weather. Some of the best free camping you'll ever see is along the beaches of Mexico's Baja and west coasts. You could write an entire book just about Mexico's beaches, in fact, it's been done.

If beaches aren't your thing don't despair. The interior of Mexico is full of attractions. Many *norteamericanos* (Mexican term for Canadian and U.S. citizens, also known as *gringos*) are drawn to the superior climate and cultural attractions of Guadalajara, Lake Chapala, San Miguel de Allende, Álamos, Guanajuato, and Cuernavaca. All have populations of permanent residents from the United States and Canada.

Bustling Mexico City is now or will soon be the largest city in the world, it is easy to visit from nearby campgrounds. Less well known colonial or neoclassical cities like Querétaro, San Luis Potosí, Zacatecas, Aguascalientes and Oaxaca also make fascinating destinations.

Perhaps you want to explore, to get off the beaten path. There are enough remote rugged byways in Mexico to keep you busy for years. Consider the desert roads of the Baja Peninsula, the hiking trails of the Copper Canyon, and the often impassable jungle tracks of Lacandón Chiapas and the Yucatán. The campgrounds listed in this book aren't remote, but some make good bases or jumping-off points for more rugged locales.

Probably most of us have limited contact with the Mexican people who have settled into the United States and Canada. Traveling in your own vehicle and living off the local economy will give you lots of chances to meet people from all social classes. Many of these folks will have had little contact with norteamericanos. We're confident that you will be amazed by the attitudes and abilities of these people who many of us would consider disadvantaged and downtrodden. As a whole you'll find the Mexican people to by friendly, cheerful, helpful and very family oriented. The chance to meet and understand the people of Mexico, who comprise a growing segment of the population of our own countries, is one of the best reasons of all to visit Mexico.

Pre-Columbian Mesoamerican archeological sites are scattered throughout the country. If you are fascinated by history you'll love Palenque (everyone's favorite), Teotihuacán, Monte Albán, Chichén Itzá, Uxmal and photogenic Tulúm. These sites are only an introduction, there must be at least a hundred major archeological attractions in various stages of preservation and reconstruction in Mexico. In fact, there are so many sites that you may even discover one yourself.

The Catholic religion has been heavily involved in Mexico since the very beginning of the Spanish conquest. For this reason you will find lots of religious buildings throughout the county. Probably most interesting are the churches, cathedrals, and monasteries of what are often called the "colonial cities" and the missions of the Baja Peninsula and northwestern Mexico. It can be rewarding to visit the remote missions of the Baja or study the architecture of Mexican churches.

Mexico is well-known as a shopping paradise, particularly for crafts. Well represented in the municipal markets, *tianguis* (open-air markets), and shops are pottery, clothes, furniture, metalwork, rugs, hammocks, baskets, masks, *alebrijes* (fantastic wooden or papier-mâché animals), and lots more. It is much easier to bring your treasures home in your own vehicle than in a suitcase.

For outdoors-oriented sports types the Baja Peninsula and west coast offer some of the best deep-sea fishing in the world. Scuba and skin divers love the Cancún coast, particularly Cozumel. Sail-borders congregate near Los Barriles on the Baja. The entire Baja west coast is a surfing paradise. Ocean kayakers travel the length of the Baja east coast. Hikers join the Tarahumaras in the remote Copper Canyon. Bird hunting has long been popular in Sonora and Sinaloa. These are just a sampling of the available outdoor pleasures.

MEXICO IS EASY TO VISIT

There can be no foreign country that is easier to visit than Mexico. You need simply drive your rig to one of many border towns, spend an afternoon securing Mexican insurance and doing last-minute shopping, and then cross the border the next morning. Within a few hours you'll be far from the hectic border area and will reach your first night's stop well before dark.

For your visit to Mexico you'll find there are few formalities and little documentation needed. You'll need little more than the camping vehicle you use at home and documentation showing that you are a U.S. or Canadian resident. There is no need for a passport or visa. There are now procedures in place when you cross the border to insure that you bring your vehicle back out of Mexico, they don't want you to sell it without paying the proper taxes. All together border formalities seldom take over a half-hour, the details are covered in Chapter 3 - Crossing The Border.

MEXICO IS INEXPENSIVE

There is no doubt that it costs less to travel in Mexico than it does in the U.S. or Canada. The actual costs vary from year to year, they depend upon the value of the peso in relation to the U.S. and Canadian dollars. It seems that the Mexican government likes to escalate the value of the peso during election years, then allow it to float to a more reasonable level immediately afterwards.

When camping you live off a different economy than jet-flying tourists. You'll shop with Mexican citizens for food and gasoline. About the only thing you'll buy that is priced for norteamericanos is your campsite. Even these tend to be less expensive than those outside Mexico, and certainly they are in much more attractive and exotic locations.

MEXICO HAS ALL OF THE SERVICES YOU NEED

Modern Mexico is a far cry from what it was just 10 years ago. There has been massive consumer-oriented investment. In larger towns almost everyone shops at huge modern supermarkets. Gasoline stations are popping up everywhere, they have unleaded gasoline and diesel. Campgrounds are located conveniently in most localities where you'll want to stay, and with this book you'll have no problem finding them. Most have full hookups so you can be very comfortable.

MEXICO HAS GOOD ROADS, AND THEY GET BETTER EACH YEAR

During the last 10 years there has been a huge road-building effort undertaken in Mexico. Modern super-highways now link most sections of the country. Most of these, unfortunately, are toll highways but there are usually free alternatives. Take a look at the Toll Roads section of the Details, Details, Details chapter. Certainly you'll never have to drive on a gravel road unless you want to get off the beaten path.

MEXICO HAS WONDERFUL WEATHER

Mexico's weather is the main reason many people head south. During the winter you can easily find tropical weather in Mexico. If hot weather doesn't appeal just head for the highlands. Guadalajara and Cuernavaca are both said to have spring-time weather year-round.

Mexico can also be a good summer destination. If you want to get away from the sweltering humidity of the central United States just head for colonial Mexico. There you'll find little humidity and warm but comfortable summer temperatures.

MEXICO IS A LAND OF ADVENTURE

Has traveling the freeways of the U.S. and Canada begun to bore you? Would you like to actually use that four-wheel-drive on your new rig? Do you dream of a campsite with no-one else around? Would you like to spend some time in a place where the nearest telephone is a full day's travel away? If you answer yes to any of these questions then Mexico is the place for you.

This is not to say that you will find adventure if you are not looking for it. Travelers sticking to the beaten path of Mex. 15 down the west coast will hardly know they're not in the U.S. But venture off the beaten track and Mexico can indeed be a land of adventure.

Consider the following. The people speak a different language than you do, often it is not Spanish. There may be freeways but there are also thousands of miles of back roads and jeep tracks. Much of the population in remote areas is composed of Indians living in near stone-age conditions. Many of the people you will meet off the beaten track are almost entirely isolated from modern culture.

The truth is that even if you stick to major roads and camp only in formal campgrounds your visit to Mexico is likely to be an adventure you'll never want to forget.

SAFETY AND POLITICAL STABILITY

Probably the main reason that Mexican campgrounds aren't overrun with folks from north of the border is that people have fears about their safety in Mexico. Remember that the unfamiliar is often scary. People from Europe think that the United States is one of the most violent places in the world, yet most U.S. citizens have little contact with any kind of violence.

We are convinced that Mexico is no more dangerous than the United States or Canada. During our travels we have never been the victims of any kind of violence. Nor have we ever had anything stolen from us (except perhaps some change at gas stations). We've talked to many people and few of them have ever had any problems either.

Just like in your own home country you must take certain precautions. We talk about some of these in the Safety and Security section of Chapter 2.

Another perceived problem in Mexico is lack of political stability. We often hear on the news that there has been political violence or that there are demonstrators on the streets of Mexico City. The truth is that Mexican politics are different than the ones we are accustomed to. As a traveler you can easily avoid this type of political unrest if you want to. After all, your home is on wheels and any type of political violence is front page news so you should have plenty of warning.

MEXICO OFFERS LOTS TO DO - SOME POSSIBLE ITINERARIES

Probably the best way to actually show you what Mexico has to offer is to outline a few popular expeditions. Thousands of people each year follow itineraries similar to the Baja Peninsula and Down the West Coast ones outlined below. The Grand Coastal Tour is popular with travelers who have the time to visit both the Yucatán Peninsula and the west coast. If you are interested in Mexican history and culture you'll love the Colonial Mexico itinerary. The time given for each itinerary is the bare minimum required to do the entire trip, but each can be shortened by turning back north before reaching the southernmost point. Each can also be easily stretched to three or four months by adding days in the destinations mentioned or by making side trips. As you review the itineraries you should use our index at the back of the book to find more detailed information.

THE BAJA PENINSULA
(17 days)

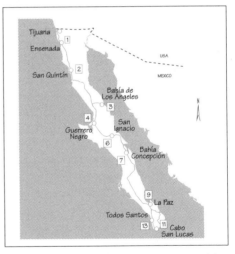

The 1,060 mile (1,731 km) long Mex. 1 stretches the entire length of the Baja Peninsula, from Tijuana in the north to Cabo San Lucas at the far southern cape. The two-lane highway gives access to some of the most remote and interesting country in the world including lots of desert and miles and miles of deserted beaches. Outdoorsmen love this country for four-wheeling, boating, fishing, beachcombing, and just plain enjoying the sunshine.

This proposed itinerary takes 17 days and allows you to see the entire length of the peninsula. There are layover days at Guerrero Negro, Bahía Concepción, La Paz, and Cabo San Lucas. Many travel days require only a morning of driving leaving lots of time to relax and explore.

The most tempting modification to this itinerary will be to spend more time at each stop. There are also many additional stopover points along this route, just take a look at the campground map at the beginning of each one of our campground chapters. Finally, it is possible to take a ferry from either La Paz or Santa Rosalía to the Mexican west coast where you can turn north for home or head south for more fun.

Day 1 - Tijuana to Ensenada - 67 miles (109 km), 2 hours driving time - This first day you cross the border at Tijuana. You probably won't even have to stop when entering Mexico because vehicle permits aren't required on the Baja. There's a four-lane toll road that follows the coast all the way to Ensenada. Once you arrive you will park and visit the *Migración* (Immigration) office near the entrance to town to get the tourist permits that are required since you will be in Mexico over 72 hours. You completed the drive to Ensenada before noon so there's plenty of time to look around town and pick up some groceries at one of the large modern supermarkets. Instead of spending the night at a campground in town you decide to stay at the beautiful Estero Beach Hotel/Resort campground beside the ocean a few miles south of Ensenada. You can celebrate by having dinner at the excellent hotel restaurant.

Day 2 - Ensenada to San Quintín - 116 miles (190 km), 3 hours driving time - This will be another short day so there's really no hurry to get started. A few miles south of Ensenada take the side trip to La Bufadora blowhole where waves spurt into the air at a point along the rocky coast. Back on the main road you pass through rolling hills with the countryside getting dryer as you head south. At San Quintín you have a choice of campgrounds, try the Old Mill Trailer Park if you want full hookups and a restaurant or maybe the El Pabellón to sample a simple ejido-run campground with miles of windswept beach out front.

Day 3 - San Quintín to Bahía de Los Angeles - 219 miles (358 km), 7 hours driving time - This is a longer day's drive so get a fairly early start. You'll want to stop and explore the cactus and rock fields in the Cataviña area before leaving Mex. 1 and driving east on a good paved road to Bahía de Los Angeles for your first glimpse of the Gulf of California. There's not a lot to the town itself, perhaps this is a good opportunity to head north of town and free camp along the water. If you have a small boat you might give the fishing a try. This is also great kayaking water.

Day 4 - Bahía de Los Angeles to Guerrero Negro - 121 miles (198 km), 3.50 hours driving time - Today's destination is back on the other side of the peninsula, the salt producing company town of Guerrero Negro. You'll spend two nights here because you want to visit the Gray Whale birthing lagoon (Scammon's Lagoon) south of town. Spend the first night at the Malarrimo R.V. Park and visit their well-known restaurant. The second night you can spend at the primitive camping area right next to the lagoon after a day in a panga on the lagoon with the whales.

Day 6 - Guerrero Negro to San Ignacio - 89 miles (145 km), 2.5 hours driving time - San Ignacio is a true date-palm oasis in the middle of desert country. Perhaps by the time you arrive the El Padrino will have finished their new campground in the palms. If not their old one will do, before dark stroll down to the plaza at the center of town to do some people watching and take a look at the old mission church.

Day 7 - San Ignacio to Bahía Concepción - 95 miles (155 km), 3 hours driving

time - Today, once again, you return to the Sea of Cortez side of the peninsula. You'll pass two interesting towns en route, Santa Rosalía and Mulegé. Neither has much room for big rigs so don't drive into either of these little towns. At Santa Rosalía you might leave your rig along the highway and take a stroll to see Eiffel's church. You'll probably have a chance to explore Mulegé later since it is quite close to the evening's destination at Bahía Concepción. Many people decide to end their journey at this point and go no further since the oceanside camping along beautiful Bahía Concepción is many folk's idea of camping paradise. We'll assume that you decide to only stay for two nights. Hah!

Day 9 - Bahía Concepción to La Paz - 291 miles (470 km), 8 hours driving time - Since you are all rested up after that time along the Bahía you decide to get an early start and blast on through all the way to La Paz. Don't forget to drive into Loreto for a quick look around, this was the first permanent Spanish settlement on the peninsula. You'll have to ignore the golf course too, even though you'll see people teeing off as you pass.

You will find your progress along the coast to be quite scenic but slow, especially as you climb up and over the Sierra Gigante, but once on the plains to the west the roads are flat and straight allowing you to make good time. A late arrival in La Paz is not a problem because there are lots of campgrounds to choose from. You can take it easy the next day and explore this most typically Mexican of Baja cities.

Day 11 - La Paz to Cabo San Lucas - 145 miles (236 km), 4 hours driving time - Today you will arrive in the true tourist's Baja. Take the long route to the Cape area by following Mex. 1 around the east side of the Sierra de la Laguna. You'll have made reservations at one of the campgrounds near Cabo San Lucas to ensure a place to base yourself. Consider yourself pre-warned that the Cape area probably won't appeal as a place to spend much time after all you've seen on the way south.

Day 13 - Cabo San Lucas to Todos Santos - 50 miles (81 km), 1.5 hours driving time - A short drive north along the west coast on Mex. 19 will bring you to San Pedrito R.V. Park on the coast south of Todos Santos. This is an excellent place to either spend several weeks along a beautiful Pacific beach or to prepare yourself for the trip north.

Day 14 through 17 Todos Santos to Tijuana - 963 miles (1,572 km), 28 hours driving time - You really have two choices for the return to the border. Many folks catch a ferry from La Paz to Topolobampo near Los Mochis and then drive north on four-lane Mex. 15 to cross the border at Nogales near Tucson, Arizona. Others simply drive back the way they've come. By putting in decently long days of driving you could make the trip in four days with overnight stops at Ciudad Constitución (254 miles), San Ignacio (255 miles), and El Rosario (304 miles).

GRAND COASTAL TOUR
(also Chiapas and Oaxaca)
(45 days)

The Grand Coastal Tour is a fascinating way to spend the winter. You travel down Mexico's eastern Gulf Coast, spend some time on the Yucatán Peninsula near Cancún, penetrate the fascinating Indian regions of Chiapas and Oaxaca, and then finish by tracing the popular west coast of Mexico.

Make no mistake, this is a **long trip**. Forty-five days is adequate but a full two to three months would be much more fun. A forty-five day schedule gives one day layovers for relaxing or sightseeing on the Costa Esmeralda and at Uxmal, Mérida, Cancún, Palenque, San Cristóbal de las Casas, Oaxaca, Puerto Escondido, Acapulco, Manzanillo, and Puerto Vallarta. Six days are set aside to relax along the Caribbean coast south of Cancún. This isn't really much because on many days you will drive long hours and on layover days there is lots of sightseeing to do. In all you will drive more than 4,600 miles (7,500 km) inside Mexico.

It is easy to modify this itinerary to make it shorter or longer. One easy modification would be to cut out the Yucatán, Chiapas and Oaxaca by cutting across the Isthmus of Tehuantepec on Mex. 185. This would cut the trip down to 22 days, but it would also mean that you wouldn't visit three of the most interesting regions of Mexico. Better would be to drive directly to Palenque from Villahermosa and bypass only the Yucatán, reducing the trip to 27 days. Other modifications will be obvious to you after a little study, they would include numerous opportunities to head inland and visit colonial cities.

Day 1 - Reynosa to Ciudad Victoria - 197 miles (322 km), 6 hours - The first day's drive to Ciudad Victoria is conveniently short. The best crossing from the US is probably the new bridge near Pharr, Texas. It doesn't open until 10 AM, you should be there soon after so that you have plenty of time to get to Ciudad Victoria before dark. Border formalities shouldn't take more than an hour, especially if you've visited Sanborn's first to have your documentation prepared for an express crossing. From near the border follow Mex. 2 a few miles west toward Reynosa and then follow Mex. 97, Mex. 180, and Mex. 101 south to Ciudad Victoria. These are all decent two lane (except for a few miles of four-lane near Reynosa) free roads. Ciudad Victoria and the Victoria Trailer Park are a good, comfortable introduction to Mexico.

Day 2 - Ciudad Victoria to Tampico - 148 miles (242 km), 4 hours - This is a short driving day. Make a late departure from Ciudad Victoria and travel down

Mex. 85 to Tampico. You'll cross the Tropic of Cancer not long after your start. Follow the instructions we give for finding the Campestre Altamira to avoid driving in busy downtown Tampico.

Day 3 - Tampico to Costa Esmeralda - 209 miles (342 km), 7 hours - You may doubt that it will take you 7 hours to drive only 209 miles, and it may not! The roads in this section of Mexico are heavily traveled by trucks and need lots of repairs. If you happen to catch them after their almost-annual reconstruction you may cruise right through in a much shorter time, but don't count on it.

Once again you are on mostly two-lane free roads as you bypass Tampico and then follow Mex. 180 south. Make sure to bypass Tuxpan on the shortcut through Alamo. You'll probably find unavoidable heavy traffic through Poza Rica but it won't last long and soon you'll arrive at the much slower-paced Costa Esmeralda north of Nautla. If you are like us you'll decide you've earned at least one day's layover here. A good way to occupy your time if you tire of the beach is a visit to Papantla to see the Voladores or to the famous El Tajín archeological site with its Pyramid of the Niches.

Day 5 - Costa Esmeralda to Veracruz - 100 miles (164 km), 3 hours - This is a short drive down an increasingly tropical coast to Veracruz, one of Mexico's most historical cities. You'll pass Mexico's only nuclear reactor at Laguna Verde. North

TRAILER PARK QUINTA ALICIA ON THE COSTA ESMERALDA

of Veracruz you could make a decision that would cut at least two days off this trip. There is now a new very nice toll road that bypasses Veracruz and Catemaco. Many people now rip right on through to Rancho Hermanos Graham RV park north of Villahermosa. If you plan to do this make sure you make an early start and bring lots of money, the toll road is very expensive.

Day 6 - Veracruz to Catemaco - 105 miles (171 km), 3 hours - A short drive south on old Mex. 180 will bring you to the hill village of Catemaco. The short driving day will give you lots of time to wander this interesting little town, perhaps take a boat ride, and enjoy a good sleep in the cool mountain night air.

Day 7 - Catemaco to Villahermosa - 109 miles (178 km), 3 hours - The distance given for this day's drive is actually only to Rancho Hermanos Graham RV park. You may want to drive on to visit the La Venta Museum in Villahermosa. You can stay in Villahermosa or return to the RV park in the evening.

Day 8 - Villahermosa to Isla Aguada - 209 miles (341 km), 8 hours - We've added two hours to this day's driving time to account for a stop at the La Venta Museum in Villahermosa. The road into Villahermosa is almost all four-lane parkway, but after leaving town on Mex. 180 to the coast you'll find that the road narrows and the driving is much slower. Recently some bypasses have been constructed around a few of the villages on this route which does help some, but in others the road passes right through the center of the village. There's plenty of room and few vehicles but you must drive slowly and watch for kids, turkeys and pigs. There are now toll bridges across the lagoon mouths on this route, no ferry travel is required. Isla Aguada is another very small village, many people decide to spend several days enjoying the laid-back pace and walking along the beaches looking for shells.

Day 9 - Isla Aguada to Campeche - 104 miles (170 km), 3 hours - Follow Mex. 180 along a mostly deserted coastline to the old city of Campeche. Avoid the toll road that starts south of Campeche, it is expensive and won't save much time at all, our directions for finding the campground assume that you will arrive on the free road.

Day 10 - Campeche to Uxmal - 105 miles (171 km), 3 hours - Our favorite route between Campeche and Uxmal follows small back roads to the Edzná archeological site and then north on Mex. 261 to Camping Sacbe some 9 miles (15 km) south of Uxmal. In the evening attend the Sound and Light show at Uxmal, it is a great introduction to one of the most interesting Yucatán sites. You can spend the next day at Uxmal and at other nearby sites like Kabah and the Loltún Caves. Once again, you could easily spend several more days and still not see everything.

Day 12 - Uxmal to Mérida - 48 miles (79 km), 2 hours - Another short driving day will take you north to Mérida. Use the ring road to easily pass around to the north end of town and the Rainbow RV Park. Visits to central Mérida for sightseeing and shopping, to Celestún to see the flamingos, or perhaps to Progreso and the north coast will easily fill the next non-driving day.

Day 14 - Mérida to Chichén Itzá - 70 miles (115 km), 2.5 hours - After a short day's drive to Piste you have all afternoon to explore the Chichén Itzá site. Once again you have a choice of free or toll roads, we prefer the free road, it is much more interesting.

Day 15 - Chichén Itzá to Cancún - 122 miles (200 km), 3.5 hours - Follow the free road to Cancún (or the toll road if you're in a hurry). Consider touring Valladolid or the Balankanche Caves en route. Once you reach Cancún base yourself at Trailer Park Mecoloco. It is convenient to the Isla Mujeres ferries and, if you don't have a convenient vehicle, to busses into Ciudad Cancún town and on out to the Hotel Zone.

Day 17 - Cancún to Paa Mul - 50 miles (82 km), 1.25 hours - When you've had your fill of Cancún head out to a campsite on the long tropical coast to the south. For hookups take a look at Cabañas Paa Mul. After a night or two there you may decide to move to one of the smaller places to the north or south.

Day 24 - Paa Mul to Chetumal - 183 miles (298 km), 5 hours - Well rested from at least a week on the coast it is time to move on. The Cenote Azul Trailer Park is a popular stop for those interested in making an early start the next day. Take a swim in the huge Cenote Azul across from the campground.

Day 25 - Chetumal to Palenque - 298 miles (487 km), 8.5 hours - This is a long day's drive on virtually empty two-lane roads. Escárcega is the only town of any

THE JUNGLE AT PALENQUE

size along the way. Make sure to get an early start. Don't be surprised if you are stopped several times during the day by army patrols wanting to check your papers. You are very close to the Guatemala border. In Palenque many people like to stay at the Mayabell because it is so close to the ruins and is a good place to hear the howler monkeys during the night, but if you have a large rig you might find more maneuvering room at Los Leones Trailer Park.

Day 27 - Palenque to San Cristóbal de las Casas - 108 miles (177 km), 4.5 hours - The small and sometimes steep paved highway between Palenque and San Cristóbal should be adequate for any size rig under normal conditions. We've driven it in a large motor home pulling a tow vehicle. Just take it slow and easy. The route passes through many mountain Indian towns, you'll see many people along the road carrying firewood or on their way to the market towns. In San Cristóbal large rigs will want to stay at the Bonampak, but travelers with smaller vehicles will probably prefer the Rancho San Nicholás since it is a slightly shorter walk from the center of town.

Day 29 - San Cristóbal de las Casas to Tehuantepec - 232 miles (379 km), 7 hours - Another long day's drive on two-lane roads will bring you to Tehuantepec. En route you'll pass through Tuxtla Gutiérrez, a bypass will let you avoid the worst of the traffic. Neither campground in Tehuantepec is actually near town so you may want to drive on in and take a look around the square. Larger rigs should probably park along the main road and not venture in since turning might be difficult.

Day 30 - Tehuantepec to Oaxaca - 154 miles (251 km), 5 hours - The drive today involves a long climb on hot two-lane roads. Watch your engine temperature and don't hesitate to give your rig an occasional rest. Don't expect much traffic. Oaxaca itself is one of Mexico's most enchanting large cities. There's the Monte Albán archeological site just outside town, the surrounding crafts villages, and the old and attractive central area.

Day 32 - Oaxaca to Puerto Escondido - 190 miles (310 km), 7 hours - This route follows Mex. 175 as it climbs up and over the coastal range, don't take it unless you are certain that your rig can handle some pretty extreme grades, both up and down. Again, we've done it in a large motorhome with a tow vehicle, but we took it very slow. Once you reach the coast you have a choice of seaside resort towns, east for Bahías de Huatulco, straight for Puerto Angel, or west to Puerto Escondido, our personal favorite. All have very different personalities and all have RV parks of one kind or another but big rigs are best accommodated in Puerto Escondido. They're close enough together that you can easily take a look at all three.

Day 34 - Puerto Escondido to Acapulco - 246 miles (402 km), 7 hours - Two-lane Mex. 200 along the coast between Puerto Escondido and Acapulco varies in quality, but it won't seem bad after all you've been over. Acapulco is a huge place and you have a large variety of decent campgrounds available to you.

Day 36 - Acapulco to Playa Azul - 231 miles (377 km), 7 hours - The section of road between Acapulco and Manzanillo is pretty remote, they don't see a lot of campers. Many people bound for Acapulco actually come through the interior.

There is really only one formal campground along this long stretch of beautiful beaches, Playa Azul. Many sources warn against free camping on one of the many tempting beaches, others say they do it all the time with no problems.

Day 37 - Playa Azul to Manzanillo - 221 miles (362 km), 7 hours - Once again this is a fairly long segment through country that doesn't get many tourists. At Tecomán, south of Manzanillo you'll find a toll road that leads past Manzanillo. We don't use it because the free road is fine, and we like to drive through Manzanillo because the Comercial Mexicana there is a good place to pick up supplies. You probably won't want to camp in Manzanillo itself, the good campgrounds lie along the coast to the north. Mileage for this day is calculated to Melaque, 39 miles (64 km) north of Manzanillo.

Day 39 - Manzanillo to Puerto Vallarta - 134 miles (218 km), 4.5 hours - Mex. 200 north to Puerto Vallarta runs inland for much of the distance, then you descend out of the mountains and find yourself on the steep coast just south of town. Watch carefully as you make the final descent toward central PV, the bypass goes right and is easy to miss. PV itself has two good campgrounds and there are many more along the coast to the north.

Day 41 - Puerto Vallarta to Mazatlán - 287 miles (469 km), 9 hours - Not long ago traffic had to climb into the mountains and pass through Tepic on this segment, now there is a near-sea level route running near San Blas from Las Varas through Zacualpan, Platanitos, and Miramar which connects with Mex. 15 north of Tepic. Mex. 15 north to Mazatlán continues to be mostly two-lane although it is bound to be widened soon. Mazatlán offers many RV parks, this is one of the most popular RV destinations in Mexico.

Day 43 - Mazatlán to Los Mochis - 259 miles (423 km), 6 hours - There is four-lane road all the way to the border from Mazatlán. We recommend using this toll road for the entire distance, except the section between Mazatlán and Culiacán. The alternate Mex. 15 Libre is fine, it will take you an hour to an hour and a half longer, and it will save you a ton of money. The Culiacán - Mazatlán Maxipista is one of the most expensive roads in Mexico. North of Culiacán all RVs are currently (1997) charged as cars, although this might change, and the toll road is the way to go. You might consider leaving your rig in Los Mochis for a few days while you ride the Chihuahua-Pacific Railroad along the Copper Canyon.

Day 44 - Los Mochis to Guaymas/San Carlos - 220 miles (359 km), 5 hours - You'll make good time on this section of road, there are just a few places (Navojoa, Ciudad Obregón) where you'll have to slow as you pass through town. Guaymas/San Carlos is a fishing port with several RV parks, many people stop here and don't go any farther south.

Day 45 - Guaymas/San Carlos to Nogales - 257 miles (419 km), 7 hours -Your final day on the road should be a breeze. Drop your vehicle papers at the station that is on the highway about 19 miles (31 km) south of Nogales. After turning them in follow signs to the truck crossing west of Nogales. You may have up to an hour wait at the border, lines going into the U.S. tend to be much longer than those coming out. You won't believe how smooth the roads in the US will feel after 45 days and 4,500 miles in Mexico, but things will seem so sterile!

COLONIAL MEXICO
(26 days)

This is an unusual tour, relatively few campers spend much time touring the interior. On the other hand, if you are interested in the Mexican culture this route will give you an amazingly complete took at the country's historical cities. In 26 days you will cover 2,150 miles (3,500 km) and visit 13 important cities. The interior is one of our favorite parts of Mexico.

You will probably quickly notice that the route does not touch the coast even one time. If you are addicted to sun and sand this can be easily remedied. From many points on this route; particularly Puebla, Cuernavaca, Patzcuaro and Guadalajara; the coast can be reached in one reasonably comfortable day of driving.

Day 1 - Nuevo Laredo to Saltillo - 193 miles (315 km), 6 hours - After spending an hour or so crossing the border head south toward Monterrey. We recommend the free road, it won't slow you down much on this relatively short day. When in doubt just follow the trucks, they are well aware of which toll routes are economically practical. When you reach Monterrey drive on past the new toll ring road and take the older free one, it too is a comparative bargain. From Monterrey to Saltillo the road is a free highway with at least four lanes at all times, one of the best free roads in Mexico. The campground in Saltillo is conveniently located near a major supermarket and buses to central Saltillo pass right out front. Go into town and see your first cathedral and central square, Saltillo's is considered the best in northern Mexico.

Day 2 - Saltillo to Matehuala - 157 miles (257 km), 3.5 hours - Head south on Mex. 54 toward Matehuala and San Luis Potosí. You'll find toll roads with the occasional free road close alongside. If there's no alternative free road the toll road rates tend to be reasonable. Matehuala doesn't have much to offer except a decent campground in a convenient location. The 19th century silver town of Real de Catorce makes an interesting side trip from Matehuala but a visit takes most of a day to accomplish.

Day 3 - Matehuala to San Miguel de Allende - 255 miles (416 km), 6 hours - Once again you drive south on good roads that let you make excellent time. Mex. 54 easily bypasses San Luis Potosí, again follow the trucks for the best route. You'll leave Mex. 54 on a much smaller but still paved and adequate side road to reach San

Miguel. As you approach from the east make sure to watch for the bypass, it is signed for Celaya. Both San Miguel campgrounds lie to the south of town, you don't want to try to navigate central San Miguel's streets in even a small vehicle.

San Miguel is a favorite town of norteamericanos living in Mexico. It is also conveniently located for day trips to Guanajuato and Cd. de Dolores Hidalgo. We've given you two free days to explore here, they will probably not be enough.

Day 6 - San Miguel de Allende to Querétaro - 38 miles (62 km), 1.5 hours - Make an early start so that you arrive at Querétaro's Flamingo Hotel with plenty of time to explore the city. Querétaro is one of Mexico's most attractive and historic cities.

Day 7 - Querétaro to Mexico City - 132 miles (215 km), 3 hours - From Querétaro to Mexico City you will be on four to six lane toll road the entire distance. This is a government-operated toll road with a reasonable price so enjoy yourself. Catch the Tepotzotlán off ramp just past the last toll booth for Pepe's RV Park. This is one of Mexico's most important campgrounds, the only one left in the Mexico City area. You can stay here and easily catch a bus to the nearest subway station. The three hour round trip can be tiring, we recommend that you spend a couple of days in a reasonably-priced Mexico City hotel. Check with the campground host for recommendations. Don't forget to tour Tepotzotlán itself, the museum here is one of the best colonial period museums in Mexico.

Day 11 - Mexico City to Puebla - 98 miles (160 km), 3.5 hours - Don't forget to pick the right day for your transit around northeast Mexico City, take a look at the license plate rules and driving instructions for this route in our Mexico City section. Once you are established on Mex. 150 heading east to Puebla the toughest part of your day is over. This excellent toll road sweeps you up and out of the Mexico City bowl and right into Puebla. Spend a day in Puebla expanding your Talavera dish collection and enjoying some of the best food Mexico has to offer.

Day 13 - Puebla to Cuernavaca - 109 miles (178 km), 3 hours - From Puebla head west on Mex. 150 toward Mexico City, but catch Mex. 15 south to Cuautla past Ixtaccíhuatl and Popocatépetl volcanoes. From Cuautla to Cuernavaca there are several routes and also several excellent campgrounds. This region is the Morelos Valley and is something of a playground for Mexico City residents, it also has great historical importance. Morelos is filled with spas and balnearios, archeological sites, and colonial buildings. Taxco, the silver town, is an easy day trip from Cuernavaca.

Day 16 - Cuernavaca to Valle de Bravo - 144 miles (235 km), 5 hours - Rather than heading north through Mexico City to reach Valle de Bravo it is easier to take a more roundabout route. Drive south on Mex. 95 (either the toll road or the free road) toward Taxco. Then cut north on Mex. 55 through Ixtapan de la Sal to Toluca. Bypass Toluca on the ring route (actually surface streets in the outskirts of the city but not too bad) to Mex. 15 headed west toward Morelia. Just past Villa Victoria follow the road south to the holiday town of Valle de Bravo.

Day 17 - Valle de Bravo to Pátzcuaro - 181 miles (296 km), 7 hours - Getting an early start head north again to Mex. 15 and follow this twisting but extremely scenic road west to Morelia. Follow the bypass south around Morelia to catch the excellent free highway southwest to Pátzcuaro. Pátzcuaro is an enchanting little town, well known for its crafts but also an excellent base for touring one of the most interesting and scenic regions of Mexico.

Day 20 - Pátzcuaro to Guadalajara - 200 miles (326 km), 6 hours - From Pátzcuaro drive north to Quiroga and then continue your journey along Mex. 15 to Guadalajara. Rather than driving on in to Guadalajara when you near the city spend the night in more relaxed Villa Corona or Chapala.

Day 23 - Guadalajara to Aguascalientes - 153 miles (250 km), 4 hours - From Guadalajara the itinerary begins to trace its way back northward. There are a variety of routes north to Aguascalientes including a toll road. We recommend Mex. 54 to Jalpa and then Mex. 70 to Aguascalientes. If you base yourself at the Hotel Medrano in Aguascalientes you can easily explore the central district of the city.

Day 24 - Aguascalientes to Zacatecas - 80 miles (130 km), 2 hours - Zacatecas is a short day's drive north on two-lane free Mex. 45. Zacatecas is a relatively small city, and is almost undiscovered by tourists although it rivals Guanajuato in attractions. We like to stay at the Motel del Bosque which is conveniently located for a stroll into town or a ride on the overhead tram.

Day 25 - Zacatecas to Saltillo - 228 miles (373 km), 5.5 hours - Mex. 54 will take you north to Saltillo and your last night before returning to the US.

Day 26 - Saltillo to Nuevo Laredo - 193 miles (315 km), 6 hours - Don't forget to turn in your vehicle documents at the checkpoint on the highway before reaching Nuevo Laredo.

DOWN THE WEST COAST
(24 days)

The popularity of this tour is due to excellent roads and lots of good RV parks in a variety of oceanside cities, towns, and beachside locations. Mex. 15 from Nogales is a reasonably priced four lane toll road almost all the way to Mazatlán, farther south the roads are two-lane but not bad. From the first day there are excellent campgrounds with modern hookups. If you would like a small taste of Mexico with little in the way of inconvenience, this is the tour for you. We've allowed at least one layover day at each stop to make this a leisurely trip.

Day 1 - Nogales to Bahía Kino - 239 miles (391 km), 7 hours - You can now pick up both your visa and vehicle permit at the highway checkpoint 19 miles (31 km) south of Nogales. Plan on about an hour to accomplish both, then drive south on four-lane Mex. 15 to Hermosillo. Follow signs through town for Bahía Kino, Hermosillo's traffic it busy but its boulevards are for the most part not difficult to drive even in a big rig. There is a long bypass around the southern edge of the city, it is the best route if you are headed south directly to Guaymas, but when bound for Bahía Kino we prefer to drive directly through the city. Bahía Kino offers many campgrounds and is a popular destinations for fishermen and campers who are looking for a quiet destination not far from the border.

Day 3 - Bahía Kino to Guaymas/San Carlos - 153 miles (250 km), 4 hours - Retrace your steps to Hermosillo and then turn south to Mex. 15 and the twin towns of Guaymas and San Carlos. Our favorite place to stay is the Hotel Playa de Cortés at Miramar beach, between the two. It is a historic and attractive facility and only a short drive from shopping in Guaymas.

Day 5 - Guaymas/San Carlos to Álamos - 157 miles (257 km), 4 hours - Álamos will be your only chance on this itinerary to visit an old mining town. They're quite common in the interior. Drive south on Mex. 15 until you reach Navojoa, then turn inland. Álamos has been adopted by many norteamericano residents, it offers good restaurants and tours of restored colonial homes.

Day 7 - Álamos to Los Mochis - 127 miles (208 km), 3.5 hours - South again on Mex. 15 is Los Mochis. From here you can take a a two-day ride on the Chihuahua-Pacific Railroad to see the Copper Canyon.

Day 10 - Los Mochis to Mazatlán - 259 miles (423 km), 6.5 hours - Follow the toll highway south only as far as Culiacán. Drive right by the entrance to the very expensive Maxipista toll road and follow Mex. 15 Libre south to Mazatlán. Mazatlán is many folk's idea of the perfect destination with all of the advantages of a major city and many good RV parks as well.

Day 13 - Mazatlán to San Blas - 180 miles (294 km), 6 hours - From Mazatlán south you are on two-lane free roads. Just before the highway begins climbing toward Tepic follow the small highway toward the ocean and San Blas. Here you'll probably first start to feel like you are in the tropics, you can make an expedition in a small boat to see tropical birds and alligators.

Day 14 - San Blas to Puerto Vallarta - 107 miles (175 km), 4 hours - From San Blas south to Puerto Vallarta you have a huge choice of campgrounds suitable for a short stop or month-long sojourn. Most are in very small towns. The road south from San Blas through Miramar and Zacualpan is small and slow until it reaches the main coastal road, Mex. 200, and Las Varas. Puerto Vallarta itself has two excellent campgrounds conveniently located for enjoying this popular resort.

Day 17 - Puerto Vallarta to Manzanillo - 173 miles (282 km), 5 hours - Like the coast north of Puerto Vallarta, that north of Manzanillo offers many camping possibilities. Most of these are less formal and don't offer the same quality facilities as those farther north. On the other hand the pace is even more relaxed and the beaches even less crowded.

Farther south along the coast the campgrounds are much more scarce and the distances longer. Take a look at the Grand Coastal Tour to see what lies farther south.

Day 20 through Day 24 - Return to Nogales - 1,173 miles (1, 914 km), 35 driving hours - In returning to Nogales we do less sightseeing. Overnight stops on the way north are at one of the campgrounds north of Puerto Vallarta, then Mazatlán, Los Mochis, and Guaymas.

If you enjoyed this tour you're ready for a much longer one next year.

CHAPTER 2

DETAILS, DETAILS, DETAILS

BUDGET

For most travelers the important budget items will be insurance, campground fees, gasoline, tolls, food, and entertainment expenses. The amount of money you spend really depends upon how you live so we will not attempt to set out a standard budget. Most people who spend time in Mexico find that it is much less expensive than a similar stay in the United States or Canada.

See the Insurance section of Chapter 3 for information about how to get an insurance quote. Your U.S. automobile insurance will not adequately cover you in Mexico.

Campground fees vary with region. On the Baja Peninsula and near the border we find that prices are usually denominated in U.S. dollars. This means higher prices because there is no benefit from the recent slow but constant devaluation of the peso. Prices along the west coast, in Guaymas, Mazatlán, and Puerto Vallarta are also high by Mexican standards because the traffic will bear it. In the interior and southern Mexico prices are lower. Each campground listing in this guide gives a price range for the campground, see Chapter 4 for more information about this. During the winter of 1996/1997 we spend four months traveling throughout Mexico in a van-type RV (19 feet long) staying in a different campground each night always using full hookups, we averaged $9.12 U.S. per day. It is usually possible to negotiate a lower rate for longer stays, often much lower.

Gasoline prices in Mexico have recently been similar to those in the U.S. On the first of each month they have been increasing a small amount in pesos which roughly equals the devaluation of the peso against the U.S. dollar. In March 1997 U.S. dollar per gallon prices were as follows: Nova (low octane leaded) $1.40, Magna-Sin $1.43 (low octane unleaded), Premium Unleaded $1.60, Diesel $1.09). See the Fuel and Gas Stations section below for more information.

Tolls are a cost of driving in Mexico that most of us are not accustomed to. You can choose to avoid toll roads if you like. This is a complicated subject so see the detailed discussion below under Toll Roads.

We find that our grocery bills in Mexico run about 75% of what they would in the U.S. This will vary considerably depending upon what you eat and where you buy your food. Fruits and vegetables are a bargain, meat and fish tend to be cheaper than in the U.S. and Canada, canned and processed foods more expensive, beer is a deal. See the Groceries section below for more information.

Campgrounds

Mexican campgrounds vary immensely. In the interior and less traveled areas you will often consider yourself fortunate to find a hookup behind a hotel. The nicest campgrounds tend to be nearer the border and in popular areas of the Baja Peninsula and the west coast.

Bathroom facilities in Mexican campgrounds are often not up to the standards of Canadian and U.S. private campgrounds. Cleanliness and condition vary widely, each of our campground descriptions tries to cover this important subject. Campers in larger rigs probably won't care since they carry their own bathrooms along with them. Other campers might keep in mind that many of the campgrounds they frequent in the U.S. and Canada, especially in national, state, or provincial parks, have pit toilets and no shower facilities. The majority of Mexican campgrounds in this guide provide at least flush toilets and some kind of shower.

In rural Mexico it is usually not acceptable to put used toilet tissue in the toilet bowl, a waste-paper basket is usually provided. Toilet tissue creates problems for marginal plumbing and septic systems, it plugs them up. Travelers who have visited other third-world countries have probably run into this custom before. You will have to bring along your own toilet tissue, few places in Mexico provide it.

On the Yucatán Peninsula and in southern Mexico campgrounds usually have cold showers. Air temperatures are often so warm that a cold shower actually feels pretty good. If you absolutely HATE cold showers try this: take along a wash cloth and give yourself a sponge bath, only stick your head under the shower to wash your hair. It is actually bearable.

Most of the larger campgrounds in Mexico, especially in the areas that are well traveled by RVers, have hookups for electricity, water and sewer. Almost all of the primary campgrounds covered in this book have them but the actual condition of the outlets, faucets, and sewer connections may not be very good. We find that in many campgrounds the hardware wasn't great when installed, and maintenance doesn't get done unless absolutely necessary. It is a good idea to take a look at the connections on a parking pad before pulling in, you may want to move to another one.

Mexico uses the same 110-volt 60-cycle service that we use in the U.S. and Canada so your RV won't have to be modified for Mexico. Many campgrounds only have small two-slot household-type sockets so be sure that you have an adapter that lets you use these smaller sockets. Most sockets do not have a ground, either because the plug is the two-slot variety without the ground slot, or because the ground slot

SUNRISE ON THE CARIBBEAN CAMPGROUND IN CHETUMAL

is not wired. Test the electricity at your site before plugging in. You can buy a tester at your camping supply store before heading south that will quickly indicate the voltage and any faults of the outlet. This is cheap insurance. Make yourself a two prong adapter that can be reversed to achieve correct polarity and that has a wire and alligator clip so you can provide your own ground.

We've used laptop computers extensively and had no problems with the electrical current in Mexican campgrounds. Full-size desktop computers might be a different story. Currency flucuations, spikes, and grounding problems are likely to affect them more.

Air conditioner use is often a problem in Mexico. Don't count on using one except along the west coast, the northern Gulf of California, and some Baja campgrounds. Even if 50-amp. service is offered by the campground heavy air conditioner use can cause voltage drops because most campgrounds do not have adequately-sized transformers.

Water connections are common, but you may not want to trust the quality of the water, even if the campground manager assures you that it is good. See the Drinking Water section of this chapter for details on how to cope with this.

Sewer connections in Mexican campgrounds are usually located at the rear of the site. You should make sure that you have enough hose to reach several feet past the rear of your rig before you come south. You probably won't be able to buy any sewer hose south of the border.

Caravans

An excellent way to get your introduction to Mexico is to take an escorted caravan tour. Many companies offer these tours, by our count there are about 200 caravans into Mexico each year. These range from luxury tours taking several months and costing multiple thousands of dollars to tours of less than a week for a fraction of that price.

A typical caravan tour is composed of approximately 20 rigs. The price paid includes a knowledgeable caravan leader in his own RV, a tail-gunner or caboose RV with an experienced mechanic, campground fees, many meals and tours at stops along the way, and lots of camaraderie. Many people love RV tours because someone else does all the planning, there is security in numbers, and a good caravan can be a very memorable experience. Others hate caravans, and do so for approximately the same reasons.

Remember that there will be a lot of costs in addition to those covered by the fee paid to the caravan company including fuel, insurance, maintenance, tolls, and groceries. We hear lots of good things about caravans, but also many complaints. Common problems include caravans that do not spend enough time at interesting places, delays due to mechanical problems with other rigs in the caravan, and poor caravan leaders who do not really know the territory or speak the language. A badly run caravan can be a disaster.

We've given the names, addresses and phone numbers below of some of the leading caravan companies. Give them a call or write a letter to get information about the tours they will be offering for the coming year. Once you have received the information do not hesitate to call back and ask questions. Ask for the names and phone numbers of people who have recently taken tours with the same caravan leader scheduled to be in charge of the tour you are considering. Call these references and find out what they liked and what they didn't like. They are likely to have some strong feelings about these things.

Adventure Caravans, 101 Rainbow Dr., Suite 2434, Livingston, TX 77351 (800 872-7879).

"Baja Winters" Caravans, 10537 Whitman Ave. N., Seattle, WA 98133 (800-383-6787).

Caravans Voyagers, 1155 Larry Mahan Street, Suite H, El Paso, Texas 79925 (800-933-9332).

Carnival Caravans, P.O. Box 3370, Sumas, WA 98295 (800-556-5652).

Eldorado Tours, P.O. Box 1145, Alma, Arkansas 72921 (800-852-2500).

Point South RV Tours, 11313 Edmonson Ave., Moreno Valley, CA 92555 (800-421-1394).

Tracks to Adventure, 2811 Jackson Ave., El Paso, TX 79930 (800-351-6053).

You might also check with the owner association of the type of rig you drive, we've recently run into caravans composed of Airstreams, Bounders, and Roadtreks.

Incidentally, caravans use CB channel 11 or 13.

CASH AND CREDIT CARDS

Mexico, of course, has its own currency, called the peso. During the 96/97 season there were about 7.75 pesos per U.S. dollar. The currency has been relatively stable with a slow devaluation rate since a large devaluation in 1994. Some visitors, particularly on the Baja Peninsula, never seem to have any pesos and use dollars for most purchases. They pay for the privilege, prices in dollars tend to be higher than if you pay in pesos. Outside the border areas and the Baja dollars are not readily accepted.

Cash machines are now wide-spread in Mexico and represent the best way to obtain cash. If you don't already have a debit card you should take the trouble to get one before heading south, make sure it has a four-digit international pin (personal identification number). Both Cirrus (Visa) and Plus (Master Card) networks are in place, not all machines accept both. Given a choice we would choose Cirrus, it seems to be more widely accepted. The transaction charge during the 96/97 winter season was usually $2.00 U.S. Don't be surprised if a machine inexplicably refuses your card, both bank operations and phone lines are subject to unexpected breakdowns. If you can't get the card to work try a machine belonging to another bank or just go directly to a teller inside the bank. You should bring a back-up card in case the electronic strip stops working on the one you normally use. Most cards have a maximum daily withdrawal limit, usually about $400 U.S. Many Mexican machines seem to impose their own limit of about $200 U.S.

Traveler's checks are a decent way to carry money for emergencies. You never know when your debit card might inexplicably stop working.

Visa and Master Card credit cards are useful in Mexico. Restaurants and shops, particularly in tourist areas, accept them. Outside metropolitan and tourist areas their acceptance is limited. Pemex stations accept only cash and supermarkets usually don't accept credit cards. It is also possible to get cash advances against these credit cards in Mexican banks but the fees tend to be high.

CHILDREN

Children love camping, and Mexico has great beaches and other recreational possibilities. Mexicans love children so yours certainly won't feel unwelcome. Each year during the winter we meet more families who are traveling while home-schooling, during the summer there have always been a lot of kids. Can you think of a better place to learn Spanish?

It is entirely possible to travel with children during the school year. Home-schooling is now quite popular and most school districts will allow it, especially if it is only for a year or so and the object is to travel in an educational place like Mexico. Policies vary, you may find that the school district will provide a lesson plan, give you assistance with your own, or require the use of a correspondence school. Check with your state department of education about the legalities and procedures. Don't forget about the advantages of a laptop computer with CD ROM drive. There is more and more reference and educational material available in a compact format on disk. Home-schooling requires discipline but can be very rewarding.

Drinking Water and Vegetables

Don't take a chance when it comes to drinking Mexican water. Even water considered potable by the locals is likely to cause problems for you. It is no fun to be sick, especially when you are far from the border in an unfamiliar environment. There are several strategies for handling the water question. Many people drink nothing but bottled water. Others filter or purify it in various ways.

We use a simple system. We purify all of the water that goes into our rig's storage tank with common bleach. Then we use a filter to remove the bleach taste, the microorganisms in the water have already been killed by the bleach. This means that we never hook up permanently to the local water supply, we always use the stored water in our rig. The advantage of this method is that you do not need to keep a separate supply of drinking water underfoot. The filter we use is commonly offered as standard equipment on many RV's, it is manufactured by Everpure. Other charcoal filters probably work equally well to remove the taste of bleach.

The procedure we use is called superclorination. Add 1/6 ounce (1 teaspoon) of bleach (sodium hypochlorite) per each 10 gallons of water. The easiest way to do this is to measure it into the same end of your fill hose that will attach to or go into your rig. Check the bleach bottle to make sure it has no additives, Clorox and Purex sold in Mexico are usually OK. You can tell because they have instructions for water purification right on the label.

Some people do not like putting bleach in the water tank because it gives a slightly slick feeling to their shower water. We find this acceptable and really hardly noticeable if we don't bleach the water too heavily. Everpure includes a test kit with their filter hardware that will let you test the water after bleaching it so that you learn to achieve the proper dosage. They also include a cute little squeeze bottle to make measuring easy.

Occasionally, even if you bleach your water and use a filter, you will pick up a load of water that doesn't taste too good. This is usually because it contains salt. A filter won't take this out. You can avoid the problem by asking about water quality before filling up, especially at campgrounds near the ocean.

If you don't want to bleach your water the best alternative is to drink bottled water. Everywhere in Mexico you can buy large 19-liter (approximately five-gallon) bottles of water. They are available at supermarkets, from purified-water shops, or from vendors who visit campgrounds. Drinking water purchased this way is very inexpensive, you can either keep one of the large bottles by paying a small deposit or actually empty them into your own water tank. If you do that, though, your showers become pretty pricey.

Another source of potential stomach problems is fruit and vegetables. It is essential that you peel all fruit and vegetables or soak them in a purification solution before eating them. Bleach can also be used for this, the directions are right on the label of most bleach sold in Mexico. You can also purchase special drops to add to water for this purpose, the drops are stocked in the fruit and vegetable department of most supermarkets in Mexico.

DRIVING IN MEXICO

If there were only one thing that could be impressed upon the traveler heading south to drive in Mexico for the first time it would be "drive slowly and carefully". The last thing you want in Mexico is an accident or a breakdown, driving slowly and carefully is the best way to avoid both of these undesirable experiences.

Mexico's roads are getting better. There are now long stretches of superhighway, the quality and engineering of some of these highways will amaze you. On the other hand, many Mexican roads are of a lower standard than we are accustomed to. Surfaces are poorly maintained, potholes are common, roads are narrow, signage is often poor or lacking. Cautious driving will mean fewer flat tires and broken springs.

The quality of Mexican drivers varies, of course. We think that on average, as a group and with lots of exceptions, they tend to be more aggressive than they should be considering the quality of the vehicles and roads. Many Mexican vehicles would not be allowed on the roads in the U.S. or Canada. They are slow, have poor brakes, lights that don't work, and bald tires. It is very common for tires to blow out, often because they have been run to the cord.

As you travel cross-country on two-lane roads you will probably be astounded by the aggressiveness of bus and truck drivers. Here's a piece of advice, never get into a race with a bus driver, their rigs are powerful and drivers fearless to a fault. They will not give up and commonly are involved in accidents, don't contribute to the problem.

Do not drive at night. There are several reasons for this. Animals are common on roads in Mexico, even in daylight hours you'll find cows, horses, burros, goats, pigs and sheep on the road. At night there are even more of them, they're attracted by the warm road surface and they don't have reflectors. Truckers like to travel at night because they can make good time in the light traffic. Some of these guys are maniacs, in the morning you'll often see a fleet of tow trucks lined up along the edge of a highway trying to retrieve one from a gully. Truckers also often leave rocks on the road at night, this is done to keep someone from hitting them when they break down, or to block the wheels when stopped on a hill. Often these rocks aren't removed, they're very difficult to see in time at night. Finally, driving at night means that if you have a breakdown you're going to be in an unsafe position. Mexican roads are good places to avoid after dark.

No discussion of driving in Mexico is complete without a discussion of traffic cops and bribes. Traffic cops (and many other government functionaries) are underpaid, they make up for it by collecting from those who break the law. This is not condoned by the government, but it is a fact of life. Norteamericanos usually feel uncomfortable with this custom and as a result they are difficult targets for cops with a *mordida* habit. Unfortunately some cops do not yet know this.

The best way to avoid the mordida trap is to scrupulously follow all traffic laws. Even if everyone around you is breaking the law you should follow it. If only one person in a line of cars gets arrested for not stopping at a railroad crossing you can be sure that it will be you. Here are a few of the many pitfalls. Obey all speed limits, especially easy to miss are those at schools and small towns along a highway. Stop at the stop sign at railroad crossings even though no one else will. In many towns the heavy traffic is directed to stay on the laterals or follow a special route marked "tráffico pesado" (heavy traffic) or "tráffico pasado" (through traffic). Watch for these signs because if you are in an RV these truck routes probably can be interpreted as applying to you. Do as the trucks do.

In the event that you do get stopped we recommend against offering a bribe. It is possible that you might get yourself in even worse trouble than you are already in. If you can't talk your way out of a fine the normal practice is to accompany the officer back to his headquarters (bringing your vehicle) to pay the fine. Most fines are quite reasonable by norteamericano standards. Occasionally a police officer will suggest that such a trip can be avoided by paying a reasonable fee to him on the spot, let your conscience be your guide.

If you park in a town or city and find your license plates gone when you return you will probably be able to find them at the local police office. Police routinely remove plates of illegally parked vehicles to make sure that the owner comes in to pay the fine. If the curb is painted red it is a no parking zone, yellow means parking during "off" hours, and white means its OK to park at all times.

Everyone's least favorite thing is to get involved in an accident. In Mexico there are special rules. First and most important is that you had better have insurance. See the Insurance section in Chapter 3. Your insurance carrier will give you written instructions about the procedure to follow if you get into an accident. Take a look at them and discuss questions with your agent before you cross the border to make sure you understand exactly how to handle an accident before it happens.

ENGLISH-LANGUAGE BOOKSTORES AND MAGAZINES

We recommend that you do your shopping for both travel guides and recreational reading before you cross the border. Stores with good selections of English-language books are virtually nonexistent in Mexico. We've included a list of recommended travel guides under Travel Library below.

There is a much better situation with regard to English-language newspapers.

Kiosks in most cities carry *USA Today* and other major U.S. newspapers. There is an English-language newspaper published in Mexico City called *The News*. It also is available in larger cities. News magazines like *Time* and *Newsweek* publish Latin American editions in English, they also are available in larger cities and tourist towns.

Ferries

Regular ferries make runs between the Baja Peninsula and the mainland. These boats provide a convenient way to avoid retracing your steps if you drive down the Baja. The ferries are operated by Grupo Sematur de California S.A. de CV, a private company. The fares are not cheap, especially for a large rig. There are three routes: La Paz - Mazatlán, La Paz - Topolobampo/Los Mochis, and Santa Rosalía - Guaymas. Fares are charged for each person and for the vehicle, the rate for the vehicles varies with length. Passenger classes include Salón (you don't have a cabin, there are areas with reclining airline-type seats), Turista (shared cabins with bunks), Cabina (private cabins with toilets) and Especial (deluxe cabins). The fares below are in U.S. dollars. Vans fall under the automobile classification while motorhomes are trucks.

The La Paz - Mazatlán run takes about 18 hours, the ferries leave at about 3:00 P.M. from each end and arrive about 9:00 A.M. This run has the nicest boats. Fares effective March 1, 1997 were: Salón $20.69, Turista $41.24, Cabina $61.68, Especial $82.27. Selected vehicle fares were: automobiles to 5 meters $223.07, automobiles to 6.5 meters $289.96, automobiles with trailer to 9 meters $401.36, automobiles with trailers to 17 meters $757.30, trucks to 10 meters $458.21, trucks to 13 meters $596.06, trucks to 15 meters $687.52, motorcycles $55.93.

The La Paz - Topolobampo/Los Mochis run takes about 10 hours, the ferries leave each end about 8:00 A.M. and arrive about 6:00 P.M. daily. These boats are popular with truckers and don't have a lot of amenities. Fares effective March 1, 1997 were: Salón $13.86, Turista $27.53, Cabina $41.24, Especial $54.90. Selected vehicle fares were: automobiles to 5 meters $136.34, automobiles to 6.5 meters $176.82, automobiles with trailer to 9 meters $244.80, automobiles with trailers to 17 meters $461.30, trucks to 10 meters $284.09, trucks to 13 meters $369.09, trucks to 15 meters $425.40, motorcycles $30.23.

The Santa Rosalía - Guaymas run takes about 7 hours and boats run on Tuesday and Friday westbound, Sunday and Wednesday eastbound. The ferries leave each end about 8:00 A.M. and arrive about 3:00 P.M. Fares effective March 1, 1997 were: Salón $13.85, Turista $27.53, Cabina $41.24, Especial $54.90. Selected vehicle fares were: automobiles to 5 meters $156.85, automobiles to 6.5 meters $203.75, automobiles with trailer to 9 meters $281.74, automobiles with trailers to 17 meters $530.98, trucks to 10 meters $304.63, trucks to 13 meters $395.52, trucks to 15 meters $456.47, motorcycles $39.61.

You should make reservations for the ferries by calling a Mexican toll-free number (91-800-6-96-96). Local numbers are: La Paz (112) 5-38-33, Santa Rosalia (115)

2-00-14, Mazatlán (69) 81-70-21, Topolobampo (681) 2-01-04. Tickets must be picked up at the ferry office on the day before sailing. Remember that you must have vehicle documents in order to travel to the mainland, they can be obtained in La Paz but it would probably be best to get them at the border to make sure you have everything you need. All of the rates, schedules, and policies seem to change frequently so don't be surprised if they have changed by the time you are ready to go.

FREE CAMPING

By free camping we mean camping outside an organized campground. In Mexico the term is really a misnomer, often there are costs involved in free camping. You often have to pay a "tip" or buy a meal to really feel comfortable in a free camping spot.

A grizzled old-timer we met in Pátzcuaro explained Mexican free camping pretty well in just a few words. When we asked him if there was a campground where he'd spent the night he said "What? A campground in Mexico? We just find a wide street with a streetlight to park under and ask the first person to come along if it is OK to park there. They always say yes." Once you have permission it is a good idea to get to know your neighbors, that way they might watch out for you.

Security is a real issue when you camp outside formal campgrounds. RVs, and to a lesser extent vans, stand out. You will be noticed and an RV is uniquely vulnerable. Any thief knows you have lots of valuable stuff in that vehicle. The best free camping spots are patrolled in some way. Several rigs traveling together are much safer than one alone. Most importantly, however, never park alongside the highway.

Here are a few possibilities for free camping: balnearios, gas stations, restaurant parking lots, tourist attraction parking lots, streets near police stations (ask for permission at the station, they may have a better suggestion), city squares, front and back yards of houses, ranchos and farms, and beach areas. One popular guide even suggests garbage dumps, we think the author is kidding. You'll find others as you spend more time in Mexico.

FUEL AND GAS STATIONS

Choosing the brand of gas you're going to buy is easy in Mexico. All of the gas stations are Pemex stations. Pemex is the national oil company, it is responsible for everything from exploring for oil to pumping it into your car. Gas is sold for cash, no credit cards. There are usually two kinds of gas, Nova in blue pumps which contains lead, and Magna Sin, in green pumps, which does not. You'll probably be using Magna Sin, it seems to have a low octane rating of about 86 or 87. Expect a lot of pinging. A new higher octane lead free has recently become available near the border. It has a higher octane rating and is much better than Magna Sin but also more expensive.

Diesel is carried at most stations. It is said to have a high sulfur content so you should change your oil more often than you do at home, probably every 2,000 miles or so.

All gas sells for the same thing all over the country so it will do you no good to search for the best price for gas. The only exception to this is very small stations in very remote places. Gas in these establishments is often pumped out of drums and can cost many times the Pemex price. With proper planning you won't ever use one of these places.

Gas stations are not as common in Mexico as they are in the U.S. and Canada. Some towns have no station, others only a few. Sometimes it is obvious that there should be more stations in an area because the lines are terrible. In years past there was often a problem finding unleaded gas, called Magna Sin, in remote places. Many stations did not carry it. Now almost all stations have it.

The rule of thumb in Mexico used to be that you should fill your tank whenever you burned half a tank. Stations were scarce and sometimes they wouldn't have gas when you reached them. This is still a good idea on the Baja and in more remote places. Even though most stations now have a Magna Sin pump they are sometimes out of gas. If an unexpected RV caravan decides to stop for gas at a remote station it can easily drain the tanks dry until more arrives.

Almost everyone you meet in Mexico has stories about how a gas station attendant cheated them. These stories are true. The attendants don't make much money and gringo tourists are easy prey. You can avoid problems if you know what to expect.

The reason that the attendants are able to cheat people is that there are no cash registers or central cashiers in these stations. Each attendant carries a big wad of cash and collects what is displayed on the pump. Don't expect a receipt. Until the stations install a control system with a separate cashier there will continue to be lots of opportunities for attendants to make money off unwary customers.

Some people think that the pumps in Mexican stations are calibrated to give you less gas than you pay for. We have two tanks in our rig and always run one dry before starting the next so we can tell if we are being sold more gas than we can really hold. We have never had that happen in Mexico (but it has happened in the states) so we do trust the pumps. The problem in Mexico is the crafty attendants.

The favorite ploy is to start pumping gas without zeroing the pump. This way you have to pay for the gas that the previous customer received in addition to your own. The attendant pockets the double payment. The practice is so widespread that at many stations attendants will point to the zeroed pump before they start pumping. Signs at most stations tell you to check this yourself.

There are several things you can do to avoid this problem. First, get a locking gas cap. That way the attendant can't start pumping until you get out of the rig and unlock the cap. Second, check the zeroed meter carefully. Do not get distracted. If several people try to talk to you they are probably trying to distract you. They'll ask questions about the rig or point out some imaginary problem. Meanwhile the pump doesn't get zeroed properly.

MODERN PEMEX GAS STATIONS ARE BECOMING QUITE COMMON

While the gas is being pumped stand right there and pay attention. Another trick is to "accidentally" zero the pump and then try to collect for an inflated reading. If you watch carefully you will know the true reading and won't fall for this. Sometimes the pump gets zeroed before the tank is full, so don't just assume that you can chat because you have a big tank.

Many pumps still show prices in old pesos. There are many more zeros than there should be. This really confuses gringos and is a favorite tool of the pump bandits. You'll ask for fifty pesos worth, the attendant will stand and pretend to pump while you are distracted and not watching carefully. When the pump reaches 5 pesos he'll cut it off and you'll pay him 50. He'll be 45 pesos richer and you'll have purchased less than a gallon of gas. Avoid confusion by checking the liter reading, then multiply by the per liter price to find the proper peso amount. It also helps to check your gas gauge before paying.

The process of making change presents big opportunities to confuse you. If you are paying in dollars, which is common on the Baja, have your own calculator handy and make sure you know the exchange rate before the gas is pumped. When paying do not just give the attendant your money. He'll fold it onto his big wad of bills and then you'll never be able to prove how much you gave him. We've also seen attendants quickly turn their backs and stuff bills in a pocket. Hold out the money or lay it out on the pump, don't let him have it until you can see your change and know that it is the correct amount.

All attendants will not try to cheat you of course. You'll probably feel bad about watching like a hawk every time you fill up with gas. The problem is that when you let down your guard someone will eventually take advantage of you, probably soon and not later. It is also customary to tip attendants a peso or two, we think honest attendants deserve to be tipped more.

GREEN ANGELS

The Mexican government maintains a large fleet of green pickups that patrol all major highways searching for motorists with mechanical problems. Usually there are two men in the truck, they have radios to call for help, limited supplies, and quite a bit of mechanical aptitude. Most of them speak at least limited English. The service is free except for a charge for the cost of supplies used. The trucks patrol most highways two times each day, once in the morning and once in the afternoon. You can call for help from the Green Angels, the nationwide toll-free telephone number is 91-800-9-03-00-92 except in Mexico City where it is (5) 2-50-82-21. They also monitor CB channel 9.

GROCERIES

Don't load your rig with groceries when you head south across the border. There is no longer any point in doing so. Some Mexican border stations are checking RVs to see that they don't bring in more than a reasonable amount of food. Modern supermarkets in all of the large and medium-sized Mexican cities have almost anything you are looking for, often in familiar brand names. You can supplement your purchases in the supermarkets with shopping in markets and in small stores called *abarrotes, panaderías, tortillarías,* and *carnecerías* (canned goods stores, bakeries, tortilla shops, and butcher shops).

Mexican supermarkets are much like French hypermarkets (or a modern Wal-Mart). Names to remember are Comercial Mexicana, Gigante, Ley, Soriana, and yes, even Wal-Mart. In addition to all kinds of groceries they carry clothing, hard goods, electronics, hardware, and almost everything else. To get to the groceries you must push your cart past lots of other temptations.

Compiling a list of things that are hard to find in a Mexican supermarket gets more difficult every year. About the only things we have difficulty finding now are good dill pickles, cheddar cheese, canned tomatoes, decent peanut butter and any type of carbonated soda not manufactured by the Coca-Cola Company (Coke has an amazing Mexican distribution system).

Almost any population center, from the largest city to the small regional market towns, has a market building with stalls selling fruits, vegetables, meats, and even fully cooked meals. Surrounding the market building may be even more temporary stalls. The sights, sounds and especially smells will both attract and repel you. Most of us would hesitate to purchase anything from the butcher stalls, even if the butcher has a clue about the cuts sold north of the border. Fruits and vegetables are another story. Those available in supermarkets cannot usually compare with the quality and selection available in the markets. Besides, dickering in the market is one of the real pleasures of Mexican living

Very small towns with no normal grocery store aften have a small government store called a Conasupo. Gringos can shop in them too..

HEALTH MATTERS

The health hazards of traveling in Mexico are not particularly intimidating. You might want to take a look at the section of this chapter titled Insects and Other Pests. Two other things you'll want to be aware of are the extremely warm temperatures in the summer, particularly in the south, and the high altitudes of the interior. Give yourself time to acclimatize before pushing yourself.

Health care south of the border is readily available and quite good. Many doctors practicing in the U.S. were trained in Mexico, the standards are high. Language is seldom a problem. Mexico has socialized medicine, the government health organization is called the IMSS. Many norteamericanos who live in Mexico have joined the IMSS and use it for all of their health care, the price is quite reasonable by U.S. or Canadian standards. These IMSS facilities are not supposed to treat non-members but we often hear about travelers getting excellent emergency treatment in remote places where the IMSS may be the only alternative. There are also many private doctors and hospitals throughout the country and their prices are very reasonable. For recommendations check with long-term residents in trailer parks, with hotels, or with tourist offices.

Prescription medicines are also readily available in Mexico. Many things that require a doctor's prescription north of the border do not require one in Mexico but this does not apply to narcotics of any kind. Costs are said to average about 20% of that in the U.S. Many residents from north of the border shop for their medicine in Mexico.

Getting insurance reimbursement for costs in Mexico is sometimes problematic. Medicare from the U.S. will not reimburse Mexican expenses. Some private insurance does pay or reimburse Mexican expenses, check with your broker or carrier. If your insurance does not cover you in Mexico you should check into supplemental coverage. We are told that Canadians are better served by their government health coverage, it will cover Mexican expenses but not those incurred in the U.S. You'll want to check into this if it applies to you.

Another popular insurance is coverage for air transportation out of Mexico in the case of major medical problems. Often this inexpensive coverage is offered as an add-on to your automobile insurance.

HOLIDAYS

Mexicans love holidays, most mean at least a minor fiesta. Some of the major ones result in big migrations to the ocean and mean full campgrounds. Most national holidays are celebrated almost everywhere with street fairs and firecrackers. Individual towns have their own fiesta days, we've tried to mention some of these in our individual city descriptions.

The two long winter holidays are the Christmas holidays and Semana Santa or Holy Week. The Christmas Holidays run for about a week on each side of the new year. You can expect significant numbers of Mexican families in the campgrounds, especially along the ocean, during this week. Semana Santa is the Easter holiday. Even more people seem to celebrate this one at the beach. Be prepared for a lively and interesting week.

HOTELS

While you are traveling in Mexico, even if you are in an RV, don't forget that you are not limited to spending the night camping. Mexican hotels and motels can be inexpensive and convenient alternatives to campgrounds. In many parts of the country campgrounds are scarce, especially along the east coast and in the interior. Hotel prices are reasonable when compared to those in the U.S., particularly if you stay in places oriented toward Mexican customers. Many hotels and motels outside central urban centers have enough parking space for larger rigs and good security. You may even be able to park on the hotel or motel grounds and stay in your own rig. Often management will string an electric cord. Travelers driving smaller RVs and cars have the advantage, they can stop for the night at virtually any hotel and have no parking problems. All RV drivers should exercise caution when visiting hotels because overhead clearance is often restricted at entry gates and parking areas. Park out front and walk in to scout the situation. There is often an alternate entrance for larger rigs.

INSECTS AND OTHER PESTS

Large areas of Mexico are covered with desert and jungle, if you live outdoors you're bound to run into some unfamiliar bugs. Most aren't a problem but you should be alert. Tent campers in particular should be on constant watch for scorpions, tarantulas, and other poisonous spiders. Mosquitoes and small biting flies can also be a problem. Probably the best insurance is a good insect-tight tent. Always check shoes and clothes for stinging insects and tarantulas before putting them on. Campers, especially tent campers, who are planning to camp in tropical areas should consider malaria pills. Your personal physician at home can prescribe them.

For RVers the largest problem is usually ants. You shouldn't be surprised if your rig gets invaded. You can help avoid this by not leaving food and water out. Fix small water leaks so they don't become a magnet for ants in dry desert climates. When parked you should make sure that your rig isn't being brushed by branches and leaves. Many people also put ant powder around their tires. If you do find yourself with an ant problem don't panic, they are easy to get rid of if you have the right tool. We've been extremely pleased with the effectiveness of the small ant baits sold in many U.S. supermarkets. Ants go into these little plastic stick-ons and pick up insecticide which they take back to the nest, within a day or so the ants start disappearing, within a week they're gone. We've not seen these in Mexico even though they may be available, make sure to take some with you when you go south because they may be impossible to find in Mexico.

LAUNDRY

Getting your laundry done in Mexico shouldn't present much of a problem, unless you want to do it yourself. There are laundromats in most larger towns and cities, ask at the campground for directions. In most places you leave your laundry and pick it up the next day, prices are very reasonable. Only on the Baja and on the West Coast will you find campgrounds with coin-operated machines that you can use yourself, we've indicated their presence in the campground descriptions.

MAIL

Mail service to and from Mexico is not great. We find that letters from Mexico often take several weeks to reach their destination in the U.S. or Canada.

To receive mail in Mexico there are really two options: have it addressed to the campground or to general delivery, known as *Lista de Correos*, at the local post office. We recommend that you use the post office method unless you are very sure (actually discuss the issue with the campground manager) that you have a good campground address. Campground addresses do change and many campgrounds are not set up to reliably receive mail for their guests.

Here's a tip for addressing mail to Mexico. Mexico uses zip codes that look just like those in the U.S. If you are not careful your mail will go to the U.S. zip code instead of to Mexico. Always put the zip code on Mexican mail before the state name and precede the number with the letters C.P. This will alert postal machines and workers and should reduce the problem.

Mexican post office boxes are addressed as Apdo. or Apdo. Postal. Many of the campground addresses in this guide include Apdo. numbers. If they do, you do not need to include street address information when sending mail to them, it is only included here to help in finding the campground.

MAPS

For the last five years or so it has been difficult to find good maps for use in Mexico. Even if you do find one of the few good maps it is likely to be out of date because roads, especially big toll roads, are being built at a very rapid pace. They often don't show up on maps, and if they do show up they are often in the wrong place.

In years past the best map was a booklet of road maps published by Pemex. If you see someone with one of these you can be sure that he is an old timer. Sometime you even meet someone who has an extra, they were readily available and not at all expensive at one time. If someone gives you one of these booklets you owe them "big time". There are two versions of the Pemex map book, the first one was published in 1986, a second version published in 1988 is better, it has many good tourist city maps too. Unfortunately these road atlases were published before many of the toll roads were in existence. They remain the best source of information about secondary roads.

The American Automobile Association (AAA) publishes the best easy-to-find road map available in the states. It is a one-sheet map but is relatively up-to-date and accurate.

In 1997 a new road atlas of Mexico began appearing in Mexican stores called the *Guia Roji Atlas de Carreteras*. It is better than any previous Guia Roji we've seen. This red-colored atlas was widely available in book stores and at newsstands in larger cities. Recently it has even been available at some stores in the U.S. A similar guide called the Guia Verdi (green-colored) also appeared at some newsstands, the maps were the same. These atlases are almost up to date and almost accurate, they're the best thing to be available on Mexican roads for some time.

Guia Roji also publishes a larger 17 by 11 inch format *Gran Atlas de Carreteras* that has one state on each page. For the most part it seems to be drawn with the same accuracy as the *Atlas de Carreteras* mentioned above except that small states are shown in amazing detail. There is a smaller but similar atlas called the *Atlas de los Estados de la Repúbilica Mexicana* and published by HFET, S.A. de CV but it is very difficult to find.

The Secretaría de Comunicaciónes y Transportes and Secretaría de Turismo have recently published a Tourist Road Map that is not bad. It has a lot of detail and shows most of the new toll roads. You may receive a copy if you send for information from the tourist offices. If not you can probably flag down a green angel and buy one from him, we did.

Topographical maps produced by the Mexican government are available in Mexico from offices of the INEGI (Instituto Nacional de Estadistica, Geografía, y Informatica) in each state capital in the country. Not all offices have all available maps at all times however. These come in both 1:50,000 and 1:250,000 scales.

Hikers and explorer types like the 1:1,000,000 maps produced by International Travel Maps (ITMB) 245 West Broadway, Vancouver, B.C., Canada V5Y 1P8; (604) 687-3320. They cover the Baja Peninsula, the Yucatán, the Gulf Coast and Southern Mexico. ITMB also publishes a 1:3,300,000 scale map of all of Mexico.

It is possible to order maps by mail, both highway and topographical, from several outlets in the U.S. Three that we like are Seattle's Wide World Books & Maps (1911 N. 45th, Seattle, WA 98103, 206-634-3453), Tucson's Map and Flag Center (3239 North First Ave., Tucson, AZ 85719, 800-473-1204 or 520-887-4234), and Map Link (25 East Mason Street, Santa Barbara, CA 93101; 800-627-7768 or 805-965-4402).

PROPANE

Either propane or butane is available near most larger towns or cities. The LP Gas storage yards are usually outside the central area of town. Ask at your campground for the best way to get a fill-up, in many locations truck will deliver to the campground. We've also seen people stop a truck on the street and get a fill-up.

We're accustomed to seeing only propane in much of the U.S. and Canada because butane won't work at low temperatures, it freezes. In parts of the southern U.S. and the warmer areas in Mexico butane is common and propane not available. This probably won't be a problem, most propane appliances in RVs will also run on butane. Make sure you use all the butane before you take your RV back into the cold country, however.

The fact is that you may never need to fill up with LP Gas at all. We find that if we fill up before crossing the border we have no problem getting our gas to last four months because we only use it for cooking. Some people run their refrigerators only on gas because they fear that some of the new electronic refrigerators can be damaged by the varying electrical voltage common to Mexican campgrounds. You may want to check into this, it is virtually impossible to get an RV refrigerator fixed in Mexico.

PUBLIC TRANSPORTATION

Much of the population of Mexico depends upon public transportation, they just don't have automobiles. Public transportation usually means busses, but taxis are usually available and sometimes reasonably priced, and Mexico City even has an extensive (and cheap) subway system.

Between cities bus travel is extremely inexpensive and convenient. First class busses run frequently, you'll see hundreds of them on the road. Second class busses run the same routes but aren't nearly as convenient, they stop constantly. You'll see lots of these too. Try taking advantage of the busses to do a little sightseeing. For example, we think busses from Puebla, Cuernavaca, or even San Miguel de Allende are a good way to visit Mexico City.

Inside cities busses make a great way to get around if you don't want to drive or haven't brought along a tow car. Leave the rig safe in the campground and catch a bus. These can take several forms. They may be normal city busses (often a converted school bus) or they may be collectivos (Volkswagen combis). In a normal bus you just pay the driver as you board. It is a good idea to ask if the bus really goes where you think it does. For example, if you are going to the city center say "¿ a centro?" (to the center?). Collectivos are much the same except that you often climb aboard and then pass your money through the hands of other passengers after pulling away from the stop. Bus and collectivo stops often aren't marked but you'll see groups of people standing waiting. Often you have to wave the bus down or it won't stop.

RESERVATIONS

You may want to make campground reservations before leaving Canada or the U.S. Many popular destinations do fill up during the months of December, January, February, March and early April. Travelers who definitely want to stay in one particular campground or want to have a particular location in a campground (like on the water) should make the attempt. We say "make the attempt" because reservation-making is often a matter of luck. Our campground descriptions indicate those where reservations are suggested and give the reservation phone number. The process is not generally simple, Usually it involves a phone call and then a letter with check or money order. We recommend that you not just send a letter or check without talking to someone at the campground. Often the most reliable way (or only way) to make a reservation is to make arrangements in the spring when you leave the campground for your stay the next year. Snow birds who always go back to the same place usually do this, they'll arrange to be in the same slot year after year.

Now the other side of the coin. We **never** make reservations and seldom have a problem getting into a campground. During the busy season (January through the end of March) we often have to settle for a less-desirable slot or campground when traveling the popular Baja or the west coast. There is also one campground on the Yucatán where reservations are recommended, that is Paa Mul. Occasionally you will find a campground to be full in other places because a caravan happens to be in town, but our experience is that there is usually room to squeeze one more rig in for the day or so that the caravan is in town.

SAFETY AND SECURITY

Mexico would be full of camping visitors from the U.S. and Canada if there was no security issue. Fear is the factor that crowds RVers into campgrounds just north of the border but leaves those a hundred miles south pleasantly uncrowded. People in those border campgrounds will warn you not to cross into Mexico because there are bandidos, dishonest cops, terrible roads, and language and water problems. The one thing you can be sure of when you get one of these warnings is that that person has not tried Mexican camping him/herself.

First-time camping visitors are almost always amazed at how trouble-free Mexican camping is. Few ever meet a bandito or get sick from the water. The general feeling is that Mexico is safer than much of the U.S., especially U.S. urban areas. After you've been in Mexico a few years you will hear about the occasional problem, just as you do north of the border. Most problems could have been easily avoided if the person involved had just observed a few common-sense safety precautions. Here are the ones we follow and feel comfortable with.

Never drive at night. Night driving is dangerous because Mexican roads are completely different at night. There are unexpected and hard-to-avoid road hazards, there are aggressive truck drivers, and there is little in the way of formal security patrols. If there are really any bandidos in the area they are most likely to be active after dark.

Don't free camp alone except in a place you are very sure of. Individual free campers are uniquely vulnerable. Many folks don't follow this rule and have no problems, it is up to you.

Don't open the door to a knock after dark. First crack a window to find out who is knocking. Why take chances. We've talked to a number of people who wish they'd followed this rule, even in campgrounds.

Don't leave your rig unguarded on the street if you can avoid it. Any petty crook knows your rig is full of good stuff, it is a great target. We like to leave ours in the campground while we explore. Use public transportation, it's lots of fun.

There are a couple of security precautions that you can take before leaving home, you probably have already taken them if you do much traveling in your rig. Add a dead bolt to your entrance door, some insurance policies in the states actually require this. If possible install an alarm in your vehicle, it can take a load off your mind when you must leave it on the street.

A final tip — don't park under any coconuts, they make a big dent if they fall on your rig or your head!

Spanish Language

You certainly don't need to be able to speak Spanish to get along just fine in Mexico. All of the people working in campgrounds, gas stations and stores are accustomed to dealing with non-Spanish speakers. Even if you can't really talk to them you'll be able to transact business.

On the other hand Mexico is a great place to learn Spanish. In many campgrounds you'll find groups of people who bring in a tutor and study on a regular schedule. There are also lots of Spanish schools scattered around the country. Best-known as good places to sturdy Spanish are San Miguel de Allende, Guadalajara, Álamos, Mexico City and Oaxaca but most larger cities have language institutes. A less formal arrangement with a Spanish speaker also works well, you can teach English and learn Spanish.

Telephones

Telephone service is rapidly improving in Mexico but is still expensive. Almost all cities now have Telmex phones on the street that you can use to call home for a reasonable fee, if you know how. Other companies, like AT&T, have started competing with Telmex so the improvement should continue. If a town does not yet have the street-side phones it usually has a phone office. You go in and the operator will dial for you and send you to a booth. When you are finished she'll get the charge and you pay her with cash.

It seems like every country has a different system of area codes and telephone numbers. Mexico is no exception. Each city has an area code in Mexico, it can have one, two, or three digits. Here are some of them: Mexico City 5, Guadalajara 3, Mazatlán 69, Puerto Vallarta 322, Cabo San Lucas 114. You can see that they vary considerably, look at the numbers given for campgrounds in our campground chapters, we give area codes. The individual phone numbers also have a varying number of digits, there can be 5, 6, or 7 so that there are a total of 8 digits when the area code is included. You can find a listing of area codes in the front of Mexican telephone books.

To call into Mexico from the U.S. or Canada you must first dial a 011 for international access, then the Mexico country code which is 52, then the Mexican area code and number. Often businesses will advertise in the U.S. with a number which includes some or all of these prefixes. Now that you know what they are you should have no problems dialing a Mexican number.

To call the U.S. or Canada out of Mexico from a Telmex phone you normally dial 95, then the area code and individual number. You can do this from most Telmex street-side phones (often labeled as Ladatel). You'll not get a very good rate by doing this, however. You can also dial Mexican numbers from these phones, the prefix to do this is 91. You also dial 91 before Mexican 800 (toll-free) numbers. Street-side phones take coins or special Ladatel prepaid cards, they are available in drug stores and other places.

The best way to call out of Mexico is to use a special access telephone number which will connect you with AT&T, MCI, Sprint, or other service provider. Calls done this way are the least expensive, in early 1997 we were paying less than $2.00 per minute for calls to the states. It isn't cheap but it is better than the alternatives. Make arrangements for doing this before leaving home, your long distance provider probably offers the service and can give you a special card, security code, and instructions for making these calls. AT&T will set you up at 1-800-331-1140, ext. 732. The same system is used for making calls throughout the world. You don't have to insert money into the phone to make this type of call except perhaps a small coin to get things started. The AT&T access number is 95-800-462-4240, MCI is 95-800-674-700, Sprint is 95-800-977-8000.

In the past the least expensive way to call home has been to call collect. This is still a good way to go. To do so from a street-side phone dial 9, an English-speaking operator will come on and help you. You can also make these calls using the access numbers given directly above.

The latest scourge to hit the telephone-starved traveler to Mexico is credit card-accepting phones placed conveniently in most tourist areas. Many Mexican businesses have allowed these things to be installed as a convenience to their customers since a normal phone is almost impossible to obtain. Unfortunately they are a real problem, the rate charged is often in excess of $8 U.S. per minute for calls to numbers outside Mexico. We have talked to several unsuspecting users who found charges of several hundred dollars on their credit card statements when they returned home. You can pick up any of these phones and ask the English-speaking operator for the initial and per-minute fee. Hopefully these rates will go down as people wise up and learn to ask.

TOLL ROADS

During the last decade or so Mexico has built many fine roads. These new highways are loved and hated. They're loved in part because they make virtually the entire country easily accessible to visitors. They're hated because they are toll roads, and the tolls are some of the highest in the world.

Typically tolls are charged based upon the number of axles on your vehicle. Here are the early 1997 rates converted to dollars from a toll booth for a segment of Mex. 15D between Tepic and Guadalajara: Automobiles $6.97, 2 *ejes* (axles) $10.19, 3 and 4 axles $13.16. Some interpretation is necessary. If you have single wheels on the back of a van it qualifies for the automobile rate. If you have duals on the back of a van or small RV (but only one axle in the rear) you qualify for the 2 axle rate. If you are an RV with 2 axles (front and rear) pulling a car you pay the four-axle rate. A normal pickup pulling a two-axle fifth wheel pays for 4 axles. This toll booth is one of four on the Tepic-Guadalajara run which is a total of about 140 miles (225 km). The rate for an automobile to travel the entire distance in January 1997 was 203 pesos or $26.19 U.S., about $.19 U.S. per mile. You can see that traveling by toll road can be a significant cost especially in an RV with lots of axles.

The tolls charged on the Tepic to Guadalajara toll road are typical of those on the newest highways. It is a beautiful four-lane superhighway that cuts across rugged mountains. The highway is also typical in that there is a perfectly free alternate route. Unfortunately the alternate is in very poor condition and full of trucks. It will take you at least twice as long to drive from Tepic to Guadalajara on the free road. You'll use lots more gas, you'll have a much higher chance of having mechanical trouble or an accident, and the wear on your rig will be significantly higher.

It has been the government's policy to have a free road alternate whenever a toll road is built. Sometimes the free road is the best route and sometimes the toll road is best. If there is no alternate route the toll road is often government owned and tolls are reasonable. All of this makes choosing a route quite complicated. When we are driving a big rig (usually a motorhome with tow car) we follow the trucks. They are knowledgeable and generally do a pretty good job of making the convenience/cost tradeoff decision to our satisfaction. In a smaller vehicle like our 19-foot van we almost always choose the toll roads. You will have to determine your own tolerance for grinding up grades behind slow trucks and bouncing over potholes. Incidentally, there are almost no trucks on the Tepic to Guadalajara toll road.

As you whiz along on the toll roads with no traffic (everyone else is on the free road) you'll wonder why the toll road builders don't lower their rates to get more traffic. It seems obvious that they would make more money charging more cars smaller fees. This is a constant topic of conversation around the evening cocktail table in RV parks. One thing is sure, the road operating companies have thought of this. Would more traffic cause much higher maintenance costs? Is demand inelastic so lower prices wouldn't really make enough more people drive the toll roads? (ha!) Is this a negotiating tactic by private companies or the banks financing them to somehow get government money? We'll just have to wait and see, it is clear that the present situation of high rates and no traffic can't last.

TRAVEL LIBRARY

Don't go to Mexico without a general tourist guide with information about the places you'll visit. Even if you're in Mexico for the sun and fun you'll have questions that no one seems to be able to answer. One of the best of the guides for our money is *Mexico Handbook* by Joe Cummings and Chichi Mallen, published by Moon Publications Inc. in 1996, ISBN 1-56691-031-5. It covers cities and towns, ruins, and even a surprising number of trailer parks and camping spots.

Other guides in the same down-to-earth economy-travel vein are Lonely Planet's *Mexico: A Travel Survival Kit* , *Mexico: The Rough Guide, Let's Go Mexico*, and *Mexico & Central American Handbook* by Prentice Hall Travel.

In guidebooks as in maps the American Automobile Association is an excellent source of information. Their *Mexico Travel Book*, updated annually, covers only the cities they think worth a visitor's time. It is so well organized that we use it when we travel to make sure we aren't missing anything. In the back there's even a decent campground directory.

For a background information about Mexican history, culture and politics you should read Alan Riding's book *Distant Neighbors*. The book was originally published in 1984. It is somewhat outdated but you will be amazed at how it predicts exactly the things that are happening in Mexico today. The book is still in print and paperback editions are not difficult to find.

Baja traveler's have a wealth of books available to them. Don't read Walt Peterson's *The Baja Adventure Book* (Wilderness Press, Berkeley, CA, 1992, ISBN 0-89997-130-X) if you're not sure you really want to visit the Baja because after reading it you won't be able to stay away. *The Magnificent Peninsula: The Comprehensive Guidebook to Mexico's Baja California* by Jack Williams (H.J. Williams Publications, Sausalito, CA, 1996, ISBN 0-9616843-7-2) is just what the title says. It has lots of information about free camping spots on the peninsula, and lots of other things too. A unique map book to the peninsula is *The Baja Book III: A Complete New Map-Guide to Today's Baja California* by Tom Miller and Carol Hoffman (Baja Trail Publications, Huntington Beach, CA, 1992, ISBN 0-914622-10-2). To get some good background try reading *Into a Desert Place: A 3000-Mile Walk Around the Coast of Baja California* by Graham Machintosh (W.W. Norton & Co., New York, NY, 1990, ISBN 0-393-31289-5). Fishermen will find *The Baja Catch* by Neil Kelly and Gene Kira (Apples and Oranges, Inc., Valley Center, CA, ISBN 0-929637-01-1) to be absolutely essential. Also lots of fun if you can find them are some old books about exploring the Baja back country by Perry Mason detective novel author Erle Stanley Gardner: *Mexico's Magic Square, Off the Beaten Track in Baja, The Hidden Heart of Baja, Hovering over Baja,* and *Hunting the Desert Whale.* Try libraries and used book stores for these classics from the 1960's.

Explorers traveling the Mexican west coast will enjoy the *Mexico West Book* by

Tom Miller and Carol Hoffman (Baja Trail Publications, Huntington Beach, CA, 1991, ISBN 0-914622-09-9). It is oriented toward driving and covers the entire coast from Golfo de Santa Clara to Puerto Arista in Chiapas, it also occasionally jogs inland to places like the Copper Canyon, Guadalajara, Oaxaca and San Cristóbal de las Casas. Miller explores almost every small road to the beach, his work will make your own exploring a lot more productive.

A visit to Mexico is a great way to study Spanish. Make sure to bring along a good Spanish-English dictionary. If you want to study while on your trip we recommend Living Language's book *Spanish All the Way* (Crown Publishers, Inc., New York, NY, 1994, ISBN 0-517-58373-9). It is available in a package with four CDs, great for studying while on the road.

There is one tourist guide to Mexico that is in a class by itself. Sanborn's Insurance can provide you with detailed mile-by-mile Travelogs of almost every route in the country. These logs are prepared by "Mexico Mike" Nelson and include lots of maps and advice. They also have so much detail that most folks set them aside after a few days because they have acquired excruciating headaches. Still, they are extremely valuable at times. In the past it was necessary to buy Sanborn's insurance to get these guides, recently memberships to the Mexico Amigo Club have become available separately for about $40 per year. Membership in the Amigo Club includes free Travelogs. Mexico Mike also writes books about traveling in Mexico including *Mexico's Colonial Heart* (ISBN 1-878166-17-4) and *Mexico from the Driver's Seat* (ISBN 1-878166-04-2). These books are available at Sanborn's and also in book stores. You can contact Sanborn's at (800) 222-0158 or (210) 686-3601.

TRAVELING IN GROUPS

Many people feel more secure traveling with several other rigs in Mexico, especially if this is a first visit. In fact they are more secure. Several rigs free camping together on a beach are much less likely to be bothered than a single camper. Likewise, if one rig has mechanical problems the others can provide help, or at least help to get help. When it comes to figuring out the unfamiliar often several heads are better than one.

There is a down side to traveling together also. The truth is that three rigs traveling together will have three times the mechanical problems. We have yet to see a caravan of RVs that wasn't being slowed by at least one rig with problems. If you do decide to travel with a group of other RV's make sure that they are in good mechanical condition before you start, otherwise there may be unexpected friction.

And that brings up another point. Only compatible people should travel together. We have met several groups who teamed up when they met at the border. Often these groups split within a week. Some people like to travel fast, others slow. Some like to get up early, others late. Some have rigs in great mechanical condition, some do not. If you must have a companion rig make sure you know them well, try traveling together north of the border first. Actually, a good place to meet compatible travel partners is on a commercial guided caravan trip.

As you travel around Mexico, even if you are a single rig, you will find that you are not really alone. Everyone trades tips about good camping spots and interesting places they have visited. Mexico is an adventure and people want to talk about it. You will get to know other people and you will find that you often run into them again, usually without planning it. After all, there are a limited number of campgrounds and even a dedicated free camper uses them occasionally.

Type of Rig

The truth is that you can travel Mexico in almost any type of vehicle, anything from a bicycle to the largest bus-style RV. Each kind of rig has its own advantages and disadvantages. The best rig depends upon where you want to go; how you travel, sight see, and shop; and how much you want to spend. We've always felt that we want the largest possible rig when we're parked, and the smallest and most maneuverable when we're on the road.

Many people do visit Mexico on bicycles. We have never thought Mexico a great bicycle destination because many highways are narrow and heavily traveled. When you see a Mexican on a bicycle you will notice that he often is forced to climb off his bike and step off the road for all passing traffic, hardly the way to make much progress. The obvious way to get around this problem is to travel back roads, something easier to say than to do. In many regions there are few minor roads and the ones that do exist don't go to the places you're likely to want to visit. There are some exceptions. Many people ride Mex. 1 on the Baja Peninsula. They can do this because much of the road is not extremely busy. Other possible biking areas are the back roads in the Chiapas mountains, the Yucatán, and Oaxaca. Fortunately bike travelers in Mexico can easily use the extensive bus system to move from one area to another.

It is entirely possible to travel comfortably in Mexico with an automobile or light truck and tent. You'll want a good insect-proof tent to keep out both the flying insects you're probably familiar with at home and the stinging crawlers you may meet in Mexico. If you plan to do no backpacking there is no real reason to use a small tent, you'll be more comfortable in one that allows you to stand up. Folding cots of some kind will let you get a much better night's sleep.

If you are at all interested in exploring there are big advantages to using a smaller camping vehicle. On the Baja Peninsula there are many roads that are just not suitable for larger RVs. Four-wheel drive is nice to have on the Baja although just having good ground clearance is a big help. On the mainland a small rig is much cheaper to use on toll roads. Smaller rigs also are easier to shepherd along Mexico's narrow and often steep highways. The warm climate in this part of the world means that you can spend a lot of time outside the rig, many people bring along one of those screened tent-rooms where then can set up a card table or cots and effectively double the size of their rig.

We've traveled the highways of Mexico extensively in a 34-foot gas-powered motorhome pulling a pick-up. We had no problems and feel that any reasonably cautious person can go almost anywhere where there are paved roads. The two Achilles heels of big rigs are ground clearance and poor maneuverability. Both of these are not nearly as limiting if you know what to expect. Hopefully this book will help in that area. While on the road the key is caution. Keep the speed down so that you have complete control and slow even more when large vehicles pass you in either direction. In spots with no shoulder a wheel off the pavement could mean disaster.

Units of Measurement

Mexico is on the metric system. Most of the world has already learned to deal with this. For the rest of us it takes just a short time of working with the metric system, and there is no way to avoid it, to start to feel at home. Conversion tables and factors are available in most guide books but you will probably remember a few critical conversion numbers as we have.

For distance runners like ourselves, kilometers were easy. A kilometer is about .62 miles (actually .6124). We can remember this because a 10 kilometer race is 6.2 miles long. For converting miles to kilometer, divide the number of miles by .62. For converting kilometers to miles, multiply the kilometers by .62. Since kilometers are shorter than miles the number of kilometers after the conversion will always be more than the number of miles, if they aren't you divided when you should have multiplied.

For liquid measurement it is usually enough to know that a liter is about the same as a quart. When you need more accuracy, like when you are trying to make some sense out of your miles per gallon calculations, there are 3.79 liters in a U.S. gallon.

Weight measurement is important when you're trying to decide how much cheese or hamburger you need to make a meal. Since a kilogram is about 2.2 pounds we just round to two pounds. This makes a half pound equal to about 250 grams and a pound equal to 500 grams. It's not exact, but it certainly works in the grocery store, and we get a little more than we expected for dinner.

Here are a few useful conversion factors:

> 1 km = .62 mile
> 1 mile = 1.61 km
> 1 meter = 3.28 feet
> 1 foot = .30 meters
> 1 liter = .26 U.S. gallon
> 1 U.S. gallon = 3.79 liters
> 1 kilogram = 2.21 pounds
> 1 pound = .45 kilograms
> convert from °F to °C by subtracting 32 and multiplying by 5/9
> convert from °C to °F by multiplying by 1.8 and adding 32

VEHICLE PREPARATION AND BREAKDOWNS

One of the favorite subjects whenever a group of Mexican campers gets together over cocktails is war stories about breakdowns and miraculous repairs performed by Mexican mechanics with almost no tools. Before visiting Mexico many people fear a break-down above all else. Our experience and that of the people we talk to is that help is generally readily available and very reasonably priced. It is usually easy to find someone to work on the vehicle, it is often very hard to get parts.

Ford, General Motors, Chrysler, Volkswagen and Nissan all manufacture cars and trucks in Mexico and have large, good dealers throughout the country. Toyota does not. These dealers are good places to go if you need emergency or maintenance work done on your vehicle. However, many of the models sold in the north are not manufactured in Mexico and the dealers may not have parts for your particular vehicle. They can order them but often this takes several weeks.

Often the quickest way to get a part is to go get it yourself. One of our acquaintances recently broke an axle in Villahermosa. His vehicle is common in Mexico, but the type of axle he needed was not used in the Mexican models. Rather than wait an indeterminate length of time for a new axle he went and picked one up himself. He climbed on a bus, traveled to Matamoros, walked across the border, caught a cab to a dealer, picked up a new axle and threw it over his shoulder, walked back across the border, caught another bus, and was back in Villahermosa within 48 hours.

Avoid problems by making sure your vehicle is in good condition before entering Mexico. Get an oil change, a lube job, and a tune-up. Make sure that hoses, belts, filters, brake pads, shocks and tires are all good. Consider replacing them before you leave. Driving conditions in Mexico tend to be extreme. Your vehicle will be operating on rough roads, in very hot weather, with lots of climbs and descents.

Bring along a reasonable amount of spares. We like to carry replacement belts, hoses, and filters. Make sure you have a good spare tire. Don't bring much oil, good multi-weight oil is now available in Mexico.

RV drivers need to be prepared to make the required hook ups in Mexican RV parks. RV supplies are difficult to find in Mexico so make sure that you have any RV supplies you need before crossing the border.

Electricity is often suspect at campgrounds in Mexico. It is a good idea to carry a tester that will tell you when voltages are incorrect, polarities reversed, and grounds lacking. Always carry adapters allowing you to use small 110V, two-pronged outlets. The best set-up is one that lets you turn the plug over (to reverse polarity) and to connect a ground wire to a convenient pipe, conduit, or metal stake.

Sewer stations (dranaje) in many Mexican campgrounds are located at the rear of the site. Make sure you have a long sewer hose, one that will reach all the way to the rear of your RV and then another couple of feet. You'll be glad you have it.

Water purity considerations (see the Drinking Water title in this chapter), mean that you may need a few items that you may not already have in your rig. Consider adding a water filter if you do not already have one installed. You should also have a simple filter for filtering water before it even enters your rig, this avoids sediment build-up in your fresh water tank. Of course you'll also need a hose, we have found a 20 foot length to be adequate in most cases..

It is extremely hard to find parts or knowledgeable mechanics to do systems related work on camping vehicles. Before crossing the border make sure your propane system, all appliances, toilet, holding tanks, and water system are working well because you'll want them to last until you get home. Marginal or jury-rigged systems should be repaired. Consider bringing a spare fresh water pump, or at least a diaphragm set if yours isn't quite new. Make sure your refrigerator is working well, you'll need it and replacement parts are impossible to find.

Make sure you have all the tools necessary to change a tire on your rig. Many large motorhomes no longer come with jacks and tire-changing tools. The theory must be that it is too dangerous for an individual to change a tire on one of these huge heavy rigs. This may be true but you need to have the proper tools available so that you can find help and get the job done if you have a flat in a remote location. Mexican roads are rough and flat tires common.

WATERFRONT CAMPSITE ON THE PACIFIC COAST

If you do have a breakdown along the road what should you do? It is not a good idea to abandon your rig. RVs are a tempting target, one abandoned along the road invites a break-in. This is one good reason not to travel at night. Daytime drivers can usually find a way to get their broken-down rig off the road before night falls. If you are traveling with another rig you can send someone for help. If you are traveling by yourself you will probably find it easy to flag down a car or truck. We find that Mexican drivers are much more helpful than those in the U.S. Ask the other driver to send a mechanic or *grúa* (tow truck) from the next town. Large tow trucks are common since there is heavy truck traffic on most highways in Mexico.

WEATHER

Most of Mexico really has two seasons: a wet season and a dry season. The wet season is the summer, from approximately June through some time September or October. During this period, in many parts of the country, it rains each afternoon. Much of the country is also extremely hot during this period. If you can only visit in the summer plan on hot, muggy weather along the Gulf Coast, the Yucatán, Chiapas, and much of the west coast. On the Baja Peninsula and the deserts of northern Mexico expect extremely hot weather. Added excitement on the Yucatán and along the southern Pacific Coast may be provided by hurricane season from August through October.

The winter dry season is when most travelers visit Mexico. In a fortunate conjunction of factors the extremely pleasant warm dry season in Mexico occurs exactly when most northerners are more than ready to leave snow and cold temperatures behind. Comfortable temperatures occur beginning in November and last through May. The shoulder months of November and June may be uncomfortably warm for some people.

For year-round comfort consider the higher elevations. Guadalajara and Cuernavaca are both famous for their year-round good weather and there are many other nearby cities with similarly decent weather during almost the entire year. Even in the highlands, however, expect afternoon showers.

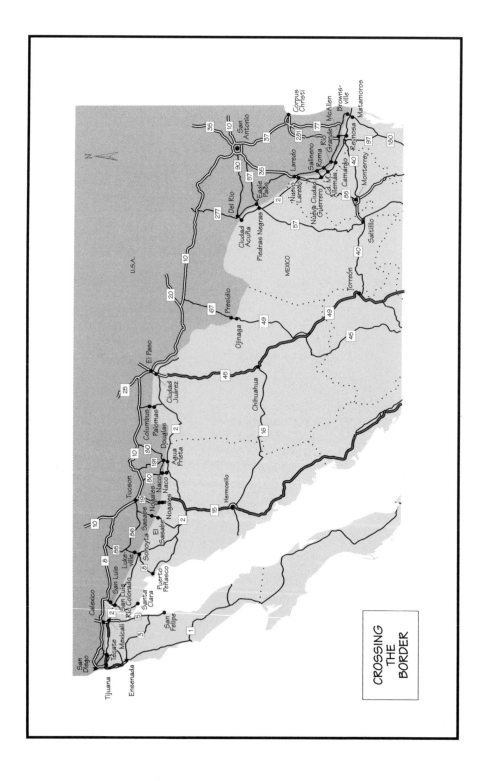

CROSSING THE BORDER

CHAPTER 3

CROSSING THE BORDER

Crossing the border into Mexico for the first time can be one of the most intimidating things you will do during your entire visit to the country. This is understandable. Mexico is so different from the U.S. that you undergo something of a culture shock the first day. When we cross the border each time we immediately notice that there is more dust, more garbage along the roadside, more people on foot, and that the roads are much poorer. Part of this is due to the fact that the border region is probably the least attractive part of Mexico. Within a few days we stop noticing these things and you probably will too. When you return to the U.S. you're likely to think that things seem sterile and uninteresting.

If you have your ducks in a row and know what to expect the border crossing will be a much less trying experience. In this chapter we'll try to give you some information to make it easier. Below you'll find sections about documentation, insurance, and what you can take to Mexico without problems. We'll even give you information about some of the more popular border crossings.

We think that the first time you go through the border crossing ritual you should arrive fairly early the day before you plan to cross and find a campground on the U.S. side. Spend the afternoon purchasing insurance and possibly having your tourist card and temporary vehicle import permit prepared by AAA or Sanborns (see below). Fill your tank with good U.S. gasoline, hit the stores for last minute purchases, and have a nice dinner. The next day cross the border about 10 A.M., after the commute rush but plenty early enough to give yourself time to reach your planned destination before dark.

PEOPLE DOCUMENTATION

Any U.S. or Canadian citizen entering Mexico for more than 72 hours must have a *tarjeta de turista* or tourist card. Don't leave home without proof of your citizenship because you will need it to get your tourist card (and are required to have it even for short visits to border areas). The best proof of citizenship is a passport but a certified copy of your birth certificate is also acceptable. If you use your birth certificate instead of a passport you will also need a picture ID like a driver's license. Even infants must have a tourist card. In some parts of Mexico it is not unusual for roadblocks to be set up to check everyone who passes for identification. The army troops at these roadblocks often speak no English and prefer passports, this seems reason enough for us to go through the trouble of getting a passport if you don't have one already.

Tourist cards are required for any visit beyond border areas or if you are going to be inside Mexico more than 72 hours. The cards are free and are issued for periods of up to 180 days. You can get them at border stations or you can pick them up before entering Mexico at Mexican government tourist offices, Mexican consulate offices, AAA (American Automobile Association) offices in Texas, Sanborn's Insurance offices and some other travel agencies near the border. If you pick up your tourist card outside of Mexico be sure to have it validated when you enter Mexico, it is not valid otherwise. The tourist cards must be returned when you leave the country. It is also possible to obtain a multiple-entry card if you plan to leave and return to Mexico. This type of card is available at border crossings.

As a practical matter the tourist card tends to take second place in importance to the vehicle documentation discussed below but that doesn't mean it can be ignored. Since you have to take care of the vehicle documentation anyway you generally will have your tourist card business done at the same time.

The Baja Peninsula is a special case. Vehicle documentation is not required on the Baja but tourist cards are. If you are on the Baja south of the Ensenada area or are anywhere on the Baja for more than 72 hours you are required to have a tourist card. Many people don't get them, either because they don't know they're required or because they are not often checked. If you get caught you are at least subject to a fine, and we have been told that campgrounds on the Baja were being spot-checked during the 96-97 winter.

Another special case is the Sonoran Free Trade Zone. This area encompasses northwestern Sonora state and includes the area east to Sonoyta and Puerto Peñasco. Visitors to this area need neither tourist cards nor vehicle import documents. It includes both Puerto Peñasco and Golfo de Santa Clara.

Many people do not worry about returning their tourist cards when they leave the country. Currently the Mexican government does not seem to keep track of tourist cards outstanding in any manner. In fact, last time we left Mexico the official we were dealing with waved us off when we tried to return our cards. Officials at border stations seldom check tourist cards since you don't even have to have one if you are planning to stay in a border town for less than 72 hours.

Vehicle Documentation

You should have the title or registration to all of the vehicles you bring to Mexico. This includes any that do not need a temporary vehicle importation permit. It also includes all vehicles brought into areas where import permits are not required, like the Baja and the northwestern part of Sonora.

In an effort to combat the illegal importation of vehicles the Mexican government has an elaborate procedure to make sure you bring yours back into the states. These procedures take some time and usually involve standing in a couple of lines, but it seems that things are better organized than when we first went through the procedure several years ago. The last time we crossed the border the entire process of vehicle and personal documentation took less than a half-hour.

To get your temporary vehicle importation permit you must have proof of citizenship, a driver's license, and the vehicle's title or registration. If you do not own the vehicle you must have a letter from the owner stating that you may take it into Mexico for a specified period of time. If your title or registration shows a leinholder (you have a loan secured by the car) you must have a letter from the leinholder stating that you can take it into Mexico for a specified period of time. You should make these letters look official. Make sure they are on letterhead and consider getting the signatures notarized. Rental cars require both a rental agreement and notarized permission letter for travel into Mexico.

You must also have a credit card (Master Card, VISA, American Express or Diner's Club) issued in the registered owner's name and issued by a U.S. or Canadian bank. If you don't have such a credit card there is an alternate procedure. You can post a bond based upon the value of the vehicle. The bonding process is complicated and somewhat expensive so go the credit card route if at all possible.

When you cross the border you should have your documentation in hand as well as two xerox copies of your proof of citizenship, driver's license, vehicle registration, and tourist card. For some reason we've never succeeded in having the right combinations of these copies even though we always give it our best shot. Never fear, there usually seems to be a handy copy machine where the operator knows exactly what you need and can produce them for a reasonable fee. You'll have your documents processed, go to a bank window where a fee of approximately $11 U.S. will be charged to your credit card, and then an official will accompany you to your vehicle where he/she will put a metallic sticker on the upper left corner of your window. This sticker must remain on the vehicle until you leave the country. When you leave you must stop and have the sticker removed at the border station. The Mexican government does keep track of this and will fine you if you don't properly return the sticker.

Camping travelers often want to stay in Mexico for several months. This can sometimes be a problem. We've recently run into people who have had trouble getting either tourist cards or vehicle permits for the length of time they request. This is a problem because getting an extension once you are in Mexico, while sometimes possible, is time consuming and a hassle. We suggest that you make every effort to get the right length of time on your tourist card and vehicle permit before leaving the border. Check your tourist card, your vehicle import permit, and your sticker. They all have an expiration date and sometimes do not match. We have never had a problem, we always request and get six months, but if we were unable to get the proper length of time on our documents we would consider giving it up for the day and trying another border crossing. The problems experienced by the people we met were isolated and may represent an individual border official's angry reaction to the recent tightening of border crossing procedures by the U.S. government.

If all of this seems complicated there is a way to simplify. Sanborn's offices and some AAA offices in border states will now help your prepare your paperwork for crossing the border, both tourist cards and vehicle permits. You can deal with someone who speaks English and when you do get to the border the process goes much more quickly. There is a fee for the service at Sanborn's and you undoubtedly need to be an AAA member to use their service. Since these people process lots of paperwork they are knowledgeable, if you have questions about your documentation you might consider giving them a call before leaving home.

VEHICLE INSURANCE

Your automobile insurance from home will not provide adequate coverage in Mexico. Insurance is not required in Mexico, but you are very foolish to do without it. Mexico follows the Napoleonic code, you are guilty until proven innocent. If you have an accident and have no liability insurance that assures the authorities that you can pay for damages it is possible that you might be detained for a considerable time. Some U.S. and Canadian policies will cover damages to your own vehicle in Mexico, check with your carrier about this.

Don't believe the old saw that all Mexican insurance costs the same, this is not true. Get several quotes and compare coverages. People who go into Mexico for just a short time usually buy daily coverage. This is extremely expensive. Some people get this short-term coverage for the week or so it takes to get to their favorite campground. Once there they park the vehicle and don't use it until they buy more short term coverage for the drive home.

Longer term coverage, for six months or a year, is much cheaper. It is comparable with the cost of insurance in the U.S. Here are names and addresses for a few of the companies that offer Mexican insurance: International Gateway Insurance Brokers, 3450 Bonita Road, Suite 101, Chula Vista, CA 91910 ((619) 422-2671); Sanborn's, P.O. Box 310, McAllen, Texas 78505 (800-222-0158), Ray Phillips Mexico Insurance (800-570-6006 or 520-570-6006); Alliance Insurance Group, 3420 E. Shea Blvd., Suite 170, Phoenix, AZ 85028 (602) 996-7600; Point South RV Tours (800-321-1394 or 909-247-1394). It is best to arrange for your long-term coverage before you arrive at the border, it may not be available at all crossings. Do some shopping by phone before leaving home.

Getting inexpensive long-term insurance coverage may involve joining a travel club. You may do so right at the insurance office or you might want to call one of these clubs for a quote: Discover Baja Travel Club (800-727-BAJA or 619-275-4225), Vagabundos del Mar Travel Club (800-47-4-BAJA), Sanborn's Amigo Club (800-222-0158), Point South Mexico Travel Club (800-421-1394).

PETS

Dogs and cats often accompany RVers to Mexico. They are generally not a problem, you just have to take care of some paperwork before leaving home. Forget about bringing birds or other pets since procedures for doing so are not in place.

Not more than 30 days before entering Mexico you must get a certificate from your veterinarian that your pet has had its shots for distemper and rabies and is in good health. The form required is 77-043, called the International Health Certificate for Dogs and Cats, it must be signed by the vet. You may also be required to have a seperate rabies inoculation permit showing that the animal has had a shot within the previous 6 months.

We've talked to many people with dogs and pets in Mexico. Most indicate that they've never been asked for anything while entering Mexico but that they are often asked for the form when re-entering the U.S.

BOATS

You will need a boat permit if you plan to use your boat for fishing (or even if you have fishing tackle on board). You can wait to get one until you get to Mexico, they are available from the Mexican Department of Fisheries (*Pesca*) offices in various port cities. In the U.S. they have an office at 2550 Fifth Avenue, Suite 101, San Diego, CA 92103. The Vagabundos del Mar Boat and Travel Club can also provide them, call (800) 474-2252.

Make sure that your vehicle insurance also covers your boat. Trailered boats and cartoppers may need to be mentioned in your insurance in order for it to be valid.

ATVS AND MOTORCYCLES

Vehicle import documents are required for ATVs and motorcycles, just as for cars and RVs. Since vehicle import licenses are not required for the Baja Peninsula or for the Sonora Free Trade Zone these are both popular off-road destinations.

FISHING LICENSES

All individuals who fish or are aboard a fishing vessel must have a fishing license. These are available at the same places as the boat permits covered above.

WHAT CAN YOU TAKE ALONG?

Campers have the ability to bring more things along with them when they visit Mexico than most people. When you cross the border you may be stopped and your things quickly checked. You are actually allowed to bring only certain specified items into Mexico duty free and most RVer probably have more things along with them than they should. Here is a list of what each person can bring, if you exceed it you may find yourself paying an import fee or duty.

- A reasonable amount of clothing and personal items including jewelry
- RV kitchen, living, and bedroom furnishings and utensils
- 3 liters alcoholic beverages
- 50 cigars or 250 grams tobacco
- $50 of gift items
- Books and magazines
- Personal medicine (bring prescriptions)
- 1 TV set
- 1 videocassette player
- 1 bicycle
- 1 row boat or kayak (no engine)
- 1 pair binoculars
- 1 camera
- 12 rolls of film for camera
- 1 video camera
- 12 blank cassettes
- 1 CB radio
- Tent and camping equipment
- Fishing tackle
- 1 portable radio
- 20 records or cassettes
- 1 musical instrument
- 5 used toys

It is quite easy for RV travelers to have a lot more on board than is actually allowed by law. Fortunately Mexican border authorities seldom are hard-nosed, in fact they usually don't do much looking around at all. Lately we have heard that people bringing large quantities of food sometimes have problems getting it across the border. Now that Mexico has such good supermarkets there is really little need to bring in food.

What You Can't Bring Along

Guns and illegal drugs. Either of these things will certainly get you in big trouble. If you travel much on Mexican highways you'll eventually be stopped and searched. Guns and drugs are exactly what they will be looking for.

It is illegal for any non-Mexican to have a firearm of any type without a special Mexican permit. These are for hunters and must be obtained through licensed Mexican hunting guides.

What Can You Bring Back

Things purchased in Mexico and brought back into the U.S. are subject to duty. There is a $400 per person exclusion for each 31 day period. Additionally, if you are over 21 you may bring back one liter of alcoholic beverages and 200 cigarettes or 100 cigars duty free. There may be a liquor tax levied by the state, Texas does this. Some things, including handicrafts, are excluded from duty. Over the $400 limit there is a 10% duty up to $1,000, then individual tariff rates are applied to each item.

We always prepare a complete list of all of our Mexican purchases. We do this so that it is obvious that we make a practice of crossing our T's and dotting our I's. Hopefully this will keep one of the U.S. officials from getting the idea that he must do a very thorough search of our vehicle which in an RV can be very time consuming.

When you come back into the U.S. you should be prepared for an agricultural inspection also. Certain food items from Mexico are not allowed to cross the border and will be taken from you. These include almost all fruit including avocados and some vegetables, eggs (unless they are boiled or cooked), pork or chicken, and some other items.

The regulations covering items that Canadian citizens can bring back to Canada are slightly different.

CHANGES TO THE REGULATIONS

All of the regulations in this chapter tend to change frequently. Don't be surprised to find that some of these rules have changed by the time you visit Mexico.

SELECTED BORDER CROSSINGS

TIJUANA,
BAJA CALIFORNIA

TIJUANA

The San Ysidro port-of-entry at Tijuana is the most popular crossing point for persons heading south onto the Baja Peninsula. This is a good crossing point if you are headed south and do not need to stop to get a tourist card or vehicle import permit. This will be the case if you are not going to take your vehicles off the Baja and if you are willing to pick up your tourist card at the Migración office in Ensenada. Otherwise you will hate this crossing point because it is so busy and crowded that parking your rig to take care of paperwork can be a nightmare, especially if you are driving a large vehicle. Coming north you should avoid this crossing point because lines can be terrible.

U.S. Highways 5 and 805 run directly south from San Diego to the San Ysidro border crossing at Tijuana. Traffic is extremely heavy because they merge just before the border crossing making it very difficult to change lanes in a big rig. Watch carefully for signs, there may be one telling RVs to use a special lane. If you do see the sign you may not be able to get into the proper lane because of traffic. This happened to us one time and seemed to make no difference at all.

Once across the border you will probably want to take the coastal road south to Ensenada. Follow signs for Rosarito and Ensenada, an off ramp leads to the highway that runs west alongside the border fence. You'll probably see men crouched behind it watching the American border patrol. Follow the road west, it soon meets another road which will take you directly to the Mex. 1D *cuota* highway (toll road) south past Rosarito to Ensenada and points south. It is also possible to follow a free road south, this is Mex. 1 or Mex. 1 Libre. We have found the routes through Tijuana to be well-signed.

There is a second Tijuana crossing point to the east of town called Otay Mesa. Access is a little more difficult than the San Ysidro crossing on both sides of the border. Going south the San Ysidro crossing is probably your best bet, but heading north Otay Mesa usually has much shorter lines. In Mexico this crossing is labeled on signs as Garita Otay Mesa. You may find access to this crossing easier if you follow the free Mex. 1 Libre from Rosarito instead of Mex. 1D. As you approach Tijuana turn right onto the Libramiento Oriente which is marked for Garita Otay Mesa and follow similar signs to the border.

TECATE, BAJA CALIFORNIA

Tecate, about 30 miles (49 km) miles east of Tijuana, offers a much more relaxed border crossing. We especially like to use the Tecate border crossing when headed north. Tecate is a small town without a lot of traffic. Mex. 3 south from Tecate to Ensenada is a good alternative for folks heading north and south, it meets the coastal road just north of Ensenada. En route you pass across scenic mountains and through vineyards in the Valle de Guadeloupe. There's even a campground near the wineries if you don't feel like driving on into Ensenada.

At the Tecate crossing there is no town on the U.S. side of the border. If you are heading south you will immediately find yourself on city streets. Parking is not difficult and there are insurance sales offices in the immediate vicinity. To find Mex. 3 just jog left one block when you are able. You'll find yourself on the street that becomes Mex. 3.

A word of warning. The Tecate crossing is not open 24 hours. It closes at midnight and doesn't open again until six in the morning.

MEXICALI, BAJA CALIFORNIA

Mexicali is the preferred border-crossing point for folks headed south to San Felipe on the Baja Peninsula's east coast. This is a big, sprawling city and traffic for San Felipe must pass directly through the middle of town. Fortunately the way is well-signed in both directions. The route follows Lopez Mateos boulevard until reaching both the east/west Mex. 2 and Mex. 5 to the south. Mex. 2 passes south of the central area of Mexicali on city streets. Where it crosses Mex. 5 things are somewhat confusing because the highway jogs through several intersections. Traffic headed north lines up along the border fence to the east of the port-of-entry. As you pass through Mexicali on your way south you'll see several large supermarkets, good places to stop for groceries since San Felipe doesn't offer anything nearly as grand.

SAN LUIS RÍO COLORADO, SONORA

San Luis Río Colorado is the normal crossing for visitors headed south for Golfo de Santa Clara. The town is convenient to Yuma, Arizona 29 miles (47 km) to the north but doesn't have much cross-border traffic. San Luis is a small town but east/west Mex. 2 runs about a block south of the border through town. There's more traffic than you would expect in a town this size. Coming from the U.S. you'll see signs for Golfo de Santa Clara as soon as you cross the border. Headed north traffic lines up along the border fence east of the crossing, just as it does in Mexicali.

SONOYTA, SONORA

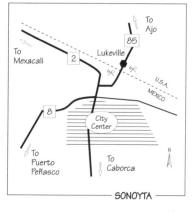

Sonoyta is the crossing for traffic headed south to Rocky Point (Puerto Peñasco). This crossing is closed from midnight to 6 A.M. It is one of the quietest border crossings of all and seldom has a line. Just south of the port-of-entry, in the small town of Sonoyta with 17,000 people, is east/west Mex. 2. San Luis Río Colorado is 124 miles (203 km) west, Santa Ana and Mex. 15 (the highway from Nogales south to the west coast) 159 miles (260 km) east. Puerto Peñasco is 62 miles (100 km) south of Sonoyta on good two-lane highway. If you are heading east you will need to pick up a tourist card and vehicle import permit. There is an office at the border to do this, there may also be an office on Mex. 2 to the east, ask at the border about this. For shopping on your way to Puerto Peñasco we suggest Ajo, Arizona, not far north of the border. As you approach the border from the north you pass through the Organ Pipe National Monument and Lukeville, Arizona. The Gringo Pass RV Park , in Lukeville, has groceries and sells Mexican insurance.

NOGALES, SONORA

Nogales is the preferred crossing for folks headed down Mexico's west coast since it is serviced by U.S. Interstate Highway 17 from Tucson to the north and serves as the beginning of Mex. 15, which is four-lane all the way to Mazatlán. The Nogales crossing is unique because you don't get your tourist card and vehicle import permit near the border crossing. Instead, there are modern facilities some 19 miles (31 km) south of the border on Mex. 15. The facility on Mex. 15 is also where you turn in your vehicle permit as you leave Mexico.

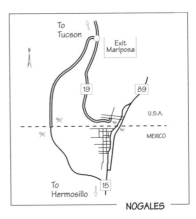

NOGALES

There are actually two crossings in Nogales. The old crossing is downtown and there is a new truck crossing west of town. We recommend that all drivers use the new truck crossing to avoid downtown traffic. Headed south on Highway 19 from Tucson you'll see the sign for the truck crossing at the Mariposa Road off ramp. Heading north you'll see a sign as you come into Nogales on Mex. 15. Nogales can be very busy with long delays for northbound traffic so it is important to pick your time of day. Weekends are usually quite busy, during the week you should try to cross in the late morning or early afternoon. This can be a problem for northbound campers driving all the way from Guaymas/San Carlos, consider an overnight at Magdalena.

Nogales, Arizona, north of the border, has lots of services and is a good place to buy Mexican insurance. Sanborn's has an office there and also an RV park. It is called the Mi Casa RV Park (2901 N. Grand Ave; (520) 281-1150) and is a popular stop for folks heading both south and north.

CIUDAD JUÁREZ, CHIHUAHUA

Ciudad Juárez is opposite El Paso, Texas. These are both large, busy cities so take it easy. There are three crossing points in Ciudad Juárez/El Paso but the one you want if you are heading south is the Cordova Bridge. To reach it head south on Highway 59 (Paisano St.) from east/west Interstate 10 through El Paso. This is the main crossing and it is where the Mexican offices are located for acquiring your tourist card and vehicle papers. Ciudad Juárez also has a checkpoint south of

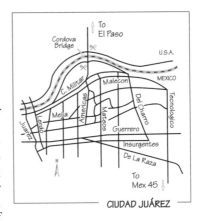

CIUDAD JUÁREZ

town on Mex. 45 like the one south of Nogales. Coming in to Ciudad Juárez from the south this is where you turn in your vehicle permit but until procedures change again you still pick up your papers in town.

Heading north towards the states after giving up your papers at the checkpoint 19 miles (31 km) south of town on Mex. 45 you will find yourself on Av. Tecnologico. This is a wide boulevard and should present no problems even for big rigs. Watch closely for the U.S.A. signs as the boulevard curves 90 degrees to the left when you near the central area of town. There is a bypass that goes off to the right (straight) and heads directly for the border crossing. If you miss it don't panic, you'll soon see other signs for the border, you can follow any of them since you've already turned in your papers.

NUEVO LAREDO, NUEVO LEÓN

Nuevo Laredo is said to be the busiest of the border crossings. The town itself is often visited by day-trippers from north of the border which probably accounts for the statistic. The crossing itself never seems as busy as Tijuana to us.

There are two bridges across the Río Grande, travelers headed south want to take the old International Bridge #1, the western-most bridge. You will probably be coming into town from the north on Interstate 35 from San Antonio. Interstate 35 will lead you directly to International Bridge #2 (also called Lincoln-Juárez bridge), the easternmost bridge if you aren't alert. Stay in the right-hand lanes. As you enter Laredo watch for signs leading to the western bridge which is also the truck crossing. You want to get about six blocks west of Highway 35 to a north-south parallel street called Salinas. This street will take you to International Bridge #1.

After crossing the bridge you want to find the customs and immigration offices to get your tourist card and vehicle import permits. Take the first street to the right and drive along the border fence until the road curves left and becomes Blvd. Lara. Now drive about .6 miles (1 km). You'll come to a statue of General Lara and see the Migración and Aduana building on the left. Turn into the big courtyard which has plenty of room for even big rigs. This is where you get your paperwork. When you are finished turn left after leaving the Migración and Aduana offices. Follow signs for Monterrey which will lead you to Mex. 85 south of Monterrey. Incidentally, the toll road to Monterrey is quite expensive and, in our opinion anyway, not worth the money. The Libre route is good enough although it will take longer.

Nuevo Laredo, like Ciudad Juárez and Nogales to the east, has a checkpoint along Mex. 85 about 21 km south of the border where you can turn in your documents if you are heading out of Mexico. Eventually you may be able to pick up documents here when heading south as you can at the Nogales checkpoint.

REYNOSA/MATAMOROS
TAMAULIPAS

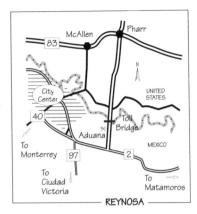

REYNOSA

Folks planning to head south along the Gulf Coast often cross the border near Brownsville. There are several crossings in this area including those in the Mexican border cities of Matamoros opposite Brownsville and Reynosa opposite McAllen. The whole area on the U.S. side of the border is extremely popular with U.S. and Canadian snowbirds. After all, this is as far south as you can go along the U.S.-Mexico border without actually going into Mexico. This is a very good place to prepare for crossing into Mexico. McAllen especially is small enough to be easy to negotiate. It is also the home of Sanborn's insurance and has many RV parks and even a Camping World RV equipment store.

There is a new crossing near Pharr, Texas just east of McAllen that is particularly good for crossing when you need to pick up tourist cards and vehicle import permits. This crossing is brand new and has little traffic. It is also in the middle of open country so you have no traffic at all to contend with. There is lots of parking room. On a recent crossing at Pharr we were the only people in line to get our vehicle permit. This would also be a good place to turn in your permits on the way out of Mexico.

When you've finished your paperwork and head south you will soon come to east-west Mex. 2. You can follow it east to Matamoros or west to Reynosa. Either way you bypass much of the city traffic in those towns.

Other Border Crossings

The crossings described above are the large crossings with the best highway connections to the north and south. There are many others, however. If you want to avoid long waits and city traffic you might prefer one of these. Make arrangements for insurance beforehand because few of the small crossing points have insurance offices nearby. Many of these crossings also have limited hours

El Sasabe, Sonora is located near Sasabe, Arizona. The crossing is open from 8 A.M. to 8 P.M. Monday through Friday and 10 A.M. to 2 P.M. on weekends.

Naco, Sonora is located across the border from Naco, Arizona and is open from 8 A.M. to midnight.

Agua Prieta, Sonora is located across the border from Douglas, Arizona and is open 24 hours a day. This is a good alternate to Nogales, Sonora.

Palomas, Chihuahua is across the border from Columbus, New Mexico and is open 24 hours a day. It is a good alternative to Ciudad Juárez if you are approaching from the west. Cut south from Deming, New Mexico on Highway 180. This road connects with Mex. 2 some 70 miles (114 km) west of Ciudad Juárez.

Ciudad Juárez - In addition to the crossings downtown there are several crossings not far southeast of the city. They are open 24 hours a day.

Ojinaga, Chihuahua is across the border from Presidio, Texas and is open from 7:30 A.M. to 9 P.M. weekdays and 8 A.M. to 4 P.M. weekends.

Ciudad Acuña, Coahuila is across the border from Del Rio, Texas and is open 24 hours.

Piedras Negras, Coahuila is across the border from Eagle Pass, Texas and is open 24 hours.

Nueva Ciudad Guerrero, Tamaulipas is across the border from Salineno, Texas and is open from 7:30 A.M. to 9 P.M. weekdays and 8 A.M. to 4 P.M. weekends.

Ciudad Miguel Alemán, Tamaulipas. is across the border from Roma, Texas and is open 24 hours a day.

Camargo, Tamaulipas. is across the border from Rio Grande City, Texas and is open from 7:30 A.M. to 9 P.M. weekdays and 8 A.M. to 4 P.M. weekends.

Reynosa, Tamaulipas is across the border from Hidalgo and McAllen, Texas and is open 24 hours a day.

Matamoros, Tamaulipas is across the border from Brownsville, Texas and is open 24 hours a day.

CHAPTER 4

HOW TO USE THE DESTINATION CHAPTERS

The focus of this book is on campgrounds, of course. A question we often hear is "Which campground is the best in Mexico?". Usually the person asking the question has a personal favorite in mind. Our answer is always the same — we like them all. No one campground is the best in Mexico because everyone likes different things. Also, the personality of a campground depends upon the people staying there when you visit. People traveling on their own in an environment they are not used to tend to be very friendly, this is one of the best things about Mexican camping. We can't tell you exactly who will be staying in each of the campgrounds in this book when you decide to visit, but we will try to give you a good feel for what to expect in the way of campground features and amenities.

Chapters 5 through 12 contain information about the many camping destinations you may visit in Mexico. The chapters are arranged somewhat arbitrarily into regions that fall naturally together for a discussion of their camping possibilities.

INTRODUCTORY MATERIAL AND ROAD MAP

Each chapter starts with an introduction giving important information about the region covered in the chapter. Usually included is something about the lay of the land, the road system, and highlights of the area. Most of this information is important to a camping traveler and much of it is not necessarily included or easy to find in normal tourist guides. On the other hand, much information that is readily available in normal tourist guides will not be found in this book. Other books do a good job of covering things like currency information, hotels, restaurants, language, and tour details. This book is designed to be a supplement to normal tourist guides, not to replace them. It provides a framework, other guides must be used to fill in the details.

The road map at the beginning of the chapter is included to give you a reference while reading about the road system and for planning purposes. There is not enough detail to use these as your primary map, see the section titled Maps in the Details, Details, Details chapter for information about available maps.

CAMPGROUND OVERVIEW MAPS

In each chapter, located just before the Selected Cities and Their Campground Section begins, there is another regional map. This map shows the cities that have campgrounds and for which there are city and campground descriptions on the pages that follow. You can use the campground overview maps as a table of contents to the cities and districts covered in the chapter.

Some of the maps also show the outline of an interesting district or region. These regions have their own individual write-up sections and are listed under the title given to the small outline maps.

Each chapter introduction also includes a distance table. Sometimes they are on the same page as the campground overview map but in chapters with many campgrounds they occupy their own page.

CITY DESCRIPTIONS

Following the introductory material in each chapter is the Selected Cities and Campgrounds section. Cities are listed alphabetically in this segment. Each city has a few paragraphs describing the local attractions, then information about at least one campground. In some cases there is also information about interesting side trips that you may wish to take while continuing to use this particular town and campground as a base. Some of the destinations are famous and well known, others less familiar but still well worth a visit.

Our descriptions of the destinations in this book are intended to give you an idea of what the city or region has to offer. They are by no means complete, you will undoubtedly need additional guides during your visit. There is no way that complete information could be included in a conveniently sized book, nor do we have the knowledge or time to write that kind of guide. Exploring travel guides is almost as much fun as exploring the destinations themselves, you will no doubt acquire a small library before you finish your travels.

We have also given population, altitude, and pronunciation information for some cities. The population and altitude information are our estimates. Population figures are difficult to obtain for Mexico since the last census was in 1980 and the population is rapidly growing and also moving about. These are our best guesses based upon many sources. Altitude figures are also estimates. While we are not linguists we do think that it is nice to be able to pronounce the names of the cities we visit, hopefully the very amateurish pronunciation guides we have included will be of some help.

CAMPGROUND MAPS

Most of the campground descriptions include a small map to assist you in finding the campground. They show enough roads and other identifying features to allow you to tie them into the highway and city maps you will be using for primary navigation. You can use these maps to assist you in your search for campgrounds, they are meant to be used in conjunction with the written directions that we have included in the campground descriptions. A picture often *is* worth a thousand words, even if it only serves to give you a general idea of the campground location. We hope these maps will do more than that, we've spent a lot of time searching for campgrounds based upon little more than a rumor. May you never have to do the same.

While the maps are for the most part self-explanatory here is a key.

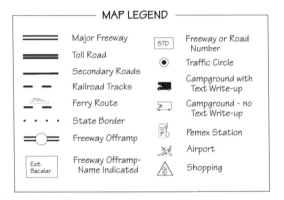

CAMPGROUND DESCRIPTIONS

Each campground section begins with address and telephone number. While it is not generally necessary or even possible to obtain campground reservations in Mexico you may want to do so for some very popular campgrounds. This is particularly true during the busy December to March season in popular areas. If reservations seem desirable or necessary we mention the fact in the campground description.

One thing you will not find in our campground descriptions is a rating with some kind of system of stars, checks, or tree icons. Hopefully we've included enough information in our campground description to let you make your own analysis.

Campground prices vary considerably. The price you pay depends upon the type of rig you drive, the number in your party, your use of hookups and sometimes even the time of year.

Generally you can expect that tents are least expensive, followed by vans and smaller RVs. The price range we give is for a van or small RV with two people using full hookups. In some places larger RVs may pay a little more but this is unusual.

A final price consideration is the value the peso against U.S. or Canadian dollars. Our prices were determined during the 1996/1997 winter season when the peso was trading at 7.75 to the U.S. dollar. The peso was gradually depreciating. Near the border, on the Baja, and on the northern west coast prices are often given in U.S. dollars so the conversion rate makes little difference. Farther from the border campgrounds often do not keep up with the depreciation of the peso so prices tend to be lower.

We've grouped campground fees into the following categories:

Inexpensive	Up to $5 U.S.
Low	Over $ 5 and up to $10 U.S.
Moderate	Over $10 and up to $15 U.S.
Expensive	Over $15 and up to $20 U.S.
Very Expensive	Over $20

All of these prices are winter high season prices for a van conversion with two people using electricity and taking a shower. You should expect to pay slightly less for tents in many places and slightly more for very large rigs.

Campground icons can be useful for a quick overview of campground facilities or if you are quickly looking for a particular feature.

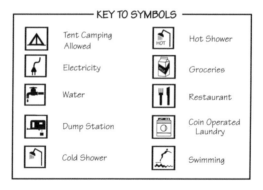

All of the campgrounds in this book accept RV's but not all accept tent campers. We've included the tent symbol for all campgrounds that do accept tents.

Hookups in Mexican campgrounds vary a great deal so we've included individual symbols for electricity, water, and sewer. For more information take a look at the written description section.

Showers in Mexican campgrounds often have no provision for hot water so we give separate shower symbols for hot and cold water. If there is provision for hot water but it was cold when we visited we list it as providing cold water only. You may be luckier when you visit.

If we've given the campground a milk carton icon then it has some groceries. This is usually just a few items in the reception area. Check the write-up for more information. The write-up will often mention a larger store located conveniently near the campground.

An on-site restaurant can provide a welcome change from home-cooked meals and a good way to meet people. In Mexico almost all restaurants also serve alcohol of some kind. Often campground restaurants are only open during certain periods during the year, sometimes only during the very busy Christmas and Semana Santa holidays. Even if there is no restaurant at the campground we have found that in Mexico there is usually one not far away.

A swimming icon means that the campground has swimming either on-site or nearby. This may be a pool or the beach at an ocean or lake.

You'll find that this book has a much larger campground description than most guidebooks. We've tried to include detailed information about the campground itself so you know what to expect when you arrive as well as information about the availability and use of public transportation for traveling into town. While most campgrounds described in this book have a map we've also included a paragraph giving even more details about finding the campground.

GPS (Global Positioning System) Coordinates

You will note that for some of the campgrounds we have included a GPS Location. GPS is a new navigation tool that uses signals from satellites. For less than $150 you can now buy a hand-held receiver that will give you your latitude, longitude and altitude anywhere in the world. You can also enter the coordinates we have given for the campgrounds in this book into the receiver and it will tell you exactly where the campground lies in relation to your position. If our maps and descriptions just don't lead you to the campground you can fall back on the GPS information.

Unfortunately we acquired our GPS right in the middle of our last tour of Mexico. That means that we were able to include GPS information for only about half of the campgrounds in this book. All of the campgrounds on the Baja Peninsula and in the interior of the country (except in the Guadalajara area) have GPS data.

If you don't have a GPS receiver already you certainly don't need to go out and buy one to use this book. On the other hand, if you do have one bring it along. We expect that GPS will actually be installed in many vehicles during the next few years so we thought we'd get a jump on things. If you are finding that our readings are not entirely accurate you should check to see which Map Datum your machine is set to use. The coordinates in this book are based upon the World Geodetic System 1984 (WGS 84) datum.

Other Camping Possibilities

We've used the heading "Other Camping Possibilities" as a catch-all for several kinds of information. If we have not had a chance to visit a campground but have heard that it exists we often put it in this section. We also list some free camping possibilities under this heading. You should keep in mind that much of what is in the Other Camping Possibilities section is information we have gathered from others and have not confirmed so do not count on it being entirely accurate. Finally, if we've spend a lot of time looking for a campground that is listed in other guides but no longer exists we'll often mention it in this section to keep you from having the same experience.

Side Trips

The "Side Trip" section included for some towns describes interesting places you may want to visit. If you have a tent or pull a trailer you can leave your camp set up at the base and avoid setting up camp each night. Even if you are in a van or motorhome and do take your camp along with you the base city always provides a place to return to if you can find no acceptable alternate campground during your side trip.

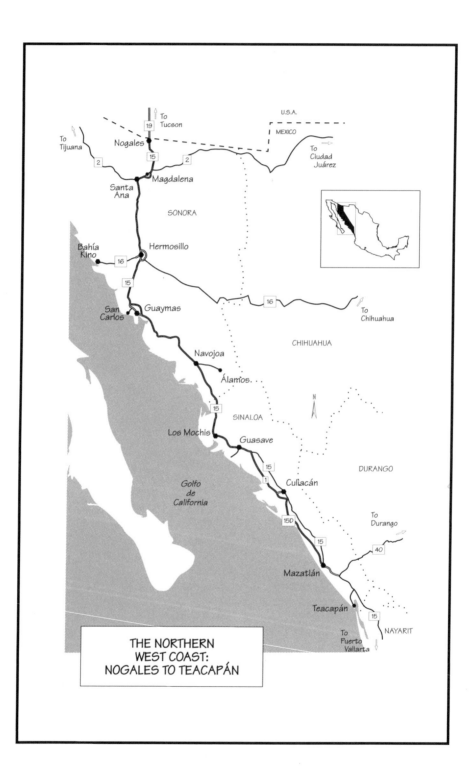

THE NORTHERN
WEST COAST:
NOGALES TO TEACAPÁN

CHAPTER 5

THE NORTHERN WEST COAST: NOGALES TO TEACAPÁN

INTRODUCTION

The northern portion of the West Coast is a premier destination for RVers in Mexico, it is second only to the northern Gulf of California in the number of camping visitors. The popularity is no mystery. Access from north of the border is easy. There are four-lane highways from the border at Nogales all the way south to Mazatlán. Dozens of full-service campgrounds serve Bahís Kino, Guaymas/San Carlos, Los Mochis, and Mazatlán. It takes only three easy days of driving to reach the farthest south of these major towns, Mazatlán.

Two states, Sonora to the north and Sinaloa in the south, define the region. These states have dry desert climates, but the big industries are fishing and agriculture. Guaymas and Mazatlán are fishing ports and there are huge areas of irrigated land, particularly around Los Mochis, Ciudad Obregón, and Culiacán. The landscape is generally flat so travel is easy. Only if you venture off the beaten path, say inland to Álamos or toward Durango, will you find mountains. The coast is often backed by lagoons and swampy areas so the road stays inland all the way to Mazatlán and then again until San Blas.

Strictly speaking the West Coast includes the important RVing destinations of Puerto Peñasco and Golfo de Santa Clara. For several reasons we feel that these destinations fit better in their own chapter, we call it the Northern Gulf of California.

ROAD SYSTEM

Four-lane Mex. 15 runs all the way from Nogales to Mazatlán. It is the arterial of the region and provides quick and easy access. It is of particular benefit to RVers with big rigs. You will hardly know you've left the states.

When you first drive Mex. 15 south you may think that the entire highway is a toll road. In actual fact there are many stretches that are free. The government of Mexico is committed to providing a free alternate to as much of the toll system as possible, so where there is not a free alternate the four-lane highway is usually toll-free. Tolls on much of the road are reasonable for cars, but RVs can really get hit hard. As we have described in the Toll Roads section of Chapter 2, the toll rates for RVs can be as much as three times the automobile rates on Mexican toll roads. The state governments recently became convinced that the dramatic drop in camping visitors to the northwestern part of Mexico during the late 80's and early 90's was due to the high tolls and several experimental programs have been used in an attempt to remedy this perceived problem. In some prior years vouchers were issued at the border allowing you to pay the car rate at many toll stations. This program was dropped for a couple of years, and then in 1996-7 the government toll roads began to charge all RVers the car rate. Hopefully this will continue. *Vamos*

A CARAVAN HEADING SOUTH

a ver (we'll see). In early 1997 the car rate to travel all the way from Nogales to Culiacán was $23. This assumes you bypass toll booths outside Magdalena and Guymas as most people do. The total distance is 600 miles (980 km) and there are eight toll booths.

Between Culiacán and Mazatlán there is a beautiful new four-lane toll road. Unfortunately it is a private toll road, a Maxipista, and the toll rates are outrageous. Only the uninformed or the rich use it. You can travel the entire route and see only RVs, express busses, and local traffic. The rate for a car to travel the 110 mile (177 km) road was $16 in early 1997, a motorhome towing a car would have paid $38. Fortunately the two-lane free highway along almost the same route is pretty good. If you take it easy the trip will take about an hour and a half longer than traveling the toll road and is almost the same distance. Headed south just drive right by the entrance to Mex. 15D on the Culiacán western bypass, you'll soon intersect Mex. 15 Libre south of town.

Travelers headed south generally make the trip to Mazatlán in three days. In the evening of the first day they stop in Guaymas having driven 257 miles (419 km), the second day they reach Los Mochis after 220 miles (359 km), and the third day of 259 miles (423 km) finds them in Mazatlán. Possible side trips on two-lane free roads to Bahía Kino and Álamos can easily make this a longer trip, as can the temptation to make multiple-day stops en route.

Highlights

There are four good oceanside destinations in this section of the book. These are Bahía Kino, Guaymas/San Carlos, Mazatlán, and Teacapán. Each has its own unique personality and amenities so take a look at the individual listings to find the one (or ones) that will please you.

The lower end of the Chihuahua-Pacific Railroad is accessible from Los Mochis. This is an excellent reason to visit the town, as is the nearby ferry port for boats to and from the Baja Peninsula. Many people leave their vehicles in one of the RV parks and make a two day train trip up through the Copper Canyon, spending the night in Creel or Chihuahua.

The old colonial gold mining town of Álamos is an unusual and very entertaining destination. It may give you a taste for visits to similar cities in other parts of the country. The side road to Álamos is paved and only takes about an hour.

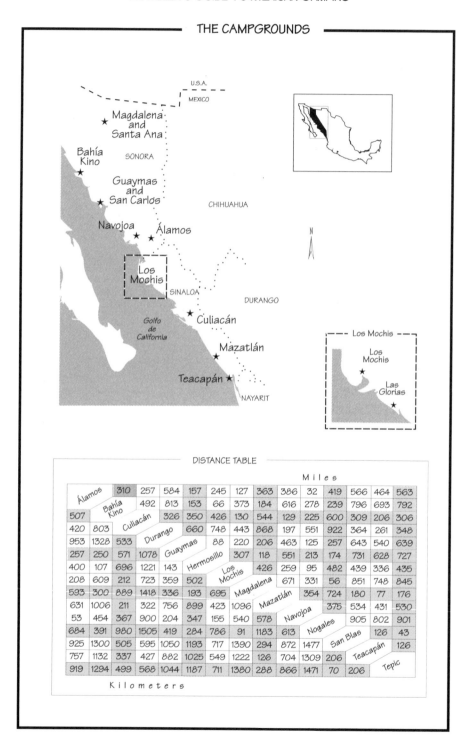

THE CAMPGROUNDS

DISTANCE TABLE

Miles

Álamos	310	257	584	157	245	127	363	386	32	419	566	464	563
507	*Bahía Kino*	492	813	153	66	373	184	616	278	239	796	693	792
420	803	*Culiacán*	326	350	426	130	544	129	225	600	309	206	306
953	1328	533	*Durango*	660	748	443	868	197	551	922	364	261	348
257	250	571	1078	*Guaymas*	88	220	206	463	125	257	643	540	639
400	107	696	1221	143	*Hermosillo*	307	118	551	213	174	731	628	727
208	609	212	723	359	502	*Los Mochis*	426	259	95	482	439	336	435
593	300	889	1418	336	193	695	*Magdalena*	671	331	56	851	748	845
631	1006	211	322	756	899	423	1096	*Mazatlán*	354	724	180	77	176
53	454	367	900	204	347	155	540	578	*Navojoa*	375	534	431	530
684	391	980	1505	419	284	786	91	1183	613	*Nogales*	905	802	901
925	1300	505	595	1050	1193	717	1390	294	872	1477	*San Blas*	126	43
757	1132	337	427	882	1025	549	1222	126	704	1309	206	*Teacapán*	126
919	1294	499	568	1044	1187	711	1380	288	866	1471	70	206	*Tepic*

Kilometers

SELECTED CITIES AND THEIR CAMPGROUNDS

ÁLAMOS, SONORA (AH-LAH-MOHS)
Population 6,500, Elevation 1,350 ft (410 m)

Álamos had a population of 30,000 people in the late 1700's. The town was the supply and cultural center for the surrounding mining area. Much of this wealth went into impressive colonial *casas* (homes) and other buildings. Later the mines closed, the town declined, and the structures deteriorated. Fortunately, in the last forty years Álamos has become popular with American and Canadian expats, many wealthy, and some of the former polish has returned. Many homes with traditional interior courtyard designs have been restored and can be toured. The town's colonial atmosphere is now protected by law.

You will want to explore Álamos on foot, the narrow streets and difficult parking make an automobile a real bother. You can easily walk from some of the campgrounds just outside town, from others you may want to take a taxi or catch a bus. One of the campgrounds, the Acosta, is located on the back side of town, staying there requires driving through Álamos, not something you should do in a rig of any size but nothing to fear if you have a car, van, or pickup camper.

The town has a museum, the **Museo Costumbrista de Sonora,** which will give you some background on the area. There are two plazas in Álamos, the first you will see is the **Plaza Alameda** which is not very impressive, it hosts a Pemex gas station and the municipal market. The nearby **Plaza de Armas** is much nicer but quieter with a central kiosk and a church, **La Parroquia de la Purísima Concepción.** It is difficult to see much of the restoration work that has been done on the many casas in Álamos, they are typically Spanish with unimpressive exteriors. Tours are sometimes available. Check at the library for information about them, Saturday tours start there and others can sometimes be arranged.

Campground No. 1

DOLISA MOTEL & TRAILER PARK
  Address: Calle Madero #72, Álamos, C.P.
  85760 Son., Mexico
  Telephone: (642) 8-01-31

Price: Moderate

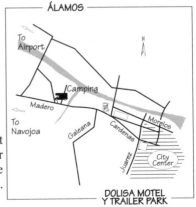

The Dolisa is the closest RV park to town that you can reach with a full-size motorhome. For that reason you will often find it full when the other Álamos campgrounds have lots of room. Caravans often fill the facility.

The campground has 42 spaces, 35 have all hookups and the others only electricity and water. A few are pull-throughs. Power is 30-amp. and air conditioners are allowed. The restrooms are clean and have hot water for showers. There is a self-service laundry with a washing machine. The walk into town from the Dolisa is about a quarter of a mile, easily done on foot.

To find the campground watch carefully as you near Álamos. It is on the left on the highway and has a good sign.

Campground No. 2

EL CARACOL RV RESORT AND RANCH
   Address: Km. 37 Carretera a Alamos,
   Álamos, C.P. 85760 Son., Mexico
   Telephone: (648) 4-26-76

Price: Moderate

We think that El Caracol has the most pleasant setting of all the Álamos trailer parks. It is in the high desert on a 2,800 acre ranch and is very quiet and peaceful. Birding is great, you should inquire about hikes and the availability of rental horses. This is the Álamos eco-campground.

There are 65 pull-through spaces at the campground. They have 30-amp. electricity, water, and sewer hookups. Most have patios and shade. The El Caracol also has a unique low-power satellite TV rebroadcast system. The restrooms have hot showers. There is a swimming pool open even in the winter and a very cute little restaurant that has been closed recently, plans are in the works to open it again. An hourly bus that stops at the front gate will whisk you in to Álamos to look around. The owner speaks excellent English.

As you approach Álamos watch for the sign. The campground is on the right 9 miles (14.5 km) before you reach the town.

Campground No. 3

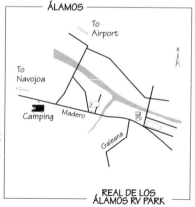

REAL DE LOS ÁLAMOS RV PARK
   Address: Morelos 31, Álamos, C.P. 85760
   Son., Mexico
   Telephone: (642) 8-00-02

Price: Moderate

This newest of Álamos' campgrounds is about a mile (1.6 km) from town on the right as you arrive. There's lots of room for big rigs.

The campground's 51 back-in spaces all have

30-amp. electric, water, and sewer hookups. They are arranged around the perimeter of a large field next to the highway. The restrooms have hot showers. This campground doubles as the local balneario (swimming resort), it has a pool. Unfortunately the pool isn't kept up during the winter.

As you approach Álamos watch for the Real de los Álamos on the right. You pass it before you reach the El Dolisa.

Campground No. 4

ACOSTA RANCHO TRAILER RV PARK
   Address: Apdo. 67, Álamos, C.P. 85760
   Son., Mexico
   Telephone: (642) 8-00-77, (642) 8-02-46
   Fax: (642) 8-02-79

Price: Low

ALAMOS

ACOSTA RANCHO
TRAILER RV PARK

The Acosta is a nice little campground in a quiet setting within walking distance of downtown Álamos, it is on the far side of town and unfortunately large rigs have a tough time negotiating Álamos' streets. If you are smaller than 25 feet and not towing you should have no problems.

The campground has 18 back-in RV slots, all have 30-amp. electricity, water, sewer, patio and most have some shade. The one restroom has a hot shower. This is also a local balneario (in the summer) and has a beautiful pool near the motel units and also a couple of lap-type pools that are empty in the winter. Groups can arrange to have meals prepared and served in the very nice dining room and the manager specializes in guided hunting trips. You can easily walk in to town from the campground, the distance is about a half-mile.

To reach the campground drive right into town. Zero your odometer as you pass the Pemex station. At the tiny glorieta in front of the Pemex you must choose your route carefully. You want to take the road to the right of the small square which you see ahead and slightly to your left. At .2 miles (.3 km) you will come to a stop sign. This is the only difficult-to-negotiate corner. Make the difficult right turn and then almost immediately turn left. Drive down this street which will eventually turn to cobblestones and make a dogleg left and cross the (hopefully) dry river bed. After the river bed you will see an Acosta T.P. sign pointing to the left at a Y, follow the indicated road until you get to a walled cemetery at .7 miles (1.1 km) from where you passed the Pemex. Follow the wall of the cemetery to the left and then right around the far end and you will see the entrance to the trailer park and motel ahead. Drive through the gate and past some houses into the trailer park. The managers are sometimes hard to find, they live in the house to the right at the far end of the trailer park.

Side Trips from Álamos

La Aduana is a nearby mining town. The mine has been abandoned but the church, **Iglesia de Nuestra Señora de la Balvanera,** remains. The church was built to celebrate a miracle which resulted in the discovery of silver in the town. A procession from Navojoa comes here on December 12 during the Festival Guadalupana. The town is located on a 2 mile (3 km) stub road off the main road into Álamos, watch for a sign for Minas Nuevas about 4.5 miles (7.3 km) outside Álamos.

Bahía Kino, Sonora (BAH-EE-AH KEY-NO)
Population 3,500, Elevation sea level

Bahía Kino or Kino Bay is really two villages. Both towns, of course, are named for the famed Jesuit missionary, Padre Eusebio Francisco Kino. Viejo Kino (Old Kino) is a traditional fishing village with dusty streets arranged around a traditional square. Fishing is from skiffs or pangas, they pull up on the beach to unload. Nuevo Kino (New Kino) is a resort with small hotels and RV parks strung along several miles of beach to the north. Only one RV park is in Viejo Kino but the old town is where many of the services are located, including the only gas station. Small grocery stores in both towns provide limited supplies, for bigger shopping trips the huge supermarkets in Hermosillo are only 66 miles (107 km) distant on a decent but not great paved road.

Kino is Seri Indian country, many live in Bahía Kino but there are also villages located to the north along the coast. You can almost always find several stands selling ironwood carvings of dolphins and other animals. There is also a museum, **Museo de los Seris**, with displays of historical photographs and traditional articles of clothing and living utensils.

The fishing is excellent off Bahía Kino and there are miles of coast to explore along rough sandy roads to the north.

Campground No. 1

Caverna del Seri Trailer Park
    Address: Apdo. 72, Bahía Kino, C.P. 83340 Son., Mexico

Price: Moderate

The Caverna del Seri is at the end of the road through Nuevo Kino. It is the largest of the campgrounds that actually allow you to park next to the sand.

The campground has 36 spaces, half are right down on the beach and the others are on a terrace above. The upper spaces have patios and some even have sun shades. All spaces have 30-amp. electricity, sewer, water, and cable TV. The restrooms are clean and have hot-water showers. There is a boat ramp and fish-cleaning house. There is also a laundry with self-service machines. English is spoken.

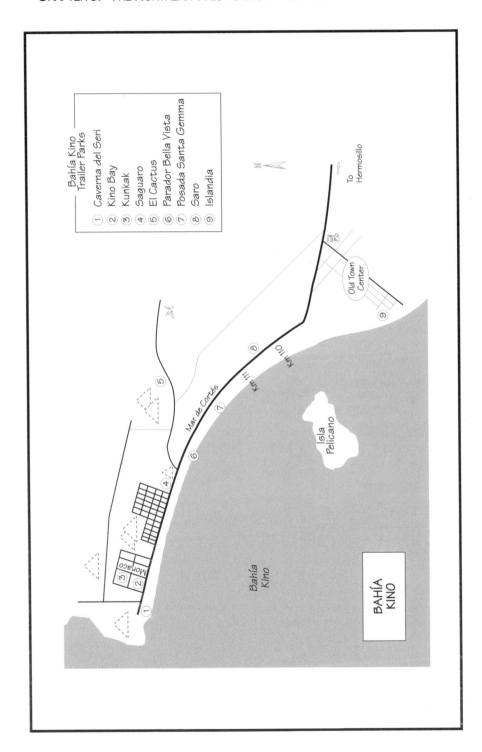

To find the campground just follow the main drag, Avenida Mar de Cortés, right to the end of the pavement. The white wall ahead is the campground, just drive around to the right and enter the gate.

Campground No. 2

Kino Bay R.V. Park
   Address: Apdo. 857, Hermosillo, Son., Mexico
   Telephone: (624) 2-02-16, (62) 80-00-00 (Hermosillo)
   Fax: (624) 2-00-83

Price: Moderate

Bahía Kino's largest trailer park is organized and well-run. This is a first-class operation so don't let the size bother you.

There are 200 full hookup spaces at the Kino Bay. These are rather barren pull-through spaces with 30-amp. electricity (air conditioners are OK), sewer, water, and covered patios. The restrooms are modern and clean, they have hot-water showers. The campground has a huge fenced storage area for boats and RV's and a fish-cleaning house that is well separated from the living areas. The folks at the reception office speak English and are very helpful. They're kept busy arranging long distance calls to the states from a small soundproof booth there.

The Kino Bay is not on the beach but the owner's house is right across the street. During the winter season it is set aside for the use of campground guests and serves as a beach-side lounge and party house.

The campground is well-signed. If you zero your odometer at the Pemex at the entrance to Viejo Kino you will find that the Kino Bay RV park is on your right at 5.7 miles (9.2 km).

Campground No. 3

Trailer Park Kunkak
   Address: Esqueda Y Deportivo (Apdo. 29), Bahía Kino, Son., Mexico
   Telephone: (624) 2-00-88, (624) 2-02-09

Price: Moderate

The Trailer Park Kunkak is one of the few campgrounds in Bahía Kino that is not on Avenida Mar de Cortés along the water. It is not far away, however, it sits almost behind the Kino Bay R.V. Park.

The camp sites of the Kunkak are arranged around an attractive central building which houses the office, lounges, library, restrooms and laundry room. There is no fence around this park, the spaces are attractively arranged and separated by rock walls and plants. The 60 spaces have 30-amp. electricity (air conditioners are OK), water, and sewer. Restrooms are modern and clean, they have hot water showers.

The well-liked owner speaks English and loves to talk politics.

To find the campground zero your odometer at the Pemex station at the entrance to Viejo Kino. At 5.6 miles (9 km) turn right on Monaco and drive a block inland alongside the small pitch-and-putt golf course, the trailer park will be on your left.

Campground No. 4

SAGUARO R.V. PARK
Address: Apdo. 50, Bahía Kino, Son., Mexico
Telephone: (624) 2-01-65

Price: Moderate

The Saguaro is one of the older trailer parks in Kino Bay, it is also one of the better maintained and managed places in town. It sits across the road from the beach, many people prefer to keep their rigs away from the salt water.

The campground has 20 spaces, they have 30-amp. electricity, sewer, water, and satellite TV hookups. Eighteen of them have covered patios and many are pull-throughs. Parking is on gravel but the driveways are paved. The restrooms are older but extremely clean, they have hot water showers. There is a laundry with a self-service washer, a recreation/meeting room, and an outdoor patio area. The Saguaro also has four rental rooms. English is spoken at this campground.

To find the campground zero your odometer at the Pemex station at the entrance to Viejo Kino. At 4.4 miles (7.1 km) you'll see the Saguaro on the right near the foot of the small hill.

Campground No. 5

EL CACTUS TRAILER PARK
Address: Camino a P. Chueca Km. 2, Bahía Kino, Son., Mexico
Telephone: (62) 16-16-43 (Hermosillo)

Price: Moderate

The El Cactus is not located in Bahía Kino at all, it sits alone in the desert about a mile from the ocean. If you like your peace and quiet this is the place for you.

The El Cactus has 29 spaces. All are back-in sites with electricity, sewer, water, satellite TV, and patios. Some have a little shade. The restrooms are clean and have hot water showers. There is a swimming pool. The campground is surrounded by a chain-link fence and lots of desert. Only limited English is spoken.

To reach the El Cactus zero your odometer as you pass the Pemex in Viejo Kino. Turn right at 4.3 miles (6.9 km) just before the small hill, there is a sign for the El Cactus Trailer Park. Follow the gravel road for .9 miles (1.5 km), the trailer park is on the left.

Campground No. 6

Parador Bella Vista Trailer Park
Address: Mar de Cortés and Cochorit (Apdo. 27), Bahía Kino, Son., Mexico
Telephone: (624) 2-01-39

Price: Moderate

The Parador Bella Vista is a small beachside trailer park. The maneuvering room is limited but somehow a few big rigs manage to get in here each year.

There are 17 spaces in the campground but only 15 are usually used so that larger rigs will fit. All have 20-amp. electricity, sewer, and water hookups. All of the spaces are back-in (or pull-in), about half overlook the water and the other half are along the highway and have patios, some with sun covers. The restrooms have hot showers and there is a laundry with a self-service machine.

To find the Bella Vista zero your odometer as you pass the Pemex in Viejo Kino. The campground is on the left at 4.1 miles (6.6 km).

Campground No. 7

Posada Santa Gemma Trailer Park
Address: Alatorre No. 912, Colonia Pitic, Hermosillo, C.P. 83150 Son.,
Mexico (Res.)
Telephone: (624) 2-00-26

Price: Moderate

This is another small campground next to the beach. The Posada Santa Gemma is also a motel.

There are 14 spaces, all are back-in or pull-in with 30-amp. electricity, sewer, and water. They all also have covered patios. About half overlook the ocean and the others are along the highway. The restrooms are small but adequate and have hot-water showers. The motel has a small store but no laundry.

To find the Santa Gemma zero your odometer as you pass the Pemex in Viejo Kino. The campground is on the left at 3.3 miles (5.3 km).

Campground No. 8

Saro Trailer Park.
Address: Avenida Mar de Cortés, Bahía Kino, Son., Mexico
Telephone: (624) 2-00-07

Price: Low

You can't get much simpler than the Saro Trailer Park. There are seven back-in spaces along the north wall of an almost-empty dirt-covered lot. Each space has electricity, sewer, and water. Restrooms are new, clean and have hot showers. Across the street, on the ocean side of the road is the small Saro Hotel which has rooms and a popular Italian restaurant. The owner, Saro, (he's Italian, of course) emphasizes that his is the least expensive trailer park in Kino Bay.

To reach the Saro Trailer Park zero your odometer as you pass the Pemex in Viejo Kino. The campground is on the right at 3 miles (4.8 km).

Campground No. 9

ISLANDIA MARINA TRAILER PARK AND BUNGALOWS
   Address: Guaymas y Puerto Peñasco (Apdo. 36), Bahía Kino, C.P. 83340
   Son., Mexico
   Telephone: (624) 2-00-81

Price: Moderate

The Islandia is the only one of the Kino Bay trailer parks located in Viejo Kino. The location in the old town is the campground's biggest attraction and it also may be it's biggest problem, it just depends upon what you like.

The family-run water-front campground has 72 spaces with 30-amp. electricity, sewer, and water. Not all of the utilities are in usable condition, this is an old park and needs some tender loving care. Some spaces are along the water but most sit back away from the beach. Restrooms are old and in poor repair but have hot showers. They are in an inconvenient remote location at the back corner of the campground. There's a self-service laundry with two washers and a boat ramp. There are also several rental bungalows scattered around the property. You can easily walk to the center of town in a few minutes. The town has dusty streets, a square, several small stores and restaurants, and small fishing boats pulled up along the beach.

To get to the campground turn left just after the Pemex as you enter Viejo Kino on the main road from Hermosillo. Turn onto the paved road and follow it all the way through town until it rises to go onto the beach. Turn right just before the rise and drive three blocks until the road reaches the campground fence. Turn to the right and follow the fence around to the entrance.

CULIACÁN, SINALOA (KOO-LEE-AH-KAHN)
Population 550,000, Elevation 275 ft (84 m)

Few of the drivers who bypass Culiacán on the way south to Mazatlán know that the city is anything more than a large agricultural center. Culiacán was founded in the 16th century by the most-hated of the conquistadors, Beltrán Nuño de Guzmán, and today is the state capital of Sinaloa. It is a prosperous city intent upon building a more attractive environment for citizens and visitors.

You won't find a lot of tourist attractions in Culiacán. One worth a visit is the **Museo del Arte de Sinaloa** which has works by Diego Rivera, Pedro Coronel, Rufino Tamayo and López Sañez. Meteorites are in the news recently, one said to be the second largest ever recovered is in the **Parque Constitución**. A major river-front park is being built with walkways and restaurants, this will help make the town attractive, particularly to campers staying at the nearby Hotel Los Tres Ríos.

If you are traveling on Mex. 15D you will bypass Culiacán and only see the town from a distance. About half way around the west side is the intersection where the Maxipista toll road south to Mazatlán takes off to the right, easy access to downtown Culiacán goes to the left at the same intersection, see the instructions for reaching the Tres Ríos Hotel given below. If you want to travel the free road south continue straight at this intersection, in 6.0 miles (9.8 km) you will intersect Mex. 15 Libre.

Campground

HOTEL LOS TRES RÍOS
  Address: Carretera México Nogales Km.
  1423, Culiacán, Sin., Mexico
  Telephone: (67) 50-52-80

Price: Low

The Tres Ríos isn't a destination campground, but it makes a convenient place to stay if you find yourself near Culiacán when night falls.

There are 32 RV parking slots with electricity, water, and sewer hookups in a fenced field behind the hotel. All are back-in sites, a couple have paved patios and big rigs have lots of room once they've threaded their way through the hotel parking lot. There isn't much shade or vegetation in the campground itself but the hotel has a pleasant pool area. The bathrooms at the pool double for the RV park, they have hot-water showers. The hotel also has a restaurant and a disco, fortunately the disco is on the far side of the grounds. No English is spoken. Tents are OK. There is a Ley supermarket next door on one side and a huge Wal-Mart and Sam's Club on the other.

The hotel is located on the east side of Mex. 15 Libre so it is easy to find if you are following the free highway through town instead of using the bypass. Watch carefully if headed north and you will see the hotel .3 miles (.5 km) north of the river bridge, just past the Wal-Mart. Driving south it is just past the Ley supermarket but you can't enter from southbound lanes, you'll have to pull into the Wal-Mart parking lot to turn around.

The easiest access, however, is from the west. At the intersection of the bypass and the Mazatlán toll road zero your odometer and follow signs toward Culiacán (also labeled Mex. 15 libre). At 2.1 miles (3.4 km) you will see a Ley supermarket on your right and then an intersection. Go straight through, you'll cross some railroad tracks at 2.6 miles (4.2 km) and see a big movie theater called the Cinepolis on the right at 5.1 miles (8.2 km). At 5.7 miles (9.2 km) slow to pass under some railroad tracks and turn sharply right immediately after them. The road will come to a big glorieta at 5.9 miles (9.5 km). You want to drive all the way around it so that you are heading back the way you came in. The river bridge is at 6.5 miles (10.5 km), you'll see the Wal-Mart on the right at 6.8 miles (11 km) and soon see the entrance to the Los Tres Ríos Hotel on the right. Pull into the driveway, bear left around the buildings, check in at the hotel office, and pull through the cobblestone parking lot to the RV park behind.

Side Trips from Culiacán

The Culiacán area is devoted to farming but people do need their time at the beach, you might want to take a look at the long beaches at **Altata**, **Playa el Tambor**, and **Playa Las Arenitas**. It can be fun to explore roads toward the ocean all along this coast. Most trips involve long drives across agricultural land and then through flats with shrimp farms. Often they end at small fish camps or villages on deserted beaches. There are definitely opportunities for free camping with no amenities other than an occasional palapa restaurant.

The colonial mining town of **Cosalá** is an excellent side trip from either Culiacán or Mazatlán. To get there drive 34 miles (55 km) east from an intersection on Mex. 15 Libre that is half way between Culiacán and Mazatlán. This town could be another Álamos, except that no one has restored it. It has its own historical museum and is known for hand-crafted saddles.

GUAYMAS AND SAN CARLOS, SONORA
(GWAY-MAHS AND SAWN KAHR-LOES)
Population 160,000, Elevation sea level

You can think of Guaymas and San Carlos as twin cities, fraternal twins, they are not at all alike. Guaymas itself is an old port, the first supply depot was set up here by the Jesuits in 1701 although they were driven out later by the tough and resistant Seri Indians. Today the major industry is fishing. Guaymas has a modern Ley supermarket which is the best place to lay in supplies in the area.

North of Guaymas is San Carlos, center of the tourism industry. The recent completion of a four-lane boulevard through San Carlos has really changed the ambiance. The dust is gone, now the town seems to be making real progress toward being an upscale resort. There are marinas, hotels, a golf course, and restaurants. There are also two good trailer parks.

Between Guaymas and San Carlos is the small town of Miramar. The main reason you will want to know this is that Miramar is home to the most popular RV park for visitors passing through the area, the venerable Hotel Playa de Cortés.

Campground No. 1

HOTEL PLAYA DE CORTÉS TRAILER PARK
  Address: Bahía de Bacochibampo (Apdo.
  66), Guaymas, Son., Mexico
  Telephone: (622) 1-01-35
  Fax: (622) 1-01-35

Price: Expensive

HOTEL PLAYA DE CORTÉS
TRAILER PARK

When the Hotel Playa de Cortes opened its campground spaces it carved the heart out of the overnight stop business in Guaymas. This is definitely the best place to pull into for a good night's sleep if you're headed for points farther north or south. Lots of people also think this is a good place to put down the anchor and spend a month or two, especially after they find out about the low monthly rate.

The Hotel Playa de Cortes was built in 1936 as a railway resort hotel and is still a class joint. It is located in Miramar, half way between the San Carlos cutoff from

COAST NEAR GUAYMAS/SAN CARLOS

Mex. 15 and the town of Guaymas. Behind the hotel is a nice RV parking area with 55 very long full-hookup back-in slots. Each has its own patio and long fifth-wheelers will find that they do not need to unhook. There is an extra charge if you use your air conditioner. The park advertises that it specializes in big rigs and there is even a sign out front asking smaller rigs not to ask to stay. This probably just means that everyone is expected to pay the full freight since vans seem to be welcome. Tents, on the other hand, are nowhere to be seen. This is a full-service hotel, it has a restaurant, bar, swimming pool, tennis courts, boat rental, and launching facilities if you've brought your own boat. There are no permanents.

The hotel is located at Playa Miramar, a beach community between Guaymas and Bahía San Carlos. Take the off ramp from Mex. 15 just west of Guaymas and follow the wide road 1.9 miles (3.1 km) to its end. You'll be at the hotel. Just through the gate turn to the left to enter the campground.

Campground No. 2

LAS PLAYITAS TRAILER PARK
   Address: Apdo. 327, Guaymas, Son.,
     Mexico
   Telephone: (622) 1-51-96

Price: Low

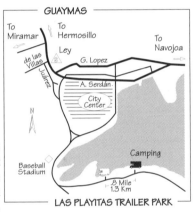

LAS PLAYITAS TRAILER PARK

One of two trailer parks located across Guaymas Bay from town, Las Playitas is quiet and friendly. According to the manager the place has been here for thirty-five years and in its heyday was very popular with fishermen. Today the fishing isn't as good and swimming in the bay just isn't done so the business has largely gone elsewhere. Take a look however, you may find the quiet and slow pace at Las Playitas to your liking. It also has low monthly rates.

The campground has 100 back-in spaces with electricity, sewer, and water. The restrooms are old but clean and have hot water showers. The campground has a restaurant and bar, a swimming pool (empty when we last visited in February) and a dock and boat launching facilities. A bus goes in to Guaymas every half-hour from a stop nearby.

To reach the campground turn toward the south from Mex. 15 through Guaymas at the stop light in front of the Ley supermarket. Zero your odometer here. Go .1 mile (.2 km) and turn left onto Blvd. Benito Juárez. Follow this boulevard through a right at a Y at .7 miles (1.1 km) and another right at 1.2 miles (1.9 km). There's a stop light at 2.2 miles (3.5 km), turn right toward Las Playitas. You'll pass a baseball stadium on your right and at the Y at 2.5 miles (4 km) turn left following signs toward Las Playitas. You'll pass the Bahía Trailer Court at 3.5 miles (5.6 km) and then come to the Las Playitas Hotel and Trailer Park at 4.3 miles (6.9 km) on the left.

Campground No. 3

BAHÍA TRAILER COURT
    Address: Apdo. 75, Guaymas, Son., Mexico
    Telephone: (622) 2-35-45

Price: Low

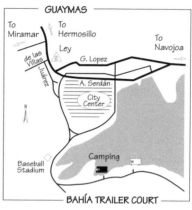

GUAYMAS

BAHÍA TRAILER COURT

Like the Las Playitas this is a campground built to serve the fishermen who no longer come in very large numbers. It too has a quiet, pleasant ambiance and is well worth considering as a base for your stay in Guaymas.

The Bahía has about 65 spaces. Many have had permanent structures built on them. About half of the spaces remain available for travelers, each has a patio, electricity, sewer, and water. The restrooms are old but clean and maintained, the campground also has a meeting hall, boat ramp and dock. Buses pass every half-hour for Guaymas.

To get to the Bahía Trailer Court follow the instructions given above for reaching Las Playitas. The campground is on the left before you reach Las Playitas.

Campground No. 4

HACIENDA TETAKAWI R.V. TRAILER PARK
    Address: Apdo. 71, San Carlos/Guaymas,
        C.P. 85406 Son., Mexico
    Telephone: (622) 6-02-20
    Fax: (622) 6-02-48

Price: Expensive

SAN CARLOS

HACIENDA TETAKAWI
R.V. TRAILER PARK

The Hacienda Tetakawi is a Best Western Hotel with a huge trailer park in the rear. You'll find a lot of people here who return every year and stay for the entire season. The campground is right across the new boulevard from the beach and there is now a sidewalk for taking a stroll.

There are about 125 spaces, many are pull-throughs and they have patios, electricity (30-amp.), sewer, water and cable TV hookups. Air conditioner use is OK. The bathrooms are clean and well-maintained, they have hot-water showers. There is a swimming pool with a bar up front next to the motel and a fish-cleaning room at the rear of the park. English is spoken at the hotel front desk and there is a bus that runs along the waterfront and into Guaymas every quarter-hour.

Zero your odometer as you take the cutoff from Mex. 15 toward San Carlos. You will be driving on a nice four-lane highway that is virtually empty. At 5.3 miles (8.6 km) you will see the Totonaka Trailer Park on the right and a tenth of a mile later the Hacienda Tetakawi, also on the right.

Campground No. 5

Totonaka Trailer Park and Apartamentos
   Address: Apdo. 950, San Carlos, Son., Mexico
   Telephone: (622) 6-03-23, (622) 6-04-81

   Price: Expensive

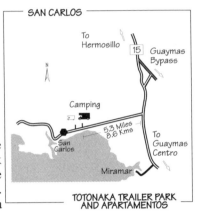

The Totonaka Trailer Park is much like the Tetakawi next door. Back in the trailer park itself you'd be hard pressed to tell one from the other if there weren't a fence between them. Instead of a hotel out front the Totonaka has a laundromat and a restaurant.

The campground has about 130 spaces, these are back-in spaces with patios, electricity, water, sewer and cable TV. The park has a cobblestone central avenue with packed gravel side streets and parking areas. Restrooms are old but serviceable, they have hot water showers. There is a swimming pool at the front of the campground. The folks in the office speak English.

To find the campground just follow the instructions given above for reaching the Hacienda Tetakawi. The two campgrounds are right next to each other.

Other Camping Possibilities

If you drive through San Carlos toward the beaches and hotels to the west you'll see quite a few rigs free camping at Playa Piedras Pinta. Looks like a good spot.

Los Mochis, Sinaloa (los MO-chees)
Population 200,000, Elevation near sea level

Los Mochis is something of a transportation crossroads. If you are traveling south on Mex. 15 this is probably where you'll spend your second night. Topolobampo, Los Mochis' port, is probably the best place to cross to/from the Baja Peninsula. The ferry runs daily. Also, Los Mochis is the western end of the famous Chihuahua-Pacific Railroad with trains along the Copper Canyon to Chihuahua.

This is a farming town. The surrounding countryside is extensively irrigated using the waters of the Río Fuerte. Sugar-cane is the main crop although you will see many marigolds being grown too. These are used as chicken feed to yellow the yolks (much of the feed goes to the U.S.). This is also the reason often given for the yellow color of the plucked chickens seen in Mexican supermarkets.

While in town you may want to visit the huge sugar refinery (**Ingenio Azucarero**) to see how the process works. The gardens at the former home of the town's founder, an American named Benjamin Johnston, are now a park. There's also a local museum, the **Museo Regional del Valle del Fuerte**. The Los Mochis area is a popular hunting destination for ducks, geese, doves and deer. Fishing out of Topolobampo and inland behind the dams near El Fuerte is also excellent.

Campground No. 1

HOTEL EL CANGREJO MORO AND RV PARK
  Address: Apdo. 342 Playa Las Glorias,
  Guasave., C.P. 81000 Sin., Mexico
Telephone: (68) 68-58-48 (Los Mochis)
Fax: (687) 2-31-31

Price: Low

This newest addition to the trailer parks in the Los Mochis area is special. This is a place to stop and spend some time. It is in the small beach-side community of Las Glorias some 26 miles (42 km) south of Guasave on Mex. 15 which is about 62 miles (100 km) from Los Mochis. People in a hurry to get to southern destinations probably won't take the time to drive out but many folks are beginning to make this their final destination for the entire winter .

The trailer park has been installed around an older hotel building, in the front and behind. There are 55 camping spaces, all are back-in and have electricity, sewer, and water but no patios and little shade. This has rapidly become a very popular destination because there is a beautiful pool, a well-used bar with a pool table, a good palapa restaurant, and miles of sandy beach out front. Additional spaces are planned. The management is very friendly and English is spoken. So far the showers are in unused hotel rooms, separate rooms are set aside for the boys and girls. Supplies are very limited in Las Glorias, you will have to drive to Guasave or even Los Mochis for anything more than the basics. The hotel sometimes provides a bus for shopping trips into Guasave.

To reach this trailer park leave Mex. 15 at Guasave and follow the signs south from town toward Las Glorias. The route passes through farming country, it is full of tractors and old pickup trucks driving very slowly so be patient. The road is paved all the way to Las Glorias and well-signed. 26.1 miles (42 km) after leaving Mex. 15 you will enter tiny Las Glorias, in another .7 miles (1.1 km) you will see a sign for the trailer park pointing right down an unpaved but divided boulevard. The campground is .7 miles (1.1 km) down this road on the left.

Campground No. 2

RÍO FUERTE TRAILER PARK
  Address: San Miguel Zapotitlán, Sin.,
    Mexico
  Telephone: (68) 15-64-65 (Los Mochis)

Price: Moderate

GPS Location: N 25° 57' 33.0", W 109° 03' 24.7"

The Río Fuerte is popular because it has a nice country setting and is much quieter than the two other trailer parks in Los Mochis. It is the first of the Los Mochis trailer parks that travelers see as they drive south.

There are 57 camping sites here, all have full 30-amp. electrical service, water, and sewer. Many are pull-throughs and have patios. The campground is a grassy meadow with some shade trees. Restrooms are modern and clean and have hot water showers, there is a nice little pool. The nearby village of San Miguel has a weekly market on Saturday morning and a few small stores. Bus service from San Miguel will take you in to Los Mochis to the supermarkets if you don't want to drive. There is usually someone who speaks English at the campground.

The Río Fuerte campground is about .2 miles (.3 km) off Mex. 15 some 10.8 miles (17.4 km) north of the main Los Mochis exit. Heading south it is 1.6 miles (2.6 km) south of the toll booth. It is on the west side of the road, just north of the Río Fuerte, with the turn-off marked by an uncompleted overpass, if you are headed north you have to cross the median on an unofficial retorno.

Campground No. 3

COLINAS RESORT HOTEL AND TRAILER PARK
  Address: Carr. Internacional No. 15 y Blvd.
    Macario Gaxiola, Los Mochis, Sin.,
    Mexico
  Telephone: (68) 11-81-11, (68) 12-01-04
    (Res.)
  Fax: (68) 11-81-81

Price: Moderate

GPS Location: N 25° 48' 46.8", W 108° 57' 31.0"

The Colinas Hotel is a favorite with caravans, you will often find it full. The draw may be the hotel facilities or it may just be that this is the easiest trailer park in Los Mochis to find. The hotel is perched on top of a hill to the right of Mex. 15 as you enter Los Mochis from the south, you can't miss it.

The campground sits on level ground on the north side of the hill. It is a level fenced gravel area with 53 spaces. Each has 30-amp. service, water, sewer, and a patio. The use of air conditioners is allowed, you will need them because there is no shade here. Bathrooms are modern and clean, showers are hot. There is a palapa-style meeting room at the campground and a long stairway up to the hotel. Once up the hill you'll find a great view, a restaurant and coffee shop, swimming pools, tennis courts, and even an amusement park. Someone who speaks English is generally available and reservations are recommended.

The hotel is just south of Los Mochis near the Km. 202 marker. It sits on a hill on the east side of the road, the entrance is just north of the hill, as is the campground. A big Pemex is just across the highway on Blvd. Macario Gaxiola which is the road to the railroad terminal for trips to the Copper Canyon and also to Topolobampo for the ferry to La Paz.

Campground No. 4

LOS MOCHIS COPPER CANYON R.V. PARK
  Address: Apdo. 1201, Los Mochis, Sin.
  Mexico
  Telephone: (68) 2-00-21 (Reservations)
  (68) 12-68-17 (Trailer Park)

Price: Moderate

GPS Location: N 25° 49' 13.2", W 108° 58' 25.8"

The Copper Canyon R.V. Park is showing its age and is surprisingly noisy because it is located next to the main road between Mex. 15 and downtown Los Mochis. There is usually room here if the other trailer parks in town are full. Caravans like this park for Copper Canyon trips.

The trailer park has 100 pull-through spaces off gravel driveways. Each has electricity, sewer, water and a patio. There is limited shade. Restrooms are older ones with separate rooms each having stool, sink, and hot shower. There is a small restaurant and the campground specializes in tours of the Copper Canyon via. the railroad. People leave their rigs here while making the two-day trip. Bus service downtown is available on the main road in front of the campground.

To find the Copper Canyon R.V. Park follow the signs off Mex. 15 for Los Mochis. This road is Blvd. A. L. Mateos. As you leave the interchange you will see the campground on your right in about 1 mile (1.6 km).

Side Trips from Los Mochis

A short 48 mile (78 km) drive inland is the old colonial town of **El Fuerte**. Founded in 1564 this town of 25,000 was a way station on the Camino Real and has its share of colonial architecture. Some people say this is the way Álamos would be if it had not been restored. In fact, El Fuerte is a bustling supply center for the surrounding agricultural area. The Chihuahua-Pacific Railroad runs through town and some people catch the train here to avoid the boring section between Los Mochis and El Fuerte.

Los Mochis is a popular base for trips on the **Chihuahua-Pacific Railroad**. People leave their vehicles in the various campgrounds (the Los Mochis Copper Canyon or the Colinas) and spend two days on the trip. They overnight in either Chihuahua or nearer to the Copper Canyon, perhaps in Creel. You can arrange a tour through one of the campgrounds or do it yourself and save a bundle.

MAGDALENA AND SANTA ANA, SONARA
(MAHG-DAH-LEH-NAH AND SAHN-TAW ANN-AW)
Population 15,000, Elevation 2,275 ft (692 m)

Magdalena and Santa Ana are located within a few miles of each other some 54 miles (87 km) south of the border town of Nogales. Magdalena is an agricultural and mining town also known as the site of the grave of **Father Kino**. There is a fiesta in honor of San. Francisco Xavier from September 22 to October 4 each year.

Santa Ana is little more than an important crossroads, Mex. 2 which crosses Northern Mexico meets Mex. 15 here. Santa Ana is also the site of a Yaqui Indian gathering during the Fiesta of St. Anne from July 17 to 26. The Yaquis sometimes perform their famous deer dance during the fiesta.

These two towns are included here because they make a good stopping point if you cross the border late and want to spend the night or if you want to rest up before crossing into the U.S when headed north. They both have a campground, and Magdalena has a good-sized supermarket. A drive through Magdalena also saves you a few dollars on tolls, there is a toll station where Mex. 15 passes town.

Campground No. 1

PUNTA VISTA R.V. PARK
    Address: Carretera Internacional #15 and
      Allende, Santa Ana, Son., Mexico
    Telephone: (632) 4-07-69

Price: Low

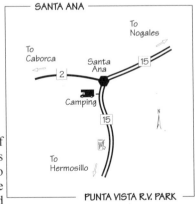

This small trailer park near the intersection of Mex. 15 and Mex. 2 is a godsend for folks who just don't feel like driving all the way to Kino Bay or Guaymas after dealing with the border crossing in Nogales. It is also a good place to rest up before crossing if you are headed north.

The Punta Vista has 12 spaces, 7 have 20-amp. electricity, sewer and water, 5 have electricity only. The parking arrangement is flexible. There's plenty of room for a big rig or two to park without unhooking, the campground is seldom full. There's no official bathroom for the campground but if the rental casita isn't in use it has a bathroom with a cold shower. The owners speak English.

The campground is right on Mex. 15. It is .6 mile (1 km) south of the intersection where Mex. 2 heads west and is on the west side of the highway.

Campground No. 2

MOTEL KINO
   Address: Ernesto Rivera Magallon #100,
   Magdalena de Kino, Son., Mexico
Telephone: (632) 2-36-84, (632) 2-36-83

Price: Low

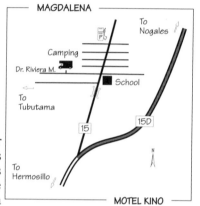

This is an alternative to the Punta Vista for folks seeking a campground between Nogales and Hermosillo. Knowledgeable travelers drive through Magdalena to avoid the toll gate on the four-lane highway bypass and save a few dollars so you're likely to be passing within a quarter-mile of the Motel Kino trailer park anyway.

The campground is located beside the motel in a fenced, gravel-covered lot. Fourteen RV slots are arranged around the perimeter but there is no shade. Each RV slot has 20-amp. electricity, sewer, and water. The one restroom is clean and modern and has hot water showers. You're likely to be one of only a few people who spend the night here so there's really going to be no reason to unhook or back into a space. The motel has a restaurant and a bar and English is spoken at the desk.

If you are driving south on Mex. 15 zero your odometer as you leave the toll road at the exit north of town. You will find yourself entering town at about 3.5 miles (5.6 km) and see the VH supermarket on the right at 4.3 miles (6.9 km). You will pass through town and drive by two Pemexes, the first on the left and the second on the right. .2 miles (.4 km) after the second Pemex and at 4.9 miles (8 km) on your odometer you will come to a stop light. Turn right here on Dr. Riviera M., it has a sign for the Motel Kino, and drive .1 mile (2 km) to the motel which is on the right.

Coming from the south take the Magdalena exit from the toll road and you will see the left turn for Dr. Riviera M. at 1.5 miles (2.4 km). The turn-off for Magdalena is 9 miles (14.5 km) north of the intersection of Mex. 15 and Mex. 2 from the west and is marked as the Libre route to Nogales.

MAZATLÁN, SINALOA (MAH-SAHT-LAHN)
Population 400,000, Elevation sea level

Mazatlán is the top RV destination on Mexico's west coast if you judge by the

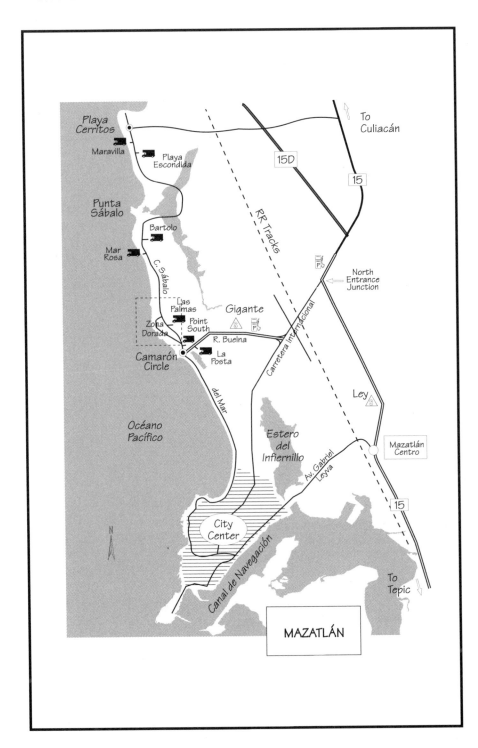

number of camping spaces available (we count nearly 700). It is also Mexico's top west-coast port. This is a bustling town that mixes everyday living with tourist activities. There is plenty to see and do and any service you require is available. Mazatlán is interesting also in that it has an acceptable climate year-round. Although temperatures do get warm in the summer July is the top tourist month here.

All of the RV parks in town are strung out in northern Mazatlán in the **Zona Dorada (Golden Zone)** tourist area and even farther north. Only a few are actually on the beautiful beach that runs all along this stretch but all are within easy walking distance of it. There are also large supermarkets and shopping malls nearby. One road, Calz. Camarón Sábalo, runs along just inland from the coast and all of the RV parks are easily accessible from it. If you drive south on Calz. Camarón Sábalo the name changes and it will take you to old Mazatlán.

Visitors tired of the glitzy Zona Dorada can find relief in downtown old Mazatlán. You'll find the restored **Plazuela Machado**, the **Plaza Republicana**, and the **Plazuela Zaragoza** here, also the **Mercado José Pino Suárez**, a municipal market. If you haven't visited a municipal market yet don't miss this one. Virtually every Mexican town of any size has one and they are filled with wonderful colors and smells. They are a great place for an inexpensive meal. Mazatlán also has a museum, the **Museo Arqueológico** and an aquarium, the **Acuario Mazatlán**.

The city is known for its **Carnaval,** the third largest in the world after Río de

FREE CAMPING IN MAZATLÁN

Janeiro and New Orleans. Like the others it is the week before Ash Wednesday when Lent starts. This, of course, means that it is variable but always in late February or March.

Since Mazatlán is often the first major city visited by campers new to Mexico a thorough description of the route to the beach-area campgrounds will probably be appreciated. As you approach Mazatlán from the north on either the toll or free roads you will see a sign in the middle of nowhere for Mazatlán Playas. On the toll road it is 12 miles (19 km) south of the toll booth, on the free road it is between the Km 11 and 12 markers. You can take this road to reach the far north end of the boulevard along the coast called Calz. Camarón Sábalo. This is a low-traffic and easy way to drive to the campgrounds. On the toll road headed north you cannot access this road.

If you are coming into Mazatlán from the south or miss the northern playas access road have no fear, campground access is really not difficult. From the north 1.4 miles (2.2 km) after the Mex. 15 Libre and toll roads meet you will see a Pemex on the right. .1 mile south of the Pemex the highway jogs left, you should go straight heading for Mazatlán centro. We'll call this the North Entrance Junction. If you approach Mazatlán from the south stay on the main highway past the first marked exit for Mazatlán centro. Eventually you'll see a big Ley store on your left, the North Entrance Junction is 2.2 miles (3.5 km) after the Ley store and goes to your left.

Zero your odometer at the North Entrance Junction. Drive south on a wide boulevard, in .7 mile (1.1 km) it will rise and cross some railroad tracks. Just at the bottom of the descent after the railroad tracks there is a confusing sign pointing right which appears to indicate that the first cross street goes to Zona Hosteleria, don't take this right. Take the next major right, your odometer will read 1.1 miles (1.8 km). You are now on Calz. Rafael Buelna and will pass many businesses including a huge Pemex on the right, a bullring, and a Gigante supermarket, also on the right. The road T's at the beach at 3 miles (4.8 km) on your odometer . This T is really a glorieta and is called Camarón Circle. Directions to all Mazatlán campgrounds from Camarón Circle are given below in the individual campground descriptions.

Campground No. 1

LA POSTA TRAILER PARK
   Address: Rafael Buelna No. 7 (Apdo. 362),
   Mazatlán, Sin., Mexico
   Telephone: (69) 83-53-10

Price: Moderate

GPS Location: N 23° 14' 25.5", W 106° 26' 35.2"

The La Posta is one of the largest trailer parks in Mazatlán and probably the easiest to find. It

is also conveniently close to the Zona Dorada restaurants and shops.

This trailer park has 180 camping spaces, all have electricity, sewer, and water. The use of air conditioners is prohibited. Most slots have patios, there is limited shade. Restrooms are older but well-maintained and have hot water showers, there is a swimming pool. Grocery shopping is convenient, both a Gigante and a Comercial Mexicana are within walking distance.

This is the only campground in town that is not north of Camarón Circle. As you approach the circle from the east you will see La Posta on your left but cannot enter because you are on a divided street. Instead go on to Camarón Circle, pass all the way around, and then drive .1 miles (.2 km) back in the direction you came from and turn right into the campground.

Campground No. 2

POINT SOUTH MAZATLÁN TRAILER PARK
   Address: 11313 Edmonson Ave., Moreno
   Valley, CA (Reservations)
   Telephone: (800) 421-1394 (USA)

       Price: Moderate

GPS Location: N 23° 14' 26.9", W 106° 26' 45.6"

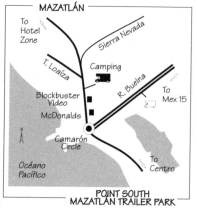

Point South is one of the best-run and most popular of the companies that guide caravans into Mexico. They have their own campground in Mazatlán and it is open to the public if there is room.

This campground has 54 spaces, all with 30-amp. electrical service, sewer, water, and patios. Shade is limited and the entire campground is surrounded by a high wall. The restrooms are modern, clean, and have hot water. Security here is the best in Mazatlán, there is always a guard and a closed gate. English is spoken and the campground is conveniently located right in the middle of the Zona Dorada.

The entrance to this campground is unmarked and easy to miss. From Camarón Circle drive north for .1 miles (.2 km), the entrance is a few driveways past the Blockbuster Video sign at the stop light. You will see a steel grill gate blocking the entrance drive.

Campground No. 3

LAS PALMAS TRAILER PARK
Address: Ave. Camarón Sábalo 333 (Apdo.
1032), Mazatlán, C.P. 82110 Sin., Mexico
Telephone: (69) 13-53-11

Price: Moderate

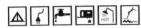

GPS Location: N 23° 14' 40.1", W 106° 27' 07.0"

Las Palmas is another well-hidden Mazatlán campground. This is an older campground but still very popular because it is conveniently located in the Zona Dorada.

The Las Palmas has about 70 spaces. They are in a palm grove behind a building just east of the main road through the Zona Dorada. Each slot has electricity, sewer, water and a patio. Bathrooms are old but have hot water for showers and there is a pool and meeting room. The campground has no security to speak of and seems unattended, it is often difficult to find someone to pay.

The entrance to the campground is easy to miss. It is marked only by a small circular yellow sign mounted high on a telephone pole. From Camarón Circle drive .6 miles (1 km) north, the entrance is on the right across from the Guadalajara Cafe.

Campground No. 4

MAR ROSA TRAILER PARK
Address: Av. Camarón Sábalo 702 (Apdo.
435 Playas del Sábalo), Mazatlán, Sin.,
Mexico
Telephone: (69) 13-61-87

Price: Expensive

GPS Location: N 23° 15' 24.4", W 106° 27' 37.5"

The Mar Rosa is one of three trailer parks in Mazatlán that are located right next to the beach. This and the fact that it is near the Zona Dorada must be the justification for a price that is the highest on the west coast of Mexico (not including Baja).

The campground has 65 back-in spaces off sandy driveways. All sites have electricity, water, and sewer. Bathrooms are modern and clean and have hot water. A central building houses a self-service laundry with three washers and two dryers. The campground is fully fenced including a wire fence in the front along the beach.

The Mar Rosa is 1.6 miles (2.6 km) north of Camarón Circle on the left, it is just past the Holiday Inn. You can easily turn into the campground from north or southbound lanes.

Campground No. 5

SAN BARTOLO TRAILER PARK
   Address: Apdo. 480, Mazatlán, C.P. 82000
   Sin., Mexico
   Telephone: (69) 13-57-55
   Fax: (69) 16-61-50

   Price: Moderate

GPS Location: N 23° 15' 43.0", W 106° 27' 51.6"

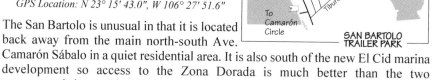

The San Bartolo is unusual in that it is located back away from the main north-south Ave. Camarón Sábalo in a quiet residential area. It is also south of the new El Cid marina development so access to the Zona Dorada is much better than the two campgrounds located farther north.

The campground has 47 spaces arranged in a long triangle-shaped fenced lot. All are back-in spaces and have electricity, water, and sewer. Air conditioner use is not possible when the campground is full, it causes voltage drops. There is limited shade. The restrooms are old but have hot water and hand clothes washing facilities with a walled clothes drying area. There is a small palapa-style meeting or lounge area.

To find the campground drive 2.1 miles (3.4 km) north from Camarón Circle and turn right on Calamar. There is a good sign on the corner. The campground is just ahead, one block from Av. Camarón Sábalo on Pulpo.

Campground No. 6

BUNGALOWS AND TRAILER PARK PLAYA
   ESCONDIDA
   Address: Av. Sábalo-Cerritos No. 999
   (Apdo. 682), Mazatlán, Sin., Mexico.
   Telephone: (69) 88-00-77
   Fax: (69) 82-22-55

   Price: Moderate

GPS Location: N 23° 17' 10.7", W 106° 28' 17.9"

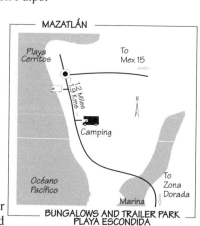

The huge Playa Escondida Trailer Park is far north of the Zona Dorada but has pretty good facilities. There is generally room here if the other Mazatlán campgrounds are full.

The campground has 236 spaces, all with electricity, sewer, water, and patios.

There is also a free satellite TV connection at each space. It is in a palm grove so there is some shade. This large campground fronts on the beach but stretches far inland. Only a few slots are on the beach side., the others are on the inland side of the divided parkway serving this area. Bathrooms here are old but usually have hot water, there is a big pool, tennis courts, a restaurant, and a small meeting room.

Find the Playa Escondida by driving north from Camarón Circle. The road now circles far inland across two large bridges before coming back to the beach strip. The campground is 5.4 miles (8.7 km) north of Camarón Circle with the entrance on the right.

Campground No. 7

MARAVILLA TRAILER PARK
   Address: Alfredo Tirado, Apdo. 1470 Playa de Sábalo-Cerritos, Mazatlán, Sin., Mexico
   Telephone: (69) 4-04-00

Price: Moderate

GPS Location: N 23° 17' 50.1", W 106° 28' 48.6"

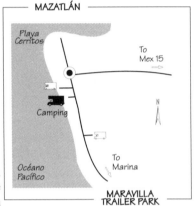

The Maravilla is a not-so-well-kept secret in Mazatlán. It is located far north next to the beach, you'll almost forget that you are in Mazatlán at all.

This is a small campground. There are about 30 back-in spaces near the beach with limited room for maneuvering (although 40 footers sometimes find room) and 9 new easier to enter back-in slots near the road. Park on the boulevard outside and walk in to make sure there is room if you have a big rig because turning around can be difficult, particularly if you are towing. Each space has electricity, water, and sewer. The lower area has shade but plants in the upper back area need time to grow. The bathroom cubicles have a toilet and warm shower but are old. They've needed a shower curtain for years but somehow no one ever gets around to installing one so the floors tend to be a mess of wet sand. There is a building between the beach and the campground with the owner's residence and a meeting room. Out front is a beautiful beach. Busses run frequently in to town so the isolated location is really no hardship. Only basic English is spoken by the owner but the campers here do a pretty good job of taking care of business. Reservations would be nice but are difficult to make unless you are actually at the trailer park and want to make them for the next season.

The Maravilla is located 6.4 miles (10.3 km) north of Camarón Circle. If you are coming from the south you will need to go on to a retorno and come back, no problem since there is virtually no traffic this far north.

Other Camping Possibilities

Tent campers might want to take a voyage to **Isla de la Piedra**. This is really the long peninsula to the south of town which has a few palapa restaurants, coconut palm groves, and lots of beach. Tent camping is allowed. This is one of the popular destinations for tourist cruises out of Mazatlán.

Free-camping RVers will find a popular location at the beach just north of the Maravilla RV park. Water vendors make this place a regular stop, there's a place to dump your holding tanks into the city sewer system, bus service to central Mazatlán runs nearby, and there is security in numbers. Many people use this place and the local police do not seem to mind.

Navojoa, Sonora (NAH-VO-HOH-AH)
Population 85,000, Elevation 125 ft (38 m)

Navojoa is the largest Mayo Indian center. It is located right on Mex. 15, the road to Álamos runs east from the city. It is the hub of an agricultural region and is known for several Mayo celebration days including the feast of St. John the Baptist on June 24, Day of the Dead on Nov. 1 and 2, and the feast of Our Lady of Guadalupe. These are celebrated in the *barrio* (neighborhood) of Pueblo Viejo. The surrounding region is popular for dove, deer and duck hunting and the town is a good place to buy Mayo crafts including baskets and masks. Navojoa has supermarkets and service stations.

Campground

ALAMEDA TRAILER PARK
Address: Apdo. 205, Navojoa, C.P. 85800
    Son., Mexico
Telephone: (642) 1-23-43

Price: Low

If you find yourself near Navojoa when darkness falls and turn into the Alameda Trailer Park you'll usually find a hard core of norteamericanos hidden beneath the trees in this campground. They've been coming here for years, primarily for the bird hunting.

The Alameda has about 80 spaces. Last time we visited only about 50 at the back of the campground were usable, the ones nearest the road were filled with the equipment of a road paving crew that was working out of the campground. The back spaces have electricity, sewer and water and air conditioners were being used. All of the slots have patios and there is lots of shade. The restrooms are old, dirty and poorly maintained but did have hot-water showers.

The campground is located just south of the Río Mayo *puente* (bridge) on the west side of the road. As you approach Navojoa from the north you will cross the bridge as you enter town, turn right at the first road after the bridge and then almost immediately turn right into the campground entrance. If there is no one at the entrance office building just drive on in and to the left, you'll probably find several rigs in the back and the watchman will find you to collect.

Teacapán, Sinaloa (tee-ack-ah-PAN)
Population 1,000, Elevation sea level

Teacapán is little more than a fishing village set at the end of a long peninsula that serves to enclose a virtually land-locked mangrove-lined estuary. The lagoon abounds in fish and bird life. You can rent a panga and guide in the village for birding, fishing, and crocodile watching. Kayaking is also excellent. On the outside of the peninsula is a long, empty beach. Dolphins are often seen near the estuary mouth. Teacapán has little in the way of services other than a restaurant or two, a Pemex station, and a few small grocery stores. There is a large supermarket in Escuinapa, about 23 miles (37 km) from Teacapán.

Campground No. 1

Rancho Los Angeles
   Address: Escuinapa, C.P. 82400 Sin.,
   Mexico
   Telephone: (695) 3-16-09 (Escuinapa)

   Price: Moderate

Teacapán is getting a brand-new beach-front RV park. Rancho Los Angeles is about 8 miles (13 km) north of town, has installed hookups, and promises to soon complete a nice restroom, laundry facilities, and landscaping. *Vamos a ver* (we'll see), but things look good so far.

Right now there are utilities for 23 full-hookup sites installed along the beach, 22 of these fronting on the sand. The restroom and laundry building is under construction. The campground is about a mile from the road, you enter and drive through a cluster of ranch buildings and then follow a good road (the one on the far right) through a coconut palm plantation to the beach. A hacienda-style building with pool and restaurant is already in operation, campers have full access to it.

There are limited supplies available at Rancho Los Angeles and in Teacapán, Escuinapa has a Ley supermarket. Busses run along the road in front of the Rancho so you don't even have to drive.

The campground has a good sign on the main road to Teacapán. You will see it on the right 15.2 miles (24.5 km) after you cross the railroad tracks when leaving Escuinapa, it is 8.2 miles (13.2 km) from the Pemex on the outskirts of Teacapán.

Campground No. 2

Trailer Park Oregon
Address: Vicky Stephens, Teacapán, Nay., Mexico
Telephone: (695) 4-51-66

Price: Low

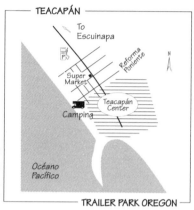

TRAILER PARK OREGON

The Trailer Park Oregon is located near the water in the village of Teacapán. This is the place to stay if you want to walk to local restaurants or stroll around town in the evening.

The campground is a grassy lot with ten slots, all have patios and connections for electricity, water, and sewer. The park is fenced but gates are not closed at night, there isn't much concern in Teacapán about big city crime problems. The restrooms are barely adequate, showers are cold. The owner's house adjoins the campground and she speaks some English and is quite helpful.

From the Pemex at the entrance to town drive toward the center. In .3 mile (.5 km) at the fourth crossroads (Calle Reforma Poniente) turn right and drive toward the water. In .2 mile (.3 km), just before you reach the water you will see the campground on your left. The roads in town are rough cobblestones and uneven dirt with puddles but passable for all rigs.

Campground No. 3

Rancho Las Lupitas Trailer Park
Address: Apdo. 22, Teacapán, Nay., Mexico

Price: Low

RANCHO LAS LUPITAS TRAILER PARK

Just before you reach Teacapán you will see a small group of buildings on the right and perhaps a few RV's. This is Rancho Las Lupitas Trailer Park. There are 10 spaces with electricity, water, sewer, patios and some shade. Most of these are pull-through slots. The one restroom is clean and has a hot water shower. The owner speaks English and provides guided boat trips on the nearby estuaries for fishing and birding. He is developing another campground on the estuary to be called Camachin or Big River.

From the Pemex at the entrance to Teacapán drive north away from town for .8 mile (1.3 km). The campground is on the left.

Campground No. 4

PLAYA LAS LUPITAS

Price: Low

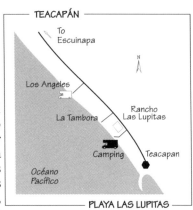

If you turn toward the beach on the next road south of Rancho Las Lupitas you will come to a group of RVs parked along the beach under coco palms in a place that reminds us of Boca de Iguanas near Manzanillo. One of the names for this place is Playa Las Lupitas. Services are very limited, there are a well and toilets, nothing else. Campers here tend to stake out a spot for the season and dig a hole for their gray water drain. They know electricity isn't really necessary when you have a good beach. The one in front of the campground fronts the mouth of the estuary and is sheltered and not too wide, but walk around the point to your right and there are miles of beautiful open beach and sand.

From the Pemex station at the entrance to Teacapán drive north away from town for .6 mile (1 km) and turn left down the dirt road toward the beach. You will drive through fields and soon come to the beach. The road has ruts and dips but you'll usually find that large fifth-wheels have made it to the beach.

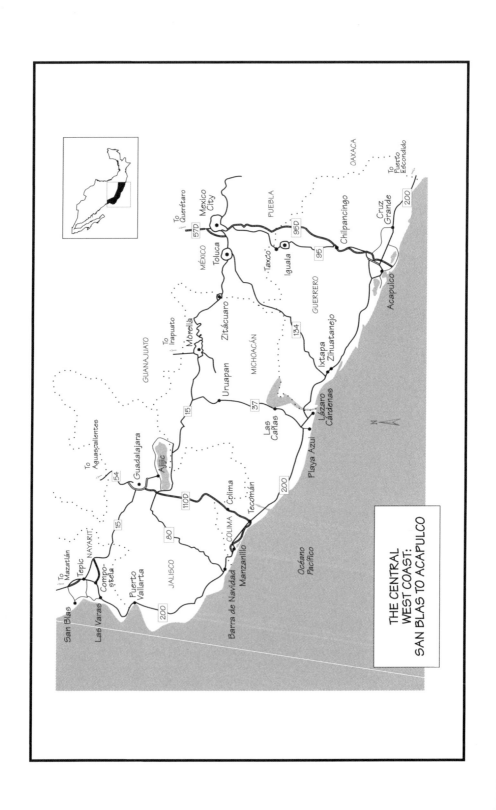

THE CENTRAL
WEST COAST:
SAN BLAS TO ACAPULCO

CHAPTER 6

THE CENTRAL WEST COAST: SAN BLAS TO ACAPULCO

INTRODUCTION

In this guide we've broken the very popular Mexican west coast into three parts. The section from the U.S. border to Mazatlán (actually just south of Mazatlán) is in Chapter 5. This chapter covers the section south of San Blas, the part of the coast south of the point where the four-lane Mex. 15 heads inland to Guadalajara and the narrow two-lane Mex. 200 takes over. Finally, Chapter 9, Chiapas and Oaxaca covers the far south.

The attractions of this part of Mexico aren't difficult to enumerate: miles of empty beaches, months of terrific weather, some of Mexico's most famous resorts, great fishing, and dozens of excellent oceanside RV parks filled with friendly people. The west coast isn't heavy on cultural attractions, don't expect much in the way of cathedrals or archeological sites.

The easiest access to this part of the coast is not necessarily down the west coast from Nogales. The distance down the coast from Nogales to Puerto Vallarta is about 1,000 miles (1,600 km), from Matamoros across central Mexico the distance is about 875 miles (1,400 km). Driving distance from the border to Acapulco is about 1,600 miles (2,580 km) along the coast, but across central Mexico from Matamoros and through Mexico City it is 975 miles (1,575 km). Even if you opt to make a lengthy bypass of Mexico City this route is clearly quicker and easier than the coastal route.

Your sense of direction may play you false on this coast. From Puerto Vallarta to the south the coast bends eastwards and is actually running northwest - southeast. The Sierra Madre Occidental (Western Sierra Madre) back the coast at varying distances. Where they are near the ocean there are rocky headlands and smaller (but still long by most standards) beaches, where the sierras retreat there are marshes, lagoons, and long sandy beaches.

As you travel south you will find that by the time you reach San Blas you are definitely into the tropical region of Mexico. Although there are some dry areas there are also many sections that are jungle-like. Even during the winter the weather can be quite hot, especially farther south near Manzanillo. The ocean is definitely warm enough for swimming.

ROAD SYSTEM

It would be hard to get lost in this area of Mexico. There is really just one major highway, Mex. 200. For the most part it is a two-lane road. The quality of the surface changes from year to year and section to section. Most of it is narrow and you shouldn't expect to average more than 35 miles an hour (55 km per hour) or so when traveling on it.

In the north, near Tepic, Mex. 200 begins in the mountains. The grades are steep and there are many trucks. Fortunately it is now possible to bypass this section. There is a quiet little road out to the coast near San Blas, then south to an intersection in Las Varas. Most RVers now use this road as they travel north and south along the coast.

Toll roads are scarce. Along the coast there is only one, a 45 mile (73 km) stretch running from north of Manzanillo southeast to Tecomán. The road is nice but hardly necessary, the free road running just inland is not bad. Other toll roads connect the coast with inland destinations. The most famous is Mexico's first major toll road, the one running from Acapulco to Mexico City. This is a very impressive but expensive road, the tolls are outrageous. We've traveled the free road, which runs along almost the same route but passes through Taxco, in a large motorhome with tow car with no problems. Another toll road runs inland from Tecomán through Colima to the Guadalajara area and a third connects Tepic with Guadalajara. This road also has a short section west of Tepic that makes the climb on Mex. 15 from the San Blas cutoff into Tepic much easier than it was in the past. This Tepic to Guadalajara road is another expensive one, but the free road along here is poor, full of trucks, and slow. It is one toll road that we recommend. A short section of two-lane toll road connects the larger Tepic to Guadalajara road with Mex. 200 at Compostela allowing traffic from Guadalajara to Puerto Vallarta to bypass Tepic. This is a less expensive government-run toll road and is also recommended.

There are several smaller roads running north into the highlands from the coast. These roads, Mex. 80, Mex. 37, and Mex. 134, while narrow and full of curves, are all used by travelers with large RVs. The trick is to take it slow and give yourself plenty of time. Many people bound for this southern coast travel through the interior of Mexico to get here and use these small roads to filter down to the ocean.

HIGHLIGHTS

The resort cities and beautiful waters and beaches of this coast are its highlights. In the far south is the queen of Mexican resorts, Acapulco. In recent years the popularity of Acapulco has dimmed and resorts farther north have taken over. First among these was and still is Puerto Vallarta. Newer and not nearly as popular among RVers is Ixtapa/Zihuatanejo. Manzanillo, despite the movie *10,* is more supply center and commercial port than resort, and little Playa Azul isn't known to airline tourists at all. All of these places, with the possible exception of Ixtapa/Zihuatanejo, make excellent destinations for campers and RVers. They have good campgrounds and lots of attractions to keep you just as busy as you want to be.

In addition to the well-known resorts there are many quiet little villages with great beaches and swaying palms. Some have RV campgrounds with reasonable facilities. Those along the coasts north of Manzanillo and Puerto Vallarta come to mind. Others offer a palapa restaurant or less, you can make camping arrangements with whomever seems to be in charge. Often the deal involves eating a few excellent meals in a nearby restaurant.

ACAPULCO

THE CAMPGROUNDS

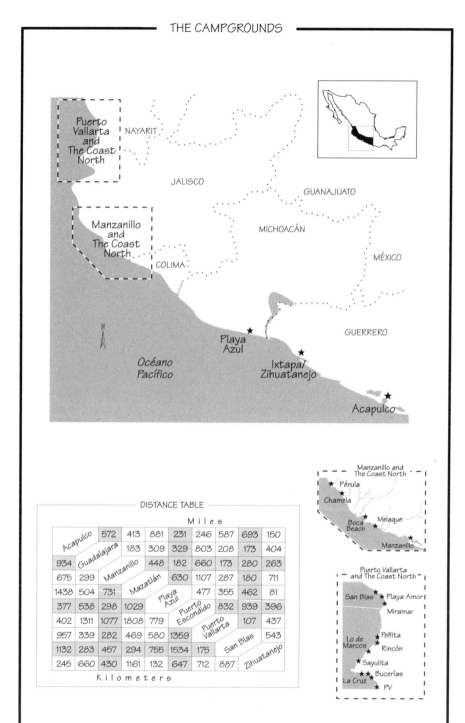

NAYARIT

Puerto
Vallarta
and
The Coast
North

JALISCO

GUANAJUATO

Manzanillo
and
The Coast
North

MICHOACÁN

COLIMA

MÉXICO

Océano
Pacífico

GUERRERO

Playa
Azul

Ixtapa/
Zihuatanejo

Acapulco

Manzanillo and The Coast North

Pérula
Chamela
Boca Beach · Melaque
Manzanillo

Puerto Vallarta and The Coast North

San Blas · Playa Amor
Miramar
Lo de Marcos · Peñita
Rincón
Sayulita
Bucerías
La Cruz
PV

DISTANCE TABLE

Miles

Acapulco	572	413	881	231	246	587	693	150
	Guadalajara	183	309	329	803	208	173	404
934		Manzanillo	448	182	660	173	280	263
675	299		Mazatlán	630	1107	287	180	711
1438	504	731		Playa Azul	477	355	462	81
377	538	298	1029		Puerto Escondido	832	939	396
402	1311	1077	1808	779		Puerto Vallarta	107	437
957	339	282	469	580	1359		San Blas	543
1132	283	457	294	755	1534	175		Zihuatanejo
245	660	430	1161	132	647	712	887	

Kilometers

SELECTED CITIES AND THEIR CAMPGROUNDS

Acapulco, Guerrero (ah-kah-POOL-ko)
Population 525,000, Elevation sea level

Everyone wants to visit Acapulco. It is the largest, oldest, and most famous of Mexico's resorts. Acapulco wasn't built from virtual scratch in recent years like the Fonatur resorts of Cancún, Ixtapa, and Bahías de Huatulco. It has quite a bit of history and is even a bit seedy in places, but Acapulco is one of the world's great resort cities with beautiful beaches, lots of shops and restaurants, and lots to do. Essentials stops on your tourist agenda are few, you'll probably want to see the **La Quebrada cliff divers** and visit the beaches and restaurants. A short driving tour to Puerto Marqués gives a great view of the bay and city.

Acapulco is also much more RV-friendly than many Mexican resorts. There are quite a few RV parks here, some in excellent locations. Shopping for essentials is easy, all the large Mexican supermarket chains are present, so are Wal-Mart and Price Club.

Driving around Acapulco is not bad if you have a small vehicle. Roads aren't narrow, but traffic is heavy with lots of taxis so you have to be alert. Bringing an RV through town is possible but not necessary, you can pass around most of Acapulco pretty easily by using outer roads that serve as a bypass.

Campground No. 1

ACAPULCO TRAILER PARK
    Address: Playa Pie de la Cuesta (Apdo #1),
      Acapulco, C.P. 39300 Gro., Mexico
    Telephone: (74) 60-00-10
    Fax: (74) 60-24-57

        Price: Front Row - Moderate,
        Middle and Back Rows - Low

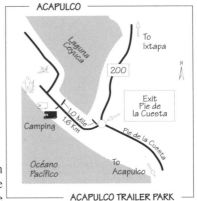

Among traveling campers there is no question that Acapulco Trailer Park is the favorite campground for a short stay in Acapulco. The reason is that if you arrive in Acapulco from the northwest you never have to enter Acapulco at all with your own rig. This campground is located in Pie de la Cuesta which is on the beach about 5 miles (8 km) northwest of Acapulco.

The Acapulco has 38 spaces on the ocean side and 12 spaces on the lagoon side. They are arranged under coconut palms on packed sand. All have electricity, water, and sewer service. The park is fenced and the gate is kept closed, there is a small grocery store at the entrance that is also the camp office. Some of the sites can be used as pull-throughs if the park is not full. There are restrooms and cold showers.

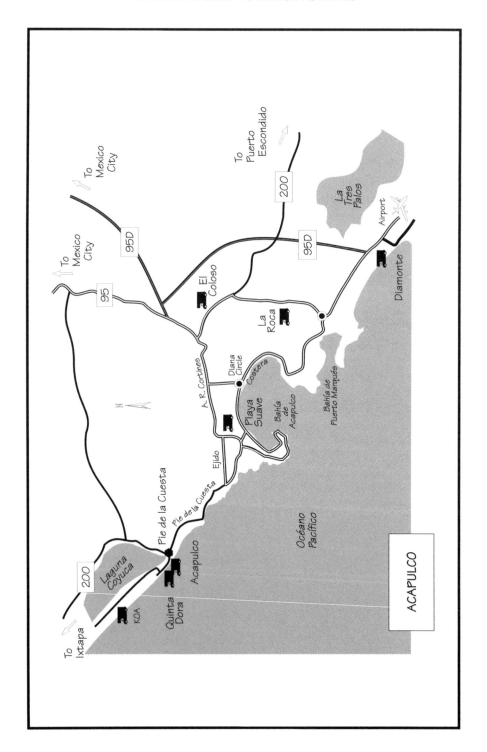

ACAPULCO

Some English is spoken.

The beach in front of Pie de la Cuesta is famous for its sunsets. It is really a beautiful place. Unfortunately it is not a good place to swim, the surf is so powerful here that swimming is dangerous. If you park at the front of the park along the beach the crash of the waves may actually shake your rig. This is not unpleasant, it just reminds you to stay out of the water. The lagoon side is a better place to swim, it is also popular for water skiing.

The somewhat remote location of the campground is not much of a problem. There are several restaurants in Pie de la Cuesta and access to Acapulco is easy by bus or taxi.

About 5 miles (8 km) outside Acapulco on Mex. 200 heading west you will see signs pointing left toward the water for Pie de la Cuesta and Base Area (there is a Mexican Air Force base past the campground). The campground is on your left 1.0 mile (1.6 km) down this road.

Campground No. 2

QUINTA DORA TRAILER PARK
  Address: Playa Pie de la Cuesta (Apdo.
  1093), Acapulco, C.P. 39300 Gro., Mexico
  Telephone: (74) 60-11-38

Price: Low

When you find the Acapulco Trailer Park you've also found the Quinta Dora. It is located about 100 yards (or meters) past the Acapulco. It also is on both sides of the road with a big sign.

Acapulco recently had a hurricane, and while the damage has been repaired at the Acapulco, the Quinta Dora ocean side is still in pretty sad shape. There are 12 sites on this side, all with full hookups. Some are large enough for big rigs. Security is lacking here but residents report no problems.

The lagoon side of the park is another story, it's cute as a bug and well-fenced. Only van-sized rigs will fit. There is room for 16 rigs, 8 sites have full hookups, 8 more lack sewer. There are restrooms with cold water showers and a very small restaurant. The owner speaks some English.

Campground No. 3

ACAPULCO WEST KOA
  Address: Carr. Pie de la Cuesta-Barra de
  Coyuca Km 4 (Apdo. 4-80), Acapulco,
  C.P.39580 Gro., Mexico
  Telephone: (74) 83-78-30
  Fax: (74) 83-22-81

Price: Moderate

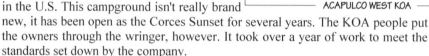

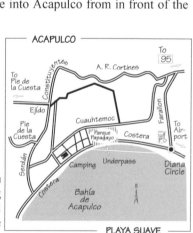

Yes, this new park is a good old KOA, just like
in the U.S. This campground isn't really brand
new, it has been open as the Corces Sunset for several years. The KOA people put
the owners through the wringer, however. It took over a year of work to meet the
standards set down by the company.

The campground is located along the beach much farther west than the Pie de la
Cuesta Campgrounds. There are 43 full hookup sites, clean restrooms with hot
water showers, a small restaurant and bar, a swimming pool and water slide, a
children's play area with wading pool, convenience store and full security. In short,
just about what you would expect at a KOA. In addition there are miles of beach
just out front. Limited English is spoken.

The campground is located on the same road as the Acapulco and Quinta Dora
Trailer Parks, just much farther out. From the intersection where the Pie de La
Cuesta road leaves Mex. 200 drive 1.25 miles (2 km) and turn right (the Air Force
Base gates are straight), drive around the end of the airport, pass a small
supermarket at 1.7 miles (2.7 km) and you will see the familiar KOA sign on the
left at 3.9 miles (6.2 km). There is bus service into Acapulco from in front of the
campground.

Campground No. 4

PLAYA SUAVE
  Address: Av. Costera Miguel Alemán No.
  276 (Apdo. 165), Acapulco, Gro., Mexico
  Phone: (74) 82-11-63

Price: Low

The Playa Suave is the only campground in
Acapulco that is within convenient walking
distance of the tourist strip on Costera Miguel
Alemán and of the beach. Probably everyone
would stay here if they could just find it.

The Playa Suave has 38 sites, all with electricity, water, and sewer. Each site also has its own toilet and cold shower in a private cubicle. All sites are paved with patio areas, palm trees provide quite a bit of shade. This campground was built during the days of smaller rigs, now giant fifth-wheels with pull-outs fill the place, their maneuvers when entering and leaving can be quite entertaining for onlookers and frustrating for the owners. Big rigs will only find this worthwhile if they plan to stay for a long period. The area is fenced and the gate is kept closed. There is 24 hour security, if the gatekeeper isn't at the gate you can be sure he's close by. If you walk out the front door you are right on La Costera, cross the street and you are on the beach. One more benefit is that you can conveniently walk to a Comercial Mexicana, a Bodega A, a Sears, or a Gigante. All are just down the street. Reservations are recommended. The manager is on-site during the day and speaks English.

Here's how find the campground. Zero your odometer at the Diana statue at the corner of La Costera Miguel Alemán and Paseo del Farallon. Drive west along La Costera and the beach. At .8 miles (1.3 km) you go into an underpass. At 1.2 miles (1.9 km) you will see a Gigante on the right, soon after that you will see a Bodega. These will tell you that you are getting close, slow down. Although the trailer park address is on Miguel Alemán the park really fronts on the next street north, Vasco Nuñez de Balboa. You must turn right at the street light at 1.45 miles (2.4 km) on Capitán Mala Espina or one of the streets on either side. Drive one block up Mala Espina, turn left, and you will see the Playa Suave about half way down the block on your left. Vasco Nuñez de Balboa is a wide, quiet street. Take your time looking and you will see the park even if you haven't taken exactly the right street off La Costera. The street address is Costera Miguel Alemán No. 276 (just in case you still have to hire a cab to lead you to it).

Campground No. 5

TRAILER PARK EL COLOSO
   Address: Av. Lázaro Cárdenas Km 2 1/2, La
   Sabana, Mpio. de Acapulco, Gro., Mexico
   Telephone: (74) 41-84-97

Price: Low

This is the most convenient place to stay if you are coming in to town from the east, up Mex. 200 from the Puerto Escondido area. The huge suburban campground is well-run and has good facilities, unfortunately it has no beach and is located somewhat out of the way. Nonetheless, it has some faithful long-termers who think it is an excellent place to live. Monthly discount rates are available.

This trailer park is a large grassy area with trees for shade. It has 150 spaces with electricity, water, and sewer. A wall surrounds the entire trailer park and there is a gate for security. There are two sets of clean restrooms with hot showers. There is also a swimming pool with a big water slide. The campground has a restaurant (with a dance floor) and there is a small grocery store out front. No English is spoken.

Busses pass right in front of the campground so transportation to downtown Acapulco or much nearer shopping is not a problem.

Coming from Cuernavaca or from Acapulco zero your odometer at the corner where Mex. 200 from the east meets Mex. 95 going in to Acapulco from Cuernavaca. Drive east on Mex. 200. The El Coloso will be on your left at 1.5 miles (2.4 km).

Coming from the Puerto Escondido on Mex. 200 zero your odometer as you pass the cutoff to the left for Bahía Puerto Marqués and Aeropuerto. The El Coloso is on your right at 1.3 miles (2.1 km).

Campground No. 6

DIAMONTE ACAPULCO RV PARK
   Address: Carretera Acapulco-Aeropuerto,
   Copacabana 8, Acapulco, Gro., Mexico
   Telephone: (74) 66-02-00

Price: Low

DIAMONTE ACAPULCO
RV PARK

This is a nice park with the right price, unfortunately it is not near the beach or downtown. If you can reconcile yourself to the location you will probably like it here. It would be a comfortable and inexpensive place to spend some time. There are more long-term residents here than at the other trailer parks in town.

The entrance road runs about .5 miles (.8 km) back into a large coconut palm grove where the park is located. It is a very large fenced area with room for lots of rigs. There are about 40 spaces with electricity, water, and sewer, and also another 10 with electricity and water. There are lots more with no services. The park has restrooms and showers with hot water. There is also a nice swimming pool.

To find the trailer park zero your odometer near Bahía Puerto Marqués where the short road between Mex. 200 and the airport road (Carretera al Coloso) meet. Drive east toward the airport. At .5 miles (.8 km) you will see a big Price Club on the left. The entrance road to the trailer park is on the right just past the entrance to the Mexico City toll road at 2.1 miles (3.4 km). You may not see the sign at first, it is very large and located on a tall column.

Campground No. 7

TRAILER PARK LA ROCA
Address: Carretera al Coloso, Km. 3,
Acapulco, Gro., Mexico
Telephone: (74) 81-00-53, (74) 82-08-27

Price: Low

The La Roca is probably the least-known and least-used trailer park in Acapulco. You might even have the place all to yourself.

There are about 20 back-in spaces under good shade trees with patios. About half of these have their own little bathrooms with cold showers and toilets. Electricity, water, and sewer are available, the electricity at some sites is both 110V and 220V so be careful, they are marked. The campground is surrounded by a wall with a gate. The place is well-trimmed and clean but when we visited the pool was empty.

The campground is located on the short road east of Acapulco between Mex. 200 and the airport road. This is called the Carretera al Coloso. If you start at the intersection with Mex. 200 the La Roca is on the right at 2.3 miles (3.7 km).

IXTAPA/ZIHUATANEJO, GUERRERO (EES-TAH-PAH/SEE-WAH-TAH-NEH-HOH)
Population 40,000, Elevation sea level

Zihuatanejo was here long before Ixtapa resort was built. It was originally a fishing village, but now it is more of a tourist resort. There are small hotels and people staying in Ixtapa come over for a visit to the beach or the restaurants.

From Mex. 200 it is about 2 miles (3.3 km) on a divided boulevard to the center of the old part of Zihuatanejo. This is a nice road, you can tell that a lot of money was spent to upgrade the streets when tourism hit town. Once you reach the old town the streets are much smaller and you won't want to bring a large RV down here. Zihuatanejo has lots of restaurants and shopping, you can spend several enjoyable hours strolling around.

East of town is the Playa Ropa area. The instructions for finding Las Cabañas will show you how to get there. This is a popular beach but the streets behind it are even more restricted than those in town.

Nearby Ixtapa is another of those Fonatur instant resorts, just like Cancún and Bahías de Huatulco. If you've seen both of those you'll understand when we tell you that Ixtapa is behind Cancún and ahead of Bahías de Huatulco on the development timeline.

You can make a quick tour of Ixtapa in your RV by driving through. You'll probably be able to find a spot to park for a few hours if you want to look around but there are no longer any campgrounds in Ixtapa.

Campground

CAMPING LOS CABAÑAS
  Address: Playa la Ropa, Zihuatanejo, Gro.
  Telephone: (755) 4-47-18

Price: Low

ZIHUATANEJO

This is the only formal campground remaining in Zihuatanejo. It is very small with room for maybe 4 vans. Larger vehicles won't fit. It is located in the Playa La Ropa area.

Los Cabañas is very small, and very cute. It is a shaded dirt pad in a back yard. There are electrical outlets and water is available. Several rest rooms with flush toilets and cold water showers are attached to the back and side of the house adjoining the camping area. It is a cozy place to camp within a couple of short blocks of Playa Ropa.

From Mex. 200 follow the southern entrance into Zihuatanejo, zero your odometer at the point where you leave Mex. 200. This is a four-lane divided road. Follow signs to the Zona Hotelera (Hotel Area). At .2 miles (.3 km) the road curves right, at .4 miles (.6 km) it curves left, at .5 miles (.8 km) it curves right again. At .7 miles (1.1 km) take the left turn for the Zona Hotelera. This actually takes you around the block so you are heading back the way you came. Now take a right turn at a Y at .8 miles (1.3 km). You will come to a traffic circle at 1.0 miles (1.6 km), continue straight here. Follow the road up a hill, take the right at 1.3 miles (2.1 km). Now the signs change to say Zona Hotelera La Ropa. The road curves to the right and left around a bluff and then down towards the Playa Ropa area. At 2.0 miles (3.2 km) at the statue of the dolphins turn right and then take the far right fork of the streets ahead of you. Almost immediately you will see a sign for Los Cabañas and then see the campground on the right.

Other Camping Possibilities

The Playa Linda Hotel and Trailer Park in Ixtapa has been closed for several years. It is still listed in some guides, don't waste your time looking for it.

The Playa Ropa area of Zihuatanejo has been the home of several trailer parks in past years. You'll see references to Pepe's or the Playa La Ropa Campground. Both are closed. However, the area seems to be a prime one for a campground for larger rigs. If you are nearby and want to stay on this section of coast you might check the area just to make sure another one hasn't popped up. There was a parking area with a hand-painted sign saying Co-op Camping last time we visited, several rigs were there.

13.3 miles (8.3 km) north of the northern Ixtapa entrance road there are trailer park signs pointed toward the beachside village of Trancones. There are several palapa restaurants there, they have space for camping but no hookups. The road is 2.3 miles (3.7 km) long and was once paved, but no longer.

1.4 miles (2.2 km) north of the Trancones cutoff there is another sign toward the beach, this one offering a trailer park with hookups. We haven't visited but have talked to people who report that there is indeed a campground there.

MANZANILLO (COLIMA) AND THE COAST NORTH (MAHN-SAH-NEE-YOH)
Manzanillo population 110,000, Elevation sea level

RVers who have formed their expectations of Manzanillo from the movie *10*, which was set here, will be disappointed by Manzanillo. There are beautiful hotels and beaches, just like in the movie, but you'll never see them if you stay on the main road.

Manzanillo has an industrial side and a tourist side. This is one of the largest west coast cargo ports in Mexico, the port area spawns lots of trucks heading inland. Unfortunately the one campground in Manzanillo is itself near the port area and shares the atmosphere. The main reason for spending the night is that the drive to the next campground south, Playa Azul, is a long one.

If you do decide to stop in Manzanillo you can have a good time. South of the port is the real town of Manzanillo. There is a pretty little square here, an evening visit is enjoyable. North of the port area there are many beaches, hotels, and restaurants. The nicest hotels are actually off the main road on the Peninsula de Santiago. There is also an excellent modern Comercial Mexicana mall north of town, it provides supplies for campers all along this coast.

Don't give up on Manzanillo just because there is limited camping in town. There are some very popular places along the 50 miles (80 km) of road to the north. Many people look forward all summer to their annual migration to places like Boca de Iguanas and San Patricio Melaque.

Campground No. 1

LA MARMOTA TRAILER PARK
   Address: Crucero Pez Vela, Carretera a
   Minatitlán Km. 0, Manzanillo, Col.,
   Mexico
   Telephone: (333) 6-62-48

Price: Low

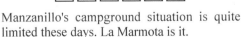

Manzanillo's campground situation is quite limited these days. La Marmota is it.

There are 24 back-in spaces with electricity, water, and sewer, each site has a paved pad

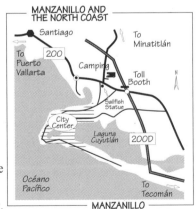

MANZANILLO AND THE NORTH COAST

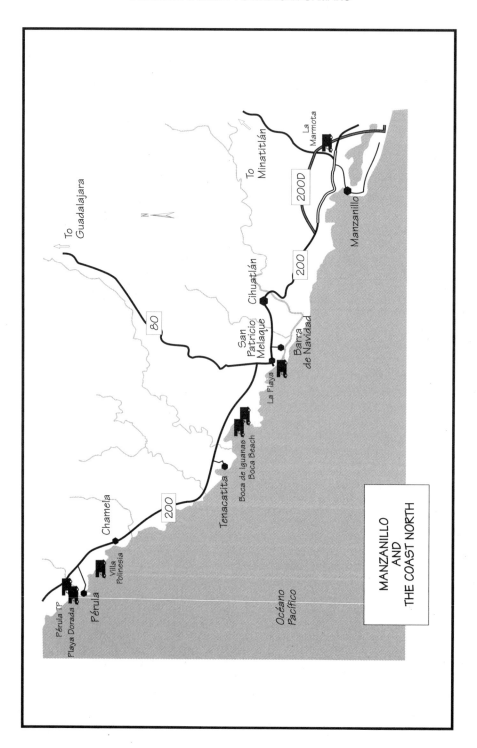

To Guadalajara

To Minatitlán

La Marmota

200D

Manzanillo

200

80

San Patricio Melaque

Cihuatlán

Barra de Navidad

La Playa

Boca de Iguanas
Boca Beach

Tenacatita

200

Chamela

Villa Polinesia

Pérula

Pérula TP

Playa Dorada

Océano Pacífico

MANZANILLO
AND
THE COAST NORTH

and patio. The campground is a fenced compound with room for more rigs to free camp if all of the spaces with services are filled. There are also many motel-style rooms. Restrooms with cold water showers are barely adequate. There is a pool, but it has never been in use when we have visited in the winter. Dust from traffic is a problem here. A small restaurant is on the road in front of the campground.

La Marmota is located about 100 yards toward Minatitlán from the Crucero Pez Vela (Sailfish Intersection), so named because it has a large sailfish statue marking it. This crossing is just west of Manzanillo Town and near the port.

Campground No. 2

TRAILER PARK LA PLAYA
   Address: Apdo. 59, San Patricio Melaque,
   C.P. 48980 Jal., Mexico
   Telephone: (335) 5-50-65

   Price: Low

The La Playa is deservedly popular. It has a beach-side location, easy access, full hookups and is located in San Patricio Melaque so you can shop, visit restaurants, and stroll around the small friendly town in the evening.

There are 45 spaces with electricity, water and sewer. All of the sites have paved patios. Some of the sites are right above the beach. Restrooms have flush toilets and cold showers. There is a fence and a gate that is kept closed at night, but there is no fence on the beach side so the fence really serves no purpose except to keep people from using the campground as a thoroughfare. There are enough people around that security isn't really a problem as long as you keep smaller items locked up so they don't grow legs. Little English is spoken. Reservations are recommended.

The La Playa is located in the town of San Patricio Melaque. Turn toward the beach from Mex. 200 on the town's main cobblestone street. Unfortunately the street is not marked, it has a *ferretería* (hardware store) on one corner and the *Refraccionaria* Wynter (an auto parts store) on the other. The cutoff is .2 miles (.3 km) east of the point where Mex. 200 makes a right-angle turn to head away from the ocean. You'll know you are on the right street when you see the town's square on your left at .2 miles (.3 km). The campground is on the right at .4 miles (.7 km), on the beach. If you've taken the wrong street you can always drive along the street running parallel to the beach, but one block back.

Campground No. 3

Boca de Iguanas

Price: Low

This is a large camping area in a grove of palm trees right on the beach. The 1.7 mile access road has a bad reputation, but don't let it put you off. There are no sections that present obstacles to passage for any rig (except the last 20 yards, see below) and in 10 minutes you're there. This same road provides access to the Boca Beach Trailer Park. These two campgrounds sit at the western end of a beautiful wide three-mile-long beach.

Boca de Iguanas is a large sandy area in a grove of palms. There are scattered electrical outlets and water taps, if you have a long cord and lots of hose you'll be able to find a way to hook up. Restrooms with flush toilets and cold water showers are provided. There is no dump station, long-termers use the toilets for black water.

Boca de Iguanas and it's next-door clone, Boca Beach, make up a very comfortable winter community of campers from north of the border. They sit on a beautiful isolated beach and even have a restaurant located between them. Things start to get crowded soon after Christmas as the snowbirds arrive and stake out their spots. Reservations are not taken.

The entrance road to Boca de Iguanas is near the 17 Km. mark of Mex. 200 some 10.3 miles (16.6 km) north of the point where Mex. 80 from Guadalajara meets Mex. 200 near Melaque. The entrance road is rough gravel and dirt with some difficult-to-negotiate sections, especially if it has been raining. Usually, however, rigs have no problem making it as far as the campgrounds. Unfortunately, Boca de Iguanas Trailer Park sits in front of a wet area that drains across the campground entrance. There is no bridge, and if the tides, winds, and rain conspire the entrance can be very difficult to negotiate. Take a close look before committing yourself or you may find yourself calling for a *grúa* (tow truck).

Campground No. 4

BOCA BEACH
    Address: Apdo. 18, San Patricio Melaque,
    Jal., Mexico
    Telephone: (338) 1-03-93

    Price: Low

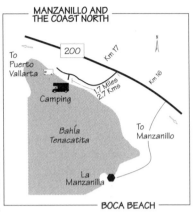

MANZANILLO AND THE COAST NORTH

BOCA BEACH

This is the campground formerly known as Tenacatita Trailer Park. It is located right next to Boca de Iguana. Of the two campgrounds this is now the most popular, Boca de Iguana's problem entrance and refusal to take reservations have led to a decline in its fortunes.

There are about 75 spaces under palm trees. Many of the sites border the beach. Most sites have electricity and water, some have sewer. The restrooms have flush toilets and cold water showers. Many campers keep small boats on the beach out front for fishing in the bay. Limited English is spoken and reservations are accepted.

To find Boca Beach just follow the directions given above for Boca de Iguanas. You'll come to the Boca Beach entrance just before you reach that of Boca de Iguanas.

Campground No. 5

VILLA POLINESIA
    Address: Carretera No. 200 Km. 72,
    Chamela, Jal., Mexico
    Telephone: (3) 1-22-39-40 (Guadalajara)
    Fax: (3) 1-21-25-34

    Price: Low

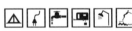

MANZANILLO AND THE COAST NORTH

VILLA POLINESIA

Villa Polinesia is an unusual campground. It is a resort fronting a beautiful beach with a few nice palapa-style bungalows and meeting areas in front, strange little concrete tents behind, and then a trailer park behind all this. Usually the place is almost empty which makes it a really nice place to stay.

There are 25 camping spaces arranged in a long row. All have electricity, the ones at the far end of the line have water and sewer also. An unusual feature here is that many of the sites have palapas that you can either park under or use to lounge out of the sun. There are handy restrooms and cold-water showers.

To reach Villa Polinesia take the road toward the beach near the 71 Km. marker. These kilometers markers start at the Melaque Junction near San Patricio Melaque so the turnoff is 44 miles (71 km) north of the Melaque junction. Drive .9 miles (1.5 km) along this unpaved but otherwise fine road following signs left into the campground.

Campground No. 6

PÉRULA TRAILER PARK
   Address: Pérula, Jal., Mexico

Price: Low

This trailer park has a devoted following. They arrive soon after Christmas (or even before) and don't leave until the end of March. After that, they report, it just gets too hot. It is one of two trailer parks in the small town of Pérula.

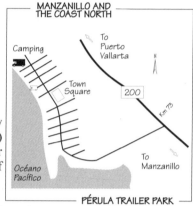

There are 19 spaces, all have electricity, sewer, and water. Good clean restrooms with cold showers are provided. The spaces are all back-ins and have patios. The ground is sandy and there is little shade. Last time we visited there was a big TV with satellite hookup in the central lounge area which is open to the breezes and looks out over the ocean. The campground is right next to a beautiful big open beach and fishing is said to be excellent. Limited supplies are available in the village and there are a few small restaurants.

One of the Pérula cutoffs is just south of the Km. 73 marker on Mex. 200. Follow the gravel road for 1.2 miles (1.9 km) until you enter the village. Continue straight ahead, you'll soon see the square on your right, the trailer park is on the left on the fifth cross-street after the square.

Campground No. 7

HOTEL, BÚNGALOWS Y TRAILER PARK "PLAYA
   DORADA"
   Address: Pérula, Jal., Mexico
   Telephone: (328) 5-51-32,
      (3) 1-22-68-53 (Guadalajara)
   Fax: (328) 5-51-32

Price: Low

This is a brand-new trailer park associated with the small hotel just across the street. It fronts the ocean and is the second of two trailer parks in this little town.

There are 9 spaces, all back-in and all with lots of room for big rigs. There isn't much shade, the owner explains that customers prefer maneuvering room to shade. All sites have electricity, water, and sewer. The restrooms are spotless and have hot water showers. If you are looking for some shade you have access to the swimming pool at the hotel next door which has plenty and is quite nice. There is also a small store at the hotel. The owner speaks excellent English and will probably correct yours if you aren't careful.

To reach the campground turn off Mex. 200 near the 73 km marker. Follow the gravel road 1.2 miles (1.9 km) until you reach the village. Continue straight ahead past the square, the campground is to the left at the second cross street after the square. It is well signed.

Other Camping Possibilities

At the north end of San Patricio Melaque is a large gravel parking lot next to the water filled with free campers. Don't be surprised to find at least 50 rigs in here. Some people spend all season at this one location. Unfortunately the sanitation standard here is questionable, there are no toilet facilities or formal dump stations.

Also in San Patricio Melaque we are told that there is a new campground that we missed during our last visit. It is apparently located in town south of the La Playa a few blocks and near the beach. It is small and has hookups.

The Tenacatita campground next to Boca de Iguanas campground recently changed its name to Boca Beach. They did this because people were confusing it with Tenicatita beach, a popular free camping beach a few miles to the north. Tenicatita beach is reached from near the 28 km marker off Mex. 200 about 7.4 miles (12 km) north of the road to Boca de Iguanas and Boca Beach. It is about 5 miles (8 km) in to the ocean.

The El Tecuán Hotel turnoff is just south of the 33 Km marker on Mex. 200 north of the Melaque Junction. There is a long twisting but paved road to the hotel. This place used to have a very popular campground, then it closed. There were various rumors involving drugs, movies, and airplanes. Now there are no camping facilities but dry camping is reportedly sometimes allowed.

As you drive along Mex. 200 you will see a large trailer park sign just north of the Villa Polynesia cutoff. This is the Chamela Hotel. It has 5 spaces at the back of the property overlooking groves of trees and the ocean in the far distance. When we stopped it looked like no one had camped here in ten years. The place has a pool that was full of slime and a tennis court. There are many more appealing places nearby. No one was around to quote a price but you could probably spend the night here if you were desperate, not likely since there are several good campgrounds quite near.

PLAYA AZUL, MICHOACÁN (PLI-YAH AH-SOOL)
Population 5,000, Elevation sea level

What can you say about Playa Azul. It isn't even in most guide books. Still, this is the state of Michoacán's claim to fame in the beach resort category. There aren't any other beach resorts in the state. AAA and most authorities claim that this is the only safe place to camp on the coast between Ixtapa and Manzanillo.

Playa Azul is a sleepy but pleasant little town with a good beach. Relaxing in the sun will be the main thing on your daily agenda here. There are a few restaurants, the best one is probably in the Playa Azul Hotel but there are others along the beach and in town. This is a resort frequented primarily by Mexican families, a pleasant change and one that will help your budget.

You may want to visit the much larger nearby industrial town of Lázaro Cárdenas because it has supermarkets and larger stores. Busses and VWs run between Playa Azul and the city.

Campground

PLAYA AZUL HOTEL
    Address: Av. Venustiano Carranza s/n,
    Playa Azul, C.P. 60982 Mich., Mexico
    Telephone: (753) 6-00-24

    Price: Low

PLAYA AZUL

The Playa Azul Hotel and its trailer park are an oasis in a long stretch of road with few RV Parks suitable for larger rigs. Located only a half-block from the beach this is a worthwhile rest stop or even a decent semi-long-term destination.

The campground sits behind the hotel. There is room for about 10 larger rigs. Electricity, water, and sewer are all available, although not necessarily at all sites. Several restrooms with cold showers are provided for the campground. The hotel has two nice pools and a restaurant. Little English is spoken by the staff but there may be a long-term camper or two to help you out with translation or logistics questions. You're only a half block from the beach. Have fun!

From Mex. 200 you must drive a short stub road to reach Playa Azul. At 2.7 miles (4.4 km) from Mex. 200 you will enter the town, there is a small Pemex with decent access on the left, directly ahead you will see that the road ends at the beach. The grid of streets branches off to the right and left. Turn left one block before reaching the beach. Drive one block, turn right on a rough dirt street, the campground entrance is half way down the block on the left. There is a gate that is sometimes closed, ring the bell or walk around to the hotel to register.

PUERTO VALLARTA (JALISCO) AND THE COAST NORTH
(PWERT-TOE VAH-YAHR-TAH)
Population 250,000, Elevation sea level

Puerto Vallarta (also known as PV) is a full-scale, extremely popular tourist destination with all that that entails. Hundreds of thousands of people each year

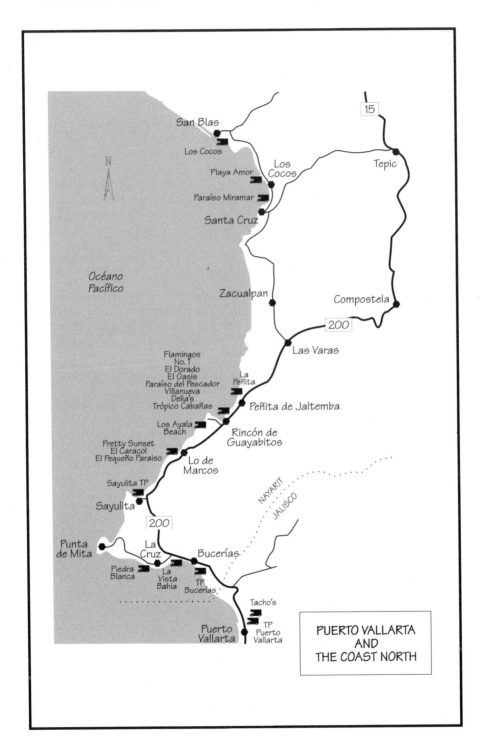

PUERTO VALLARTA
AND
THE COAST NORTH

visit for a week at a time, they come by jet and cruise ship. Every tourist service you can imagine is offered: great restaurants, booze cruises, tours, para-sailing, time-share sales, you name it. The whole thing can be hard to take for more than a few days at a time, but never fear, a slower-paced paradise of small towns and quiet beaches stretches to the north.

In Puerto Vallarta the crowded downtown area is the center of activities. There's a malecón along the waterfront for strolling, across the street and up the hill are restaurants and shops along small cobblestone streets. The selection of Mexican crafts in Puerto Vallarta is one of the best in Mexico and prices aren't really too bad. South of downtown and the Río Cuale a hotel and restaurant area backs Playa de los Muertos while to the north toward the airport are big hotels, more beaches, and a marina and golf course. Big rigs are a real problem in the old town, use a tow car or bus to get there, you'll be glad you did because streets are narrow and parking very limited. If you approach PV from the south you can avoid most of the traffic by following a bypass that runs around the back side of the old town. Just watch carefully for the sign pointing right as you enter town.

A few miles north of Puerto Vallarta but still along the shore of Banderas Bay is Bucerías. Between the highway and the beach are wide cobblestones streets lined with many expensive homes, most have high walls so you really can't get a good look. There are small restaurants and stores so if you stay in Bucerías you probably won't visit PV very often.

The small town of Sayulita, some 27 miles (43 km) north of Puerto Vallarta, is about the quietest place you're likely to find in this area. The beach is a popular surfing destination (swimming is only good when the waves are down), there are a couple of good restaurants, some tiny grocery stores, and that's about it.

A short distance to the north is the slightly larger oceanside town of Lo De Marcos. It is neatly arranged along cobblestone streets and has an excellent swimming beach. Here you'll also find small restaurants, hotels, and shops.

North again is Rincón de Guayabitos. This town seems to cater more to Mexicans than norteamericanos, you'll see many family groups on the beach. Prices tend to be lower than in PV. There are many restaurants and hotels, as well as a variety of small stores. This is also a popular fishing destination for campers, with nine campgrounds in town RVers are obviously an important part of this community.

Moving north again, we leave Mex. 200 in the town of Las Varas and drive through tobacco farms and then rolling hills until we reach the water again near the tiny towns of Aticama, Los Cocos, Miramar and Santa Cruz. There are a couple of campgrounds along here and the mosquitoes aren't quite as bad as in nearby San Blas.

San Blas today is a small fishing village but one with a surprising amount of history. The town was an important port even in the 1500s. The Manila galleons visited and expeditions north to California departed from here. You can still visit the ruins of an old Spanish fort just inland. San Blas also has beaches, they start south of town near the campground. Behind San Blas is an area of swamps and

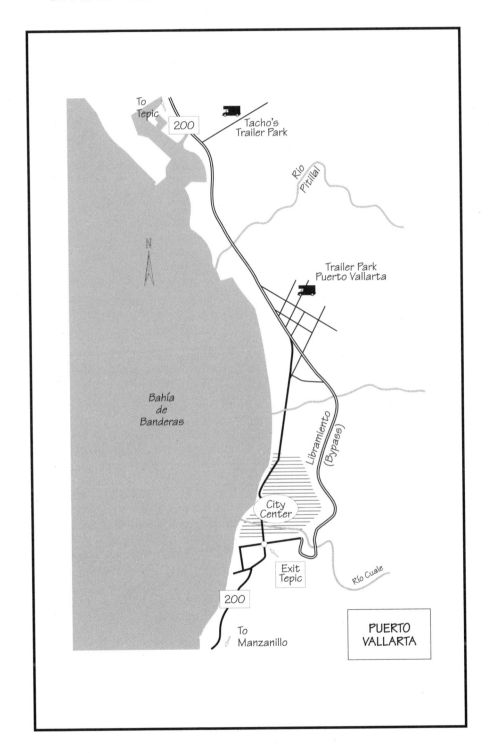

lagoons, small boats are available to take you exploring and birding. The swamps are also responsible for another memorable San Blas attraction, the mosquitoes. Be sure you bring bug dope and have good screens on your rig if you stay in the San Blas campground.

Campground No. 1

Tacho's Trailer Park
   Address: Camino Nuevo al Pitillal (Apdo.
   315), Puerto Vallarta, Jal., Mexico
   Telephone: (322) 4-28-28

Price: Moderate

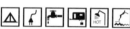

Tacho's is the big rig trailer park in Puerto Vallarta. The campground's wide cobblestone streets make access easy and the widely spaced sites with patios are very pleasant. The location north of town and outside the busy traffic area is also a plus.

The campground has about 150 spaces, each with electricity, water, and sewer. All are back-in sites. The clean restrooms have hot showers. There is a nice big pool here to make up for the distance from the beach. You'll have to use your own car or public transportation to reach beaches, shopping, or downtown.

The key to finding this trailer park is locating the correct intersection north of Puerto Vallarta. From the north watch for the airport on your right. The left turn to El Pitillal and the trailer park is 1.6 miles (2.6 km) south of the airport. You must make your turn from the lateral lane on the right so watch carefully ahead for the overhead sign for El Pitillal (a Puerto Vallarta suburb). From the south the intersection for the right turn to El Pitillal and the trailer park is 1.8 miles (2.9 km) north of the point where the ring road around old PV joins the four-lane (plus laterals) road north out of town and .2 miles (.3 km) north of a Pemex on the left. From the south you also must make the right turn from a lateral but access is easy and the turn easier to see as you approach. Once you make the turn toward El Pitillal the trailer park is .5 miles (.8 km) ahead on the left. The park has its own turn lane so the entry is easy.

Campground No. 2

TRAILER PARK PUERTO VALLARTA
   Address: Calle Francia #143, Colonia
   Versailles, Puerto Vallarta, Jal., Mexico
   Telephone: (322) 4-28-28

Price: Moderate

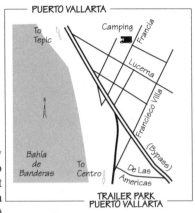

For the most convenient place to stay to enjoy PV's delights you should give the Puerto Vallarta Trailer Park a try. It is located almost within walking distance of downtown (really a pretty good hike of about 2 miles (3.3 km)) and with great access to busses and supermarkets.

The trailer park has 49 spaces, several are pull-throughs for big rigs while most are back-in sites. This is a walled campground in a close-in PV suburb. There is no gate and poor security but this is apparently not much of a problem here. All sites have electricity, water, sewer, and patios. They are close together. Shade is abundant, in fact the campground is much like a *vivero* (gardening nursery). The bathroom building is only adequate but the showers are now plenty hot (new water heaters were installed in 97). Campers can use the pool at the Playa Las Glorias, about 10 minutes away.

The campground is not on a main road and there are no signs so it is not easy to locate. It sits not far from the point where the ring road and the four-lane road north out of town meet. The easiest landmark to find is the four-story white Plaza del Sol Hotel on the east side of the road. The road just north of the hotel is Francia, drive 2.5 blocks east, you'll see the unsigned entrance to the campground on the left.

Campground No. 3

TRAILER PARK BUCERÍAS
   Address: Apdo. 148, Bucerías, Nay, Mexico
   Telephone (329) 8-02-65 Fax: (329) 8-03-00

Price: Expensive

A camper we met at Boca de Iguanas once warned us that Bucerías was the most expensive campground on the coast. "They know what they've got" he told us.

Bucerías has about 45 spaces with full hookups and a few more with electricity only.
There is plenty of room for big rigs and all of the full-service sites have patios. The restrooms have hot showers, the women's is particularly cute. There is a brick fence

completely around the park, great for security but blocking any beach view. The beach is the park's best feature, this is the closest ocean-side park to Puerto Vallarta, but not by much. English is spoken and reservations are a must during the high season.

The trailer park is located next to the beach on the south side of Bucerías. The easiest access from Mex. 200 is on the road to the Hotel Costa Flamingo (watch for a big DIF sign too) near the 142 Km. marker. You'll pass a bull ring on the right and then should turn right at the last possible road in front of the hotel. The trailer park is on the left in the third block after this turn.

Campground No. 4

La Vista Bahía Condominium and Trailer Park
  Address: Apdo. 64-A, Puerto Vallarta, Jal, Mexico
  Telephone: (329) 8-01-37

      Price: Expensive

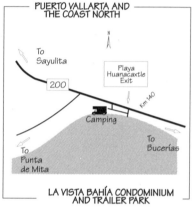

LA VISTA BAHÍA CONDOMINIUM AND TRAILER PARK

The Vista Bahía is small and usually fully reserved during the January to March high season (reportedly for several years in advance), but since it is near the highway and such a nice place you should always stop on your way by to see if there is a free space. We think the atmosphere here is more like a Mediterranean villa than a trailer park.

There are 23 sites, 11 on one end of the buildings and 12 newer ones on the other. The campground sits on a low bluff above a beach that extends far to the north and south. Sites have electricity, water, sewer and patios, they are all back-in slots. The bathrooms are clean and modern with lots of hot water. Two beautiful swimming pools sit in front of the condominiums and above the ocean, you'll probably be spending quite a bit of time there. The only drawback to the campground is the presence of the nearby highway, road noise is quite noticeable. Campers here often hike into nearby Bucerías for groceries and busses on the highway go into Puerto Vallarta. English is spoken and reservations are definitely recommended.

You drive into this campground from near the Km. 140 marker north of Bucerías. There is a sign for Bahías de Huanacaxtle and an entrance to a lateral access road. Turn right to drive parallel to the highway for .4 miles (.6 km), the campground will be on your left.

Campground No. 5

TRAILER PARK PIEDRA BLANCA
   Address: Calz. Independencia Nte. 914,
   Guadalajara, Jal. Mexico (Reservations)

   Price: Moderate

The Trailer Park Piedra Blanca is located next to the beach near the small town of La Cruz de Huanacaxtle, when someone recommends that you stay at La Cruz this is the place they're talking about.

The campground is situated next to the beach. There are 26 sites, all with patios and electricity, water and sewer. The bathrooms are adequate and have hot water. You may find this campground slightly easier to get into than Bucerías and La Vista Bahía during the high season, but only slightly. Some English is spoken and reservations are accepted.

To reach the trailer park take the Punta de Mita road just north of the Km. 138 marker on Mex. 200 north of Bucerías. After 1.5 miles (2.4 km) you will reach La Cruz de Huanacaxtle and at 1.9 miles (3.1 km) you should turn 90 degrees left and drive about 200 yards on a dirt road to the entrance gate on your right. Open the gate and drive down the long entrance (make sure someone isn't coming in the opposite direction, this is a one-lane road). Check in at the hotel office on the far side of the pool and parking lot.

Campground No. 6

SAYULITA TRAILER PARK
   Address: Apdo. 11, La Peñita de Jaltemba,
   C.P. 63726, Nay., Mexico
   Telephone: (327) 5-02-02

   Price: Low

This campground is a real find. It is located next to a beautiful beach in the so-far-undiscovered village of Sayulita. The owner makes his guests promise only to recommend it to nice people, we assured him that our readers would qualify.

There are 34 sites in this campground, all with full electricity, water, and sewer hookups. The sites have patios and shade. Amenities are shared with 7 bungalow units and are generous. The bathrooms are tiled and very clean with lots of hot water. A TV room and patio provide a place for people to get together and two more terraces provide places for Ping-Pong and surfer watching. Someday there may be a pool but right now no one seems to miss it. The beach is one of the prettiest around and increasingly popular for surfing. When the surf is down it makes a great place to swim. Sayulita village has several places to buy groceries and also a couple of excellent restaurants.

During the off season you can arrange reservations with Thies and Cristina Rohlfs, Revolucion 349, C.P. 54030 Tlalnepantla, Mexico. The telephone number is (5) 5-72-13-35 and the fax number (5) 3-90-27-50. Call the campground itself to reach them from November to March. English is spoken.

The road to Sayulita is near the 123 Km. marker north of Puerto Vallarta. A paved road leads .9 miles (1.5 km) to the village. Turn right following campground signs down a dirt street just after entering the village, the campground is at the end of the street.

Campground No. 7

PRETTY SUNSET TRAILER PARK
   Address: Camino a las Minitas s-n, Lo de
   Marcos, Nay., Mexico
   Telephone: (327) 5-00-55

Price: Low

This is the newest of the trailer parks in the village of Lo de Marcos. It is little more than a line of 8 sites stretching from the road to the beach. Still, each site has its own patio, shade, electricity, water, and sewer. There's plenty of room to park long rigs. The bathrooms are new and clean but showers (so far) are cold. There's a watchman on duty at the gate and all of the campers we talked to loved the place. The beach out front may have something to do with that.

This is the first of three campgrounds you will find as you drive south out of the little village of Lo de Marcos. From Mex. 200 the turnoff for Lo de Marcos is near the 108 Km. marker. If you zero your odometer as you turn off the highway you will reach the village square at .5 miles (.8 km) and the road doglegs left just beyond it. Drive until you see the ocean ahead, you want to turn left two blocks from the beach at .7 miles (1.1 km). The road soon becomes paved (it was cobblestone before) and at .8 miles (1.3 km) you will see the campground on the right.

Campground No. 8

EL CARACOL BUNGALOWS & TRAILER PARK
Address: Apdo. 89, La Peñita de Jaltemba,
C.P. 63726 Nay., Mexico
Telephone: (3) 686-04-81 (Guadalajara)

Price: Low, Moderate with air con. use

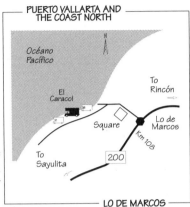

El Caracol is the luxury trailer park in Lo de Marcos. This campground is usually full during the high season so if you want to stay here you had better make reservations.

There are sixteen parking slots but three are taken by permanently installed rigs. They all have electricity, water, sewer, patios, and plenty of shade. This is a very tidy facility with cobblestones for paving. Bathrooms are very clean and showers are hot. There are even special areas for hanging your wash to dry that are screened from the view of passersby. There is a patio area separating the campground from the beach, it has tables and a small wading pool.

El Caracol is on the same road as the Pretty Sunset Trailer Park described above. Just drive .2 miles (.3 km) farther and you will see the trailer park on the right.

Campground No. 9

BUNGALOWS, TRAILER PARK, Y CAMPAMENTO EL
 PEQUEÑO PARAISO
Address: Carrt. Las Minitas No. 1938, Lo de
 Marcos, Nay., Mexico
Telephone: (327) 5-00-89

Price: Low

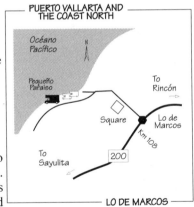

The El Pequeño Paraiso is the largest of the Lo de Marcos campgrounds, but not by much. There is actually lots of room here but much is not being used. There are about 20 developed back-in sites, all with electricity, water, sewer, patios, and shade. The bathrooms are not fancy but they are clean, they have cold water showers. The campground also has some rental motel-style bungalows.

To reach the campground follow the directions given above for the Pretty Sunset Trailer Park. Once there continue on for another .3 miles (.5 km) and you will see El Pequeño Paraiso on the right.

Campground No. 10

KAMPAMENTO LOS AYALA BEACH
Address: Sr. Sergio Sovar M., San
Guanguey #2, Tepic, Nay, Mexico
Telephone: (32) 13-33-07 (Tepic)
Price: Low

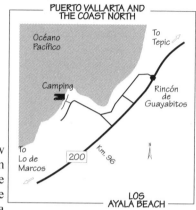

Kampamento Los Ayala Beach is a brand-new campground that wasn't quite finished when we visited in February 1997. At the rate the owner was working it won't be long before the area has a spiffy new campground. Los Ayala Beach is just south of Rincón de Guayabitos, you might even think of this as one of that cluster of campgrounds. People at the campground say the beach here is better.

Right now the campground has 9 spaces with electricity, water, and sewer. Later there will be 12 of them. Construction was under way on the buildings between the sites and the beach so time will tell how they turn out but the bathrooms were nearing completion and they looked great. There will be lots of tile and hot water.

The Los Ayala cutoff is just south of the entrances to Rincón de Guayabitos. If you zero your odometer as you leave the highway you will reach the village at 1.3 miles (2.1 km). Take the first right toward the beach and you will see the campground directly ahead.

Campground No. 11

TRAILER PARK TRÓPICO CABAÑAS
Address: Retorno Palmas s-n, Junto al Cocos, Rincón de Guayabitos, Nay.,
Mexico
Telephone: (17) 12-33-24 (Torreón)
Price: Moderate

The Trópico Cabañas is the farthest south oceanside trailer park in Rincón de Guayabitos. This campground is very much fishing oriented, it is also a favorite of big rigs since the parking slots are especially long.

There are 30 spaces in this campground, all with electricity, water, and sewer. The entire campground is paved and there is a boat ramp. The bathrooms are very clean and there are hot water showers. This is a popular campground and reservations are recommended.

The campground is the only one on the Palmas Returno.

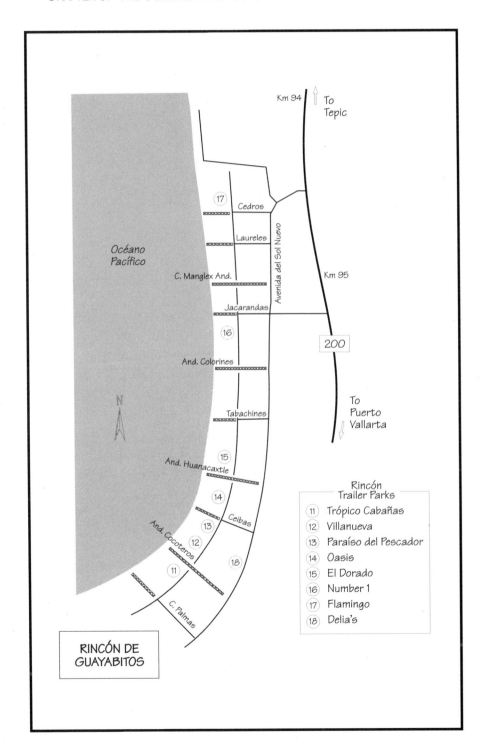

Campground No. 12

TRAILER PARK VILLANUEVA
Address: Retorno Ceibas No. 10, Rincón de Guayabitos, Nay., Mexico
Telephone: (327) 4-03-91

Price: Moderate

This is another fisherman's campground, but it is much more relaxed than those to the north and south. The gate isn't kept locked and the ground cover is cobblestones and sand, not cement. Palm trees provide lots of shade.

There are about 30 spaces with all utilities and patios. Bathrooms are adequate and there is hot water. As you would expect there is a boat ramp but this campground also has a beach-side open air restaurant. Some of the campers here have been coming to Rincón for decades.

The campground is located off the Ceibas Returno. This is a popular location, two other campgrounds are also located on this one.

Campground No. 13

PARAÍSO DEL PESCADOR TRAILER PARK AND BUNGALOWS
Address: Retorno Ceibas s-n (Apdo. 8), Rincón de Guayabitos C.P. 63727 Nay., Mexico
Telephone: (327) 4-00-14, (47) 13-36-15 (León)

Price: Moderate

Complete with boat ramp, Paraíso del Pescador is another fisherman's favorite. There are 40 spaces in a fully paved, carefully-gated beach-side campground. All sites have electricity, sewer, and water. Most have patios. The bathrooms are beautifully clean, have lots of tile and hot water showers. The manager speaks some English.

Paraíso del Pescador is located on the Ceibas Retorno.

Campground No. 14

OASIS TRAILER PARK
Address: Retorno Ceibas s-n, Rincón de Guayabitos, Nay., Mexico
Telephone: (327) 4-03-61

Price: Moderate

The Oasis is the most expensive of the Rincón campgrounds. It is also the newest. The parking area is completely paved and has hookups for 19 rigs. Palms provide limited shade. There is plenty of room for big units. Between the camping area and the beach are two buildings, but in front of them is a sunning area and a small hourglass-shaped pool. The bathrooms are modern and there is hot water. This campground has it's own boat ramp.

The Oasis is located on the Ceibas Retorno.

Campground No. 15

T.P. EL DORADO
  Address: Retorno Tabachines s-n, Rincón de Guayabitos, Nay., Mexico
  Telephone: (327) 4-01-52

Price: Moderate

This is the last campground with its own boat ramp as you go north along the beach in Rincón. Fishing is important here but so is lying in the sun.

The El Dorado has 21 spaces arranged around a central parking area. All sites have patios and full hookups. There is a sunning platform above the beach at the front and campers have access to a nice pool at a small hotel across the street that is owned by the same people. Bathrooms are tucked away behind the owner's house but are clean and showers have hot water.

The El Dorado is located on the Tabachines Retorno.

Campground No. 16

TRAILER PARK NUMBER 1
  Address: Retorno Jacarandas s-n, Rincón de Guayabitos, Nay., Mexico
  Telephone: (327) 4-03-04

Price: Moderate

The Trailer Park Number 1 has recently been spruced up and is now really quite nice. There are back-in parking slots for 15 units with plenty of shade and a grassy area in the middle. The bathrooms are nice but offer only cold water showers, hot water may come next year. This campground also has its own palapa restaurant next to the beach. The owner here speaks English.

The Trailer Park Number 1 is located on the Retorno Jacarandas.

Campground No. 17

FLAMINGO TRAILER PARK
  Address: Apdo. 58, Rincón de Guayabitos, Nay., Mexico

Price: Low

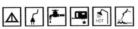

At the far north end of the Rincón strip is the Flamingo Trailer Park. This trailer

TRAILER PARK NUMBER 1 AT RINCÓN DE GUAYABITOS

park is showing its age but has its own attractions. There are about 30 spaces with hookups in varying stages of repair. The Flamingo probably has the nicest beach of all of the trailer parks in town, Rincón's beach gets wider as you go north. Bathrooms are adequate and the showers are hot. We've recently seen caravans using this campground, probably because it is the only one in Rincón with any room during the busy season.

The Flamingo is on the Retorno Cedros, this is the first one you come to after entering the main entrance to Rincón and turning left on Avenida del Sol Nuevo.

Campground No. 18

DELIA'S TRAILER PARK
   Address: Avenida Del Sol Nuevo s-n, Rincón de Guayabitos, Nay., Mexico
Price: Low

Delia's is the least expensive of the Rincón trailer parks and the only one not on the beach. Delia's is definitely showing its age. There is room for about 10 rigs in dense vegetation behind the main building. Most have electricity, water, and sewer. The bathroom has a hot shower.

The entrance to Delia's is off Avenida del Sol Nuevo, not one of the returnos. There is poor signage, watch closely as you drive between the entrances to the Ceibas and Palmas Retornos.

Campground No. 19

LA PEÑITA TRAILER PARK
Address: Apdo. 22, Peñita de Jaltemba, C.P. 63726 Nay., Mexico

Price: Moderate

This campground is a little different than the others in the area. It is located on a small hill above, but close to, a nice beach. The facilities have a rustic feel to them and the folks are friendly.

Campsites are spread all along the hillside on terraces. There are about 130 spaces, most have full utilities and some have patios. There is lots of shade and some sites have great views of the coast and beach below. Restrooms have hot showers and there is even a swimming pool. The many fishermen at this campground must either go down the road to launch their boats or manhandle them across a wide beach below the campground. The town of Peñita, about a mile south, provides adequate shopping.

The entrance to this campground is well-signed and is right on Mex. 200 between the 91 and 92 Km. markers. This is just north of the town of Peñita de Jaltemba.

Campground No. 20

PARAISO MIRAMAR RV-TRAILER PARK
Address: Calle Cerrada en Playa La Manzanila s-n, Miramar, Nay., Mexico
Telephone: (32) 12-04-11 (Tepic)

Price: Moderate

The long cobblestone driveway into Paraiso Miramar may give you pause but press on, this almost unknown trailer park is well worth the trouble.

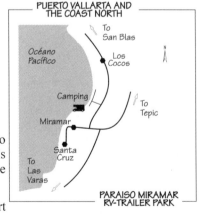

Paraiso Miramar is a small motel-style resort set above a small rocky beach. Behind and alongside the bungalows is a small RV park with about eight usable sites. Each has electricity, water and sewer. Some have cement parking pads and all are back-in spaces. The bathrooms are clean and modern and have hot water showers. This is a very pleasant camping area with well-clipped green grass and a park-like setting. In front above the ocean are small swimming/wading pools and sunning areas. The Paraiso Miramar has a cute little restaurant overlooking the ocean and the tiny towns of Miramar and Santa Cruz are just a short stroll away along the beach.

The turn-off for Paraiso Miramar is just 2.5 miles (4.0 km) south of the well-known Playa Amor RV Park (see below). The entrance road has a small sign, follow the good dirt road toward the ocean for .2 miles (.3 km), turn left at the T and drive .3 miles (.5 km) on cobblestones to the campground entrance at the end of the road. Big rigs should have no problems with reasonable caution.

Campground No. 21

PLAYA AMOR RV PARK
  Address: Playa Los Cocos, Aticama, Nay., Mexico

Price: Low

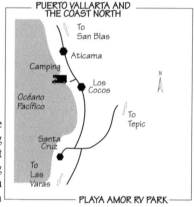

PUERTO VALLARTA AND THE COAST NORTH

To San Blas
Aticama
Camping
Los Cocos
Océano Pacífico
To Tepic
N
Santa Cruz
To Las Varas

PLAYA AMOR RV PARK

The Playa Amor has seen better days, the facility is somewhat run down. It is getting quite a bit of traffic lately, however. Now that there is a paved route bypassing Tepic along the coast many people spend the night at Playa Amor, it is a good place to break the drive from Mazatlán to Puerto Vallarta. A lot of other people like Playa Amor for itself, this is one of the few places where you are almost guaranteed to find a free site on a low bluff overlooking the ocean, even during the high season.

Playa Amor really has two different camping areas. One has 38 spaces with electricity, water, and sewer. Another area next door has 35 spaces with only electricity and water. This second area is usually reserved for caravans, they often spend a day or two here on the way up and down the coast. Some sites in both areas have patios and some are pull-throughs. The bluff sites seem to be eroding away, take a look before you park too near the edge! The bathrooms are barely adequate, they need a lot of cosmetic work, but there are hot water showers. English is spoken.

Playa Amor is located on the highway between San Blas and Santa Cruz to the south. This road heads south at a junction some 1.3 miles (2.1 km) east of the bridge at the edge of San Blas. The campground is 8.5 miles (13.7 km) south of the junction, you will drive through the small town of Aticama about a mile before you reach it.

Campground No. 22

TRAILER PARK LOS COCOS
   Address: Av. Temiente Azueta, San Blas,
   Nay., Mexico
   Telephone: (328) 5-00-55

Price: Low

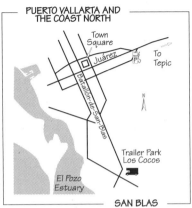

Given the fact that San Blas has an unfortunate reputation for harboring hordes of biting insects it is probably not too surprising that Los Cocos always has lots of room. The campground itself, set in a grove of coco palms, is pleasant enough. It sits within walking distance of both the town of San Blas and the beach.

The sign out front says there are 100 spaces in the campground. There must be at least that many, the campground is a large flat well-clipped grass field under coco palms with services islands widely spaced in rows throughout the campground. Each has electricity, water, and sewer. There are no patios or roadways so every site can be a pull-through. The bathrooms are poor, they have hot water showers but unfortunately harbor even more mosquitoes than you will find outside. When you arrive check in with the bartender in the bar out front, that's the office. There is a low fence around the campground and a gate that is closed at night.

As you enter San Blas on Mex. 74 you will pass over a bridge and in .6 mile (1.0 km) be confronted with a three-way fork. Take the middle street passing under an arch. Drive straight ahead until you come to the square, turn right and pass around it counter-clockwise for 270 degrees, you really wanted to turn left on the road on the far side of the square but big rigs can have trouble making the turn. In .7 miles (1.2 km) you will see the Los Cocos straight ahead behind a fairly respectable-looking bar. Make a left turn just beyond to pass down a side road and turn into the campground gate.

Other Camping Possibilities

Kampgrounds of America (KOA) is once again moving into Mexico in a big way, the Puerto Vallarta KOA was not open for business when this book went to press in March 1997 but it was very close. This will be a large campground built new to KOA standards. It is located north of Puerto Vallarta and south of Bucerías on the east side of Mex. 200 near the 139 Km. marker. You can easily see it from the highway.

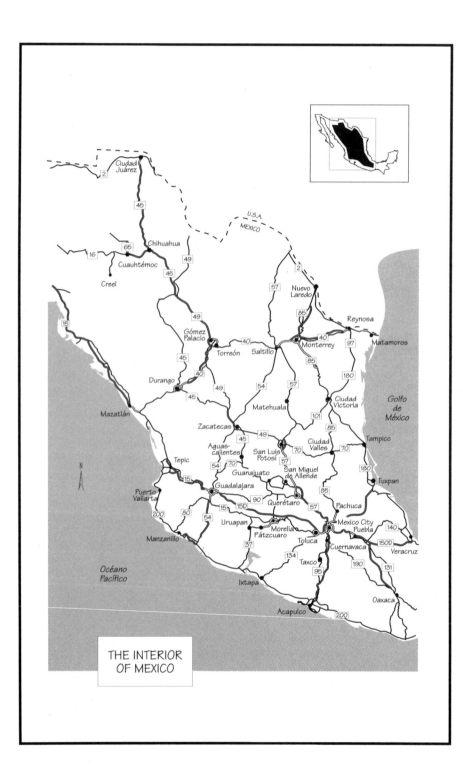

THE INTERIOR
OF MEXICO

CHAPTER 7

THE INTERIOR OF MEXICO

INTRODUCTION

This chapter covers a huge area, much larger than any of the other chapters in this book. The interior, as organized here, has 28 cities with good camping accommodations. If you are new to Mexico it is no easy task to arrange a picture of the interior in your mind.

Most of the interior is comprised of high plateau or mountains. Two mountain ranges define the borders of the northern portion. The Sierra Madre Occidental are in the west and the Sierra Madre Oriental in the east. Between them is a highland plateau, far from flat, that slopes gradually upward toward the south. This area is called the Altiplano. At the U.S. border the altitude is about 4,000 feet, but in the south near Mexico City it is 8,000 feet.

At the south end of the plateau is a unique east-west volcanic fault area called the Cordillera Neo-Volcánica. It runs from the Cape Corrientes, near Puerto Vallarta on the west coast, to the Tuxtla mountains near Veracruz on the east coast. Following the fault from west to east you will find some of the highest and most active volcanic mountains in the world including Ceboruco, Nevado de Colima, Pico de Tancitaro, Paricutín, Nevado de Toluca, Popocatépetl, Iztaccíhuatl, La Malinche, and Pico de Orizaba. Within the folds of the Cordillera are the cities of Tepic, Guadalajara, Morelia, Pátzcuaro, Uruapan, Toluca, Mexico City, Cuernavaca, and Puebla.

Almost all of the towns covered in this chapter are above 4,000 feet in altitude, many are over a mile high. This means that the weather, especially during winter evenings, can be brisk. Daytime temperatures are quite comfortable. During the summer the northern desert cities can be very hot while farther south and higher up temperatures are milder. Both the Guadalajara area and the Cuernavaca area are known for their year-round springtime climates.

ROAD SYSTEM

Most of the cities with camping facilities in the northern interior sit astride one of three major routes south to Mexico City.

The farthest west of the three routes is Mex. 45 and 49. This highway crosses the border at El Paso/Ciudad Juárez and runs south through Chihuahua, Torreón, Durango, Zacatecas, and Aquascalientes to the Guadalajara and Bajío (Guanajuato, San Miguel de Allende, Querétaro) regions. Much of this route is fast toll roads but often there are alternate free roads.

The next road corridor to the east is Mex. 57. This highway crosses the border at Eagle Pass, Texas/Piedras Negras but it is also easily accessed through Monterrey from Laredo/Nuevo Laredo and McAllen/Reynosa. Along this route are the cities of Monterrey, Saltillo, Matehuala, San Luis Potosí, San Miguel de Allende, and Querétaro. This is the quickest route from the border to Mexico City. Much of it is toll road, there are often alternate free routes.

The farthest east of the interior road corridors is the old Pan American Highway, Mex. 85. This was once an important route but is sinuous and slow, most people only drive selected sections of the route now. It crosses the border at Laredo/ Nuevo Laredo and runs through Monterrey, Ciudad Victoria, and Cd. Valles to Pachuca and then Mexico City.

There are many east/west highways connecting these three corridors. One of the most popular is Mex. 40 which runs from McAllen/Reynosa to Mazatlán through Monterrey, Saltillo, Torreón, and Durango. Between Durango and Mazatlán this highway descends the famously scenic "Devil's Backbone" which is steep in places, use your engine for braking and take it slowly. Trucks use this route so most RVs should be OK.

Once you reach the Bajío, an east-west breadbasket region with some of the most famous and attractive cities in Mexico you have a choice of several east-west routes. These routes actually run between Guadalajara, Mexico's second largest city, and Mexico City itself. The northernmost is a combination of Mex. 90, Mex. 45, and Mex. 57 and runs from Guadalajara, passes south of Guanajuato and San Miguel de Allende, to Querétaro and on to Mexico City. Much of this highway is toll road. The second is the new Guadalajara to Mexico City toll road, Mex. 15D which starts in Guadalajara, passes just north of Morelia, then through Toluca to Mexico City. The third is the old free Mex. 15. This slow but extremely scenic two-lane road runs from Guadalajara, through Morelia, across the mountains past Los Azufres and north of Valle de Bravo, to Toluca and then Mexico City.

You can see that all of these routes funnel in to Mexico City (you've no doubt heard the phrase "all roads lead to Mexico City"). This is great if Mexico City is your destination, but for many people the capital city is a huge roadblock. How do you go on to Puebla and the Yucatán or Cuernavaca and Acapulco. With the proper directions in hand this is no real problem, we've included a section which follows the Mexico City campground section below to show you several bypass routes.

From the interior there are of course many good highways to the coast. Here are a few of them. Starting in the northwest and traveling south along the Sierra Madre Occidental Mex. 2 is the traditional east - west route at the top of Mexico. Farther south there is now a scenic but slow and long paved road, Mex. 16, connecting Chihuahua with Hermosillo. Mex. 40, mentioned above, runs down the "Devil's Backbone" to Mazatlán from Durango. Mex. 15 is a major four-lane route (toll with alternate free roads) connecting Guadalajara with Tepic and then running north along the west coast all the way to the border. From Guadalajara you can also follow winding little Mex. 80 to the ocean at Barra de Navidad/San Patricio Melaque or the better toll route, Mex. 54D through Colima to Tecomán and Manzanillo. Farther south Mex. 37 runs from the Bajío through Uruapan to the coast at Playa Azul.

Eastward now, Mex. 134 runs from Toluca past Valle de Bravo to the coast near Ixtapa/Zihuatanejo. From Mexico City a major toll road, Mex. 95D passes through Cuernavaca and down to the coast at Acapulco. This is the first and most famous of Mexico's toll roads but there is also a free route. The free route is quite steep near Taxco but we've done it in a big motorhome towing a car so most rigs should have no problem if they take it easy and use their engines for braking. From near Cuernavaca 160 leads southeast, meets Mex. 190 from Puebla, and goes on south to Oaxaca. This is a long and lonely two-lane road, expect to spend two days en route unless you are in a small vehicle. A much quicker route to Oaxaca is from Puebla on a new toll road through Tehuacan, you can easily make the trip in one day on this road, it is possible to drive from Puebla to Oaxaca in about 5 hours. It also is supplemented by a free road, Mex. 131.

On the east side of the country the four-lane toll highway Mex. 150D descends to Veracruz from Mexico City and Puebla but there is also a free route, Mex. 140, that circles toward the north around Pico de Orizaba and through the interesting and little-visited city of Jalapa. Moving toward the north through the Sierra Madre Oriente we find a new toll highway from Mexico City to Tuxpan (brand new - probably open by the time you read this). There are several smaller routes through the Sierra Madre on this eastern side of Mexico. One popular one is Mex. 70 from San Luis Potosí through Ciudad Valles to Tampico. Finally, Mex. 85 from Monterrey to Ciudad Victoria actually passes through the Sierra Madre before turning back to climb toward Mexico City, the Monterrey to Ciudad Victoria section is not a bad road at all.

HIGHLIGHTS

The interior is chock full of interesting destinations. First, of course, have to be the cities. But there are also several regions with lots of interesting sights outside the cities. If you are a lover of hiking and the outdoors, don't despair, the interior has some of the best hiking areas in the country.

Mexico City (Ciudad de México) is the number one interior city. This huge metropolis, the area has somewhere in the neighborhood of 20,000,000 inhabitants, is not difficult for a camper to visit. The number two city is Guadalajara, it is even easier to visit than Mexico City and has almost as much to offer. The entire area around Guadalajara and Lake Chapala is extremely popular with norteamericanos,

GUANAJUATO STREET SCENE

many make it their home. San Miguel de Allende is another popular norteamericano hangout, it has two good RV parks. The Cuernavaca area is full of campgrounds used mostly by Mexico City residents, some are balneario (spa) campgrounds in the countryside outside Cuernavaca. Other attractive colonial cities include Guanajuato, Puebla, Tlaxcala, Morelia, Zacatecas, Querétaro, and San Luis Potosí. A smaller town loved by many tourists, it can't properly be called a city, is Pátzcuaro. This is a long list but it is difficult to leave out any of these destinations, they all have a lot to offer.

If you are more interested in the countryside your first destination should probably be the Copper Canyon. The best access point is Creel, just east of Chihuahua. Other areas of outdoors interest are Los Azufres and the monarch butterfly reserve and La Malinche volcano near Tlaxcala.

DISTANCE TABLE

Miles

Aguascalientes	600	263	754	367	265	153	113	273	220	313	360	197	323	233	388	181	308	103	165	285	225	382	301	316	273	343	80
979	Chihuahua	800	154	954	408	721	712	872	585	899	480	797	908	832	974	764	428	640	765	756	807	968	883	286	873	942	520
429	1306	Ciudad Valles	954	345	465	366	288	429	277	291	318	403	237	438	348	284	371	160	297	498	327	328	330	512	479	380	280
1231	252	1558	Creel	1108	563	875	867	1026	739	1053	634	951	1062	987	1129	918	582	794	919	911	961	1123	1037	440	1027	1097	674
600	1557	564	1809	Cuernavaca	618	389	278	192	431	55	621	239	108	275	109	186	562	314	224	521	167	124	94	664	315	144	432
433	667	760	919	1009	Durango	386	378	538	423	563	345	462	571	498	639	429	293	306	431	348	473	633	549	151	538	599	186
250	1177	597	1429	635	631	Guadalajara	181	239	323	334	481	164	363	200	410	220	429	206	234	132	264	404	295	437	167	310	201
184	1163	471	1415	454	617	296	Guanajuato	189	246	224	434	114	234	149	299	92	405	129	53	314	135	293	211	429	190	260	192
445	1424	700	1676	314	878	391	309	Los Azufres	436	138	628	75	192	111	213	195	601	318	233	372	238	207	99	589	151	87	352
360	955	453	1207	704	691	528	402	712	Matehuala	377	209	361	386	396	452	241	157	118	255	456	285	446	367	299	437	418	238
511	1468	475	1720	89	920	546	365	225	615	Ciudad de México	566	185	54	220	75	132	507	259	170	467	113	69	39	610	261	89	378
588	783	520	1035	1014	563	786	708	1026	342	925	Monterrey	553	551	589	642	434	52	317	454	614	477	636	553	194	629	603	280
322	1301	658	1553	391	755	268	186	123	589	302	903	Morelia	239	36	260	119	526	243	157	296	163	254	146	513	76	146	277
528	1482	387	1734	177	933	592	382	313	630	88	900	390	Pachuca	274	111	142	516	268	180	495	129	91	93	625	315	143	386
380	1359	716	1611	449	813	326	244	181	647	360	961	58	448	Pátzcuaro	296	155	562	279	193	332	198	290	181	549	40	181	312
634	1591	569	1843	178	1043	669	488	348	738	123	1048	425	182	483	Puebla	207	582	334	245	542	188	20	115	685	336	165	453
296	1247	463	1499	304	701	360	150	318	394	215	708	195	232	253	338	Querétaro	407	124	38	353	43	201	119	475	195	170	244
503	698	605	950	917	478	701	662	982	257	828	85	859	843	917	951	664	Saltillo	275	412	562	450	576	526	141	602	576	228
168	1045	261	1297	512	499	336	210	520	192	423	517	397	438	455	546	202	449	San Luis Potosí	137	338	167	328	250	356	319	300	120
270	1249	485	1501	366	703	382	86	380	416	277	741	257	294	315	400	62	673	224	S.M. de Allende	366	81	239	157	481	233	208	245
466	1235	813	1487	851	568	216	512	607	744	762	1002	484	808	542	885	576	917	552	598	Tepic	396	536	427	499	299	442	333
367	1318	534	1570	273	772	431	221	389	465	184	779	266	211	324	307	71	735	273	133	647	Tequisquiapan	182	152	518	239	202	287
624	1581	536	1833	202	1033	659	478	338	728	113	1038	415	149	473	33	328	941	536	390	875	297	Tlaxcala	108	679	330	159	447
491	1442	539	1694	153	896	482	345	161	600	64	903	238	152	296	187	195	859	408	257	698	248	177	Toluca	594	222	50	363
516	467	836	719	1085	247	714	700	961	488	996	316	838	1020	896	1119	775	231	582	786	815	846	1109	970	Torreón	589	644	236
446	1425	782	1677	515	879	272	310	247	713	426	1027	124	514	66	549	319	983	521	381	488	390	539	362	962	Uruapan	222	353
560	1539	621	1791	235	978	506	424	142	682	146	985	238	234	296	269	277	941	490	339	722	330	259	82	1052	362	Valle de Bravo	413
130	849	457	1101	706	303	328	314	575	388	617	458	452	630	510	740	398	373	196	400	544	469	730	593	386	576	675	Zacatecas

Kilometers

THE CAMPGROUNDS

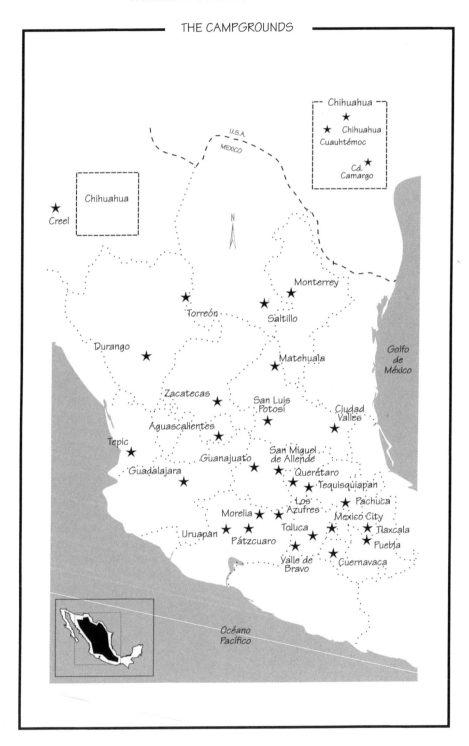

SELECTED CITIES AND THEIR CAMPGROUNDS

AGUASCALIENTES, AGUASCALIENTES (AH-GWAHS-KA-LEE-EHN-TAYS)
Population 450,000, Elevation 6,250 ft (1900 m)

The city of Aguascalientes, capital of a state of the same name, is known for its orderliness and well-being. The attractive central area of the city holds most of the sights interesting to visitors, it has colonial buildings interspersed with more modern structures, including many stores and shopping centers. The city is not known as a tourist destination, many of the visitors it does get come for the **Feria de San Marcos** in late April and early May. The surrounding region is known for producing the best **fighting bulls** in Mexico, also for its **vineyards**. Aguascalientes is named for its **hot springs**, the **Centro Deportivo Aguascalientes** described below is one of them.

Campground No. 1

HOTEL MEDRANO
   Address: Blvd. José Má. Chávez 904,
   Aguascalientes, Ags., Mexico
   Telephone: (49) 15-55-43
   Fax: (49) 16-80-76

      Price: Low

GPS Location: N 21° 52' 13.2", W 102° 17' 40.9"

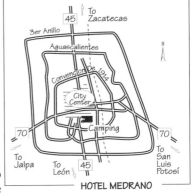

The Hotel Medrano is located just a mile or so south of central Aguascalientes. It is a place where the camping facilities aren't considered very important in the scheme of things, but with this convenient location it is difficult to complain and Aguascalientes offers few alternatives.

Camping slots are in two different locations at the Medrano. There are about four back-in parking spots on pavement at the rear of the newer part of the hotel near the swimming pool. There is electricity, sewer, and water here. Another few larger pull-through spots with very limited electricity, sewer, and water are spaced around a grassy central area in an older part of the hotel nearby. Larger rigs can maneuver into this area with care but should avoid the first area. There are no restrooms set aside for campers, a room is available with showers and toilets. The hotel has a restaurant and a pool that is not filled in the winter. You can walk to the central area of town in 15 minutes or catch a bus. Limited English is spoken at the front desk.

The easiest access to the hotel is from Mex. 45 entering town from the south. From other directions take one of the two outer ring roads around town until you meet Mex. 45 (José Má. Chávez). The hotel is on the east side of the road .8 miles (1.3 km) north of Aguascalientes Ave.

Campground No. 2

Centro Deportivo Ojocaliente
  Address: Km. 1 Carr. a San Luis Potosí,
  Aguascalientes, Ags., Mexico
  Telephone: (49) 70-06-98

       Price: Inexpensive

GPS Location: N 21° 52' 46.7", W 102° 15' 42.7"

CENTRO DEPORTIVO
OJOCALIENTE

The Centro is a balneario and sports center east of central Aguascalientes. They allow overnight dry camping. This can be a pleasant place to stay, especially if you like to swim.

There is a grassy area behind the squash courts for camping. Water is available but there are no hookups. The squash courts have restrooms with hot showers. The balneario also has swimming pools, saunas, steam baths, a restaurant, squash and tennis courts and sports fields.

This campground is most easily found if you enter town on Mex. 70 from San Luis Potosí to the east. From other directions follow the outer ring road (3er Anillo) until you reach Mex. 70. You will cross the second ring road at .9 miles (1.4 km) and see the balneario on the right in 1.4 miles (2.2 km). There is a low arch over the entrance road but RVs can use an alternate gate.

Chihuahua, Chihuahua (CHEE-WAH-WAH)
Population 520,000, Elevation 4,700 ft (1429 m)

Chihuahua is the trade center for a huge area of northern Mexico and the capital city of the state of the same name. For such a large city there is surprisingly little to interest the traveler. One attraction is the **Museo de la Revolucíon** which is probably the best Pancho Villa museum in Mexico. Chihuahua is also often used as a departure point for rides on the **Chihuahua-Pacific Railway** to Los Mochis along the Copper Canyon. Travelers with their own vehicles will probably find that Creel makes a better departure point for this trip since it has better places to leave your vehicle and allows you to cut off the least interesting portion of the trip. Chihuahua boasts a fine selection of large supermarkets so it makes a good place to stock up.

Campground No. 1

CENTRO DEPORTIVO
Address: Av. Division del Norte and Av.
Tecnologico, Chih., Mexico

Price: Inexpensive

GPS Location: N 28° 39' 20.4", W 106° 04' 53.8"

CHIHUAHUA
To Juárez
45
N
Tecnologico
Periférico
Airport
Camping
City Center
Pacheco
45
F. Mares
To Torreón
To Cuauhtémoc
16
CENTRO DEPORTIVO

Chihuahua is very short of campgrounds. The only one we can find is the parking lot of the stadium in the large Ciudad Deportivo park on Avenida Tecnologico. Camping vehicles are allowed to spend the night there, for a fee. There are no hookups but there are overhead lights. The restrooms in the stadium are available but there are no showers. Security personnel are on duty all night.

From Av. Tecnologico turn southwest on the road that runs by the southeast edge of the park, this is Av. Division del Norte. The parking lot entrance is about .1 miles (.2 km) from the corner of Av. Tecnologico and Av. Division del Norte.

Campground No. 2

MOTEL Y TRAILER PARK VILLA DEL CHARRO
Address: Carr. Panamericana 63 (Apdo. 103), C.P. 33700 Cd. Camargo, Chih., Mexico.

Price: Low

GPS Location: N 27 38' 58.4", W 105° 08' 42.9"

CHIHUAHUA
To Chihuahua
45
N
Ciudad Camargo
Camping
Km 64
Km 63
To Torreón
MOTEL Y TRAILER PARK VILLA DEL CHARRO

This campground is really a full 95 miles (155 km) south of Chihuahua near the town of Cd. Camargo, but it is the best place to overnight for travelers driving through the area along the north/south Mex. 45 highway. Access is easy and there are full hookups.

The campground has 32 pull-through slots with electricity, sewer, and water. Parking is on gravel and there are small trees to provide some shade. The dedicated restroom buildings were not in service when we visited but a motel room was available for toilet and hot showers. There are also 8 motel rooms and a children's play area.

The Villa del Charro sits on the east side of Mex. 45 near the Km. 64 marker about 1 mile (1.6 km) south of Ciudad Camargo.

Campground No. 3

LOEWEN'S R.V. PARK
   Address: Km. 14 Carr. a Col. A. Obregón,
   Cd. Cuauhtémoc, Chih., Mexico
   Telephone: (158) 1-09-79
        Price: Low

GPS Location: N 28° 31' 21.2", W 106° 54' 36.6"

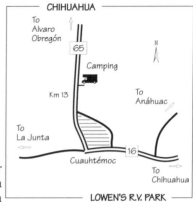

Full-service campgrounds are few and far between near Chihuahua. Loewen's is a popular stop for caravans bound for La Junta for loading onto rail cars for the Copper Canyon transit. If there is no caravan in the campground you're likely to be alone. Cuauhtémoc is a large agricultural center with a population of some 150,000 people sitting in the middle of a rich farming region famous for its apples. Mennonites farm much of the surrounding land.

There are 23 pull-through spaces in a large flat grassy field with electricity, sewer, and water hookups. Back-in sites along the perimeter also have some utilities. A nearby building has restrooms with hot showers, coin-operated laundry, and a meeting room. There are a few supplies for sale.

Mex. 16 runs west from Chihuahua 61 miles (98 km) to Ciudad Cuauhtémoc. Mex. 65 cuts off to the north from Mex. 16 both east and west of Ciudad Cuauhtémoc, they meet north of town and continue north. If you take the more direct western cut-off and drive north you will see Loewen's on the right after 8.4 miles (13.7 km).

CIUDAD VALLES, SAN LUIS POTOSÍ (SEE-OOH-DAWD VAH-YES)
Population 95,000, Elevation 300 ft (91 m)

Once an important overnight stop on Mex. 85 to Mexico City, Ciudad Valles receives fewer visitors now that there are alternatives to the slow and winding highway to the south. Today the city serves as a hub for exploring the surrounding **Huasteca region**, there is a **Huastec Regional Museum** of Anthropology and Archeology in Valles which makes a good introduction to the Indian culture and surrounding attractions. Travelers descending from the higher areas to the west and south may be surprised by the climate here, the area is known as part of the northernmost **tropical rain forest** in North America.

Campground No. 1

HOTEL VALLES
 Address: Boulevard México-Laredo 36
 Norte, Ciudad Valles, C.P. 79050 S.L.P.,
 Mexico
 Telephone: (138) 2-00-50

Price: Low

GPS Location: N 21° 59' 28.6", W 099° 00' 38.0"

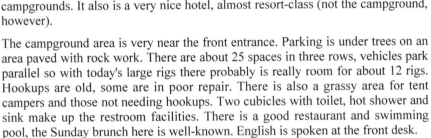

Hotel Valles is by far the most conveniently
located of the two Ciudad Valles
campgrounds. It also is a very nice hotel, almost resort-class (not the campground,
however).

The campground area is very near the front entrance. Parking is under trees on an
area paved with rock work. There are about 25 spaces in three rows, vehicles park
parallel so with today's large rigs there probably is really room for about 12 rigs.
Hookups are old, some are in poor repair. There is also a grassy area for tent
campers and those not needing hookups. Two cubicles with toilet, hot shower and
sink make up the restroom facilities. There is a good restaurant and swimming
pool, the Sunday brunch here is well-known. English is spoken at the front desk.

The campground is located on Blvd. Mexico-Laredo which is also Mex. 85 from
Cd. Victoria. From the intersection of Mex. 85 from Cd. Victoria and Mex. 70 from
San Luis Potosí to the north of town head south, the Hotel Valles will be on the left
in .4 miles (.6 km). From the south on Mex. 85 from Pachuca or Mex. 70 from
Tampico turn right in town at the corner of Blvd. Sur and Blvd. Mexico-Laredo
toward Cd. Victoria. The hotel is on the right in .8 miles (1.3 km) just after the
Chevrolet dealer.

Campground No. 2

EL BAÑITO RESTAURANT-BAR
 Address: Km. 370 Carr. 85 (Apdo. 66), Cd.
 Valles, S.L.P., Mexico

Price: Low

GPS Location: N 21° 54' 53.0", W 098° 57' 01.5"

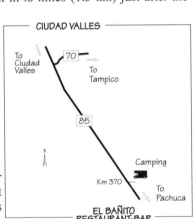

The El Bañito is a good place to let down your
hair and relax. There's nothing fancy about
this balneario, in fact we've had people tell us
that they drove by and it looked closed to
them, and this while we were actually staying there.

The campground has 24 back-in spaces with electricity, sewer, water and patios. There is quite a bit of shade and the orange blossoms next to the campground smell great in the spring. The grass isn't clipped as closely as it could be and the facilities are old and a little run down. There are several restrooms near the pools and lots of changing rooms, but, amazingly for a balneario, no showers to be seen. If you ask the manager he'll give you a key to the one cold shower, it is in an outbuilding and not available to the balneario customers, don't expect much of a shower. The two swimming pools smell of sulfur, one strongly and the other only slightly. This second pool is actually very pleasant, a morning swim before the first customers arrive about 10:30 A.M. is one of the best parts of this stop. The other is the little restaurant, we know people who come here just for the French fries.

El Bañito is south of Ciudad Valles on Mex. 85. It is on the east side of the highway very near the Km. 370 marker. This is 5.4 miles (8.7 km) south of the outer Ciudad Valles ring road.

Side Trips from Ciudad Valles

The **Tamasopo** waterfall area is located about 35 miles (57 km) west on Mex. 70 and then north about 5 miles (8 km). There are swimming areas and primitive tent camping sites.

The **Zona Arqueológica El Consuelo** is located in the other direction, 19 miles (31 km) east on Mex. 70 and then 3 miles (5 km) south from Tamuín village. These are excavations of a large Huastec ceremonial center.

Winding Mex. 85 south to Pachuca crosses remote mountains and is quite narrow in places. During certain times of the year fog is common, this isn't a route for folks in a hurry. The highway passes through the heart of the Huastec region, some interesting Huastec towns center around **Pedro Antonio de los Santos** some 31 miles (50 km) south of Ciudad Valles.

CREEL, CHIHUAHUA (CREH-EHL)
Population 3,500, Elevation 7,659 ft (2,328 m)

Creel is the gateway to the Copper Canyon area. The little town has long been short of decent RV accommodations but things may be improving, see The Lodge at Creel R.V. Park below. Activity centers on the railway station and nearby plaza, almost everything in town is within walking distance and there are restaurants and grocery stores. The real attraction is the nearby **Copper Canyon**. This is the approximate midpoint of the Chihuahua-Pacific Railway and an excellent place to catch the train to Los Mochis or El Fuerte. If you are interested in some of the best hiking and tent camping in North America this is the place. Many of the hotels in town run tour vans to various sights in the area and also offer hiking tours.

Campground No. 1

THE LODGE AT CREEL R.V. PARK (ACTUAL NAME
  NOT YET DETERMINED)
  Address: López Mateos No. 61, Creel, C.P.
  33200 Chih., Mexico
  Telephone: (145) 6-00-71
  Fax: (145) 6-00-82

  Price: Not yet determined.

GPS Location: N 27° 44' 45.5", W 107° 38' 11.9"

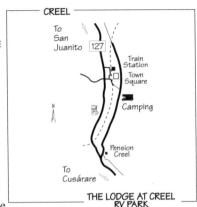

Creel has desperately needed a full-service
campground for some time and it appears that it will soon have one. The operators
of the Best Western Lodge at Creel and the Pension Creel tell us that they are going
to build a park to be in operation by October 1997. These folks have done a great
job with their other two operations so we'll take them at their word. The following
is a description of the proposed campground.

There will be thirty pull-through spaces with electricity, sewer, and water. These are
large sites, 65 by 30 feet, on gravel. There will be a restroom building with hot
showers and a clubhouse. Access for big rigs will be no problem. Attempts are also
underway to get the railroad to allow loading from a siding right in the campground,
this would make the Copper Canyon trip a piece of cake! For folks wanting to ride
the train in a normal fashion the campground is within easy walking distance of the
central square and the train station. You will be able to leave your rig here and take
the two-day rail trip with no fear for your rig's safety since the campground will
have 24 hour security. There will also be van tours available to destinations
throughout the Copper Canyon area.

As you approach Creel from the north pass through town on the paved road until
you reach the southern entrance road at the far end of town. Turn left onto this
cobblestone street, you will see the campground entrance on your right in .5 miles
(.8 km).

Campground No. 2

VALLE DE LOS HONGOS (ARARECO LAKE
CAMPGROUND)

Price: Inexpensive

GPS Location: N 27° 42' 04.5", W 107° 35' 42.4"

There is a large dry-camping area with room
for many rigs and tents near Lago de Arareco
about 3.2 miles (5.2 km) west of Creel. The
campground has pine trees and rolling hills
near the lake shore. There are pit toilets and
also some showers, but the showers were closed when we visited during March.
There are boat rentals on the lake and hiking throughout the area. The camping fee
is collected at a gate house but there is no security, Tarahumaras often wander
through selling their wares.

Side Trips from Creel

Access into the **Copper Canyon** for hiking and camping is not really difficult.
Don't attempt a serious hike, however, without proper maps and supplies. You
should use a guide or at the very least obtain a good guide book. This can be
complicated camping country because you must contend with both the country and
its inhabitants, the Tarahumara Indians. The canyons are their home and proper
etiquette is essential. Many people use the train as an access route. There are trails
or roads into the canyon from several stops including **Divisadero** where there is a
hiking trail down to the river and Bahuichivo where you can catch a bus down to
the town of **Urique** in the canyon on the river. Another good way to get into the
canyon country is the bus from Creel to Batopilas. Remote **Batopilas** has some
interesting hiking routes that are not nearly as difficult as an on-foot descent into
(and ascent out of) one of the canyons. It is also possible to drive to Divisadero in
almost any vehicle (the entire route is being paved) and high-clearance smaller
vehicles can drive farther along the rail line or make the long and dusty drive on a
different road all the way to Batopilas. Creel itself has some good hiking routes
including ones to the Cristo Rey statue overlooking town and to the San Ignacio de
Arareco mission village.

A good side trip to make in your vehicle is **Basaseachic Falls National Park.** The
falls themselves have a drop of almost 1,000 feet and there are marked hiking trails.
There are two different tent-camping areas with pit toilets in the park, they are near
the entrances, one off Mex. 16 and the other off Chih. 330. To reach the park from
Creel backtrack 19 miles (30 km) on Chih. 127 to San Juanito, then follow Chih.
330 north for about 59 miles (95 km) to the park entrance. This road also goes on
to meet Mex. 16 a few miles past the park entrance so you can continue either east
to Chihuahua or west to Hermosillo.

CUERNAVACA, MORELOS (KWER-NAH-VAH-KAH)
Population 450,000, Elevation 5,100 ft (1,550 m)

The Cuernavaca area is the weekend playground for people from Mexico City. The weather is usually warmer and far more pleasant than that of the capital since the altitude is far lower. We've certainly always had good weather when we've visited Cuernavaca. By Cuernavaca we mean the entire region around the city because the whole area is full of interesting sights and destinations, not to mention many campgrounds.

Like many Mexican cities Cuernavaca's interesting sights tend to be clustered near the central square, in this case a double one called the **Plaza de Armas** and the **Jardín Juárez**. Next to the squares on the southeast side is a large **home built for Cortés**, he lived in Cuernavaca for several years. The building is now a museum with colonial and Indian artifacts from the area. Also near the square are the **Palacio Municipal** and the **Catedral de la Asunción**. A few blocks to the west is the **Jardín Borda**, a large park with lakes and gardens. The city is well supplied with excellent restaurants.

In the surrounding area you will find many other attractions. There are several balnearios (bathing resorts) including three with campgrounds which are listed below. The ex-hacienda at **Temixco** is also worth a visit. The mountain-side town of **Tepoztlán** makes a good day-trip. It has an old Dominican convent, an archeological museum, and the **Tepozteco Pyramid** perched on the mountain above Tepoztlán and offering great views to those willing to hike the 2 miles (3 km) up from town. The **Xochicalco** archeological site is probably the most impressive in the area. It is located about 25 miles (41 km) from Cuernavaca to the south and is best known for it's **Pyramid of the Plumed Serpent**.

Campground No. 1

TRAILER PARK CUERNAVACA DIAMONTE
   Address: Mesalina S/N Trailer Park, Col.
   Delicias, Cuernavaca, Mor., Mexico
   Telephone: (73) 16-07-61

Price: Moderate

GPS Location: N 18° 56' 02.5", W 099° 12' 05.4"

This trailer park is the most popular in the Cuernavaca region for caravans and RVers passing through. Its popularity stems from its location near the toll highway and inside the city. Cuernavaca is a popular vacation and weekend retreat for people from Mexico City, the Diamonte is really designed to service those people. Up to now you probably have believed that Mexican people really don't own RVs, but a few do. This park has a big collection. Mexico City residents rent spots here on an annual

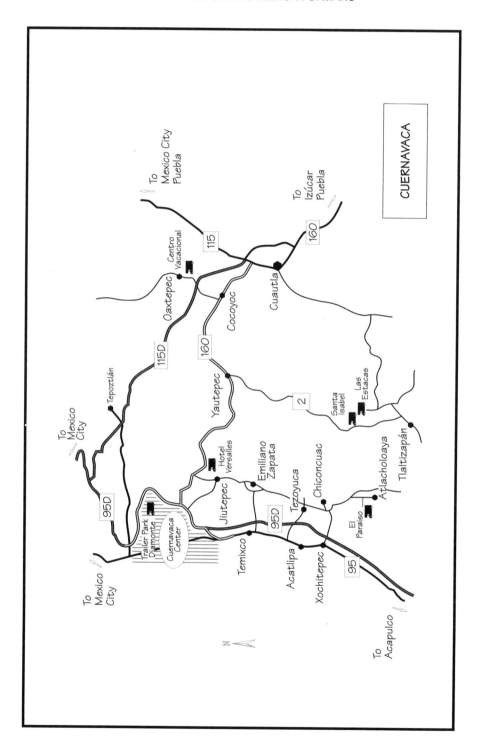

basis and come up for the weekend. The nicer spaces in the upper park are generally occupied by these permanently parked rigs. There is a separate area for those of us who are just passing through.

The temporary area is located below the main park and just above Mex. 95. Freeway noise is noticeable but not a major problem. It is a gravel parking area and could get quite crowded if all the spots were filled. There are 24 back-in spaces with electricity, water, and a dump station nearby. There are adequate restrooms with hot showers dedicated to the temporary area and others in the park above.

The key to enjoying this park is knowing that it is a beehive of activity on weekends but almost deserted during the week. The facilities are quite nice and include three swimming pools, a tennis court, and a billiard room. You'll have a great time during the quiet of the week but things are not nearly so nice on weekends when the older kids use the temporary area as a proving ground for their four-wheelers and motorcycles. There are sometimes spaces available in the upper area of the park, see if you can talk the management into putting you there. Most of these slots are small but they do have full hookups, grass, patios, and shade.

The campground is outside walking distance of central Cuernavaca. Taxis are the most convenient way to get around this crowded town. You can generally flag one down if you walk the short distance up to Diana Street.

To reach the campground take the Diana Street off ramp from Mex. 95D. Diana is just north of the Km. 89 marker and is easy to find because it has a huge Kmart right at the exit. Big signs to the north and south along Mex. 95D warn you that it is coming. Rumor has it that Kmart has sold out to Comercial Mexicana in Mexico so this may soon be a Comercial Mex. Take the Diana exit and head up the hill on Diana (left and under the toll road if you were traveling north). At .6 miles (1 km), just as you are cresting the hill, you want to take a left on Mesalina. It is marked with a trailer park sign on the left side of Diana but facing you as you come up the hill, watch carefully. Follow the entrance road as it zigzags right, then left, then right again and then left to the gate. You may have some problems raising the gate guard but eventually he'll let you in and perhaps collect some money. We've always had trouble getting someone to take ours at this park, perhaps the new office near the gate that was under construction at our last visit will help matters.

Campground No. 2

EL PARAISO DE LOS ACAMPADORES TRAILER PARK
   Address: Atlacholoaya, Mor., Mexico
   Telephone: (739) 1-34-54
   Fax: (739) 1-34-56

   Price: Low for small units,
      Moderate for large ones

GPS Location: N 18° 46' 04.1", W 099° 13' 12.0"

EL PARAISO DE LOS
ACAMPADORES TRAILER PARK

This large, well-run campground in a country setting caters primarily to Mexico City weekenders. Unlike the Diamonte there are not a lot of permanent rigs here. It would no doubt be more popular with RVers if it were easier to find. If you are a Taxco fan this is the closest campground to that city. It is also a fine campground for larger rigs, but you'll want to have a smaller vehicle to do your sightseeing, public transportation is not very accessible from here.

The El Paraiso has 150 spaces, all have electricity and water, 65 also have sewer. The spaces are grass and dirt under shade trees. There are big tiled restrooms with hot water showers. There is also a swimming pool, playground equipment and a small store. Reservations are unnecessary except during holidays, use the phone if you want to make them because the mail is slow and erratic. English is spoken.

While there are many ways to drive to this campground there is only one worth considering. The other routes are confusing, crowded, and rough. On Mex. 95D headed south you will see an exit for Xochitepec and Tezoyuca south of Km. 107 (actually right at Km. 108). There is currently no exit if you are heading north, you have to go to Km. 100 and make a U-turn at the Fracc. Las Brisas exit. Take the Xochitepec exit and after paying the toll you will come to a T. Turn right (east), pass under the toll road, and proceed for 1.1 miles (1.9 km) to another intersection. Turn right here and drive 1.2 miles (2 km) and turn right, this turn should be marked Atlacholoaya but the last time we visited the sign was missing. Proceed another .3 miles (.6 km) and turn right onto a very small but passable gravel access road, there is a trailer park sign at this road. The El Paraiso is on the left in .4 miles (.7 km).

Campground No. 3

LAS ESTACAS
   Address: Km. 6 Carretera Tlaltizapán-
   Cuautla, Tlaltizapán, Mor., Mexico
   Telephone: (734) 5-00-77, (734) 2-14-44
   Fax: (734) 5-01-59

Price: Expensive,
Moderate if you stay more than two days

GPS Location: N 18° 43' 42.5", W 099° 06' 47.6"

Las Estacas is a balneario in a class by itself. It has a half-mile crystal-clear jungle river running through the grounds. Another great feature is the beautiful RV park.

The RV park has 13 back-in spaces with electricity, sewer, and water hookups. The pads are gravel arranged off a paved driveway, well-clipped grass separates them, tall palms and other trees provide shade, and flowers complete the picture. The slots are a little short for big rigs but by now you probably are accustomed to making your rig fit into a short space, since the park is usually practically empty a long rig should cause no problems. There is also an extremely large area set aside for tent camping. Restrooms are basic but have hot water showers and are well maintained.

Las Estacas has many swimming pools, an open-air restaurant/bar, a mini-mart, miniature golf, and horse rentals. Best of all is the river. The water is cool but not cold, you can easily drift through the grounds for a half-hour using a snorkel to watch the many fish as you float along. A few deeper pools provide areas for diving and you can wave at the folks at the bar as you drift by. When you reach the edge of the property you can climb out and go back for more.

To reach Las Estacas turn south near Km. 26 of the Cuernavaca-Cuautla road (Mex. 160). Road signs point to Jojutla and Zacatepec. Note the large sign advertising Las Estacas here, you will see several of these as you approach the park. Zero your odometer here. Follow the road south, it goes through several small built-up areas until at 6.7 miles (10.9 km) there is a Y, go left following the sign for Balneario Estacas. The new section of road is one of the best that you've seen in Mexico. At 11.3 miles (18.5 km) you pass the Balneario Santa Isabel on the left. There is also an entrance to Las Estacas here, but it is for pedestrians, not RVs. At 11.9 miles (19.4 km) the road T's, go left. Watch closely now, at 14.1 miles (23.0 km) there is a concrete road on the left that goes down a short hill and meets another small road, where you turn left. This is a short cut that allows you to bypass the small town ahead where you would otherwise have to make a sharp difficult turn. If you miss the concrete road at 14.1 miles (23.0 km) just continue on for .5 mile (.8 km), make the difficult turn just past the Pemex station, and come back to this point. You will soon pass over a single lane bridge and then go straight at a Y at 14.8 miles (24.2 km). Finally at 16.0 miles (26.1 km) turn left, Las Estacas will be on the left at 17.0 miles (27.8 km).

Campground No. 4

BALNEARIO SANTA ISABEL
Address: Km. 20 Carr Yautepec-Jojutla,
Libramiento de Ticuman, Tlaltizapán,
Mor., Mexico

Price: Inexpensive

GPS Location: N 18° 43' 59.1", W 099° 06' 57.9"

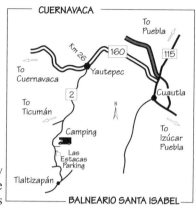

BALNEARIO SANTA ISABEL

If Las Estacas is a little rich for your blood try the balneario next door, the Santa Isabel. The amenities are much more basic but the price is right.

The Balneario Santa Isabel has lots of room for camping on two large grassy fields, some have palapas. There are no hookups other than two electrical outlets on one light pole in the middle of one of the fields. Restrooms are very basic with flush toilets and cold showers. Swimming is in two nice dammed pools, this is the same river used by Las Estacas. There is also a palapa bar on the property.

To reach the Santa Isabel turn south near Km. 26 of the Cuernavaca-Cuautla road (Mex. 160). Road signs point to Jojutla and Zacatepec. Note the large sign advertising Las Estacas here, you will see several of these as you approach the parks. Zero your odometer here. Follow the road south, it goes through several small built-up areas until at 6.7 miles (10.9 km) there is a Y, go left following the sign for Balneario Estacas. At odometer 11.3 miles (18.5 km) you will see the Balneario Santa Isabel on the left just before the Las Estacas parking and pedestrian entrance.

Campground No. 5

HOTEL VERSALLES
Address: Carretera Federal a Cuautla Km.
15.5, Cuernavaca, Morelos, Mexico
Telephone: (732) 3-00-99

Price: Low

GPS Location: N 18° 53' 29.9", W 099° 07' 43.2"

HOTEL VERSALLES

The Hotel Versalles has just four RV slots in a fenced yard next to the small motel and restaurant. They are back-in slots, electricity and water are available and each has a sewer drain. There are no dedicated restrooms but a room is available for showers and the restaurant has restrooms. There is also a decent swimming pool. There is frequent bus service along the road in front of the hotel and even a small bus station just a short distance to the east so bus transportation into Cuernavaca should be easy.

Watch for the Hotel Versalles on the south side of the Cuernavaca-Cuautla free road (Mex. 160) near the Km. 15.5 marker.

Campground No. 6

IMSS CENTRO VACACIONAL OAXTEPEC
  Address: Oaxtepec, Mor., Mexico
  Telephone: (735) 6-01-01

Price: Moderate

GPS Location: N 18° 54' 03.3", W 098° 58' 47.6"

The IMSS (Mexican social security) runs this huge balneario but anyone is welcome. There are over twenty swimming pools here, you'll want to visit just to see the place.

The RV camping area is a small grassy field with room for about 30 rigs to hook up to electricity and water, there is no sewer hookup or dump station. The sites slope, leveling may be difficult. A tent camping area next door has grassy fields with room for hundreds of tents. There are restrooms available to the campgrounds with toilets (and cold showers for the tenters), hot showers are available in the large dressing room buildings near the pools. In addition to the swimming pools there are several restaurants, a small supermarket, hotels and rental cabañas (each with a small wading pool), a geodesic dome covering a garden, play areas, rental boats on a small lake, and even an overhead tram. Virtually no English is spoken here.

The campground is located right next to Mex. 115D near Cuautla. Take the exit marked Oaxtepec near the Km. 27 marker and then turn north, you'll see the entrance almost immediately. Alternately, from Mex. 160, the Cuernavaca to Cuautla highway, turn north at the sign to Oaxtepec near Km. 36, the balneario is 1.2 miles (1.9 km) ahead after you pass under Mex. 115D.

Other Camping Possibilities

If you find that you like camping at balnearios you have some other choices. Here are a couple that advertise camping areas but that we have not had the time to check out: Balneario Los Limones in the center of Cuautla and Centro Turístico Ejidal El Bosque in Oaxtepec.

The Benedictine Monastery trailer park near Cuernavaca is apparently now closed to the public. When we visited in March of 1997 we were turned away at the gate. It's a shame to see this interesting place go, but the Cuernavaca area is hardly short of campgrounds.

Side Trips from Cuernavaca

Mexico's colonial silver town, **Taxco**, doesn't currently have a campground but it is an easy day trip from the Cuernavaca region, the distance is about 60 miles (96 km).

There's easy toll road access and also a decent free road. Parking in Taxco is difficult for big rigs so if you don't have a tow car consider taking a bus from Cuernavaca.

Once you get familiar with the long-distance bus stations you might consider another excellent bus destination from Cuernavaca, **Mexico City**. The ride takes about an hour and a half on a luxury bus and you can leave your vehicle safe in a Cuernavaca campground.

Durango, Durango (DOO-RAIN-GOE)
Population 600,000, Elevation 6,200 ft (1,885 m)

Durango is often visited by travelers crossing Mexico from Texas to the Mazatlán area. The city is known as the filming location for many westerns, there are several **movie set locations** just to the north of town that you can visit. Durango has been declared a national monument because of the colonial architecture, especially a number of churches in the central area. Durango's plaza and surrounding area are good places to explore on foot.

Campground

Campo Mexico Motel
   Address: Av. 20 de Noviembre y Heroico
   Colegio Militar. (Apdo. 96), Durango,
   Dgo, Mexico
   Telephone: (18) 18-77-44
   Fax: (18) 18-30-15

   Price: Low

GPS Location: N 24° 01' 52.7", W 104° 38' 34.6"

There is no doubt that the RV parking area is an afterthought in this motel. The hookups are old and badly in need of maintenance, several are unusable unless you are in a European rig because they are 220 volt. Despite this, the Campo Mexico is a reliable stopping point in a region with few campgrounds.

There are 14 parking spaces with hookups, they have varying combinations of electricity, sewer, and water. Six are marked as having 110 volt electricity, we used one with no problems. The remaining 8 are marked 220 volt and have normal 15-amp. plugs, we didn't check them. They are located in a very large fenced field behind the motel, there is a lot of room for rigs not needing hookups or for tent campers. The motel has no restroom for the camping area, they will let you use a room for hot showers and toilets. There is a restaurant in the motel and it has a swimming pool and playground area. A Gigante supermarket is about five blocks away.

To find the motel start at the glorieta where Mex. 45 from Zacatecas and Mex. 40

from Torreón meet. There is a statue of Pancho Villa in the center. Head southwest on Colegio Militar for .4 miles (.6 km), you'll see the large fenced field behind the motel with the camping area on the right but must pass it and then take a right around the block to reach the motel entrance. There is plenty of room for big rigs.

GUADALAJARA, JALISCO (GWAH-DAH-LAH-HAH-RAH)
Population 4,000,000, Elevation 5,100 ft (1,550 m)

Guadalajara is the second largest city in Mexico, much easier to visit than Mexico City and very rewarding. This and the climate with year-round decent weather have made Guadalajara a favorite retirement city for Americans and Canadians. The large norteamericano population also means that it is easy to find information, activities, and friends.

There are many attractions in Guadalajara, here are just a few. The center of town is the **cathedral**. It is surrounded by **four elegant squares** and many walking streets, this is probably the most attractive central area in all of Mexico. Nearby is the **Mercado Libertad**, a huge municipal market that is without a doubt also the cleanest and most attractive in the country. It takes massive self-control to walk through the food section without sitting down to at least a small snack. Probably the most important museum in Guadalajara is the **Regional Museum of Guadalajara** with archeological, crafts, and painting exhibits. It is located in the block northeast of the cathedral. You should also visit the **Cabañas Cultural Institute** at the east end of the Plaza Tapatía to see some of local artist José Clemente Orozco's frescos.

In the suburbs of Guadalajara you will want to visit famous **Tlaquepaque**. The town, a favorite with home decorators, is a source of pottery, glassware, silver, copper ware, furniture, leather goods and even sculpture. **Tonalá**, a little farther from the center of Guadalajara, is the source of some of the things you'll see in Tlaquepaque, especially pottery. Tonalá has open-air markets on Thursday and Sunday where you may find some excellent pottery bargains.

The month of October is an excellent time to visit the city. The city holds it's **Fiestas de Octubre** with continuing cultural events. During the same month the suburb of Zapopan celebrates the end of the 4-month pilgrimage of the Virgin of Zapopan with a huge bash on October 12.

Driving in Guadalajara can be confusing. The city is cris-crossed by wide boulevards, but they seem to run at odd angles. You must keep a close eye on the map. Many of the main boulevards have lateral streets running along both sides. You are not allowed to turn from the center lanes, either left or right. This is confusing at first, watch to see what other drivers are doing.

The area around Guadalajara is full of interesting destinations. Two are especially popular with RVers since there are convenient campgrounds nearby. Lake Chapala is south of Guadalajara about 24 miles (38 km). You can reach it by driving south on Mex. 23 or Mex. 54 past the San Jose del Tajo campground. The PAL campground is in Ajijic near the north shore of the lake. About 15 miles (24 km)

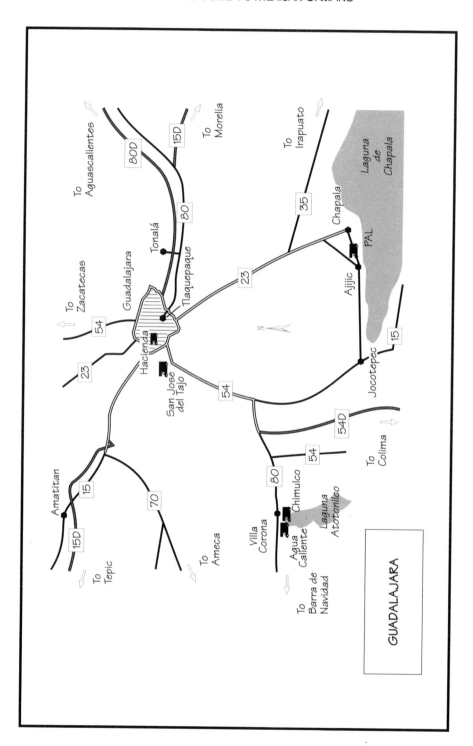

east of the lake there are two campgrounds in the hot-water-spring town of **Villa Corona**. All of these campgrounds are listed below in this section.

Campground No. 1

HACIENDA TRAILER PARK
    Address: Circunvalación Pte. 66, Ciudad
    Granja (Apdo. 5-494), Guadalajara, C.P.
    45000 Jal., Mexico
    Telephone: (3) 6-27-17-24, (3) 6-27-18-43
    Fax: (3) 6-27-28-32

Price: Low

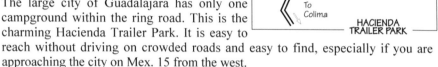

The large city of Guadalajara has only one campground within the ring road. This is the charming Hacienda Trailer Park. It is easy to reach without driving on crowded roads and easy to find, especially if you are approaching the city on Mex. 15 from the west.

The Hacienda has 98 spaces with patios arranged along cobblestone paths under spreading shade trees. All spaces have electricity, water, and sewer. These are all back-in spaces. The central building houses the bathrooms with hot showers, a lounge, billiard room, and laundry room. The adjoining swimming pool is especially well-maintained and surrounded by comfortable lounge chairs. English is spoken at the check-in desk and the people are particularly helpful.

Access to downtown Guadalajara by bus is convenient and inexpensive. The number 45 bus stops at the circle about 100 yards away and will drop you in central Guadalajara in 45 minutes. Coming back make sure to take the 45 with the Granja sign. Shopping is equally easy. There are huge Wal-Mart and Price Club stores a 25-minute walk from the campground, you can also use the number 45 bus to reach them.

To find the campground start at the point where the ring road (Anillo Periférico) and Mex. 15 from Tepic meet (actually Mex. 15 passes over the ring road). Zero your odometer at this point and head southeast into town on Av. Vallarta which is the continuation of Mex. 15. Av. Vallarta is a boulevard with lateral roads along the side, you should get on the lateral as soon as possible. In 1 mile (1.6 km) you will see a Nissan Dealer on the right. Turn right just after the dealer, proceed .4 mile (.6 km) to a traffic circle, as you go to the right around it take the second exit (there is a sign here for the campground) and you will find the campground on the right in about .2 mile (.3 km).

Campground No. 2

SAN JOSE DEL TAJO TRAILER PARK
Address: Km. 15 Carr Guadalajara-Colima
(Apdo. 31-242), Guadalajara, Jal., Mexico
Telephone: (3) 6-86-17-38

Price: Moderate.

Located just a few miles outside the Guadalajara periférico in a pleasant country setting, San Jose del Tajo Trailer Park is the campground of choice for many visitors to the area.

The campground has about 175 spaces, all back-in with patio and paved parking pads. All sites have electricity, water, and sewer. There is also quite a bit of shade. The campground has hot water showers in the clean rest-rooms, a swimming pool, satellite television, a large meeting room/lounge, and a popular nearby restaurant. There is a large Gigante supermarket just down the road. English is spoken at the desk. Tent camping is only available from May to September.

To find the campground take the exit for Mex. 15 (Morelia, Colima) from the Guadalajara periférico. This is a four-lane highway. At 2 miles (3.2 km) you will see a Gigante supermarket on the right, slow down at 2.5 miles (4 km) and watch for the entrance road on the right. You should see it on the right at 2.7 miles (4.4 km), turn in and follow the cobblestone road for .6 miles (1 km) to the campground.

Campground No. 3

PARQUE ACUATICO CHIMULCO
Address: Apdo. 25, Villa Corona, C.P.
45730 Jal, Mexico
Telephone: (377) 8-02-09, (377) 8-00-14
Fax: (377) 8-01-61

Price: Low

If you've been missing your evening bath this is the place for you. Chimulco has many hot pools, they empty them each night and refill them each morning with hot water from natural springs. The use of the pools is included in the price, they even fill a special pool for the use of the campers each evening after the day-trippers have gone home.

This combination water park and trailer park has about forty-nine camping sites. About half are pull-through and half back-in. All have patios, electricity, water, and sewer. Pines provide shade. The bathrooms are clean and have hot water showers, in fact, the water from all of the faucets at the camp sites is hot. There is a meeting room reserved just for the campground. Limited English is spoken at the office but resident campers will fill you in on anything you need to know about the park or surrounding region. Shopping in Villa Corona is limited but residents find they can get by with a weekly visit to the Tuesday village market and daily visits to the nearby *tortillería* (tortilla shop).

To reach Villa Corona and Chimulco head south from the Guadalajara periférico on Mex. 15. Zero your odometer when you do this. At 2.7 miles (4.4 km) you will pass the entrance to the San Jose del Tajo Trailer Park. Continue along this four-lane highway until you come to a Y at 15.9 mile (26.0 km), take the left fork

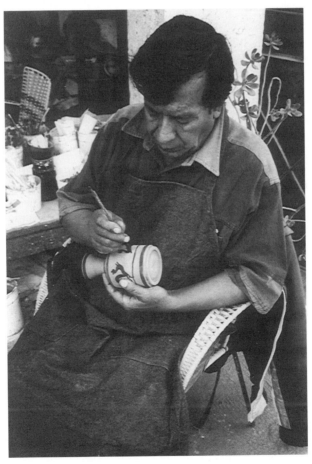

TONALÁ CRAFTSMAN AT WORK

following signs for Barra de Navidad (Mex. 80). At 16.2 miles (26.5 km) at another Y go right continuing to follow the signs for Barra de Navidad (Mex. 80). Finally, at a third Y at 18.4 miles (30.0 km) go right following Mex. 80 and Villa Corona signs. There is a railroad crossing at 21.3 miles (34.8 km), you pass the road right to Buenavista at 21.8 miles (35.6 km) and enter Villa Corona (population 12,000) at 24.3 miles (39.7 km). Watch carefully for Chimulco signs, you turn left at 24.5 miles (40 km) onto a cobblestone road, turn right at the T, and then reach the entrance to the park at 25.2 miles (41.1 km). Tell the person at the entrance booth that you want the trailer park, they'll give you an instruction slip in English that says to drive in and check in at the nearby office. Then you can pull into the trailer park.

Campground No. 4

AGUA CALIENTE PARQUE ACUATICO
   Address: Km. 56 Carr. Guadalajara-Barra
   de Navidad, Villa Corona, Jal., Mexico
   Telephone: (377) 8-00-22

   Price: Low

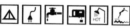

GUADALAJARA

Chimulco Exit

1 Mile
1.6 Km

80

To Cocula   Camping   Villa Corona   To Bellavista

Laguna Atotonilco

AGUA CALIENTE PARQUE ACUATICO

Just a few miles down the road from Chimulco is another water park, Agua Caliente. Agua Caliente also offers camping.

There are 67 sites, all with patios and all with electricity, water and sewer. Some are pretty small. The camping area is in a fairly thick pine grove, lots of shade. The restrooms have hot showers. Use of the huge water park is included in the camping fee. Long term rates here are extremely low, which may explain the large number of permanently located Mexican rigs in this campground, about a third of the spaces are filled with rigs only used on weekends. No English is spoken here.

To find this campground follow the directions given for the Chimulco Trailer Park. When you reach Villa Corona remain on Mex. 80, drive directly through town, and 1.0 mile (1.6 km) west of the turn-off for Chimulco you will see Agua Caliente on the left. Do not enter at the main entrance, the campground entrance is on the far end of the big parking lot.

Campground 5

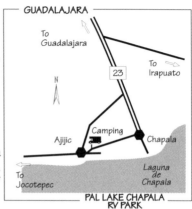

PAL LAKE CHAPALA RV PARK
   Address: Apdo. 84, Chapala, C.P. 45900 Jal,
     Mexico
   Telephone: (376) 6-04-40

Price: Moderate

The north shore of Lake Chapala has been a resort area since the mid-nineteenth century. The only trailer park in the area is the PAL RV Park, and it's a good one.

The park has 106 back-in spaces. All have patios and there's plenty of space for big rigs. All sites have 30-amp. electric, water, and sewer. Air conditioners are OK in this park, but you probably won't need them with Chapala's near-perfect weather. This campground is famous for it's spic-and-span tiled bathrooms, they have hot showers. There is a beautiful clean swimming pool, a laundry, and a club house with terrace. You will be impressed by the beautiful brick "lean-to's" that have been built to surround several permanently located rigs in this park. The people at the front desk speak English well, they'll answer all your questions.

LAKE CHAPALA

There is a small supermarket within easy walking distance and both Chapala and Ajijic are not far away.

To most easily find the campground follow Mex. 23 south from the Guadalajara *periférico* (ring road). Just before reaching Chapala watch for the Chapala bypass as the road descends to the lake, it is marked as going to Ajijic and Jocotepec. Follow the bypass for 3.6 miles (5.8 km), it terminates at the Chapala-Ajijic road. Turn left, the campground is on your left in .2 miles (.3 km).

GUANAJUATO, GUANAJUATO (GWAH-NAH-HWAH-TOH)
Population 77,500, Elevation 6,700 ft (2037 m)

Of all the colonial cities in Mexico, Guanajuato is probably the most interesting and fun to visit. Its small size and cramped bottom-of-a-ravine location combine to make it a walker's paradise. The town is a maze of crooked little streets, alleys, and even tunnels. Guanajuato was a colonial silver mining town, one of the more important cities of that era and on a par in importance with cities like Querétaro, San Miguel de Allende, Zacatecas, and San Luis Potosí. Most of these cities have grown and lost their colonial atmosphere. Guanajuato hasn't had room to grow so it has retained a great deal of charm. Guanajuato has been declared a **national monument** and is a popular destination for Mexican and international tourists so there are many restaurants, interesting shops, and things to see.

Guanajuato doesn't have much in the way of large flat areas for a central plaza so instead it has several smaller ones, **El Jardín de La Unión** and **Plaza de la Paz** are the largest. Sights of interest in town include the historically important **Alhóndiga de Graniditas**, the **statue of Pípila** overlooking town, the **Mercado Hidalgo**, and any number of churches, museums, and shops. Slightly farther from town are the **La Valenciana** mine and church and the ghoulish **Museo de las Momias** (Mummy Museum). Both of these destinations can be reached by bus from central Guanajuato.

The small streets that are so attractive to walkers are a nightmare for drivers. Do not take a large RV anywhere near central Guanajuato. Unfortunately, travelers headed for Dolores Hidalgo or to the Morrill Trailer Park must find their way around town. The periférico on the east side of town (allowing you to circle counter-clockwise) is accessible from the south, which is the direction of approach for most visitors, but it is definitely the long, scenic route. The periférico on the west is more direct but is only accessible by driving through a section of town. This route is OK for rigs up to small RV size, follow signs for Dolores Hidalgo. Young men standing along the road just outside town will undoubtedly try to flag you down and offer to guide you to local hotels, you should probably ignore them since they are unlikely to know the location of a campground.

Travelers with only RVs for transportation should use a bus to get into the central area of town or, if their rig is small enough, stay at the Morrill RV Park which is close enough to the central area to make walking practical.

Campground No. 1

MORRILL TRAILER PARK
    Address: Carretera Escenica y Subida de
    Mellado, Guanajuato, Gto., Mexico
    Telephone: (473) 2-19-09

Price: Low

GPS Location: N 21° 01' 31.1", W 101° 15' 07.5"

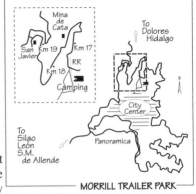

Perhaps you've heard rumors of this place but never been able to track it down. Here are the directions you need to find the only Guanajuato campground within walking distance of town. We think this campground is only suitable for rigs up to 24 feet, if yours is larger please check it out on foot before committing yourself.

There are about 8 parking spaces with electricity, sewer, and water hookups arranged on a terrace on the hillside above Guanajuato. There is a second terrace below for tents. The restrooms are old but tiled and clean and have hot water showers. There is a gate and the steep terraces provide pretty good security, the managers live on the property. You can walk downtown in 15 minutes via a tunnel at the bottom of the hill, ask someone in the trailer park for detailed directions. Guanajuato has a Comercial Mexicana store in the central area so supplies are easy to find. You may want to take a taxi back up to the campground, however, since the climb is challenging.

The campground is located just off (below) the Panoramica near the Mina de Cata and the Km. 17 marker. The easiest access is from the highway to Dolores Hidalgo. If you are approaching on the other highway from San Miguel de Allende and Silao you can either follow the Panoramica counterclockwise for almost 17 kilometers or drive through town following signs for Dolores Hidalgo and Mina de Cata. The Panoramica leaves the highway to Dolores Hidalgo just outside town near the Parador San Javier and is marked Panoramica and M. de Cata. Zero your odometer at the Parador San Javier. As you drive clockwise around town you'll reach the Mina de Cata at 1.2 miles (2 km) and reach the road going downhill to the right to the trailer park at 1.7 miles (2.7 km). If you pass over some railroad tracks you've gone too far. Drive down the hill a short distance to a Y and stop. The trailer park is just to the left, unfortunately this is a one-way road coming up the hill. Easiest access to the trailer park is along this route so send someone down the hill to stop traffic and then head down the left fork. You might also want to walk down to take a look before committing yourself. The trailer park is the second gate on the left. If you are coming around the Panoramica in a counter-clockwise direction watch for the railroad tracks after the Km. 16 marker, the road to the campground is the first one on the left after passing over the tracks.

Campground No. 2

BUGAMVILLE TRAILER PARK
  Address: Km. 9.5 Carr. Guanajuato-J Rosas,
  Guanajuato, Gto., Mexico
        Price: Low

GPS Location: N 20° 56' 42.0", W 101° 15' 31.7"

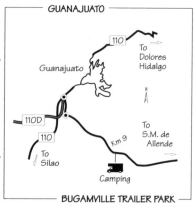

This place is also known as the Cactus or Buganvilia, but the sign out front says Bugamville. It is suitable for large rigs and often used by caravans.

There is room for at least a hundred rigs on a flat open graded area with no shade. The only hookups available are water, there are about 20 of these. You may be able to run an extension cord from one of the five motel-style rooms at the entrance. The restroom is small and not too clean when we visited, it does have a hot water shower. The manager reports that there is a dump station, we didn't see it. There is a cute little restaurant. Access to Guanajuato is by busses that pass the gate.

The campground is located off the road from Guanajuato to Juventino Rosas and San Miguel de Allende. The entrance road has a sign, it is on the south side of the highway very near the 9 Km. marker. The campground is about .2 miles (.3 km) back from the highway.

Other Camping Possibilities

Travelers with large rigs which can not fit into the Morrill RV Park in Guanajuato often stay in one of the San Miguel de Allende RV parks. The bus trip to Guanajuato takes less than two hours and is inexpensive, this is a great way to avoid Guanajuato parking hassles.

LOS AZUFRES, MICHOACÁN (LOES AH-SOOF-RAZE)

Los Azufres (the Sulfurs) is an area of sulfur hot springs located some 75 miles (123 km) east of Morelia along Mex. 15. While Los Azufres itself probably isn't of more than passing interest to the traveler it is included here because campgrounds in this area are few and far between. Mex. 15 between Morelia and Toluca is extremely scenic and not to be missed. Attractions along the way include the **Mirador de Mil Cumbres** (thousand peaks viewpoint), the **Monarch Butterfly wintering area** at El Rosario, and the **Los Alzati** archeological site.

From the campground at Balneario Erendira (see below) you can continue up the hill toward Los Azufres National Park. If you have zeroed your odometer at the point where the Balneario Erendira entrance road meets the highway you will come to the road to the Motel Tejamaniles at 3 miles (4.9 km), take a right at the Y at 3.6 miles (5.9 km), and come to the Campamento Turístico at 4 miles (6.5 km). This is the park, don't expect much and you won't be disappointed. Next door is the Balneario Doña Celia which looks nice, we didn't visit because it was closed when we were in the area. Farther along the road are many geothermal wells that have been drilled to produce power.

Campground

CABAÑAS Y BALNEARIO ERENDIRA
   Address: Morelos Pte. 43, Cd. Hidalgo,
   Mich., Mexico (Res.)
   Telephone: (715) 4-01-69

Price: Inexpensive

GPS Location: N 19° 45' 21.7", W 100° 41' 27.7"

Like most other popular balnearios this one is loud and crowded on weekends and holidays, but during the week you're likely to have it mostly to yourself. The minerals in the pools give them a disturbing green color, but they're warm and there's no smell.

The balneario has no formal RV spaces but has several flat grassy areas suitable for RV parking. Some have good shade. Larger rigs will end up in a less secluded area near the restaurant where busses park because the access road to the normal camping area is steep, you'll have to decide if you can handle it. In the various areas there is room for at least 10 RV's during the week, but you probably won't have any other campers for company. It is possible to run an electric cord to one of the many lamp posts but don't count on much juice, a hair dryer will trip the breaker. The restrooms are balneario-style with group shower rooms but have fairly warm water and are clean when they're not getting heavy use. There are two small groups of pools, they're open at all times so you can take an early or late dip. There are a few rental cabañas but most visitors are day-trippers. There is also a restaurant.

From Mex. 15 some 2 miles (3.3 km) west of Cd. Hidalgo near the 148 Km. marker the road to Los Azufres goes north. Turn left onto the rough gravel Erendira driveway at 8.6 miles (13.9 km). You'll reach the gate in .3 miles (.5 km). They'll check you in there.

Other Camping Possibilities

The Campamento Turístico at Los Azufres National Park has tent camping, you would probably be allowed to camp overnight in the parking lot if you have an RV but access is poor for rigs over about 22 feet long. There is a cafeteria, a playground, some pools and a bathroom with hot shower. There is also a private balneario next door which may allow tent camping.

The motel Tejamaniles which is about 3 miles (4.9 km) beyond Balneario Erendira is said to offer dry camping for RVs and tent camping.

We have talked with folks who have parked their RV overnight in the square in front of the auditorium in Angangueo near the butterfly reserve (see Side Trips below). Other camping possibilities in that area include the parking lots for visitors to the reserve.

Side Trips from Los Azufres

The Monarch butterfly reserve, the **Reserva Mariposa Monarca**, near El Rosario has become a top tourist destination during the past few years, and for good reason. During the months of December through March millions of Monarchs cling to the drooping branches of trees in this small reserve waiting for warmer weather. On sunny days, especially during February and March, they warm up and begin to fly, actually filling the air with the sound of their wings.

The road to El Rosario, Ocampo and Angangueo leaves Mex. 15 toward the north at San Felipe which is about 4.4 miles (6.8 km) west of Zitácuaro. The paved road climbs (but not too steeply for RVs) for 7.9 miles (12.9 km) to Ocampo. Just before reaching Ocampo you will see grassy fields alongside the road being used for parking, if you have a big rig this is probably the best place to park, trucks will take you up to El Rosario and the reserve for a fee from here. It may also be possible to dry camp here overnight if you are willing to pay for the privilege. Visitors with maneuverable high-clearance vehicles can drive in to El Rosario from Ocampo themselves, the distance is about 8.5 miles (14 km). Alternately, you can drive on from Ocampo following the paved road another 6.5 miles (10.5 km) to the mining town of Angangueo where there is limited parking but also a rough track suitable for hiking in to El Rosario. Small trucks are also available in Angangueo to take you into El Rosario for a fee. We've heard of folks getting permission to camp overnight in front of the municipal auditorium in the center of town when they arrived too late in the evening to go to the reserve before dark. Tent camping is allowed near the reserve.

New Mexican travelers coming from the west won't have had many opportunities to visit archeological sites. The road to **Los Alzati** leaves Mex. 15 about 1.3 miles (2 km) east of San Felipe (the turn-off for the Monarch reserve). Los Alzati is a Matlatzinca Indian city which was at the height of its power about 900 A.D. and has a huge pyramid.

MATEHUALA, SAN LUIS POTOSÍ (MAH-TEH-WAH-LAW)
Population 55,000, Elevation 5,300 ft (1,611 m)

There are two good reasons to stop in Matehuala. The first is that this is a very convenient stop if you are traveling north or south on Mex. 57. The other is that this is the best place to overnight if you are planning a trip to **Real de Catorce**. See the Side Trip section below.

Campground

LAS PALMAS MIDWAY INN
  Address: Carretera Central Km 617 (Apdo.
  73), Matehuala, S.L.P., Mexico
  Telephone: (488) 2-00-01
  Fax: (488) 2-13-96

Price: Moderate

GPS Location: N 23° 39' 40.1", W 100° 38' 04.1"

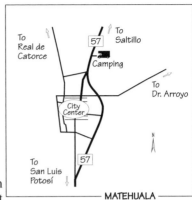

The Las Palmas has 24 back-in spaces with
electricity, water and sewer hookups and about
6 more with electricity and water. Since the campground will probably not be full
there is a good chance that big rigs can park sideways and avoid unhooking or
backing. The campground is actually a large oiled gravel lot behind the hotel and
has its own older restroom building with hot showers. The hotel has a restaurant,
swimming pool, 2 lane *boliche* (bowling alley), mini-golf, children's play area, and
a 1.7 km paved bike trail. English is spoken at the front desk.

The hotel is located on the east side of Mex. 57 north of town. It is .2 miles (.3 km)
north of the north entrance intersection and difficult to miss because there is a huge
sign.

Side Trips from Matehuala

During the 1800's **Real de Catorce** was a thriving silver-mining town with a
population of 40,000. Then came the lower silver prices in the first part of the 20th
century and the town was virtually abandoned. Today there are about 900
inhabitants and Real de Catorce is virtually a ghost town except at the end of
September and beginning of October when over 100,000 people visit the town for
the festival of San Francisco pilgrimage.

Driving to Real de Catorce can be something of a trial. You might want to just take
a bus or tour from Matehuala. To drive yourself go west 17 miles (27 km) past the
town of Cedral on a paved highway, then 15 miles (25 km) south on a rough
cobblestone road. Just before reaching Real you must drive through a 1.4 mile (2.3
km) tunnel. This is a one-way passage, tolls are taken and traffic is regulated so that
you won't meet someone coming the other way inside the tunnel. That means that
you can wait up to 20 minutes before being allowed to continue.

CIUDAD DE MÉXICO, DISTRITO FEDERAL
(SEE-OOH-DAWD DAY MAY-HEE-KOH)
Population 20,000,000, Elevation 8,000 ft (2,432 m)

For most travelers the idea of visiting Mexico in their own vehicle is more than a
little intimidating. Aren't there terrible traffic jams, pollution, predator cops,
confusing traffic laws and perhaps even criminals? The truth is that Mexico City

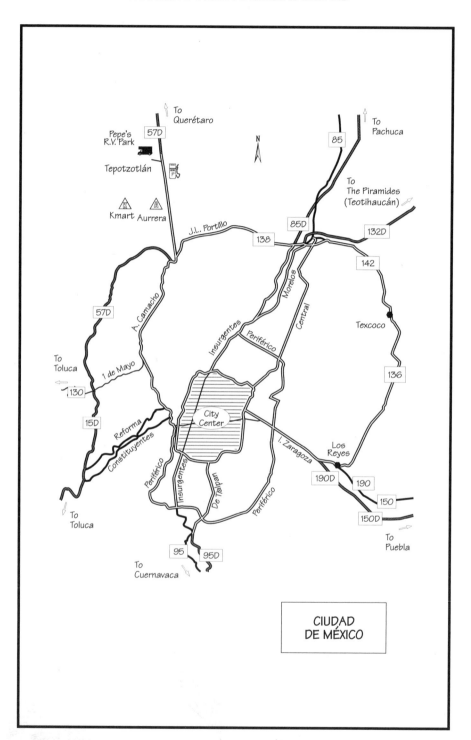

CIUDAD
DE MÉXICO

does indeed have all of these things, but a visit, perhaps even an extended visit, is well worth the trouble.

This is perhaps the largest city in the world. No one really knows how many people live there. The sights and activities in Mexico City place it on a level with other world capitals including London, Paris, New York and Tokyo as far as tourist interest is concerned. Sure there are problems, but remember, 20,000,000 people deal with them on a daily basis. The fact is that once you actually arrive you will be amazed that you were ever concerned. Most visitors never have a problem.

When you visit Mexico City it is important to do it right. First, and most importantly, don't drive into Mexico City for your visit. Base yourself either at the northern entrance of the city at Tepotzotlán where there is an excellent campground, or in one of the Cuernavaca campgrounds. Use the excellent bus service from both locations to get downtown. Consider spending several days in a reasonably priced hotel. Get a good guidebook and pack light. When you get to the city exercise normal precautions like you would in any major city. Only visit well-traveled places. Don't stay out late at night. Don't drink too much. Don't carry any more valuables than you can afford to loose and keep credit cards, passports, and most of your cash in a belt safe. Don't carry anything of value in a purse, in fact, avoid carrying one at all if possible. And finally, a special Mexico City precaution, don't take a taxi that you have hailed on the street, only use one that you have ordered by phone.

There are really too many attractions in Mexico City for even inadequate coverage in this book. The most popular ones include the **Ballet Folklórico de México**, the **National Museum of Anthropology**, the **Shrine to the Virgin of Guadalupe**, the **Zona Rosa**, the **Zócalo** and surrounding area, **Chapultepec Park** and the **University**. This only scratches the surface. Transportation is easy, there is an extensive subway and bus system which can be supplemented by cautious use of taxis.

Campground

PEPE'S R.V. PARK
    Address: Eva Sámano de López Mateos No. 62, Tepotzotlán, Edo. de México, Mexico
    Telephone: (5) 8-76-05-15, (5) 7-05-24-24 (Res.)

           Price: Moderate

GPS Location: N 19° 43' 26.3", W 099° 13' 15.7"

Pepe's is the only Mexico City trailer park left (that we are aware of). It is situated in the small town of Tepotzotlán, about 25 miles (40.8 km) north of the center of the city. The campground makes a convenient base for your visit to this amazing city, and you don't have to take your own vehicle anywhere near the terrible traffic.

There are about 80 full service back-in spaces with 30-amp. electricity, sewer, and water hookups. Virtually the entire spacious park is paved with attractive red bricks, there are some grassy areas for tent or van campers. A large and a small restroom area are both clean and modern and have hot water showers. The park is fenced and gated and has continuous 24-hour security. English is usually but not always spoken. Caravans use this campground quite a bit but there are so many spaces that reservations are not usually necessary.

The trip into town is quite easy. A city bus stops at a nearby stop, an hour-long bus ride takes you to the nearest subway station, and then you can travel easily and very cheaply to any area of the huge city. The owner of the RV park also owns a travel agency, you can make arrangements at the campground for tours of the city and surrounding areas or book a room for an overnight stay downtown. You can also use the agency to make reservations at the RV park: Mallorca Travel Service, Paseo de la Reforma No. 105, México, D.F., telephone (5) 7-05-24-24 or fax (5) 7-05-26-73. Don't forget to explore Tepotzotlán. This is an interesting little town with it's own important tourist attraction, the **Museo Nacional de Virreinato**, which includes the beautiful church of San Francisco Javier. This is an excellent museum of the colonial period. Don't miss the museum or the gilded church interior.

Finding the campground is not difficult with decent directions. As you drive south on Mex. 57D toward Mexico City you will pass through the last toll booth at Km. 44. Take the first exit after the toll booth, it is just .1 mile (.2 km) south and is labeled Tepotzotlán. At the end of the off ramp zero your odometer and turn right (west) toward town. Drive to odometer .1 mile (.2 km) and turn right onto an avenue under high-tension electrical cables (look up). Turn left at odometer .3 miles (.5 km). You will find yourself on an uneven brick road with lots of topes. Follow it up the hill and past a long rock wall on the left. Turn right at 1 mile (1.6 km), there is usually a sign for the trailer park visible here if you look carefully. There is lots of room to make the turn although you may have to wait for other traffic, semis and big busses make the turn all day long so even if people stare they really are accustomed to big rigs coming through here. At odometer 1.1 miles (1.8 km) there is a Y, take the right fork. You will see the campground entrance on your left at 1.7 miles (2.7 km). The gate will probably be closed, you can ring the bell to get someone's attention.

Other Camping Possibilities

Don't forget that Mexico has lots of excellent reasonably-priced bus service, especially to Mexico City. You can easily visit the city for several days by taking a bus and staying in an inexpensive but conveniently located hotel. Here are the approximate travel times by bus from several cities with good campgrounds: Cuernavaca - 1.5 hours, Puebla - 2 hours, Querétaro - 3 hours, San Miguel de Allende - 4 hours, Acapulco - 5 hours, Guadalajara - 7 hours.

Side Trips from Mexico City

Teotihuacán is probably the most impressive archeological site in Mexico, especially if size is what impresses you. The huge Pyramid of the Sun and smaller

PYRAMID OF THE SUN AT TEOTIHUACÁN

Pyramid of the Moon rival those in Egypt. You can drive to Teotihuacán easily, follow the first portion of our driving log around northeastern Mexico City in the section below. You can also catch a tour bus from Mexico City, check with a travel agency about this.

Tula is another archeological site, this one much smaller but known for its Atlanteans, carved fifteen-foot-high stone warriors. To get there from Pepe's follow Mex. 57 north for 8.3 miles (13.4 km) and then a secondary highway north another 21.5 miles (34.7 km) to Tula. As you approach the town of Tula watch for signs for Las Ruinas or Parque Nacionál Tula. A smaller and sometimes rough road will take you another 7.9 miles (12.7 km) to the ruins.

Driving Through or Around Mexico City

Mexico City is a wonderful destination, but when you decide to continue south you have a problem. How do you get through the city? This is probably one of the big reasons many people don't visit Mexico City on their way to other destinations in the south like Chiapas or the Yucatán. They hate the idea of driving through the largest city in the world.

It is really quite amazing, but true, that there is no toll ring road allowing motorists coming south on Mex. 57 to easily bypass the city and continue south on Mex. 150 to Puebla and beyond or to Mex. 95 to Cuernavaca. Most other cities in Mexico now have bypasses, why not the capital?

We don't know the answer to that question, but we do know several useful routes around and through the city.

You should be aware that in an effort to fight pollution Mexico City has extended rules making it illegal to drive your vehicle in the city on certain days. These rules are based upon the last digit of your license plate and apply to all vehicles. The digits and days are as follows: 5 or 6 - Monday, 7 or 8 - Tuesday, 3 or 4 - Wednesday, 1 or 2 - Thursday, 9 or 0 - Friday. Do not drive your vehicle in Mexico City on these days. If you are pulling a trailer or tow car use the towing vehicle's license number. The rules do not apply as far out as Tepotzotlán so you can arrive at Pepe's RV park on any day. The covered zone also does not extend far enough from Mexico city to apply to the Pachuca bypass route or the Toluca bypass route described below. However, they do apply to the northeastern Mexico City bypass route and also the route directly through Mexico City.

EASTERN BYPASS ROUTE
THROUGH PACHUCA

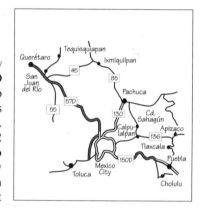

To bypass Mexico City to the east follow Mex. 45 from an intersection with Mex. 57D just a few miles south of the San Juan del Río exits. This is known as the Palmillas intersection but probably not marked as such. Mex. 45 meets Mex. 85 after 56 miles (92 km). Turn south on Mex. 85 and drive to Pachuca, a distance of 51 miles (84 km). Now follow two-lane highways southeast through Ciudad Sahagún to meet Mex. 136 at Calpulalpan and then east to Tlaxcala, altogether a distance of 92 miles (150 km). Puebla and Mex. 150D are then only about 18 miles (30 km) farther south, you can then easily travel east to the coastal route on Mex. 150D. This entire bypass route is relatively quiet and easy to drive, only the city bypass south around Pachuca is at all challenging. The entire drive should take about 5 hours.

WESTERN BYPASS ROUTE THROUGH TOLUCA

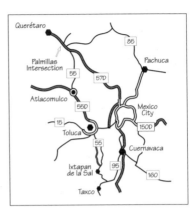

The western bypass of Mexico City starts on Mex. 57 very near the Palmillas intersection, just south of the exit for the eastern bypass. Follow Mex. 55 south to Atlacomulco, then join Mex. 55D south to Toluca. From Toluca Mex. 55 continues south to a point near Taxco where you can join Mex. 95 and travel back north to Cuernavaca or south to Acapulco. This bypass, from Mex. 57 to Mex. 95, is about 150 miles (250 km) long and takes about 5 hours. This route is busier than the eastern route and has several sections of toll roads. You must also follow the bypass around Toluca which can be busy, and pass through Ixtapan de la Sal, which is easy. Still, this route avoids Mexico City, a worthwhile achievement.

NORTHEASTERN MEXICO CITY BYPASS HEADING SOUTH

There is a bypass route that runs around northeast of Mexico city from south of Tepotzotlán to the toll highway running east to Puebla. The route is 40 miles (65 km) long and will take you about an hour and thirty minutes if you avoid rush hours. The ultimate time to do it would be Sunday morning. It is all on four-lane or better streets, much of it on secondary highway without stop lights.

Zero your odometer at the overpass on Mex. 57 that is just south of the toll plaza near Tepotzotlán. This is a good place to start because it is the exit associated with Pepe's RV Park, the place most people will stay while visiting Mexico City. Head south.

At 7.7 miles (12.6 km) take the exit for Ecatepec. This exit road is just past an overpass, you loop around and take the overpass over Mex. 57 so that you are headed east. You can identify the overpass because there is a big McDonald's sign nearby on the west side of Mex. 57.

For the next few miles you will be following the signs towards Ecatepec. For the first mile stay to the left as several roads, detailed below, split off from this route.

Roads split off to the right at 8.4 miles (13.7 km) (Perenorte) and again at 8.8 miles (14.4 km) (Cd. Labor). At 9.0 miles (14.7 km) you will merge left into a boulevard that you will be following for the next few miles, the street's name is J.L. Portillo but you may never see a sign identifying it.

You will follow J.L. Portillo for 8.9 miles (14.5 km), until your odometer reading is 17.9 miles (29.2 km). This street is six lanes wide with many stop lights. If you stay in the second lane from the left you should have easy sailing. Checkpoints along this road are a big Comercial Mexicana on the right at 10.3 miles (16.8 km), a big Bodega store on the left at 12 miles (19.6 km), a McDonalds, Burger King, and Kentucky Fried Chicken (did we leave anyone out?) near 14.4 miles (23.5 km), and both a Bodega Gigante store and a Comercial Mexicana at 15.9 miles (26.0 km).

As you approach 17.5 miles (28.6 km) on your odometer move to the right lane to be ready to take the exit to the right at 17.9 miles (29.2 km). This exit is marked with an overhead sign for Texcoco and Los Reyes. The route will curve to the left and run over J.L. Portillo. From here you will be following the signs for Los Reyes, although you really will have few route choices to make. The highway numbering through here is confusing, we think that this portion of the road is Highway 142, but the exit sign from J.L. Portillo says Highway 138. We really don't care which highway it is if it gets us around the city. This highway is four lanes wide and divided in most places. You will want to keep your speed down because there are many unexpected dips and heaves. There are occasional unmarked speed bumps, so watch out.

Here are some checkpoints for this portion of the route. You will pass over freeways at 19.9 miles (32.5 km) and again at 20.9 miles (34.1 km), there is an off ramp to the right for the Teotihuacán Pyramids (see the pyramid discussion in the Side Trips section of this chapter, you may want to take this exit) at 25.7 miles (42.0 km), there is a Comercial Mexicana at 34.1 miles (55.7 km) and a Cuota road to Mexico City cutting off to the right. There is a stop light at 34.7 miles (56.7 km) and you cross railroad tracks at 36.7 miles (60.0 km).

Just past the railroad tracks the highway merges left into another road, Mex. 136. Stay in the second lane from the left to avoid being forced to turn off this road. There is a Pemex on the right at 40.9 miles (66.8 km)and another small railroad crossing at 46.1 miles (75.3 km). Near here you may see signs pointing off this highway labeled Los Reyes, do not follow them, continue on straight.

At 46.9 miles (76.6 km) you will see the cutoff for the Mex. 190 free road to Puebla, do not take this exit, continue straight. You now pass through a fairly congested area but don't worry. Stay in the middle lanes and take it easy, the end is near. At 48.0 miles (78.4 km) you will see another big Comercial Mexicana store on the right.

At 48.3 miles (78.9 km) you should move to the left to follow the sign to Mex. 150D, the Cuota to Puebla. Finally at 48.5 miles (79.2 km) you exit to the right to enter Mex. 150D towards Puebla.

See how easy that was?

NORTHEASTERN MEXICO CITY BYPASS HEADING NORTH

From the Cuota road from Puebla, called both Mex. 150D and Mex. 190D, take the exit for Mex. 136, signed as Texcoco Libre. This exit is about 9.5 miles (15.5 km) from the last toll booth as you approach Mexico City from the east. Zero your odometer as you leave the freeway so you can stay in step with these directions.

You will be following signs towards Texcoco during this first section of the route. Follow these signs through a fairly congested area with three lanes in each direction, stay in the middle lane because the far left one will force you to turn and the far right one is extremely slow and crowded. The road will shrink to two lanes and then go back to three. At 1.4 miles (3.3 km) you will pass under the free road to Puebla, continue straight following the Texcoco signs.

At 11.0 miles (18.0 km) make sure you are in the left lane. From here you will be following the signs to Lecheria. At 12 miles (19.6 km) follow the Lecheria signs to the left. You will immediately have a stop sign, a railroad crossing, and speed bumps, not necessarily in that order.

You will be following this highway for about 19 miles (31 km). It is two lanes in each direction and is divided most of the way. Keep your speed down, however, because there will be unexpected swoops and bumps. Checkpoints along here are a Comercial Mexicana store on the right at 14.2 miles (23.2 km) with the entrance to a cuota road to downtown Mexico City (don't take it), an exit for Highway 132 to the pyramids at 22.7 miles (37.1 km), and a V in the road at 25.5 miles (41.6 km), go left towards Lecheria.

As you approach odometer 30 get into the right lane and take the exit to Lecheria that goes to the right. There will be a couple of good sized speed bumps and you will merge left onto J.L. Portillo.

J.L. Portillo has three lanes in each direction along much of its course, you will be following it for about 9 miles (14.7 km). This road will be slower than the one you have been traveling on, it has quite a few stop lights and more traffic, if you stay in the middle lane whenever possible you should have no problems.

Some checkpoints along this route are a Comercial Mexicana on the left at 32.0 miles (52.3 km) and many U.S. fast food places around 33.0 miles (53.9 km).

Near 37.0 miles (60.4 km) you will begin to see Querétaro signs, follow them from now on instead of Lecheria signs. You will see a Lecheria sign at 38.8 miles (63.4 km), do not follow it, continue straight ahead.

Finally, at 39.9 miles (65.2 km) you will see a sign pointing to Querétaro, Mexico, and probably also Lecheria, follow these signs over an overpass above many railroad tracks until you see the Querétaro sign at 39.8 miles (65.0 km), exit here and you will find yourself heading north away from Mexico City on Mex. 57.

If you are planning to stay in Mexico City you will want to exit at Tepotzotlán. This exit is to the right at 47.4 miles (77.4 km), you will know you are getting close when you see the marker for kilometer 42 and a Pemex station on the right at 47.2 miles (77.1 km).

Once off the freeway take the left turn so that you cross the freeway and are heading west. From here follow the directions to the campground given in the campground section.

THROUGH MEXICO CITY
HEADING SOUTH

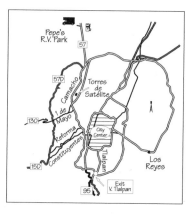

It is also not difficult to drive right through Mexico City on multi-lane highways. If you try to do this in the morning when traffic is light, say between 9 A.M. and 11 A.M., there is a good chance that you will not even run into much in the way of slow traffic. This route involves little other than staying on a major limited-access highway until it is time to get off and catch the Cuernavaca highway. We'll give a few checkpoints to give you something to watch for.

As you approach Mexico City on Mex. 57 from the north zero your odometer as you pass the Tepotzotlán off ramps just south of the last toll booth. At 7.6 miles (12.4 km) you will pass the overpass and exit for Ecatepec, this is where the route around the northeast side of the city exits as detailed above. Just past this point is an exit for an expensive new toll bypass that leads to the Toluca toll road, do not take it. The hard-to-miss Torres de Satélite monument is on the left at 16.0 miles (26.1 km). The exit for Mex. 130 to Toluca is at 18.3 miles (29.9 km). The exit for Palmas and Mex. 15D to Toluca, Morelia, and Guadalajara is at 21.1 miles (34.5 km). There is a Y at 23.8 miles (38.9 km), stay left. You'll see a Price Club on the right at 24.1 miles (39.4 km). At 32.9 miles (53.7 km) you'll see an exit for Cuernavaca and Mex. 95, do not take it. Instead take the exit for the Viaducto Tlalpan at 35.5 mile (58.0 km). Follow signs for Cuernavaca that take you to the right, merge you to the left with a lateral and then merge you left again onto the main street. At 37.2 miles (60.7 km) you'll see signs for Cuernavaca Libre and Cuernavaca Cuota, and if you merge left to Mex. 95D you'll come to the first toll booth at 40.1 miles (65.5 km).

THROUGH MEXICO CITY
HEADING NORTH

If you are heading north the route is also easy. Zero your odometer at the last toll booth of Mex. 95D from Cuernavaca. At 2.7 miles (4.4 km) follow signs right for Viaducto Tlalpan and Periférico. Go right again at 3.9 miles (6.4 km) following the signs for Periférico. At 4.3 miles (7.0 km) go right again following signs for Reino Av., Insurgentes, and Querétaro. At 4.7 miles (7.7 km) you merge left onto the Periférico and should have smooth sailing the rest of the way through the city.

Here are a few checkpoints. The Price Club is on your left at 15.4 miles (25.1 km). An exit for Mex. 15D to Toluca, Morelia, and Guadalajara is at 17.1 miles (27.9

km), there is another at 19.0 miles (31.0 km). Mex. 130 to Toluca exit is at 21.5 miles (35.1 km). The Torres de Satélite monument is on the right at 24.2 miles (39.5 km). The new Toluca toll bypass route is at 31.4 miles (51.3 km) and the exit for Tepotzotlán and Pepe's RV Park is at 40.2 miles (65.6 km). Immediately after this exit is the first toll booth of Mex. 57 to the north.

MONTERREY, NUEVO LEÓN (MOHN-TEH-RAY)
Population 2,600,000, Elevation 1,750 ft (532 m)

Busy, prosperous Monterey is the third largest city in Mexico and the capital of the state of Nuevo León. Travelers who have already had a chance to see some of the rest of the country will not be surprised to hear that Monterrey has the highest standard of living in all of Mexico. The city lies in a valley surrounded by mountains with the Río Santa Caterina bisecting the town in a east-west direction.

The huge central **Gran Plaza**, just north of the river, with its modern orange obelisk topped with a laser and called the Faro de Comercio sets the tone for the city. It is very different from the central plazas in other Mexican cities. Running for many blocks in a north-south orientation many of the interesting attractions of Monterrey surround it or are not far away. These include the Zona Rosa pedestrian mall which makes a good place to stroll and introduce yourself to Mexican shopping and also the **Catedral de Monterrey**.

El Obispado, at the western end of the downtown area near the river, was built as a bishop's residence in 1797 and has also served as a fort during the Mexican - American war of 1846, as Pancho Villa's headquarters during the Revolution, and today as a regional museum. It sits on a hill and offers good views of the city.

Lead crystal glassware fans will want to tour the **Cristalería Kristaluxus** factory and showrooms. Visitors with other interests may want to visit the giant **Cervecería Cuauhtémoc** which brews Bohemia and Carta Blanca beer. The brewery also houses a **Sports Hall of Fame** and the **Monterrey Museum**.

Monterrey fiestas include the **Feria de Primavera** which begins on Palm Sunday and lasts two weeks and the **Fiestas de Septiembre**, in September, of course. In December Monterrey hosts the **Feria del Norte de México** and also the **fiesta of the Virgin of Guadalupe**.

Maps of the Monterrey area are likely to confuse you because many of them show a bypass road that does not yet exist. A new toll bypass road scribes a semicircle around from Mex. 40 to the west, north to meet Mex. 85 from Nuevo Laredo, and then east to meet Mex. 40 from Reynosa. Unfortunately it does not extend south to meet Mex. 85. This is a very expensive toll road, fortunately there is a free bypass road just south (toward the city) that virtually parallels the toll bypass, you will probably want to use it instead. If you are coming from the north and want to get to Mex. 85 to Linares and Ciudad Victoria you will have to pass through Monterrey or follow the bypass road clockwise in order to pick up Mex. 40 into Monterrey from the east. This road passes along the north bank of the river, you will see signs for an exit to head south to Linares and Ciudad Victoria as you reach central Monterrey.

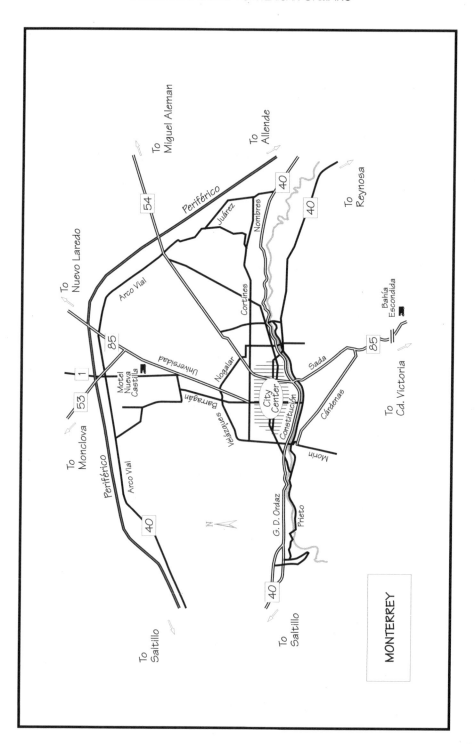

MONTERREY

Campground No. 1

HOTEL NUEVA CASTILLA
  Address: Carretera a Laredo No. 85 Km.
  15.5, Monterrey, N.L., Mexico
  Telephone: (8) 3-85-02-65, (8) 3-85-02-57
    Price: Moderate

GPS Location: N 25° 48' 45.6", W 100° 16' 06.2"

The Hotel Nueva Castilla is conveniently
located for travelers coming south from Nuevo
Laredo. It is a pretty good place to spend your
first night in Mexico, you don't have to deal with much traffic since the hotel is
quite a distance from the central area and near the ring roads.

There are 12 back-in spaces on gravel behind the hotel, 11 have electricity, sewer,
and water and one has electricity and water only. There is also a lot of room for rigs
to park with no hookups and for maneuvering. There is a modern and clean
restroom building with two cubicles, each has a toilet, sink and hot shower. The
hotel has a swimming pool and a restaurant. Exercise caution when entering, the
normal entrance is low but there is a marked RV entrance just to the left.

To find the campground just follow Mex. 85 into town. Start watching when you
pass the inner ring road, get on the lateral as soon as possible. The hotel is on the
right just after the Km. 16 marker and has a good sign.

Campground No. 2

BAHÍA ESCONDIDA HOTEL AND RESORT
  Address: Av. Eugenio Garza Sada 2116,
  Col. Roma, Monterrey, N.L.,
  Mexico (Res.)
  Telephone: (828) 5-24-00 (Resort),
  (8) 3-59-74-00 (Monterrey)
    Price: Summer - Expensive,
      Winter - Moderate

GPS Location: N 25° 24' 49.2", W 100° 07' 19.8"

The Bahía Escondida is slated to be a KOA
sometime in the near future, but it has been
open for several years and is a first-class operation. Unfortunately it is somewhat
inconveniently located 15 miles (24 km) south of Monterrey on the road to Ciudad
Victoria and is not a good place to overnight if you are heading west to Saltillo and
then south to the central area of Mexico via Mex. 54.

This very large resort has lots of amenities, the campground is very nice but hardly the center of attention. There are 26 back-in spaces with electricity, sewer, water, picnic tables, barbecues and plenty of shade. The access drive is gravel with curbs, there is well-clipped grass everywhere else. The restroom building is large, modern, clean and tiled, it has hot water showers. There is a children's play area in the camping area. Really long rigs won't fit in this campground, we estimate 30 feet to be about the maximum although you could park a tow vehicle away from your space but nearby.

Here's a short list of some of the other offerings at this resort: swimming pools (including one with waves), boat launch, restaurant, rental rooms, and a huge water slide.

The entrance to the resort is on the east side of Mex. 85 south of Monterrey near the Km. 244 marker. If you are traveling away from Monterrey you must go beyond the Km. marker, use a retorno to turn around and head back toward the city. Just beyond the Km. 244 marker take the right marked Bahía Escondida. Follow this small paved road for 1.4 miles (2.3 km) until you reach the entrance gate and office. After checking in you head down the hill to the left, take a left fork as you climb again, and follow the driveway up and over the small hill to the campground which sits down next to the lake.

Side Trips from Monterrey

Sights outside the city but in the immediately surrounding area include **Horsetail Falls**, **Huasteca Canyon**, and the **Grutas de García**.

The distance between **Saltillo** and Monterrey is only 51 miles (82 km) on a good multi-lane free highway. This means that if you would like to base yourself in one of these cities and visit the other on a day trip you can easily do it.

MORELIA, MICHOACÁN (MOH-RAY-lee-ah)
Population 430,000, Elevation 6,400 ft (1,946 m)

Morelia is the capital of the state of Michoacán, one of the most handsome state capitals in Mexico. Originally the city was called Valladolid but in 1828 it was named after the Mexican War of Independence hero General José María Morelos. The city is extremely well endowed with colonial-style buildings, building ordinances preserve what is there and restrict the construction of clashing designs in the central area.

The state of Michoacán is known for its handicrafts and Morelia has a good selection. Try both the **Casa de las Artesanías** at the **convent of the Church of San Francisco** and the **Mercado de Dulces** (Candy Market). You'll also find many smaller shops scattered around town.

The **central square** and **cathedral** are rewarding, just as they are in most Mexican colonial cities. Morelia is special, however, the cathedral is considered one of the most impressive in Mexico. Morelia also has an **aqueduct**. It is no longer in use but you'll probably see at least some of its remaining 253 arches. There are two museums to the city's namesake, **Museo Casa Natal de Morelos** (where he was born) and **Museo Casa de Morelos** (where he lived later). Morelia also has a good **zoo** and, at the modern convention center, a **planetarium** and an **orchid house**.

Morelia is also well-endowed with shopping centers, supermarkets, and discount stores so it is a good place to stock up. Several are located off the ring road in the southeastern section of town.

Campground No. 1

HOTEL MESON TARASCO
    Address: Carr. Morelia-Guadalajara Km. 7
    (Apdo. 61-A), Morelia, Mich., Mexico
    Telephone: (43)16-19-40

Price: Low

GPS Location: N 19° 41' 15.5", W 101° 16' 37.6"

The RV park doesn't get much attention at this hotel, but these are the only RV spaces we could find that actually are in Morelia. Decent alternatives are the balneario in Quiroga (described below) and the good RV parks in Pátzcuaro, which is 36 miles (58 km) away on a good highway.

The motel has five RV slots behind the main building under shade trees. Unfortunately there were only three usable electrical outlets for all of them when we visited. There was also no water although all of the parking slots had sewer drains, in fact, each had two drains. Another problem is that there is no restroom available to the RV park guests so you must be self-contained. A final problem is that access to the slots for big rigs is difficult, you could drive in just fine, but a big unit would probably have to back all the way out to the highway when leaving. If all of this doesn't bother you you'll like the rest of the features. There's an excellent restaurant and also a nice swimming pool. Bus service to Morelia runs past the front of the motel.

To reach the Hotel Meson Tarasco drive east on Mex. 15 from the Morelia ring road. You'll see it on the left near the 7 Km. marker. This is 2.3 miles (3.7 km) east of the ring road.

Campground No. 2

BALNEARIO SAN JOSÉ DE AGUA TIBIA
  Address: Lopez Mateos Y Juárez, Quiroga,
  Mich., Mexico
  Telephone: (435) 4-02-95

Price: Low

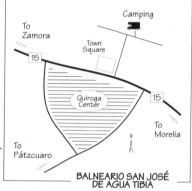

BALNEARIO SAN JOSÉ
DE AGUA TIBIA

GPS Location: N 19° 40' 05.1", W 101° 31' 30.4"

This is the town balneario in Quiroga, one of the main arts and crafts market centers around Lake Pátzcuaro in Michoacán. Quiroga is also only 30 miles (48 km) from Morelia so it is also a fairly convenient place to stay while visiting the city. There is frequent bus service into Morelia.

The balneario has two large grass fields behind its pool area. RV's can park along the edge of one field near the changing room building and run a cord for electricity. Tenters have a large area to themselves. The restrooms are old and nothing special but have hot showers. The pool here is heated using a boiler so it is heavily used all year long. Weekends at the balneario can be crowded but the camping area is slightly removed so there is some privacy. Security is pretty good since a decent fence is the only way to make sure the local teens pay for their pool use. The central plaza is only a block away so you are in a very convenient location when you stay here.

Passing through Quiroga on Mex. 15 turn north at the east side of the central plaza. The balneario is two blocks straight ahead. Large RV's may have some trouble entering the camping area because swing room is limited. We estimate that a 30 foot motorhome is about the maximum size for this campground.

PACHUCA, HIDALGO (PAH-CHOO-KAH)
Population 175,000, Elevation 8,000 ft (2,432 m)

Pachuca is one of the closest capitals to Mexico City, it is only 55 miles (88 km) away on a good toll road. It is the capital of the state of Hidalgo. Historically this is a mining area, and it continues to produce a great deal of silver, but today the town is becoming more and more industrial.

Few people visit Pachuca and it really has little to attract tourists. Many Cornish miners came to Pachuca in the 19th century so it has a personality slightly different than other Mexican cities. While the central area is on flat land much of the suburban area rises onto the mountains behind, the roads in this area are narrow and difficult to negotiate, don't get trapped on them if you are in a larger rig. A ring road around the east side of town makes it relatively easy to get to Mex. 105 northeast to El Chico.

Campground

EL CHICO NATIONAL PARK

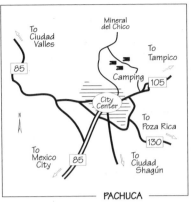

PACHUCA

El Chico National Park just north and far above Pachuca has many flat grassy areas for dry camping. Most are provided with pit toilets by locals and a small fee is charged for camping. There is also a more formal area called El Oyamel *(GPS Location: N 20° 10' 40.9", W 098° 41' 43.8")* just inside the entrance gate to the park. It is run by a local ejido and has 10 full hookup sites with electricity, sewer, and water. Also a large building with restrooms and meeting rooms. Unfortunately when we visited there was no power or water and it was only open on weekends. This could be a good campground but apparently there is not enough demand to make its operation worthwhile.

To find El Chico National Park follow Mex. 105 northeast from Pachuca. After a 2.8 miles (4.5 km) climb from the ring road you'll see a sign for Mineral del Chico to the left. Take this road and after another 3.5 miles (5.6 km) you'll pass through the park entrance and find campsites at various locations for the next several miles.

PÁTZCUARO, MICHOACÁN (PAHTZ-KWAH-ROW)
Population 45,000, Elevation 7,150 ft (2,174 m)

Pátzcuaro is a treasure. It is a town from another time and place and seems to be a favorite with everyone who visits. It is a friendly-sized town, there are adequate facilities for camping, many good restaurants, lots of shopping for crafts, and interesting side trips around the surrounding countryside.

Life in town centers around the two plazas. The **Plaza Grande** is slow-moving and shaded. Restaurants and shops occupy porticos around the perimeter. The **Plaza Chica** is much different. It is full of activity and vendors, especially during the Friday market, and the town mercado (market) is adjacent. The third location of interest is the **lake front**, it is about 2 miles (3 km) from the central area and quite near the campgrounds. There are several seafood restaurants there and two dock areas where you can catch boats to Janitzio and other villages on islands or along the lake shore.

Crafts are readily available in Pátzcuaro. The **Friday market** is an excellent place to find them, you should also check out the **Casa de los Once Patios** (house of eleven patios) where you can watch craftsmen work and buy their handiwork.

One thing not to be missed in the Pátzcuaro area is the **dance of "Los Viejitos"** (old men). Young dancers dress in masks of old men and carry canes, their dance is hilarious.

If you decide to stay in Pátzcuaro for an extended period you shouldn't forget that Morelia is just 36 miles (58 km) away on good roads. You can easily run in for a day of shopping for supplies in the big stores. Do not drive a large RV into Pátzcuaro since the streets are confusing and some would be hard to negotiate. The campgrounds are well outside the central area but small combi busses provide easy access to town.

Campground No. 1

MOTEL PÁTZCUARO
> Address: Avenida Lázaro Cárdenas 506,
> Pátzcuaro, C.P. 61600 Mich., Mexico
> Telephone: (434) 2-07-67
> Fax: (434) 2-29-84

Price: Low

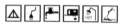

GPS Location: N 19°32' 00.5", W 101° 36' 39.2"

This is a cute little place conveniently located and with good facilities. It is best for smaller rigs, anything over about 30 feet will have some maneuvering problems although we've seen some huge rigs here.

There are 10 short back-in spaces with electricity, sewer, and water. A much larger grassy area is available for dry and tent camping. The restrooms are well-maintained and have hot water. There is a small swimming pool. The docks for boats to Janitzio are a 10 minute walk in one direction and the center of town is 30 minutes in the other. Small busses along the nearby highway provide convenient motorized transport.

As you arrive in Pátzcuaro from the direction of Morelia on Mex. 14 you will see a Pemex on the left. Zero your odometer. In .3 miles (.5 km) you will see the El Pozo Trailer Park on the right and then at 1.1 miles (1.8 km) come to an intersection. Go left here toward central Patzcuaro, the small road to the Villa Patzcuaro is on the left at 1.5 miles (2.4 km).

Campground No. 2

EL POZO TRAILER PARK
    Address: Apdo. 142, Pátzcuaro, C.P. 61600
    Mich., Mexico
    Telephone: (434) 2-09-37

Price: Low

GPS Location: N 19° 32' 45.9", W 101° 36' 02.5"

This is the first campground you'll see when you come into Pátzcuaro from Morelia. It is the best of the campgrounds in town for big rigs, there's plenty of room. It is popular with caravans.

There are 20 back-in spaces arranged on both sides of a very large grassy field. Each has electricity, sewer, and water. Restrooms are clean and well-maintained, they have hot water showers. There is a playground for the kids and busses pass in front of the campground for transportation into town or to the dock area.

As you come into Pátzcuaro from Morelia watch for the Pemex on the left. Just after the Pemex you'll see the 20 Km. marker and then the El Pozo on the right. Watch for the campground's large sign on the far side of the railroad tracks running alongside the highway.

Side Trips from Pátzcuaro

When you visit Pátzcuaro don't miss the boat trip to **Isla Janitzio**. These waterborne busses are used by both tourists and residents. The trip takes about a half hour each way. On weekends you are likely to be treated to a mariache band, be sure to kick in a few coins when they pass the hat. Once on the island you climb to the statue of Morelos on the summit of the island. The view from the base of the statue is good but you'll probably want to climb up into the torch, if only for the thrill. All the way up the hill you'll be tempted by vendors with handicrafts and wonderful smelling restaurants. You can catch any boat back to the mainland, the return is included in the price you paid on the way out.

Santa Clara del Cobre (also called Villa Escalante) is 12 miles (20 km) south of Pátzcuaro. This town is famous for its copper metalwork. You'll find most of the stores concentrated near the plaza, they're filled with plates, pots, and almost anything you can think of made of copper. Take a tour of one of the *fábricas* (factories) to see the work in progress.

Nine miles (15 km) north of Pátzcuaro near the shore of the lake is the pre-colonial village of **Tzintzuntzan**. **Las Yácatas** archeological site has five round tombs built by ancient Tarascan Indians. The village produces a green-colored pottery.

PUEBLA, PUEBLA (PWEH-BLAH)
Population 1,100,000, Elevation 7,100 ft (2,158 m)

Like many Mexican cities Puebla sits surrounded by mountains, they include the volcanoes of Popocatépetl, Iztaccíhuatl, Malinche, and Pico de Orizaba. This is a sophisticated city with an elegant colonial central area. It is also Mexico's fourth largest city. There is a lot of history in Puebla and the **food** is famous throughout the country. Puebla's mole poblano is the country's national dish. The city is synonymous with **Talavera**, both tiles and pottery.

On May 5, 1862 Mexican forces won a huge and unexpected victory here over invading French forces. The victory was a temporary one, a year later the French were back with reinforcements from home and this time they were victorious. The May 5 victory is celebrated by a well-known holiday known as Cinco de Mayo. You can visit the **fort** where all of this happened, it is located just northeast of the center of the city and has a museum.

Another very attractive town, **Cholula**, is almost a suburb of Puebla. Cholula is known for its churches, there are sometimes said to be 365 of them in this small town of approximately 50,000 people. The most unique is built atop a huge Indian pyramid. Today the pyramid looks like a pyramid-shaped hill but if you take the tour through the interior you will see that it definitely is a pyramid to rival those at Teotihuacán, in fact this one is even larger.

Campground No. 1

TRAILER PARK LAS AMERICAS
  Address: Km. 122 de la Carr. Fed. México-
  Puebla (Apdo. 49), Cholula, Pue. , Mexico
  Telephone: (22) 47-01-34

Price: Moderate

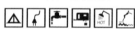

GPS Location: N 19° 04' 09.2", W 098° 17' 18.1"

Las Americas is located in Cholula, a pleasant Puebla suburb with lots to see. The famous Cholula pyramid, largest in the western hemisphere, is only a 20 minute walk from the campground. It's the tall hill to the south with the church on the summit.

The campground has 17 back-in spaces with electricity, sewer, water and patios arranged around the outside wall of a cobblestone courtyard with grass surfaces for parking. There is plenty of room for big rigs to maneuver. An additional 11 full service back-in spaces occupy the entrance courtyard, they are seldom used for camping, usually this area is used by the adjoining motel for parking. The campground has three tiled restroom cubicles with toilet, sink and shower. There is also a pool, a wading pool, playground equipment, and a dormitory room that can be rented by groups. The gate is closed at night. Access to both Puebla and Cholula by public transportation is easy, dozens of small collectivos (VW combis) ply the road two blocks away. The central Cholula square can be reached in a half-hour stroll.

To reach the campground from Mex. 150D take the Puebla exit near Km. 120 and head south following the Puebla Centro sign on Av. Hermanos Serdan after zeroing your odometer. On this big boulevard you will pass three quasi-glorietas with monuments and then come to a fourth glorieta at 2.7 miles (4.4 km). Take the road that Y's right at the far end of the monument, you will see an Aurrera store dead ahead. At the T in front of the store turn right. You are now on Prol. Reforma, the road east to Cholula. You were at odometer 3 miles (4.8 km) at the Aurrera store, you will pass under an arch and onto a bridge at 4.4 (7.1 km), pass the Km. 109 marker at 5.5 miles (8.9 km), cross railroad tracks at 6.1 miles (9.8 km), pass under the new periférico at 7.7 miles (12.4 km) and see the easy to miss Las Americas sign on the left at 8.1 miles (13.1 km) just after the Km 105 marker. If you follow the road around a gradual 90 degree left bend you've gone too far. After making the turn at the Las Americas sign you will follow a rough dirt road for two blocks and turn left. The campground is on the left about half way down the block.

Campground No. 2

HOTEL CUATRO CAMINOS
   Address: Av. Hermanos Serdan No. 406,
   Puebla, C.P. 72000 Pue., Mexico
   Telephone: (22) 24-03-91 or (22) 24-02-62

      Price: Moderate

GPS Location: N 19° 05' 35.5", W 098° 13' 43.9"

This campground has only a few spaces in the central parking area of a hotel, but it is easy to find and the only campground actually in Puebla. It has the same ownership as the Trailer Park Las Americas in Cholula.

There are eight back-in spaces with electricity, sewer, and water on a paved parking area. While there is probably room for bigger rigs here they would definitely be in the way of the motel guests. The one restroom cubicle has a toilet, sink and hot water shower. Buses pass on Av. Hermanos Serdan en route to central Puebla.

To reach the campground from Mex. 150D take the Puebla exit near Km. 120 and head south following the Puebla Centro sign. Immediately you will see the Hotel el Meson del Angel on your right and the campground, Hotel Cuatro Caminos, on your left. It is just to the north of the Chevrolet dealer with a small sign.

QUERÉTARO, QUERÉTARO (KEH-RAY-TAH-ROW)
Population 500,000, Elevation 6,100 ft (1,855 m)

The city of Querétaro has played an important part in Mexican history. Querétaro was the headquarters for the Franciscan monks as they founded missions throughout the country, the revolution against Spain was planned here, Maximilian made his last stand and faced the firing squad in Querétaro, the constitution was drafted here, and here the PRI was founded.

The colonial center is the prime attraction for visitors. It has a very Spanish flavor, Some of the center is closed to automobile traffic. You'll want to visit the central square which is called the **Jardín Obregón**, the **Ex-Convent and Church of San Francisco** which also houses a museum, the **Casa de Corregidora**, and the **Temple and Ex-Convent of Santa Cruz**. About a half-hour walk from the central area is the **Cerro de las Campanas**, a hill where Maximilian was executed. Querétaro has a still-working **aqueduct** on the east side of town which was finished in 1738.

Campground No. 1

FLAMINGO HOTEL
    Address: Av. Constituyentes Pte. 138
    Centro, Querétaro, C.P. 76000 Qro.,
    Mexico
    Telephone: (42) 16-20-93

Price: Low

GPS Location: N 24° 01' 52.7", W 104° 38' 34.6"

If a little heavy traffic doesn't bother you this is the place to stay for your Querétaro visit. The center of town is a twenty-minute stroll away.

The Flamingo has 7 camping spaces. They are arranged along the side of a cobblestone driveway next to a lawn area, in effect they are pull-throughs. All have electricity, sewer, and water hookups. The lawn is good for tent camping. The small restroom is adequate, it has a hot water shower and is relatively clean. The hotel has a swimming pool and a restaurant was under construction last time we visited.

Access to the hotel is from near the intersection of Mex. 45 and Mex. 57 on the southwest side of Querétaro. The road that the hotel sits next to (Av. Constituyentes Pte.) is the continuation of Mex. 45 Libre as it enters town after passing under Mex. 57. Unfortunately the hotel is on the north side of the boulevard and the necessary U-turn is difficult for big rigs. The best access is by taking Av. Ignacio Zaragoza east from Mex. 57 (use the laterals on 57 to access Zaragoza), turning right on Ezequiel Montes (the 7th street east of Mex. 57) or any other convenient street, to head south to Constituyentes. Once established westbound on Constituyentes you can easily make the right turn into the hotel. The entrance is tight but big rigs should be able to enter if they use care.

Campground No. 2

AZTECA PARADOR HOTEL
   Address: Km 15.5 Carr. Querétaro-S.L.P.,
   Querétaro, Qro., Mexico
   Telephone: (42) 94-05-92, (42) 94-05-93

Price: Inexpensive

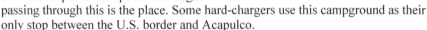

GPS Location: N 20° 34' 52.7", W 100° 23' 57.6"

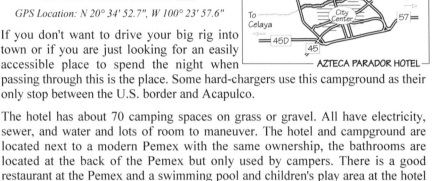

AZTECA PARADOR HOTEL

If you don't want to drive your big rig into town or if you are just looking for an easily accessible place to spend the night when passing through this is the place. Some hard-chargers use this campground as their only stop between the U.S. border and Acapulco.

The hotel has about 70 camping spaces on grass or gravel. All have electricity, sewer, and water and lots of room to maneuver. The hotel and campground are located next to a modern Pemex with the same ownership, the bathrooms are located at the back of the Pemex but only used by campers. There is a good restaurant at the Pemex and a swimming pool and children's play area at the hotel for use by camping guests. It is possible but not really convenient to catch a bus into town from along the highway out front. A tow car would work better. This is also a good place to gas up, it has excellent and honest service.

The hotel and campground are located on the east side of Mex. 57 near the Km. 15 mark. Mex. 57 is a four-lane divided highway at this point. Headed north just take the exit at the Pemex. Headed south you must continue for 1.4 miles (2.2 km) to a retorno to reverse direction and access the hotel. Another convenient retorno to the north will allow you to head south the next morning.

SALTILLO, COAHUILA (SAHL-TEE-YOH)
Population 450,000, Elevation 5,250 ft (1,596 m)

Saltillo is close to Monterrey and shares the booming industrial economy of that city. On the other hand, Saltillo is much smaller and much easier to deal with. Traffic is less of a problem and the colonial central area quite walkable. Saltillo has the best colonial center of any city near the U.S. border.

The streets are crowded and narrow, they are not suitable for big rigs. Park outside the central area and either walk or catch a bus. The town centers on a plaza, of course, in this case called the **Plaza de Armas**. The Churrigueresque **Cathedral de Santiago Saltillo** faces out onto the plaza. A few blocks away is the city market building, the **Mercado Juárez**.

Campground

HOTEL IMPERIAL DEL NORTE
  Address: Blvd. V. Carranza No. 3800,
  Saltillo, Coa., Mexico
  Telephone: (84) 15-00-11
  Fax: (84) 16-75-43

Price: Moderate

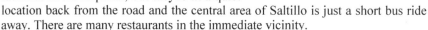

GPS Location: N 25° 27' 27.1", W 100° 59' 12.8"

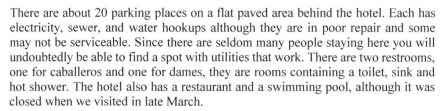

There's nothing too fancy about the camping facilities at the Imperial, but they're in a quiet location back from the road and the central area of Saltillo is just a short bus ride away. There are many restaurants in the immediate vicinity.

There are about 20 parking places on a flat paved area behind the hotel. Each has electricity, sewer, and water hookups although they are in poor repair and some may not be serviceable. Since there are seldom many people staying here you will undoubtedly be able to find a spot with utilities that work. There are two restrooms, one for caballeros and one for dames, they are rooms containing a toilet, sink and hot shower. The hotel also has a restaurant and a swimming pool, although it was closed when we visited in late March.

The Imperial del Norte is located on Blvd. Carranza to the northeast of central Saltillo. If you are approaching on Mex. 40 from Monterrey you will already be on Blvd. Carranza when you arrive. If you are arriving from the south follow the Periférico Luis Echeverria around to the northeast side of town and then take Blvd. Nazario S. Ortiz Garza north to intersect with Blvd. Carranza. From either direction watch for the Soriana supermarket on the northeast corner of Blvd. Carranza and Blvd. Nazario S. Ortiz Garza. The hotel is on the right .7 miles (1.1 km) south of this intersection, watch for a Kentucky Fried Chicken just before the hotel. Turn right into the road between the KFC and the hotel and park at the curb to check in. The campground entrance is directly ahead. Approaching from the south on Blvd. Carranza is more difficult, there is no break in the median so you must go north to a retorno which has little swing room, big rigs will probably have to pull through a Pemex station there to turn around.

Side Trips from Saltillo

The distance between Saltillo and **Monterrey** is only 52 miles (85 km) on a good multi-lane free highway. This means that if you would like to base yourself in one of these cities and visit the other on a day trip you can easily do it.

SAN LUIS POTOSÍ, SAN LUIS POTOSÍ (SAHN LOO-EES POH-TOE-SEE)
Population 550,000, Elevation 6,175 ft (1,877 m)

Few tourist seem to make it to San Luis Potosí, this really isn't a tourist city. For a long period of Mexican history San Luis Potosí was the largest and most important city of northern Mexico, today that spot is taken by Monterrey. San Luis Potosí remains an economic powerhouse however, it is a transportation center sitting astride railroads and highways.

Because it was historically prominent and powerful the center of San Luis Potosí has impressive buildings and parks. The streets tend to be narrow but quite a few are closed to traffic to make a pedestrian shopping area. There are many squares, often in the form of well-tended gardens. Centrally located ones include the **Alameda**, the **Jardín Hidalgo**, the **Plaza de los Fundadores**, and the **Jardin San Juan de Dios**. Many of these are flanked by neoclassical or republican-style buildings and connecting walking streets. The historical importance also means that San Luis Potosí is full of churches. These include the centrally located **Santa Iglesia Catedral** and the Churrigueresque-style **Templo del Carmen**, but there are many others. Important museums include a **bull-fighting museum** at the bull ring and the centrally located **Museo Regional Potosino** and **Mexican mask museum**.

Campground

EL MESQUITE
    Address: Carretera 57 a Matehuala - San
    Luis Potosí Km. 13, San Luis Potosí,
    S.L.P., Mexico
    Telephone: (48) 12-03-65

Price: Low

GPS Location: N 22° 14' 47.0", W 100° 53' 01.9"

SAN LUIS POTOSÍ

A word of warning about this campground. In early 1997 the hotel was being completely remodeled, actually being virtually torn down and rebuilt. The campground was sometimes open and sometimes not, and was often without services. It will probably be at least a year before the place is up and running again and there is some question of whether the campground will survive. The description below is pre-remodel, hopefully the campground will be at least as good after the remodel is complete.

The camping is in a grassy area to the south of the motel buildings. There are about 20 back-in spaces on grass with electricity, water, and sewer. There are no dedicated restrooms but campers are allowed to use an empty hotel room for hot showers. There is a good restaurant and a swimming pool. Busses to central San Luis Potosí pass on the highway in front of the motel.

The motel is located in the village of Enrique Estrada on Mex. 57 north of San Luis Potosí. It is on the east side of the road near the Km. 13 marker. New lateral streets have been built in the village so be sure to enter the lateral if you are approaching from the south. From the north you must now go all the way to the south end of the village and use a retorno to turn around and enter the northbound lateral lane.

SAN MIGUEL DE ALLENDE, GUANAJUATO
(SAHN MEE-GEHL DAY AL-YEHN-DAY)
Population 50,000, Elevation 6,100 ft (1,854 m)

This small colonial town is justifiable popular with North American visitors. Many have made it their home so there are lots of the kinds of amenities demanded by visitors from north of the border. San Miguel is second only to the Guadalajara area in popularity with expats. The Allende Institute which offers art and language classes is one of the major reasons for San Miguel's popularity. It draws many art and language students to the town.

Here, as elsewhere in central Mexico, a plaza marks the city center. This one is the **Plaza Allende**. Next to it is the unusual **La Parroquia** church which has French Gothic features. The central streets are narrow, hilly, and cobblestone-covered. Park outside the central area, there are few places where there is room to park inside it. Near the plaza are many shops and restaurants.

San Miguel does have a ring road bypass. It is absolutely essential that you use the bypass if you have a rig that is larger than a van because the town is a maze of very narrow cobblestone streets with few direction signs. Unfortunately the bypass is not marked well so many people, particularly when approaching San Miguel from the east, blunder into town. It is an experience they long remember.

When approaching from the east watch for the Gigante store on the right. The paved road to the left, marked Celaya, is the one you want to take to bypass town. It also takes you on an easy route to the RV parks. This intersection and road were being reconstructed the last time we were in San Miguel, hopefully the bypass will be more clearly marked when the project is completed.

Campground No. 1

LAGO DORADO TRAILER PARK
   Address: Apdo. 523, San Miguel de
   Allende, Gto., Mexico
   Telephone: (415) 2-23-01
   Fax: (415) 2-36-86

Price: Low

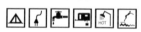

GPS Location: N 20° 54' 00.4", W 100° 46' 35.9"

The Lago Dorado is by far the nicest of the San Miguel campgrounds, unfortunately it is somewhat remote, you'll have to use your vehicle to get into town. At one time it was a KOA, the signs have been changed but still look a lot like KOA signs. While named for the nearby lake it is seldom near the water, the reservoir's dam apparently can no longer withstand the pressure of a full lake.

There are 65 camping spaces at the campground. All have electricity and water, twenty have sewer hookups and are pull-throughs. They are arranged on grass under pines that provide lots of shade, the trees are spaced just right for hanging a hammock. Some have picnic tables. The bathrooms are modern, clean, and nice, they have hot water showers. There is also a swimming pool for spring and summer use and a children's play area. English is spoken if the owner is around.

The entrance road to the campground is off the highway leading south from San Miguel toward Celaya and Guanajuato. From the intersection at the south side of San Miguel (near the La Siesta Hotel) drive south .7 miles (1.1 km). The entrance road goes right at the Hotel Misión de Los Angeles. There is a good sign. Zero your odometer here and drive down the teeth-rattling cobblestone road for .9 miles (1.4 km) to the end, turn right and follow a smaller road that crosses railroad tracks at 1.3 miles (2.2 km) and reaches the campground at 1.7 miles (2.7 km). Bus-type motorhomes (those with long wheelbases) will probably not have sufficient clearance to cross the railroad tracks.

Campground No. 2

LA SIESTA HOTEL
   Address: Salida a Celaya No. 82 (Apdo. 72),
   San Miguel de Allende, Gto., Mexico
   Telephone: (415) 2-02-07
   Fax: (415) 2-37-22

   Price: Low

GPS Location: N 20° 53' 55.7", W 100° 45' 04.9"

Many people use the La Siesta during their San Miguel stay because it is conveniently located. It is possible to walk into town from the La Siesta in twenty minutes.

The Hotel has about 45 usable back-in spaces located in a dusty lot behind the motel-style hotel units. The electric, sewer, and water connections for these back-in spaces are in poor repair. There is quite a bit of shade. A small restroom building is also in poor repair but does have hot water showers. The hotel has a restaurant and a swimming pool for summer use. English is not spoken.

The La Siesta is located next to the bypass road on the south side of San Miguel. From the intersection of the bypass and the road to Celaya go north toward town. You'll see a Ford agency on the left, the La Siesta has a much smaller sign and is on the right.

TEPIC, MÉXICO (TEH-PEEK)
Population 240,000, Elevation 3,000 ft (915 m)

Most guidebooks don't devote many words to Tepic, but it is an important stopover point for RVers. If you are traveling to Guadalajara from either Mazatlán or Puerto Vallarta you will find that Tepic is a great place to break up the long drive. The altitude cools the evening air and the atmosphere is pollution free, there is a big cigarette factory here however.

Tepic has few tourist attractions. The **State Museum** has displays of Indian crafts and also pre-Columbian ceramics. Tepic is the place to buy **Huichol and Cora Indian crafts**.

The city has several large supermarkets, including a large one with a Comercial Mexicana. To reach it follow Mex. 200 in to town from the intersection with the southern Mex. 15 bypass. Turn right at Av. Insurgentes, the store is .7 miles (1.1 km) from the turn.

There are two decent campgrounds near Tepic and one about 27 miles (44 km) southeast toward Guadalajara at Laguna Santa Maria, a lake inside an old volcanic crater.

Campground 1

TRAILER PARK LOS PINOS
    Address: 2 1/2 Kms. Sur Tepic, Carretera
    Puerto Vallarta (Apdo. 329), Tepic, Nay.,
    Mexico
    Telephone: (32) 13-12-32

Price: Low

Los Pinos is one of those places that might make you think of abandoning your rig. Their rate for camping is quite reasonable but it is almost exactly the same as the rate they charge for their motel-style rooms.

The campground is a large grassy field behind the home/office of the owners. There are 24 back-in sites. All have full utilities. Each also has level parking pads and a patio. The entire area has a high wall for security and there are 18 rental bungalows. The central driveway is cobbled so wet weather is no problem here. The small baño buildings have two private bathrooms each with each bathroom having it's own toilet, shower, and sink. Each is tiled in a different color. They are quite clean and have hot water. The owners speak a little English.

To reach central Tepic from the campground you can either walk 2.2 miles (3.5 km) north to the central square or catch a convenient bus on the road in front of the campground.

Los Pinos is easy to find. From the point where Mex. 200 meets the Libramiento passing south of Tepic drive north into town on Blvd. Xalisco, which is the street that becomes Mex. 200 as it heads south. Los Pinos is on the left exactly .85 miles (1.4 km) north of the junction. There is a gap in the barrier between lanes to allow you to turn left into the campground.

Campground 2

KAMPAMENTO KOA
　　Address: Jalisco 211, Col. Valle de
　　Matatipac, C.P. 63196 Nay., Mexico
　　Telephone: (32) 14-04-86
　　Fax: (32) 14-78-81

Price: Low

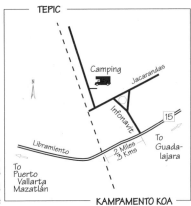

No, this isn't another member of the U.S. campground chain, or at least it isn't now. This is a huge fenced field, dotted with trees, with the swimming pool, baños, and offices in the middle.

There are 100 sites, all on grass with no driveways or patios, half with all services and half with water and electricity. The restrooms have toilets and hot showers. There is a pool here that is open to the public and popular with the local kids. The place is so big that you'll hardly notice them. In the evenings things quiet down. The park is fully fenced and the gate locked at night. Don't count on there being an English speaker here.

The Kampamento KOA has a well-deserved reputation of being hard to find. It really isn't though, if you know the secret. Zero your odometer at the point where the southern bypass around Tepic crosses Mex. 200 to Puerto Vallarta. Drive 1.5 miles (2.5 km) east toward Guadalajara. The road will rise over the railroad tracks. If you look to your left while you are at the top of the overpass you can almost see the campground right next to the tracks about a half-mile north.

Knowing that it is right next to the tracks is the secret. That's where it is, now to get to it. Take the first left after the tracks, the road is Infonavit Los Sauces (it is signed but there is no campground sign) and the turn is at 1.7 miles (2.8 km) from the intersection of the bypass and Mex. 200. In a tenth of a mile there is a Y, you'll want to go straight but can't, the road is one-way. Take the right fork and pass around a big traffic circle with a park in the middle until you have actually accomplished a left turn from Los Sauces and are headed toward the railroad tracks on Jacarandas. At 2.3 miles (3.7 km) you will reach the tracks and be forced to turn right, at 2.4 miles (3.9 km) you'll see the campground on your right. If the front gate is locked (it is sometimes if the pool is closed) try going around to the left and entering through the gate on that side. There is always someone around to check you in.

Campground 3

KOALA BUNGALOWS AND TRAILER PARK
Address: Chris French, Apdo. 493, Tepic,
C.P. 63000 Nay., Mexico
Telephone: (32) 12-37-72 (Res.)

Price: Low

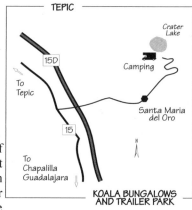

Some 15 miles (24.2 km) east of Tepic off Mex. 15 is Laguna Santa Maria, a pleasant lake located down inside the crater of an extinct volcano. Best of all, there is a trailer park there. Limited maneuvering room and the steep descent to the lake mean that rigs over 30 feet probably shouldn't try to visit this campground.

Koala Bungalow and Trailer Park has about 12 back-in spaces placed behind the motel-style bungalow building. Each space has electricity, water, and sewer. Visitors relax on the front lawn next to the lake surrounded by citrus trees. There is a children's swimming pool, a kiosk-style refreshment stand, and a boat launching ramp. Swimming in the lake, fishing, and birding are all excellent. English is spoken.

From Mex. 15 Libre some 14.6 miles (23.5 km) east of the junction of the toll and free roads near Tepic follow signs north for Sta. Maria del Oro. You'll pass over the toll road in .5 mile (.8 km) and in 6.1 miles (9.8 km) reach the town of Sta. Maria del Oro with 3,000 residents. Pass straight through town on the main road and at 7.8 miles (12.6 km) reach the crater rim which has a viewing pull-off. There is a steep descent to the lake which you reach at 12.0 miles (19.4 km). Turn left and you will find the Koala at the end of this short access road along the lake.

TEQUISQUIAPAN, QUERÉTARO (TEH-KISS-KEY-AH-PAN)
Population 20,000, Elevation 5,600 ft (1,701 m)

Tequisquiapan is a spa town that is very popular with week-enders from Mexico City. Access for them is easy, the town is just 75 miles (120 km) north on Mex. 57D and then another 12 miles (20 km) east on Mex. 120 which is a good two-lane road. It is a small town with lots of hotels, restaurants and cobblestone streets. Incidentally, this town occupies the official geographic center of Mexico.

Don't drive a rig of any size into Tequisquiapan, while good at first the roads narrow and become a trap for the adventurous. The two campgrounds below are well outside town.

Campground No. 1

TERMAS DEL REY
   Address: Carretera Tequisquiapan a
   Ezequiel Montes Km. 10, Tequisquiapan,
   Qro., Mexico
   Telephone: (5) 5-54-65-87 (Res.)

Price: Low

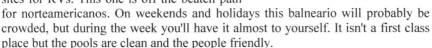

GPS Location: N 20° 37' 06.0", W 099° 54' 42.2"

Here's another example of a balneario with
sites for RVs. This one is off the beaten path
for norteamericanos. On weekends and holidays this balneario will probably be
crowded, but during the week you'll have it almost to yourself. It isn't a first class
place but the pools are clean and the people friendly.

The RV camping area has electrical and water hookups for at least twenty rigs. Tent
campers can use the grass. The RV area doubles as parking for the other balneario
visitors but you will probably be able to set up out of the way. The balneario
changing room doubles as the restrooms, they are cavernous but clean and have
warm water showers. There's a small refreshment stand open during the day and a
restaurant for busy weekends and holidays. No English is spoken.

From Tequisquiapan head northeast on Mex. 120. The balneario is on the right near
the 31 Km. marker, which is about 6 miles (10 km) out of town.

Campground No. 2

FIDEL VELAZQUEZ HOTEL AND BALNEARIO
   Address: Carretera Tequisquiapan a
   Ezequiel Montes Km. 7, Tequisquiapan,
   Qro, Mexico

Price: Inexpensive

GPS Location: N 20° 35' 32.6", W 099° 54' 08.8"

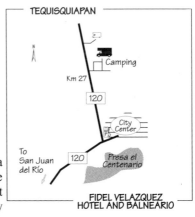

This campground near Tequisquiapan is also a
balneario. The pools are not as good as the
ones at the Termas del Rey, nor is there a giant
waterslide, but the RV camping area is very
good.

There are 45 back-in spaces with electricity, water, and sewer hookups. All are on
cobblestones with a line of trees providing some shade. You can probably pretend
these spaces are pull-throughs, there isn't likely to be a crowd except on holidays.
Big rigs are no problem. There isn't a massive changing room here, instead there are

individual tiled cubicles for toilets and showers. Water in the showers is warm (as it comes from the ground). There are two swimming pools and a restaurant for weekends. No English is spoken.

To reach the campground drive northeast on Mex. 120 from Tequisquiapan. Just after the Km. 27 marker turn right into the entrance driveway. The road surface is cobblestone. Almost immediately go right at a Y, then at .4 miles (.6 km) take a right-angle turn to the left. You'll pass alongside a vineyard and at .9 miles (1.4 km) arrive at the balneario. The camping spaces are through the gate and to the left. Look around for someone to accept your registration.

TLAXCALA, TLAXCALA (TLAS-KAH-LAW)
Population 53,000, Elevation 9,800 ft (2,979 m)

Although Tlaxcala is located just a half-hour or so north of Puebla it seems like most people never take the time to visit. This is a mistake. Tlaxcala is a small, easy to visit Indian town with colonial features. The area around the central plaza offers good shopping and several restaurants. This is an easy town to spend some time strolling around. If you have a larger rig you will probably find yourself parking some distance from the center, arrive in a smaller rig if possible. The campgrounds listed below are quite a distance from town and not really good places to use as a base for exploring the city. A visit to Tlaxcala is a good day trip from Puebla.

Campground No. 1

IMSS CENTRO VACACIONAL LA TRINIDAD
　Address: Santa Cruz Tlaxcala, Tlax., Mexico
　Telephone: (246) 1-07-00 or (800) 1-06-14
　Fax: (246) 1-06-92

Price: Low

GPS Location: N 19° 21' 34.2", W 098° 09' 08.6"

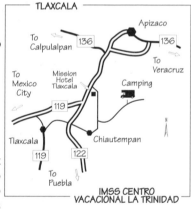

The Mexican social security department (IMSS) maintains several resorts near Mexico city to give residents a chance to get out into the country. Several have camping facilities and non-Mexican visitors are more than welcome. RV campers are something of an afterthought at this facility but don't let that stop you.

The RV camping area is actually two large brick covered parking lots above and behind the hotel building. Lamp posts have electrical outlets, there are no water or sewer hookups. A reasonably good restroom with no showers is provided for the RV area. There are lots of showers with hot water in the changing rooms for the pools. Tenters have a separate grass-covered area, this area is more heavily used than the RV area at this resort. The resort itself is very large, it is set in a reconstructed factory but is really quite elegant. It has hotel facilities, two very large pools (one inside), two restaurants, and lots of other attractions. You'll enjoy just seeing this place. Access for really big rigs could be tight but others should have no problems. Just take it easy.

From Tlaxcala follow Mex. 119 toward Apizaco. After about 5.5 miles (8.9 km) near where the 28 Km. marker should be you'll see a small exit for Atlihuetzian and Centro Vacacional Trinidad. The Mission Hotel Tlaxcala is signed at the same exit. Follow the Trinidad signs south for about 2.5 miles (4 km). RVers want the second entrance. Owners of big rigs should walk the driveway before entering to make sure there is maneuvering room.

Campground No. 2

IMSS CENTRO VACACIONAL MALINTZI
   Address: Huamantla, Tlax., Mexico

Price: Low

GPS Location: N 19° 16' 51.7", W 098° 02' 34.9"

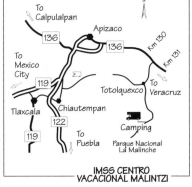

This is another IMSS resort near Tlaxcala. This one has even less provision for RVs but they are welcome, as are tent campers. The campground is a fenced and gated compound set in a pine forest, it is a 6 mile (10 km) hike to the top of La Malinche volcano from this campground.

There is a large parking lot here where RV's are allowed to park but it has no hookups. Tent campers have their own grass-covered area. There is a restroom near the tent area, it has flush toilets and showers, there is a water heater but it wasn't working when we visited. This campground also offers rental cabañas, a small grocery store, a restaurant, play fields and a children's play area.

To reach Malintzi head south on the road up the volcano which cuts off Mex. 136 at about the 131 Km. marker. After 2.6 miles (4.2 km) you will reach the small town of Totolquexco. Turn left at the intersection and drive another 3.4 miles (5.5 km) to the gated park entrance. A ranger will let you in and then it is another 1.8 miles (2.9 km) to the gated campground entrance on the right.

TOLUCA, MÉXICO (TOW-LOO-KAH)
Population 330,000, Elevation 8,800 ft (2,675 m)

Toluca has the highest altitude of any major city in Mexico. It is definitely an industrial city. The city's location means that you will probably pass through some day, either on the east-west routes between Mexico City and Guadalajara or when bypassing Mexico City on the north-south route. Tourists visit Toluca primarily for its famously huge **Friday Indian market** which offers a great selection of handicrafts. It is located near the bus station and is really open all week, Friday is just the best day. Toluca may seem like a good base for visiting Mexico City since it is so close but we recommend either Pepe's R.V. Park which is listed in this book under Mexico City or Cuernavaca.

Campground No. 1

PARQUE SIERRA MORELOS

Price: Low

GPS Location: N 19° 18' 18.9", W 099° 41' 43.5"

The Sierra Morelos is a public park located outside of Toluca to the east. It has picnic facilities, lots of play fields, and paths through pine forests. Camping facilities are minimal but this is a place you can park for the night.

There is an unmarked flat open field near a large picnic area that is used for parking by RVs. There are no hookups and the restrooms are in poor condition and not very clean but do have flush toilets. There are no showers. The park is very large and has full-time watchmen but the fences are not secure and people wander through at will. Busses stop at the gate of the park which is about a mile from the RV parking area.

The park is well signed off Mex. 15 to the east of Toluca. The road to the park goes north about 1.1 mile (1.7 km) west of the Toluca ring road. If you are driving toward the east watch for the big Coca-Cola bottling plant on your left and then watch for the sign for the left turn soon afterwards. If you pass a Comercial Mexicana on your right you've gone too far.

Campground No. 2

PARQUE EL OCOTAL
  Address: Parque El Ocotal S/N, Timilpan,
  Edo. de Méx., Mexico
Telephone: (726) 1-16-81

Price: Inexpensive

GPS Location: N 19° 48' 27.4", W 099° 45' 21.7"

It is a bit of a stretch to consider this a Toluca campground but since campgrounds in the region are scarce it is entirely possible that a visitor to Toluca will spend the night here. Toluca is the nearest large city.

The Parque El Ocotal is a state campground. There are several hundred acres filled with pine trees and walking trails. This is a government-owned wilderness campground in the tradition of those we're accustomed to in the states and Canada, except this one has a nice little hotel tucked away in one corner with a convenient and very nice restaurant.

The camping areas are open pine needle covered areas with scattered picnic tables and grills. There are also some flat parking areas for RVs. There are no hookups (you might be able to arrange to stretch an electric cord from one of the restrooms). Large rigs will have to be cautious on the interior dirt roads, this campground is really best for those under 30 feet. The restrooms have flush toilets and hot showers. There are several children's playgrounds. This is a quiet and isolated spot so you'll really feel like you are in the woods, but just over a rise is the hotel with restaurant, tennis courts, horse rentals, sauna, steam bath and Jacuzzi. There is 24-hour security at the gate to the park. No English is spoken.

From the eastern side of the Atlacomulco ring road, 44 miles (71.8 km) north of Toluca, drive east toward Villa del Carbón on Mex. 5. After 7.2 miles (11.6 km) you will reach the small village of Santiago Acutzilapan. On the far edge just past the Pemex a paved road goes north 1.1 miles (1.8 km) to El Ocotal. The attendant at the gate will let you in and take your money (but not very much).

TORREÓN, COAHUILA (TOE-RAY-OHN)
Population 450,000, Elevation 3,700 ft (1,125 m)

This is really a triple city: Torreón, Gómez Palacio, and Lerdo. Torreón is in the state of Coahuila while nearby Gómez Palacio and Lerdo are in Durango. The three cities form a railroad, farming and industrial center. Torreón is a relatively new city, founded in 1897, and has more to offer than the other two cities including parks, museums and stores.

Campground

HOTEL VILLA JARDÍN
    Address: Blvd. Miguel Alemán y Calz. J.
    Agustín Castro, Gómez Palacio, Dgo.,
    Mexico
    Telephone: (17) 15-87-77, (17) 15-81-17

        Price: Low

GPS Location: N 25° 33' 12.9", W 103° 30' 25.4"

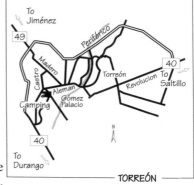

The Hotel Villa Jardín offers campers little more than four parking slots behind the motel, but there is not much else available in this area. The hotel itself is a Best Western and quite nice, the management seems to like RVers.

Parking is parallel parking along a paved driveway. There are four electrical sockets, a water faucet, and the area is lighted. It is behind the hotel and seems secure. The swimming pool is nearby and there are restrooms available with toilets and sinks but no showers. There are a tennis court and a children's play area also behind the hotel. The hotel has a restaurant and some English is spoken. A huge new Soriana supermarket is across the street.

If you are approaching from the north on Mex. 49 from Chihuahua zero your odometer as you cross the periférico and continue straight ahead. From the west or south it is best to start from this same point, take a look at the map, this is a confusing city. Fortunately there are quite a few signs for the Villa Jardín. Continue south for 1.9 miles (3.1 km) from the intersection of Mex. 49 and the periferico until you reach Independencia. Turn right and follow the road as it jogs left around a statue at 2.4 miles (3.9 km). You will come to a stop light at 3.3 miles (5.3 km). The hotel is directly ahead and to the right, the Soriana supermarket ahead and to the left.

Side Trips from Torreón

At the point where the three states of Chihuahua, Durango and Coahuila meet is the **Zone of Silence**. This is an area of remote desert. There are reports of mysterious happenings in the zone: radio signals are blocked, meteorites fall, and UFO's land. To get here drive north on free Mex. 49 about 67 miles (110 km) to a road going east. The Zone of Silence is about 55 miles (90 km) away on poor gravel roads requiring a high-clearance vehicle. You should also have a good map and supplies for the desert.

URUAPAN, MICHOACÁN (OOH-ROO-AH-PAN)
Population 190,000, Elevation 5,500 ft (1,672 m)

A semi-tropical climate has given the city of Uruapan the reputation as one of Mexico's top agricultural centers. Coffee, avocados, bananas, and oranges are grown in the region. Travelers often find this a convenient place to stop on the trip down Mex. 37 to the coast at Playa Azul. Sights worth a look in Uruapan include the **Parque Nacionál Eduardo Ruiz** and the **headwaters of the Río Cupatitzio**, and the **Plaza Principal** with the **Museo Regional Huatapera** alongside. Interesting side trips from the city include the Paricutín Volcano and Tzaráracua Waterfall.

Campground No. 1

TRAILER PARK LA JOYITA
    Address: Estocolmo No. 22, Uruapan,
    Mich., Mexico
    Telephone: (452) 3-03-64

Price: Low

GPS Location: N 19° 23' 53.4", W 102° 03' 17.6"

This is a tiny trailer park quite near central Uruapan. The facilities are old and simple but fine for a quick stopover. We think that the best feature of the campground is that it is only a few blocks from a newish Comercial Mexicana and a good multi-screen movie house. Since most U.S.

movies shown in Mexico are in their original English with Spanish subtitles you can catch up on a first-run movie while staying here and walk home afterwards.

The campground has three back-in slots with electricity, sewer, and water. There are an additional few slots with electricity and water only. All are located in a courtyard with a few motel rooms and quite a few parked cars. The restrooms are old and reasonably clean and have hot water for showers.

The campground is in the southeastern section of Uruapan. Headed south on Paseo Gral. Lázaro Cárdenas you will see the Comercial Mexicana on your left. Turn left at the second possible place after this sighting, the road is a divided boulevard here and the turn is easy if you are prepared. Drive east one and a half blocks, you'll see the campground entrance on your right. The street out front can be a little loud at night, several street-side stall-type restaurants are located there and it is a busy place on weekend nights.

Campground No. 2

MOTEL PIE DE LA SIERRA
   Address: Km. 4 Carretera Uruapan-Carapán
   (Apdo. 153), Uruapan, Mich., Mexico
   Telephone: (452) 4-25-10, (452) 4-97-12
   Fax: (452) 2-25-10

   Price: Low

GPS Location: N 19° 26' 28.4", W 102° 04' 27.4"

The Motel Pie De La Sierra is located high above Uruapan to the north. It has very nice facilities except that the RV park serves as overflow parking for the popular disco and party facilities. During the week this is the place to stay in Uruapan, on weekends you might wish that you had a quieter location.

There are 20 back-in parking spaces with electricity and water. There is sewer too, unfortunately the drains are about an inch and a half in diameter, suitable only for a small hose. Campers use the pool restrooms which are tiled and clean, they have hot water showers. This very nice hotel has a beautiful pool area overlooking town and also a restaurant/bar and game room. Also, of course, there is the disco. Access for big rigs is tight, you will want to park outside the gate and take a look to see if you can get past the two bad spots. These are at the gate itself, you have to make a quick left just inside it, and up the hill in front of the reception office where you have to make a tight 180 degree turn. This may be no problem, it just depends upon how cars are parked in the driveway. Bus and taxi service to downtown Uruapan are available.

From Uruapan drive north out of town toward Carapán on Mex. 37. You'll see the motel on the right just past the Km. 71 marker. This is 1.1 mile north (1.8 km) of the intersection in town of Mex. 37 and Mex. 14 from Pátzcuaro.

Side Trips from Uruapan

Most people have probably heard the story of **Paracutín**. In 1943 a farmer was plowing his field when the ground began shaking and a brand-new volcano began building where there had been nothing before. For 9 years the volcano erupted, in the process burying two nearby villages and rising to approximately 1,700 feet above the corn field. Today you can drive to the village of Angahuán and then walk or ride a horse with a guide to view the mountain or even visit a church that is partially buried in lava. Angahuán itself is of interest, it is a Purépecha Indian village. You can reach Angahuán by driving north on Mex. 37 from Uruapan for 10 miles (16 km) and then following a small paved road to the left for 13 miles (21 km) to the village.

The 60-meter high **Tzararacua Falls** are located about 6 miles (10 km) south of Uruapan on Mex. 37. The river here, the Cupatitzio, is the same one that arises in Uruapan at the National Park. There is a car park and many stairs leading down to the viewpoint.

VALLE DE BRAVO, MÉXICO (VAH-yay day Brah-voe)
Population 16,000, Elevation 5,950 ft (1,808 m)

The town of Valle de Bravo is another favorite weekend destination for crowds from Mexico City which is only 87 miles (140 km) distant. This upscale resort village overlooks a large *presa* or reservoir called Lake Avandaro. The high surrounding mountains are covered with pines, the town sometimes feels like it is located in Switzerland or the mountains above the French Riviera instead of Mexico. There are lots of good tourist facilities here, especially restaurants. Good campgrounds are scarce in this neighborhood but there is one place, or perhaps two, as we detail below.

Campground

EMBARCADERO LAUMASE
  Address: San Gaspar del Lago, Carr. Valle
  de Bravo-Colorines, Valle de Bravo, Méx.,
  Mexico
  Telephone: (726) 2-39-35, (726) 2-26-42
  Price: Low

GPS Location: N 19° 13' 30.1", W 100° 08' 40.5"

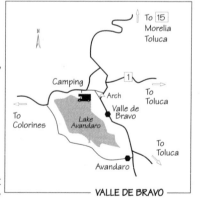

VALLE DE BRAVO

The Embarcadero Laumase is a boat launching and storage facility conveniently located for a visit to Valle de Bravo. You'll also see some Mexican RVs stored here. It is particularly good if you are driving a big rig and have a smaller vehicle for driving on into town.

There is a lot of room on a large sandy and grassy field extending to the water.

There are no hookups although the owner may stretch an electrical cord for you. Water is also available. There are nice new tiled bathrooms with hot showers. This is a popular boating facility with storage and launching, weekends and holidays are likely to be very crowded and busy. At other times things are peaceful. The restaurants and shops of Valle de Bravo are about 3 miles (4.8 km) away, busses run past the gate of the campground.

As you descend into Valle de Bravo from the north you will come to a Pemex on the left and see an arch across the road ahead. The road to Colorines is signed to the right. Turn right toward Colorines, you will see the Embarcadero Laumase on your left on the lake shore in 1.1 miles (1.8 km).

Other Camping Possibilities

The Family Ortega or Don Antonio Trailer Park is listed in some guides and does exist, unfortunately it seems to be closed much of the time and is very difficult to reach, particularly in a rig of any size. There are several back-in spaces with electricity, water, and sewer in the front yard of a beautiful house. All are on a well tended lawn, tents are welcome. We've talked to many people who have tracked this place down and no one who found someone home. Generally the gate is closed and no one answers the bell. The address is Av. de Carmen 26, Avándaro. It is not difficult to find if you know that it is in the suburb of Avandaro, which is some 4 miles (7 km) south of the arch that you reach when you enter the lake area from the north. You follow the convoluted and sometimes constricted lakeshore to get there, following occasional signs for Avandaro. When you finally reach the village you will pass a Pemex on your left, just beyond the main road turns right, go straight, this is Av. de Carmen. The campground is on the right about .2 miles (.3 km) up this road, there is a hanging sign saying Otero and you can see the camping sites in the front yard. The GPS Location is N 19° 09' 32.1", W 100° 07' 04.1". The route described is not suitable for rigs larger than van size, other routes may exist but we have not searched them out. You should not explore the Valle de Bravo area in a big rig, you could find yourself stuck in a bad situation because some roads are narrow or steep. On the other hand, if you approach as described in the instructions for finding Embarcadero Laumase and then use a small car or busses for exploring you should have no problems.

ZACATECAS, ZACATECAS (SAH-KAH-TAY-KAHS)
Population 110,000, Elevation 8,200 ft (2,493 m)

Zacatecas is a well-kept secret. It gets few visitors from outside Mexico. This colonial mining city has a spectacular site in a valley below two peaks. There is a **aerial tramway** between the two for great views of the city. The **cathedral** here is generally considered the best example of a Churrigueresque church in Mexico and the downtown area, built of rose-colored sandstone, would seem straight out of an earlier century if it weren't for the cars. Two museums in this town shouldn't be missed: the **Museo Pedro Coronel** with a large and varied art collection and the **Museo Rafael Coronel Mexican mask collection**.

Campground No. 1

HOTEL HACIENDA DEL BOSQUE
  Address: Heroes de Chapultepec 801,
  Zacatecas, Zac., Mexico
  Telephone: (492) 4-66-66
  Fax: (492) 4-65-65

Price: Expensive

GPS Location: N 22° 46' 28.2", W 102° 37' 12.8"

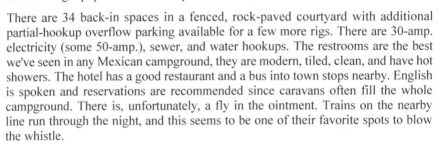

Zacatecas has a brand-new first-class campground (with a price to match). Owned by the same people who run the Motel del Bosque, the Hotel Hacienda del Bosque is becoming a popular caravan stop.

There are 34 back-in spaces in a fenced, rock-paved courtyard with additional partial-hookup overflow parking available for a few more rigs. There are 30-amp. electricity (some 50-amp.), sewer, and water hookups. The restrooms are the best we've seen in any Mexican campground, they are modern, tiled, clean, and have hot showers. The hotel has a good restaurant and a bus into town stops nearby. English is spoken and reservations are recommended since caravans often fill the whole campground. There is, unfortunately, a fly in the ointment. Trains on the nearby line run through the night, and this seems to be one of their favorite spots to blow the whistle.

The campground is at the intersection of Mex. 45 from Durango and the Mex. 54 cutoff south to Guadalajara. This is not the same intersection discussed in the driving directions to the Servicio Morelos Trailer Park below, it is about 6 miles (9.7 km) east toward Zacatecas from that one.

Campground No. 2

MOTEL DEL BOSQUE
  Address: Periférico Diaz Ordaz, Zacatecas,
  Zac., Mexico
  Telephone: (492) 2-07-45

Price: Low

GPS Location: N 22° 46' 41.1", W 102° 34' 27.9"

It would be tough to beat the location of this campground for campers interested in visiting central Zacatecas. The motel overlooks the downtown area, the walk to the central area is less than a mile. The teleférico (overhead tram) terminal to La Bufa is right below the campground.

There is room for about 6 rigs to back in on a large rock-paved area near the entrance to the motel. The spaces have electricity and water hookups, they have no view. The parking area slopes a bit so you'll have to level your rig. The one restroom is in poor repair and was not too clean when we visited, it has a hot water shower. The motel has a reasonably-priced restaurant that overlooks the town. Access to the campground is down a short winding road from the Periférico, rigs to 26 feet should have no problems although they may have to do a little careful maneuvering to make one turn. You can walk a short distance down the hill to catch a bus to the central area or walk there in less than 15 minutes.

Mex. 45 and Mex. 49 are one road running right through Zacatecas. Just northwest of the city center they climb a hill, at the top is the exit to the Periférico. Take this exit, it is marked Quebradilla, Centro, and Teleférico from both directions. The exits from both directions enter a traffic circle above the highways, follow the sign for La Bufa, there is also a sign for the Motel del Bosque painted on a wall next to this road. After .8 miles (1.3 km) you'll see the motel entrance on the right.

Campground No. 3

SERVICIO MORELOS TRAILER PARK
    Address: Panamericana Guadalajara -
    Saltillo Km. 678, Zacatecas, Zac., Mexico
    Telephone: (492) 1-03-67

Price: Low

GPS Location: N 22° 51' 40.0", W 102° 37' 26.0"

The Servicio Morelos Trailer Park has long been a popular stopover for folks heading south to Guadalajara or the coast through the interior. It is well away from any urban traffic and is an excellent place for a late arrival and early start.

The campground has 16 back-in spaces with electricity, sewer and water hookups. Since the campground is rarely crowded many people don't bother to back in and unhook. The service station out front is a big modern one with toilets but no showers. It also has a modern Telmex phone and a small store. The campground is fenced and gated. Someone will be by to collect, ask for a receipt for proof of payment.

The campground is located at the junction of Mex. 45 from Durango and Mex. 54 from Saltillo about 8 miles (13 km) northwest of Zacatecas near the 15 Km. marker of Mex. 45. Mex. 45 is four-lane with the opposing lanes about 1.4 miles (2.3 km) apart at this point, you won't be able to see the Pemex and campground if you are traveling toward Zacatecas on Mex. 45 but it is obvious from both Mex. 45 northwest-bound and Mex. 54.

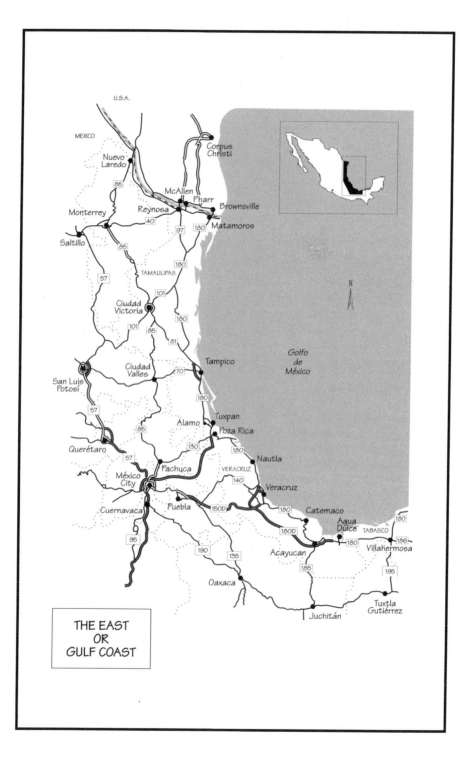

THE EAST
OR
GULF COAST

CHAPTER 8

THE EAST OR GULF COAST

INTRODUCTION

Mexico's Gulf Coast is a long semi-circle of mostly deserted beaches backed by often swampy flatlands. Unfortunately, because of the wetlands behind the beaches access is sometimes difficult or not possible. Fortunately, if you can get to the beach, it is likely to be uncrowded and very good for fishing, birding, and beachcombing. For our purposes in this book the Gulf Coast stretches from the border at Matamoros to the town of Villahermosa in the State of Tabasco, a driving distance of about 900 miles (1,470 km). The coast east of Villahermosa is covered in our Yucatán chapter.

Much of the Mexican Gulf Coast is oil country. This means that you will pass through areas that are industrial, full of trucks, and generally not very pleasant. Don't let the bad places bother you. The Yucatán and Chiapas at the end of your journey are outstanding, and even the Gulf Coast has its rewarding destinations.

Winter is the time to visit the Gulf Coast. Summer, from May to September is extremely hot and humid. Temperatures from October to April can be hot also, but bearable.

ROAD SYSTEM

The Gulf Coast serves as the shortest route south to both the Yucatán Peninsula and Chiapas. Unfortunately the roads are not great. Most are two lanes, and many stretches are heavily used by trucks and do not get nearly enough maintenance. In general the condition of roads tends to be bad at the end of the summer rainy season and gets better as they are gradually repaired during the winter dry season.

Mex. 180 serves as the main arterial. It snakes down the coast from Matamoros and eventually ends at Puerto Juárez, now a Cancún suburb. For the most part traffic along the Gulf Coast stays on 180 although there are a few short-cuts and bypasses around larger towns.

A new addition to the coastal route is a new toll road which runs from just north of Veracruz to a point near La Venta, about 80 miles (130 km) west of Villahermosa. This is one of the new private toll roads that are appearing throughout Mexico and is very expensive. It does effectively cut a day from the drive south, you can now easily drive from the campgrounds on the Emerald Coast to Rancho Hermanos Graham near Villahermosa. Unfortunately to do this you must bypass both Veracruz and Lake Catemaco, a difficult decision.

If you are not bound for the Yucatán there are several places along the coast where you might choose to turn inland. Mex. 85 (the Pan American Highway) is a good road leading from the border at Nuevo Laredo through Monterrey and then into the Gulf Coast area at Ciudad Victoria before winding its way south through mountains to Mexico City. Mex. 101 from Ciudad Victoria to the southwest is small and uncrowded as it crosses rugged mountains and desert until connecting with Mex. 80 and Mex. 57 into San Luis Potosí. Mex. 70 provides a direct route from Tampico to San Luis Potosí while Mex. 130 does the same from Poza Rica to Pachuca where you can catch a good toll road south to Mexico City. There's a well-traveled toll road from Veracruz to Mexico City, Mex. 150D. In the south, near Minatitlán, the two lane Mex. 185 cuts south across the Isthmus of Tehuantepec to the Pacific, a relatively low altitude route.

At Villahermosa travelers bound for the Yucatán face a choice of routes. Mex. 180

PYRAMID OF THE NICHES AT EL TAJÍN

goes north to the coast and crosses a string of sandy islands until reaching the Yucatán. This route now has bridges across all of the inlets and is very popular. The alternative is Mex. 186 which runs inland and passes near Palenque before heading to the northeast through Escárcega to the Yucatán. Both routes take about the same time. Many folks follow one route while bound for the Yucatán and the other on their return.

HIGHLIGHTS

The Gulf Coast is often considered little but a corridor to the south, but there are many places along the way that are destinations in themselves or well worth a short visit.

The far north near the Texas border is very popular with sportsmen. It has good fishing and hunting. Lake Vincent Guerrero to the northeast of Ciudad Victoria is known for its bass fishing as are several other lakes in the region. The coast through here also offers great fishing where it is accessible. There are campgrounds at La Pesca to the east of Ciudad Victoria.

The Emerald Coast between Poza Rica and Nautla offers several good campgrounds with an excellent beach and some good side trips. The El Tajín ruins nearby are a well-known site off the beaten track that does not get many visitors because there are no big tourist destinations nearby. The small town of Papantla is home to the flying *Voladores* you'll see performing far from home in many other parts of Mexico.

Veracruz is the traditional port for Mexico City. It has great historical importance, its own ambiance, and plenty to see and do. Fortunately there is a campground here so you can easily make an extended visit.

The Sierra de los Tuxtlas to the south of Veracruz offer a mountainous break from the sometimes monotonous lowlands. You can stay at Lake Catemaco, make day trips to the nearby towns, and take a boat tour of the lake while enjoying cool evenings.

Finally, the modern town of Villahermosa is known for its La Venta Park Museum containing giant Olmec heads in an outdoor setting. If this park helps you develop a deeper interest you might also want to visit the Museo Regional de Antropologiía at CICOM.

THE CAMPGROUNDS

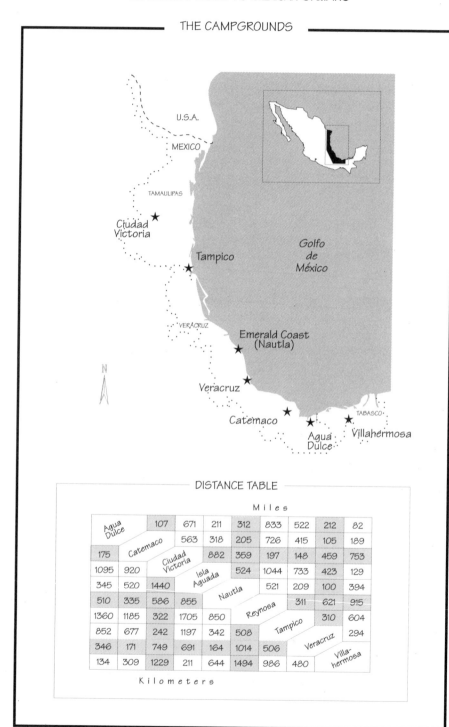

U.S.A.

MEXICO

TAMAULIPAS

Ciudad Victoria

Tampico

Golfo de México

VERACRUZ

Emerald Coast (Nautla)

Veracruz

Catemaco

Agua Dulce

Villahermosa

TABASCO

DISTANCE TABLE

Miles

Agua Dulce	107	671	211	312	833	522	212	82
	Catemaco	563	318	205	726	415	105	189
175		**Ciudad Victoria**	882	359	197	148	459	753
1095	920		**Isla Aguada**	524	1044	733	423	129
345	520	1440		**Nautla**	521	209	100	394
510	335	586	855		**Reynosa**	311	621	915
1360	1185	322	1705	850		**Tampico**	310	604
852	677	242	1197	342	508		**Veracruz**	294
346	171	749	691	164	1014	506		**Villa-hermosa**
134	309	1229	211	644	1494	986	480	

Kilometers

SELECTED CITIES AND THEIR CAMPGROUNDS

AGUA DULCE, VERACRUZ

Rancho Hermanos Graham, a popular campground located here, is covered in the Villahermosa section of this chapter.

CATEMACO, VERACRUZ (KAH-TEH-MAH-KO)
Population 41,000, Elevation 1,200 ft (354 m)

The Sierra de los Tuxtlas are a small isolated range of mountains sitting near to the coast south of Veracruz. These are volcanic mountains with lush vegetation, a pleasant change from the hot surrounding flatlands. You'll appreciate the altitude in the evenings, they are cooler than down on the flats. Mex. 180 runs right through the mountains, you can now bypass them on a toll road from Veracruz to La Venta but the tolls are high and you will probably enjoy spending at least one night at Lake Catemaco.

There are really three interesting towns in these mountains: Santiago Tuxtla, San Andrés Tuxtla, and Catemaco. You'll pass through all of them as you follow Mex. 180 but only the last has campgrounds, and it sits beside very scenic Lake Catemaco. The town has become something of a ecotourism destination lately. Boat tours on the lake are very popular, you can see a great variety of bird life and even some Asian monkeys on one of the islands in the lake. Catemaco is famous in Mexico for its brujos, or witches. You can consult with one or buy charms and herbs at the markets here to fix what ails you.

Campground No. 1

LA CEIBA TRAILER PARK
    Address: Malecón Esq. Unión s-n,
    Catemaco, Ver., Mexico
    Telephone: (294) 3-00-51

        Price: Low

For convenience to the delights of Catemaco this campground can't be beat. It is near the water-front malecón across the street from the lake. Boat tours and the central area of town are a short stroll away. The camping area here is a grassy yard next to and behind a small restaurant.

This campground does not have a lot of formal facilities. Electricity is made available by stringing extension cords. There's a bathroom with a flushing toilet and shower, nothing fancy but the water in the shower is hot. The restaurant can provide meals and they are more than happy to arrange boat tours of the lake. Since the campground really doesn't have any defined parking spaces and is somewhat uneven larger rigs might not be too comfortable here, you can take a look and if you don't think La Ceiba is suitable you can go on to Playa Azul. Tent campers will be quite comfortable.

Easiest access is from the southern-most town entrance right next to the lake, just before you cross the Puente Catemaco if you're heading south. After leaving Mex. 180 at the Puente Catemaco you'll see La Ceiba on the left in .1 mile (.2 km). This route is the easiest for all rigs once you're off the highway, but you should take a look before attempting it because rigs with a big rear overhang might have a problem with the abrupt concave angle of the road surface as it descends from the highway to the town street. The alternate route is to take the main Catemaco exit some six-tenths of a mile north and drive through the main part of town as you work you way down to the lake shore.

Campground No. 2

PLAYA AZUL
    Address: Km. 2 Carretera a Sontecompan, Catemaco, C.P. 95870 Ver., Mexico
    Telephone: (294) 3-00-01

Price: Low

Play Azul is a hotel with a few spaces set aside for RV's. It sits on the lake shore about 1.5 miles (2.4 km) from Catemaco and will work well for RV's of all sizes but is not suitable for tents.

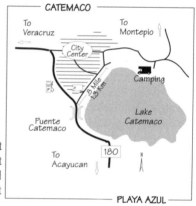

The hotel has set aside four hotel rooms as its "Trailer Park". There are no furnishings in the rooms at all, but the bathrooms are usable and there is hot water in the showers. Parking is on the flat paved drive in front of the rooms and you can string an extension cord for electricity and be comfortable. In addition to these rooms there is a parking area behind the motel that could be used for dry camping if the "Trailer Park" rooms are full.

The Play Azul has a nice swimming pool and terrace area next to the pool and a dock where launches for lake tours can embark. There's a restaurant but this often is not open.

To find the Playa Azul take the town entrance right next to the lake, just before you cross the Puente Catemaco if you're heading south, just as is described above in the La Ceiba entry. Drive along the malecón until you reach its end about .8 miles (1.3 km) from Mex. 180. Watch carefully because you might get stuck in a short road extension at the end of the malecón and be forced to back out. Turn 90 degrees left just before the extension and drive about .2 mile (.3 km) until you see a road to your right marked with a sign with an arrow for Playa Azul, which is 1.2 miles (2.0 km) away. You will see a big sign painted on the wall marking the entrance to the hotel on the right.

Side Trips from Catemaco

The town of **Santiago Tuxtla**, 16 miles (26 km) toward Veracruz on Mex. 180 has an Olmec head in the central square and a small museum with Olmec sculptures. If the museum piques your interest you may want to continue on to the important Olmec ceremonial site of **Tres Zapotes**. Take the paved Mex. 25 south from town toward Isla 13 miles (21 km) to Tibernal. From there a small road takes you north to the town of Tres Zapotes with its own museum and the site. There's not much to see at the site but many of the finds are in the museum.

San Andrés Tuxtla is the largest town in the Tuxtlas, it has a population of about 50,000. It is 7 miles (12 km) from Catemaco. You might want to visit the Santa Clara cigar-manufacturing factory there and take an informal tour. This city is the transportation hub for the Tuxtlas, if you don't feel like touring in your car you can use the local busses to get almost anywhere.

Salto de Exipantla is a 150-foot waterfall near Catemaco. The road to the waterfall cuts off Mex. 180 about 2.5 miles (4 km) on the Catemaco side of San Andrés Tuxtla. About 4 miles (6 km) down the small road you'll see some small restaurants and the beginning of the steps to the falls.

CIUDAD VICTORIA, TAMAULIPAS (SEE-OOH-DAWD VEEK-TOH-REE-AH)
Population 210,000, Elevation 900 ft (274 m)

Ciudad Victoria is a small city without much in the way of tourist attractions. Still, it is a pleasant place to kick back and get accustomed to being in a foreign country, the perfect stop for your first night in Mexico. Banking, groceries, and supplies are easy to find. You can drive around town without worrying much about traffic or finding a place to park.

The city is the capital of the state of Tamaulipas. People here work for the government, for suppliers for the agriculture in the area, or in light manufacturing. All of this activity makes Ciudad Victoria relatively prosperous by Mexican standards.

If you do feel like taking in a sight or two you might take a look at the **Anthropology and History Museum** which has a variety of artifacts from the area or take a short 25 Km. drive to **El Chorrito** waterfall where the Virgin of Guadalupe is said to have once appeared.

There is a huge new Soriana supermarket only a half-mile from the Victoria Trailer Park. It's an easy walk if you don't feel like moving your vehicle. Just turn to the left when you leave the park. You'll enjoy exploring the store and seeing the relative prices of things here compared to back home. Since this is likely to be your first stop in Mexico you will probably need money. There is a Banamex bank with a cash machine about a quarter-mile past the Soriana store.

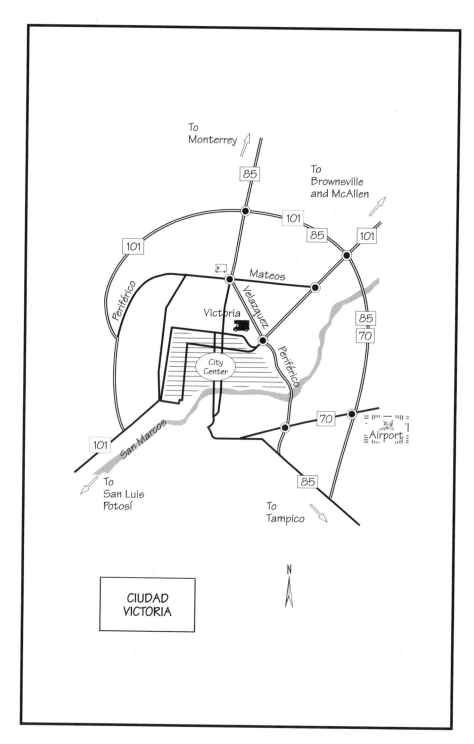

CIUDAD
VICTORIA

N

Campgrounds

VICTORIA TRAILER PARK
  Address: Blvd. F. Velazquez (Apdo. 475),
  Cd. Victoria, Tamps., Mexico
  Telephone: (131) 2-48-24

  Price: Moderate

This is a very large park with about 150 spaces with electricity, water and sewer. Many of these spaces are pull-throughs. The Victoria is a large grassy field sitting behind the owner's house. It is enclosed by a wall, there are a few small rental rooms along one side. Most sites have electricity, water, and sewer connections.

Amenities include restrooms, hot showers, a covered patio area used by caravans for get-togethers and a small gift shop.

The park's location is convenient, bus service from just in front of the park will take you downtown. Ciudad Victoria is small enough that driving into the central downtown area is no problem.

The owner/managers speak English and have done some RVing in the U.S. themselves so they are simpatico. It seems like every RVer who ever stayed in their park is on a first name basis with one or the other of them. RV tours love this place, if you're here during their season you're likely to share the campground with at least one of them. This is no problem since this is a big campground.

The best way to get to the campground, especially with a big rig, is from the point where Mex. 85 from Monterrey meets the outer bypass ring. Drive toward the center of town for 1.9 miles (3.1 km) until you reach a glorieta or traffic circle. Go around it and take the exit that is about 300 degrees from where you entered. The street is Blvd. F. Velazquez, you can recognize it because it is a divided road with trees growing in the middle. You may note some campers parked on the corner just as you enter the glorieta, this is the El Jardin Motel and Trailer Park, an alternate to the Victoria Trailer Park. Drive east on Blvd. F. Velazquez for .6 mile (1 km), the entrance to the park is on the right. Watch carefully for a cement fence with the trailer park sign painted on it, the entrance is just past the fence and is quite obscure. Don't miss it or you'll have to go on down the road and use a retorno.

Other Camping Possibilities

The only other campground in town is the **El Jardin Motel and Trailer Park**. It is near the Victoria. This place is very small but there are often several rigs there. If the Victoria doesn't suit you may want to check it out.

There are several places dedicated to sportsmen north of Ciudad Victoria near **Lake Guerrero**. These might be viable for those coming directly south from McAllen or Brownsville, Texas, especially bass fishermen.

La Pesca, on the coast directly east of Ciudad Victoria has several campgrounds. The area is reported to have very good fishing and is only a two-hour drive from Ciudad Victoria. La Pesca is also known as one of the only good surfing spots on the Gulf Coast. You might want to use it as an alternative to Ciudad Victoria if you're headed south and don't mind a small side trip. To do this you would bypass Ciudad Victoria by taking Mex. 180 and the added side trip would only be 31 miles (50 km) from the highway to the ocean.

Emerald Coast, Veracruz (near Nautla)
Elevation: Sea Level

This very pleasant coast and its continuous beach stretch for about 25 miles (40.8 km) north of the small town of Nautla. It is a popular holiday destination for residents of Poza Rica to the north and Veracruz to the south. There is an unsophisticated cluster of campgrounds, hotels and condos some 9 miles (14 km) north of Nautla. As you drive down the Gulf Coast from Texas this may be the first place you'll be tempted to stay for another day, then another, and another. The beach can be walked for miles, swimming is fine if you watch for undertow. Coconut palms run continuously for miles between the highway and the water. There are no large stores nearby but small local ones supply the basics.

Campground No. 1

TRAILER PARK QUINTA ALICIA
  Address: Carret Nautla-Poza Rica Km 84,
    Monte Gordo, Ver., Mexico
  Telephone: (232) 1-00-42

        Price: Low

The Quinta Alicia is a small campground with a very attractive location right on the beach. For such a small campground it has good facilities and the management is first-rate, this is a favorite for all kinds of campers. Even if you're in a hurry to get south you'll be tempted to stay for a few days. Space is tight for big rigs so caravans usually choose to stay in one of the other campgrounds nearby.

The campground has about forty spaces. They are located in a coconut grove between the highway and the ocean. At the entrance there is a small store with a few necessities, including beer. Eighteen level sites with electricity, water, and sewer are arranged off the entrance drive. A grassy area beyond is for those not needing utilities if the utility sites are full. There are even a few electrical outlets available for these sites. There's a well-maintained swimming pool and beyond is the beach. Swimming on the beach is fine, ask the managers about the safest places. The bathroom and shower building is clean and has hot showers. English is not spoken here.

Finding this campground is easy. There's a good sign on Mex. 180 about 7 miles (11 km) north of Nautla near kilometer marker 84. It's on the ocean side, of course.

Campground No. 2

HOTEL PLAYA PARAISO DEL TAJÍN
   Address: Carretera No. 180 Km. 83, Costa
   Esmeralda del Tajín, Ver., Mexico
   Telephone: (232) 1-00-44

Price: Low

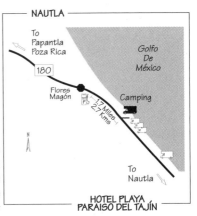

As you turn in the gate of the Playa Paraiso there's a big two story white motel building on the right. The entrance road runs around the left of the motel building, down almost to the beach, and then left about 100 yards to a very large lot filled with palms. There are at least 40 usable spaces here in varying stages of repair. Most have electricity, water and sewer. While not usually quite as popular as the Quinta Alicia the Playa Paraiso has its own charm.

Facilities at Playa Paraiso include two swimming pools which are both well-maintained. One is located in the trailer park area, the other in front of the motel. Both can be used by people staying at the trailer park. The trailer park bathroom facilities are somewhat marginal but include working toilets and showers that usually have hot water. The motel also has a restaurant.

As you enter the Costa Esmeralda campground area this is the first place you'll see. They say their address is Km 83 while the Quinta Alicia says theirs is Km 84. The distance between them is 2.9 miles (4.7 km). You figure it out.

Other Camping Possibilities

There are several campgrounds along the Costa Esmeralda near the two described above. These include the Torre Molino, El Pino Trailer Park, Trailer Park RV Center El Corsario, and the Playa Dorada. All of these are between the Playa Paraiso and the Quinta Alicia. There's also a place called the Trailer Park Neptuno less than a mile south of the Quinta Alicia.

In Poza Rica, just as you are entering town from the south on Mex. 180 you'll see the Poza Rica Inn on the right. Their sign says they take RVs. They are reported to have electricity and to let campers use a shower in one of the rooms.

Also north of the Costa Esmeralda group of campgrounds, this time about 20 miles (33 km), there's the Hotel San Carlos which has a sign outside advertising that it is a trailer park. We've not stopped to check it out or talked to anyone who has.

Side Trips

The important **El Tajín** archeological site and the town of **Papantla** make a good day-trip from the Costa Esmeralda. Papantla is a Totonac Indian town with its own unique atmosphere. You'll see quite a few Totonacs dressed in their traditional costume of loose shirts, tapered white pants, and high-heeled black ankle boots. A lot of vanilla is grown here, you'll have many opportunities to buy the pods and the liquid extract. Papantla is the home of the *Voladores*. You'll see these Indians perform their unique spectacle which involves descending on whirling ropes from the top of a tall pole in many places in Mexico, but this is their home.

The El Tajín site can be reached from both Poza Rica and Papantla. Follow the signs from Papantla for about 7.5 miles (12 km) on back roads to reach this large grouping of pyramids and ball courts, best known for its unique Pyramid of the Niches. The Voladores often perform here using a pole mounted in front of the site entrance buildings.

PAPANTLA'S VOLADORES

TAMPICO, TAMAULIPAS (TAHM-PEE-KO)
Population 650,000, Elevation sea level

The large and active city of Tampico is often bypassed by travelers on their way south. The city is a large port and oil and fishing are also important. If you do venture into town you'll find that it has an active street scene, a sort of run-down Veracruz flavor. Cruise ships actually stop here occasionally so it is difficult to say that the city holds no attraction for the tourist. The city's Huastec Museum is worth a look if you are interested in this pre-Hispanic culture. Playa Miramar is the city beach, it is located about 3 miles (5 km) north of town.

Campgrounds

CAMPESTRE ALTAMIRA
    Address: 2 km. Maxilibramiento, Tampico,
    Tamps., Mexico

Price: Moderate

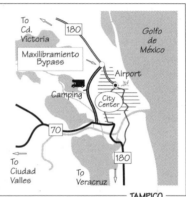

Campestre Altamira is a welcome alternative to the Tampico airport parking lot, the traditional stop-over point in Tampico for RVers heading south along the coast. It's easy to find on the Maxilibramiento bypass.

This is really a holiday resort. It has 10 individual cottages, extensive grounds with two swimming pools, a bar and restaurant, and tennis courts. It is a dry camp for RV's. The usual parking spot is a large grassy field down near the lake. When the ground is wet larger rigs will feel more comfortable parked in the driveway. We've seen as many as 20 large Bounders parked there when a caravan came through. The management may be able to arrange to have an extension cord strung to give you limited electricity. You have the use of the facilities and can use one of the cottages for a hot shower if they're not all full.

From the north follow signs for the Maxilibramiento bypass, a toll road which completely bypasses the crowded town of Tampico to the west. Campestre Altamira is about at 1.2 miles (2 km), on the right. You reach it before the toll booth so if you do want to drive through town you can return after a night in the campground and not pay a toll.

Other Campgrounds

Many people spend the night in the Tampico Airport parking lot. You'll pay almost as much to stay there as at the Campestre Altamira but it is an alternative. The airport is not hard to find. As you come into Tampico from the north on Mex. 180 continue straight at the Maxilibramiento bypass. If you zero your odometer as you pass the bypass entrance and continue to follow the main road, which is a divided boulevard, you'll come to a sort of glorieta at 3.8 miles (6.2 km). Turn left here and almost immediately you'll see the airport on your left.

We've also talked to folks who have spent the night at Playa Miramar north of town. This is probably only a viable alternative if there are several rigs.

VERACRUZ, VERACRUZ (VEH-RAH-CROOZ)
Population 550,000, Elevation sea level

Veracruz is one of Mexico's main east coast seaports, and has a long history as the gateway for entry into Mexico. The Spanish, French, and Americans have all used this port for invited and uninvited visits to Mexico.

As in most Mexican cities the central focus of life in the city for visitors is the main square, in this case the **Plaza de Armas**. Cafes are located in arcades around this small friendly square. The atmosphere is much more Caribbean than in the cities farther north. Veracruz, like other seaports such as New Orleans, Mazatlán, and Buenos Aires , has an excellent pre-Lent *Carnaval* (Mardi gras).

The drive from Balneario Mocambo to the downtown area is straightforward but really only suitable for a smaller vehicle. Use the main north-south road, Av. Adolfo Ruiz Cortines, which runs in front of the Mocambo Hotel. Follow it northwards for 5.5 miles (9.0 km) or so, it twists and turns a bit but the route is obvious. A wrong turn won't do any harm, the road runs along the seawall or malecón for much of the distance. This malecón is another Veracruz attraction. You can spend several hours strolling along it and enjoying the views of the water.

Veracruz is famous for it's seafood, but the best place to get it is not downtown. For seafood you want to go to **Boca del Río**, the small town located about three miles (5 km) south of the RV park.

Access to shopping from the Balneario Mocambo is quite good. The large Plaza de Las Americas shopping center is about half a mile away. You can see it easily from in front of the Hotel Mocambo, Vips and McDonalds signs rise far into the air. Take a right from the hotel then turn left towards the shopping center, there is a large supermarket and many other stores.

Campgrounds

BALNEARIO MOCAMBO
   Address: Playas de Mocambo s/n, Boca del
   Río, Ver., Mexico
   Telephone: (29) 21-02-88

   Price: Low

Since this is the only RV park in Veracruz it is used by most visitors. The other side of the coin is that few campers actually stop in Veracruz so the campground is usually not crowded. Many campground guides list it as having up to 100 sites. There are no utility hookups and parking spaces are not delineated so 100 campers probably

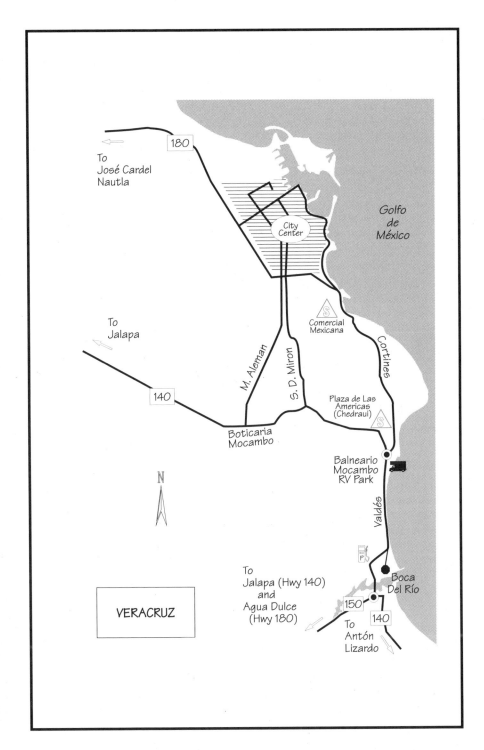

To
José Cardel
Nautla

180

Golfo
de
México

City
Center

To
Jalapa

Comercial
Mexicana

M. Aleman

S. D. Miron

Cortines

140

Plaza de Las
Americas
(Chedraui)

Boticaria
Mocambo

N

Balneario
Mocambo
RV Park

Valdés

To
Jalapa (Hwy 140)
and
Agua Dulce
(Hwy 180)

Boca
Del Río

VERACRUZ

150

140

To
Antón
Lizardo

could squeeze in here, but 40 is a more reasonable number.

Hookups, however, are not where this campground shines. The location is the attraction. Balneario Mocambo is located right on one of the nicest and most interesting beaches around Veracruz, Playa Mocambo. The grassy campground area is situated with only a small grove of palm trees between it and the beach. You will probably have no trouble securing a parking spot with a beautiful view of the water and beach activities.

The RV park is really part of a balneario, or swimming pool and beach facility, but the pools have always been empty in the winter when we have visited. Toilet facilities are basic, they're the same ones used by balneario visitors. There is no hot water for showers, lots of cold though. The park does have a dump station and you can fill with water, no guarantees on the potability. Purify it, just as you always should.

This beach is good for sunning and walking, but the most interesting activity on it is the fishing. Small skiffs pull a long net out to sea and then bring it back in a loop, then a crowd of people pull on both ends of the net from the beach to bring in the school of fish caught in the trap. As the fish are pulled ashore an even larger crowd assembles to see the results, many people buy their evening meal right there.

Access to downtown Veracruz by bus is not difficult. The busy Adolfo Ruiz Cortines runs very close to the park, and there are many busses running along it towards town and the other way towards Boca del Río and its restaurants.

Other Camping Possibilities

Some guidebooks list two other campgrounds in Veracruz, Parador Los Arcos and the Fiesta Trailer Park. Both of these places have fallen victim to development and are no longer open.

VILLAHERMOSA, TABASCO (VEE-YAH-ERR-MOH-SAH)
Population 390,000, Elevation near sea level

Villahermosa has money, you can see it in the wide boulevards and the parks. The main reason most RVers stop here is to visit the **La Venta** outdoor museum. This is a good place to learn about the Olmec culture. The museum is justifiably famous, it contains the oversized heads originally unearthed at La Venta, near the Hermanos Graham RV Park. They are set in a well-tended garden. Visitors follow a walking path around the grounds, many of the trees are identified and there is even a zoo containing Mexican animals.

La Venta is easy to find. You can actually park at the museum with a big rig if you drive past the parking area and then park along the lateral street. Even on a Sunday we had no problem finding plenty of room, we just had to walk back about 200 yards. You can also park in the La Choca parking lot as we have explained below but you'll need transportation to get to the museum.

If you need to visit a large supermarket or wish to pick up a copy of *The News* there is a shopping center with an adjoining Sanborn's on the opposite side of Blvd.

Grijalva just past Paseo Tabasco. It is well-marked with McDonald's golden arches. There is also a huge new French Carrafours supermarket with lots of parking room that you can't miss as you enter town from the west.

Campground

RANCHO HERMANOS GRAHAM
   Address: Agua Dulce, Ver.
   Telephone: (923) 3-06-66

   Price: Low

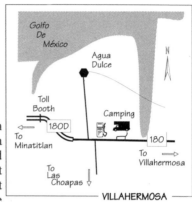

Rancho Hermanos Graham is a tradition with caravans journeying to the Yucatan, it makes a great place to stop between Veracruz and Palenque or the Yucatán. Villahermosa is just another hour and a half down the road, but there are no campgrounds with hookups there and the extremely warm weather in this part of Mexico makes electricity for the air conditioner an important consideration. The distance from Rancho Hermanos Graham to Villahermosa is about 80 miles (131 km)

Hermanos Graham can seem isolated and run-down, almost abandoned, or it can seem like a busy crossroads with lots of activity. It just depends upon the luck of the draw. If a caravan is scheduled or if the pool facility has been rented things will be in pretty good shape. Otherwise you may find long grass and no water because the pump is turned off.

The camping area sits well back from the highway so traffic noise is not a problem. The 88 serviced sites are shaded and grassy, very pleasant. If more people should show up than available serviced sites there is a lot of room for dry camping. This is a good place to meet caravanners and find out how the other half lives. On the other hand, a caravan taxes the electrical system here, if you have a lot of company you may not be able to get your air conditioner to work.

The campground has restrooms and showers, cold ones. There is a swimming pool but it is often not usable, if it has been cleaned up recently it can be quite refreshing. English is sometimes spoken, depending upon who is managing the campground when you arrive.

If you are interested in birds you should keep an eye open for parrots. At dusk you can often see them flying in pairs across the big open field behind the campground. You can recognize them because they are heavy fliers, almost like ducks, they seem to be working pretty hard to stay aloft.

Hermanos Graham is well-signed and located right on Mex. 180 near Km. 38. There are two entrance roads separated by about .1 mile, the second one is often blocked by a locked gate so take the first one through the rancho's yard and between the houses. Be careful when you try to turn here because it is very likely that as soon as you start to slow down the trucks behind you will grab the opportunity to pass, don't accidentally turn in front of them.

From the entrance the campground is about .6 miles (1 km), take the obvious right and then a left away from the road and past a pond and then a balneario or swimming pool area. You'll start to climb a small hill and see the camping sites ahead.

We hear that the campground has recently (spring 97) changed hands and is sometimes not open. Only time will tell whether this campground will remain a dependable option. If you reach the campground and it is not open you might try the large Pemex located just up the road.

Other Camping Possibilities

If you wish to actually stay in Villahermosa for the night there are two often-used locations.

We consider the idea of camping at La Choca fairgrounds to be a bit of a joke, but many people do spend the night here. It is listed in camping guides and some caravans use it. It is a large gravel parking lot with no shade and no hookups. It is also the most popular place in town for driving lessons. Entertainment for campers consists of watching the new drivers go round and round the parking lot until well into the night. An attendant will visit you and collect a fee. There are restrooms in the fairgrounds. If you do spend the night at La Choca there is a convenient nearby grocery. Just take the sidewalk to the left around the park, on the far side you will see a small supermarket across the street. La Choca might also be a good place to leave a large rig while you visit La Venta outdoor museum which is just a couple of miles away.

To find the fairgrounds when you arrive from the north on Mex. 180 begin at the first big glorieta in Villahermosa that has a statue of a man in a suit in the middle. Continue following Blvd. Grijalva but watch carefully for signs for Tabasco 2000 and La Choca. You will want to get to the right onto a lateral road so that you can use an overpass that will take you across Grijalva to the left. The signs will tell you when to do it, the best place is just after the second big glorieta with a statue of women in the center. Turn left on Paseo Tabasco and drive over Grijalva. The road almost immediately goes under a shopping center (yes, under), there's lots of room, and continues past a Holiday Inn to a glorieta. Go all the way around the glorieta so that you are heading back the way you came and almost immediately take a right onto a lateral marked with a La Choca sign. The parking lot is on your right, the entrance is on around the corner.

Some campers have been able to stay at the La Venta Museum itself. The parking area is not particularly spacious but once it has emptied for the night you should have no problem with maneuvering even a big rig. As at the La Choca fairgrounds you'll pay for the privilege. You should ask at the museum itself about the possibility of doing this.

OLMEC HEAD AT LA VENTA

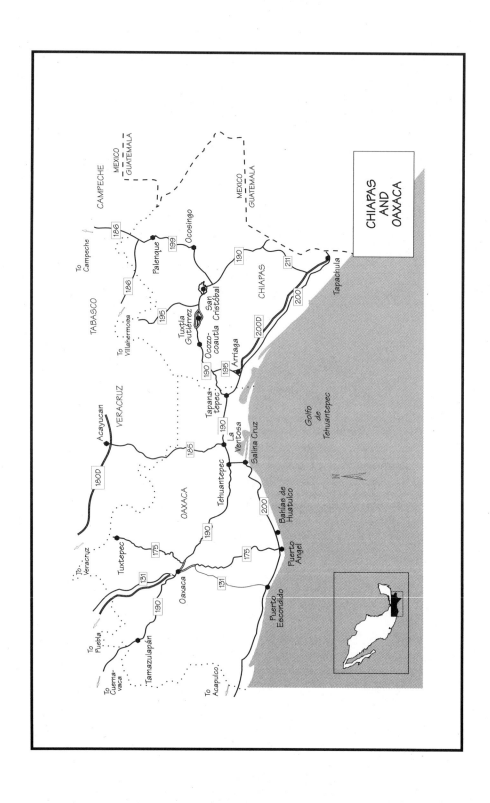

CHAPTER 9

CHIAPAS AND OAXACA

INTRODUCTION

More than anything else it is the Indian cultures that attract visitors to the southern states of Chiapas and Oaxaca. The Chiapas Indians, dressed in bright colors and descended from the Mayas, are ubiquitous throughout the region. Even if you don't visit their remote villages you will see them along the roads and in the towns, especially in San Cristóbal de las Casas. The Oaxacan Indians have a different lineage, they are descendants of the Zapotec and Mixtec cultures and are known for their handicrafts.

Geographically the southern states are composed primarily of highland areas with the low Isthmus of Tehuantepec crossing between them. In northern Chiapas the town of Palenque is at 200 feet (61 m) elevation while only 70 miles (114 km) away (as the crow flies) the town of San Cristóbal de las Casas is at 6,900 feet (2,098 m). Moving west from San Cristóbal de las Casas the country becomes lower and hotter. When they reach Tehuantepec the Oaxacan Pacific coast lures travelers with empty golden beaches while the highland valleys at over 5,000 feet near the state capital city of Oaxaca are filled with ancient archeological sites and small villages famous for their crafts.

ROAD SYSTEM

The road system in this part of Mexico is not really extensive but the area is something of a crossroads. At the Isthmus of Tehuantepec, the narrowest part of Mexico, the distance from the Caribbean to the Pacific coast is only about 125 miles (200 km). Mex. 185 runs north and south across the Isthmus from near Coatzacoalcos in the north to La Ventosa Junction near Tehuantepec. This is the easiest route for large rigs from coast to coast since the road does not gain much altitude or have steep grades. Watch for wind near La Ventosa, however.

From La Ventosa near the Pacific Coast roads lead east and west. Each soon splits with a leg heading inland and a leg following the coast. East of La Ventosa Mex. 190 soon forks into Mex. 200 (at times a toll road) along the coast through Arriaga and Tapachula to Guatemala and Mex. 190 running inland through Tuxtla Gutiérrez and San Cristóbal de las Casas. This road also eventually enters Guatemala, but branches lead north directly to Villahermosa (Mex. 195) and to Palenque and then Villahermosa or the Yucatán (Mex. 199).

West from La Ventosa junction the highway soon reaches Tehuantepec where it splits, one branch following the coast (Mex. 200) and the other (Mex. 190) climbing to the inland city of Oaxaca. These forks are joined farther west by a small steep road (Mex. 175) which descends precipitously from Oaxaca to the coast near several excellent resorts. From Oaxaca several good roads lead north into central Mexico. One is a toll road leading north to Tehuacán and Puebla. The others are Mex. 190, a slower route leading eventually to Cuernavaca and Puebla and scenic Mex. 131 north to Tehuacán and Puebla.

GRÚAS PULLING A TRUCK FROM THE DITCH

HIGHLIGHTS

The states of Chiapas and Oaxaca are blessed with some of Mexico's most interesting archeological sites. Palenque, a Mayan site set in the jungle, is easy to reach and probably most people's favorite of all of the ruins they will see in Mexico. A visit to two more remote sites south of Palenque, Bonampak and Yaxchilán, requires mounting an expedition by air or four-wheel drive. Easier to reach is Toniná near Ocosingo on Mex. 190 between Palenque and San Cristóbal.

The Oaxaca Valley was home to the pre-Columbian Zapotec and Mixtec Indian cultures. Monte Albán, located just outside Oaxaca is huge, and unusually impressive because it sits on top of a mountain. Another very popular site near Oaxaca is Mitla, known for its geometric mosaic facades.

The mountains surrounding San Cristóbal in Chiapas are filled with Tzotzil and Tzeltal Indian villages. Two near the city, San Juan Chamula and Zinacantán, are easy to visit. You will pass through others on Mex. 199 between San Cristóbal and Palenque or on Mex. 195 leading to Villahermosa. Further exploration off the main highways is not difficult, it just requires a vehicle with high clearance.

The villages around Oaxaca are known for their crafts and markets. The towns include Atzompa (green pottery), Arrazola (brightly painted wooden animals), San Bartolo Coyotepec (black pottery), Teotitlan del Valle (wool rugs), and Ocotlán (green pottery, reed crafts). Some of these towns have market days, mini-bus tours to the villages are available from Oaxaca and are really the easiest way to visit.

The Oaxaca Coast offers some of the best beaches in Mexico. Three very different destinations; Huatulco, Puerto Angel, and Puerto Escondido; all have campgrounds of some kind and many tourist amenities.

THE CAMPGROUNDS

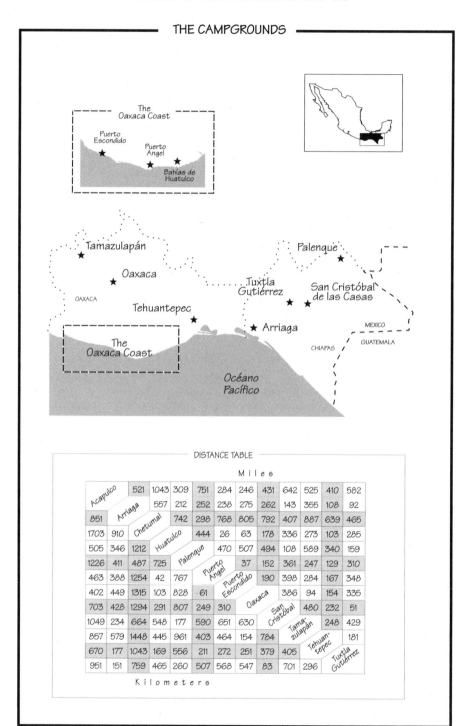

The Oaxaca Coast

Puerto Escondido · Puerto Angel · Bahías de Huatulco

Tamazulapán · Oaxaca · Palenque · Tuxtla Gutiérrez · San Cristóbal de las Casas · Tehuantepec · Arriaga

OAXACA · CHIAPAS · MEXICO · GUATEMALA

The Oaxaca Coast · Océano Pacífico

DISTANCE TABLE

Miles

Acapulco	521	1043	309	751	284	246	431	642	525	410	582
Arriaga		557	212	252	238	275	262	143	355	108	92
851	Chetumal		742	298	768	805	792	407	887	639	465
1703	910	Huatulco		444	26	63	178	336	273	103	285
505	346	1212	Palenque		470	507	494	108	589	340	159
1226	411	487	725	Puerto Angel		37	152	361	247	129	310
463	388	1254	42	767	Puerto Escondido		190	398	284	167	348
402	449	1315	103	828	61	Oaxaca		386	94	154	335
703	428	1294	291	807	249	310	San Cristóbal		480	232	51
1049	234	664	548	177	590	651	630	Tamazulapán		248	429
857	579	1448	445	961	403	464	154	784	Tehuantepec		181
670	177	1043	169	556	211	272	251	379	405	Tuxtla Gutiérrez	
951	151	759	465	260	507	568	547	83	701	296	

Kilometers

SELECTED CITIES AND THEIR CAMPGROUNDS

ARRIAGA, CHIAPAS (AHR-EE-AH-GAW)
Population 25,000, Elevation 184 ft (56 m)

Arriaga is little more than a place to stop for the evening if you are bound east along the Chiapas coast toward Guatemala or wish to explore the beaches around Puerto Arista. It does have a hotel with adequate maneuvering room to accommodate campers and RVs. Arriaga is only 27 miles (44 km) from Mex. 190 between Tuxtla Gutiérrez and Tehuantepec (via either of two different highways) and makes a decent place to spend the night if you find yourself on this stretch of road as darkness approaches.

Campground

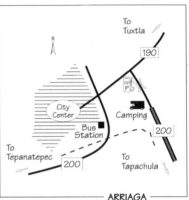

AUTO HOTEL EL PARADOR
   Address: Km 46-7 Carr. Arriaga-Tonalá,
   Arriaga, Chis., Mexico
   Telephone: (966) 2-01-99, (966) 2-01-64

   Price: Inexpensive

No one would mistake the Auto Hotel El Parador for a destination resort, but it does make a good secure place to pull in for the night. The hotel has room for three to four rigs to park on grass at the left end of the buildings as you go in the gate. Park away from the wall of the hotel because people staying in the back units drive through here. You can string a long extension cord from your rig into the laundry room for electricity. There is a cold shower and toilet for camper use, also in the laundry room. The hotel has a decent restaurant, one of the best in town, and there is a pool.

Coming into Arriaga from the southeast on Mex. 200 you can't miss the hotel. It will be on your left just before you enter town. From other directions follow signs for Tonalá, Tapachula, and Mex. 200. You will see the motel on your right just after you enter Mex. 200. This is a divided four-lane highway but there is a turn-around just past the motel so you can easily head back northwest in the morning.

OAXACA, OAXACA (WA-HAH-KA)
Population 300,000, Elevation 5,100 ft (1,540 m)

Oaxaca state has more different Indian groups than any other in Mexico, and the city of Oaxaca has more Indian influence than any other large Mexican city. This is the home of many of those handicrafts that you have been seeing in other areas of Mexico, and this is the place to buy them.

The main square (Plaza de Armas) area is a good place to start your visit. It has a personality of its own and also a lot of nearby locations to shop, including the Old Market, a block south of the square. Many crafts are offered from collections spread right on the square itself. Later you will probably visit other market locations like the Abastos Market on the outskirts of town and in surrounding villages.

Oaxaca is a great walking town. It is filled with churches and colonial houses. There are also several streets set aside just for pedestrians. Be sure to visit the **Regional Museum of Oaxaca**. It is located in the very interesting **Convent of Santo Domingo** and contains the treasure found in a tomb at Monte Albán. The Santo Domingo Church is right next door.

Oaxaca is also known for fiestas. The **Guelaguetza**, in July, is a time for regional dances. The **Night of the Radish**, on December 23, with carvings made from radishes, is one of several pre-Christmas celebrations. The **Day of the Dead** on November first and second is also an important celebration in Oaxaca.

Your daily necessities are easy to find in this large city. The newest and largest supermarket is located south of town on Avenida Universidad. To reach it drive south on Vasconcelos from Mex. 190 just west of Violeta near the Oaxaca Trailer Park. At odometer 1.1 (1.8 km) you will reach a light. Continue straight across the intersection, there will be a Pemex on the corner on your right as you enter Avenida Universidad. Continue straight for one more mile (1.6 km), you will see a shopping center on your right with a large Gigante and a McDonald's.

Campground No. 1

OAXACA TRAILER PARK
   Address: Apdo. 33, Oaxaca , C.P. 68000 Oax., Mexico
   Telephone: (951) 5-27-96

   Price: Moderate

This is definitely the most popular of the two Oaxaca campgrounds. It is a large fenced area with some shade trees. There are about 90 spaces, all with electricity, water, and sewer. None of the spaces are pull-throughs, but some are quite large. Many have patios. Those of you with big rigs will appreciate this place. The campground has restrooms, hot showers, and a meeting room.

Although located in town the campground is still about 2.5 miles (4 km) from the center, perhaps too far to walk. Busses do run close to the park so even if you don't have a small vehicle you will be able to get around.

The campground is located a few blocks north of Mex. 190 where it passes north of central Oaxaca. Turn north on Violeta, one block east of the Volkswagen dealer.

The road is marked as going to Colonia Reforma. Drive north for .5 mile (.8 km) and you will see the Oaxaca Trailer Park on the left.

Campground No. 2

ROSA ISABEL TRAILER PARK
   Telephone: (951) 6-07-70

Price: Moderate

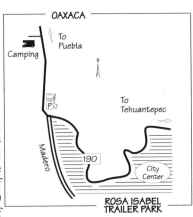

The Rosa Isabel has spaces for 60 rigs, unfortunately the arrangement of the spaces makes access for large rigs difficult. Several houses have been built in the center of the campground and they block access to many of the sites. The park is located right on Mex. 190 so it is easy to locate but a bit noisy. Most of the spaces have electricity, water, and sewer. Restrooms are available and they have hot showers.

This campground is actually outside Oaxaca in the suburb of Loma de Puebla Nueva. Many busses run on the highway so access to the Centro area is not inconvenient.

To find Rosa Isabel Trailer Park drive north from Oaxaca on Mex. 190. From the Y where Mex. 190 meets with Madero (which connects to the periférico and the south end of the city) drive 2.0 miles (3.2 km) and you will see the Rosa Isabel on the left. You cannot turn here, however. Continue another .6 mile (1 km) to a gap in the median where you can turn around.

Side Trips from Oaxaca

The very large and famous Zapotec and Mixtec archeological site **Monte Albán** is located on a hilltop about six miles (10 km) from town. Believe it or not it is different from all of the ruins you have seen so far, you won't want to miss it. There is room to park your RV at the site although you will have to climb a hill to get there.

The **Árbol de Tule** is a 2,000 year old Mexican Cyprus that is 164 feet high and 161 feet in circumference at the base. This is said to make it the largest tree in the world, it is about 2,000 years old. It sits in a church yard and you are asked for 1 peso if you want to get really close, seems like a reasonable fee to us for protecting the tree. It is located only 7 miles (12 km) from Oaxaca on Mex. 190 toward Mitla and Tehuantepec in the town of El Tule.

Mitla, much smaller than Monte Albán, is another well-known Zapotec/Mixtec archeological site near Oaxaca. The ruins are unusual because they are covered with geometric stone carvings known as mosaics. Mitla has a church built in the middle of the ruins and there is a crafts market nearby to serve the many tours that visit the ruins. Mitla is located about 27 miles (43 km) from Oaxaca, also southeast on Mex. 190 but off the main road about 2.5 miles (4 km). Also impressive is **Yagul**. It is reached by a .9 mile (1.5 km) paved road leading off Mex. 190 about 22 miles (35 km) from Oaxaca. You might also look for **Dainzú**, off the road near the 23.5 km marker and **Lambityeco**, also located near the road about 18 miles (29 km) from Oaxaca.

The villages surrounding Oaxaca are known for their crafts and folk art. They can be visited in your own vehicle or by reasonably priced bus tours available through Oaxaca travel agencies. Some of these villages have their own market days and some do not. If you don't want to visit the individual villages you can find their products in the Abastos Market in Oaxaca on Saturday.

Atzompa is the nearest village to Oaxaca, about 5 miles (8 km) west and at the foot of Monte Albán. It is known for green-glazed pottery.

Arrazola is south of Oaxaca on the short road to the village of Zaachila, about 7.5 miles (12 km) from town. Arrazola is known for its *alebrijes*. These weirdly playful carved and brightly painted figures are probably the most popular craft produced in the Oaxaca valley. The first ones were done here by Manuel Jiménez about 15 years ago, they are now widely copied in the Oaxaca area and elsewhere in Mexico. The best are still produced in this village, most go directly into galleries.

Ocotlán is a large town located about 20 miles (32 km) southwest of Oaxaca on Mex. 175. It is known for green-glazed pottery, rugs, and also for products made of reeds by inmates of the prison here. Ocotlán has an excellent market on Friday.

San Bartolo Coyotepec is known for its black pottery. The village is located south of Oaxaca about 7.5 miles (12 km) on Mex. 175 toward Puerto Angel. This style of pottery was invented by Doña Rosa Nieto in 1934. She is no longer alive but her shop is still open. You can watch a a demonstration of the process that is used to produce the black color and shine.

Santo Tomás Jalieza is known for cotton textiles. This village is off Mex. 175 just before you reach Ocotlán.

Teotitlán del Valle produces hand-woven wool products, especially rugs and serapes. It is located about 17 miles (28 km) southeast of Oaxaca off Mex. 190.

Tlacolula, 19 miles (30 km) southeast of Oaxaca on Mex. 190, also has a market, this one on Sunday. It is a close rival to the one in Oaxaca on Saturday. The town is known for its Mescal and castor oil but at the market you'll find many other products from the surrounding Indian communities.

Zaachila, south of Oaxaca and past Arrazola has an Indian market on Thursday. You will find a wide range of crafts here. There are also a few Mixtec ruins.

THE OAXACA COAST

BAHÍAS DE HUATULCO, OAXACA (WA-TOOL-KO)
Elevation sea level

If the Mexican government has its way the Bahías will some day become a mega-resort to rival Cancún and Ixtapa. The natural beauty is certainly here, there are nine bays along 22 miles (32 km) of coastline with wide protected beaches and pristine water. Rocky headlands separate the bays. There are already miles of four-lane boulevard running behind the largely undeveloped coastline. Some of the first road that was installed is already starting to look like it could use a refurbishment but several large hotel chains have taken the plunge, including Club Med and Sheraton.

It appears that the remote location of the resort is slowing development. Right now the big hotels are mostly clustered around Bahía Tangolunda to the east. Santa Cruz de Huatulco on Bahía Santa Cruz seems more of a Mexican-oriented resort, and as such is really much more interesting and fun. Tour busses from all over Mexico arrive, especially during the Christmas holidays, and visitors throng the beach, restaurants, and shops.

RVers do not currently appear to be part of the government's plan. The only real RV park, the Trailer Park Los Mangos, looks like an unwelcome afterthought but is conveniently located between Santa Cruz on the coast and La Crucecita inland.

Campground

TRAILER PARK LOS MANGOS
   Address: Boulevard Benito Juárez, Bahías
   de Huatulco, Oax., Mexico

   Price: Low

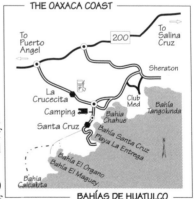

THE OAXACA COAST

To Puerto Angel
To Salina Cruz
200
Sheraton
La Crucecita
Club Med
Bahía Tangolunda
Camping
Bahía Chahué
Santa Cruz
Bahía Santa Cruz
Playa La Entrega
Bahía El Organo
Bahía El Maguey
Bahía Calcauta

BAHÍAS DE HUATULCO

When you first see Los Mangos you will probably not be impressed. Don't be put off, if your rig can manage the entrance the place will grow on you.

This trailer park has room for about 50 campers on a sandy surface in a grove of mango trees next to the road. The sites in front and some around the perimeter are suitable for smaller RVs because they are flat and the trees have more room beneath them. The majority of the sites are really tent sites. Most of the spaces have electricity, a few have water. There are fluorescent light fixtures for many sites, these can be turned off if you don't need them. There are primitive but clean restrooms with flushing toilets and cold showers available.

Larger rigs will not be able to use this place because they will not be able to

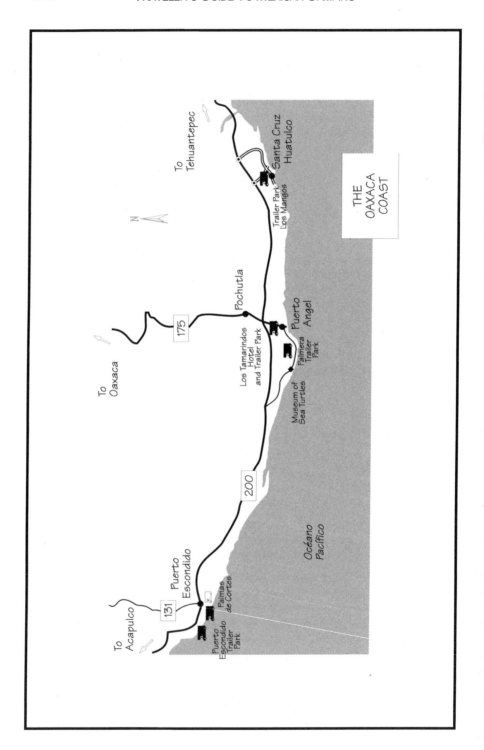

THE
OAXACA
COAST

negotiate the entrance. It is a short but steep ramp, long vehicles will bottom out. Take a close look, however, it is not as bad as it at first appears. Smaller trailers and medium-sized RVs enter and leave with no problems.

The beautiful Playa de Chahue (Chahue Beach) is about a five-minute walk from the trailer park. In the opposite direction the bayside village and port of Santa Cruz is also only five minutes away. Santa Cruz has many excellent waterside restaurants. Slightly farther away, say a fifteen minute walk, is the clean and attractive town of La Crucecita, with a small supermarket, restaurants, and shops.

If you zero your odometer at the point where Mex. 175 meets Mex. 200 near Puerto Angel and drive east, at 25 miles (40.8 km) you will see a divided six-lane road leading toward the water on your right. This is the first of two Huatulco cutoffs. Follow the road to a T at 27.5 miles (44.9 km) and turn right. Almost immediately you will see the Trailer Park Los Mangos on the right. Swing wide to enter and watch out for that ramp.

PUERTO ANGEL (PWEHR-TOE ANN-HELL)
Elevation sea level

Puerto Angel really is the small, sleepy fishing village that everyone says it is. Now you see a few mostly young Europeans and North Americans wandering around town, but this is no tourist resort.

Most of the camping action is west of town on Zipolite beach. The visitors here tend to be tenters and van campers. There is a paved road now out to Zipolite so you would expect a campground for larger RVs to follow soon. In fact, there is now a paved road that leads from Zipolite past Playa Mazunte to the west and connects with the main road some 7.6 miles (12.3 km) west of the old Puerto Angel cutoff. This is a good route for larger rigs because it avoids the steep winding descent into Puerto Angel on the main access road.

You can buy some groceries in Puerto Angel. There is a small supermarket on the west end of the town.

Campground No. 1

PALMERA TRAILER PARK

Price: Inexpensive

The Palmera is suitable for small to medium rigs. The spaces are not really marked out, but there is room for about 10 campers to scatter around on sand under the palms. There are no permanent hookups but you can reach an electrical outlet if you have a long extension cord. The campground has a restroom and

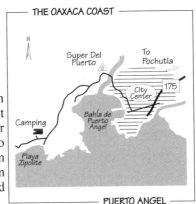

cold shower.

The Palmera is not on the water, but it is very near beautiful Playa Zipolite. You can stroll over to the beach anytime you wish.

Zero your odometer at the point where Mex. 200 and Mex. 175 meet, follow the road leading south from the intersection toward Puerto Angel. At 6.0 miles (9.7 km) you will reach the village of Puerto Angel, turn right when you get to the street along the water at 6.1 miles (9.8 km). Follow the road along the coast, you will see occasional signs for your destination, Zipolite beach. This is a decent paved road with some steep sections.

At 6.4 miles (10.3 km) you will see the Super Del Puerto on the right, this is your source for groceries in Puerto Angel. At 6.5 miles (10.5 km) and again at 7.3 miles (11.8 km) you will come to Y's in the road, go right at both of them, following the signs to Zipolite. At 7.8 miles (12.6 km) you will see the Palmera Trailer Park on the right in a grove of palm trees.

You can also reach this campground without driving through Puerto Angel from a cutoff 7.6 miles (12.3 km) west of the Puerto Angel cutoff. This entrance road is less steep.

Campground No. 2

LOS TAMARINDOS HOTEL AND TRAILER PARK

Price: Inexpensive

Los Tamarindos has 10 camping spaces and a few basic rental rooms. It is suitable only for smaller rigs. There is no room to maneuver anything larger than a van. All of the sites have electricity but no other hookups. Unfortunately the campground had no water when we were there, you will want to make sure that water is available before you decide to stay. The campground has restrooms and cold showers.

This campground is in an unfortunate location. It occupies a hot hillside with no view to speak of and it is not near the water. Most people will want to continue on down the hill in search of a place with more to offer.

Zero your odometer at the point where Mex. 200 and Mex. 175 meet, follow the road leading south from the intersection toward Puerto Angel. At 3.2 miles (5.2 km) you will see the trailer park and sign on the right.

Other Camping Possibilities

Zipolite Beach is lined with places offering rental palapas and refreshments. Many of these have room to park a smaller rig. No doubt some of these places would be happy to accommodate overnight campers. A few even have camping signs out. Most do not have a great deal of room. Puerto Angel is a place for tent campers and smaller rigs, large RVs would do better to stay in Puerto Escondido.

Side Trips from Puerto Angel

A few years ago Playa Mazunte was notorious as a place where turtles were slaughtered. Now the harvest of turtles is illegal in Mexico and instead you'll find the **Museum of the Sea Turtle** here. Drive west 3.7 miles (6 km) from La Palmera Trailer Park at Zipolite beach on the new road, you can't miss it.

PUERTO ESCONDIDO, OAXACA (PWEHR-TOE ES-CON-DEE-DOH) ─────
Population 38,200, Elevation sea level

The most mature of the Oaxaca Coast resort towns, Puerto Escondido may be a pleasant surprise to you. Once known primarily as a surfer hangout it has developed into an attractive but relaxed beach resort with all the services you could desire. There is a barricaded pedestrian street along the bay, Pérez Gasga, lined with reasonably priced restaurants, some quite good. There are also lots of places to shop for the usual tourist items. Puerto Escondido has no big stores but many smaller ones, you can pick up groceries many places including a small supermarket located at the east end of Pérez Gasga.

Campground No. 1

PUERTO ESCONDIDO TRAILER PARK (BAHÍA DE
  CARRIZALILLO)
  Address: Bahía Carrizalillo, Puerto
  Escondido, Mixt., Juq., Oax., Mexico
  Telephone: (958) 2-00-77

    Price: Moderate for view sites,
      Low without view

This large trailer park has two things going for it. First, it is the only trailer park on this coast that has lots of space with full hookups. Second, it sits on the bluff above a beautiful beach.

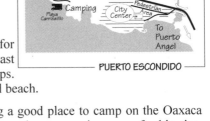

Larger RV's will have a tough time finding a good place to camp on the Oaxaca coast. Most campgrounds just don't have enough maneuvering room for big rigs. Most don't have much in the way of water or sewer hookups either.

The Puerto Escondido Trailer Park (usually known as the Carrizalillo) has at least 150 spaces, 57 of these have electricity, water and sewer, 76 more have just electricity and water, and many more have no service connections. Most sites are pull-throughs on grass, there are no patios. The restrooms have cold showers and there is a swimming pool.

CARRIZALILLO BEACH NEAR PUERTO ESCONDIDO

The park is a large grassy area on a bluff above the ocean with little shade. Carrizalillo beach, just a short climb down a steep dirt trail, is about a quarter of a mile long, rocks at each end make it accessible only from the trailer park and another better trail to the east. Access is so limited that launches from Puerto Escondido sometimes bring visitors for the day. This is one of the prettiest beaches along the coast.

Even if you know that the Puerto Escondido Trailer Park sits on a bluff above Carrizalillo beach about 2 miles (3 km) west of Puerto Escondido you may have a difficult time finding the best road to reach it. Several signs point to the beach area from the highway, but most of these roads are terrible. The area is being haphazardly developed and local drivers have worn their own dirt routes.

Zero your odometer at the Puente Regadillo (Regadillo bridge) as you enter Puerto Escondido from the east. Drive past the first entrance to the beach tourist area immediately after the bridge. At .4 miles (.6 km) you will see the cutoff to Mex. 135 on the right. At 1.8 miles (2.9 km) there is a boulevard with trees in the middle leading down towards the ocean to the left. This is Blvd. Benito Juárez but you won't see street signs until you travel a block or two. Follow this road as it bears left at 1.8 miles (2.9 km) and again at 2.0 miles (3.2 km). Turn right on Huajuapan de Leon at 2.1 miles (3.4 km) and then follow the road as it turns left at 2.2 miles (3.5

km) and then right at 2.3 miles (3.7 km), and again left at 2.4 miles (3.9 km). You will see the trailer park on the right just after the last turn. All of this is more difficult to read than to drive, you are really just following the main road.

Coming from the west watch for the Pemex on the left just after the airport cutoff. From the Pemex, Blvd. Benito Juárez is .4 miles (.6 km) on the right.

Campground No. 2

PALMAS DE CORTES

Price: Moderate

The Palmas de Cortes is located right on the beach in downtown Puerto Escondido. There are fifteen spaces for vans and small RVs set under palm trees next to the beach. There is also a tent camping area. The park is fenced but limiting unauthorized access in this area is almost impossible, if you camp here you should watch your belongings carefully. All of the spaces have electricity and there are a few water spigots. The surface is packed sand and there are no patios. Clean restrooms are provided with cold showers.

To reach the trailer park take the first left (toward the beach) west of the Puente Regadillo. When you reach the barriers marking the pedestrian area turn left. You will see the campground sign ahead down the alley and to the right. This campground is only suitable for smaller rigs. Maneuvering space inside the campground is very tight.

Other Camping Possibilities

The Neptuno Trailer Park is located on the beach near downtown Puerto Escondido. To reach the park you also take the first turn west of the Puente Regadillo just as you do when headed for the Palmas de Cortes. The Neptuno will be on your left almost immediately after the turn. This trailer park has a lot more room than the Palmas de Cortes, but even less security. It is also in a palm grove. There is probably room for 30 RVs, some spaces have electricity. Restrooms have cold showers and are usually extremely dirty. Even at the height of the Christmas holidays when the other campgrounds are packed almost no one stays here.

We have occasionally seen campers along the beach east of town along the road that runs past the Hotel Santa Fe, which has a very good restaurant.

PALENQUE, CHIAPAS (PAH-LEHN-KEH)
Population 25,000, Elevation 195 ft (60 m)

The town near the archeological site is really named Santo Domingo de Palenque, but everyone, including the signs, now calls it Palenque or Palenque Village. It is about five miles (8 km) from the ruins and the campgrounds are near the ruins, not the town. Many visitors never see the town. You won't want to drive a large rig into Santo Domingo, the roads aren't laid out for anything larger than a small bus, but you should be able to catch a bus, collectivo, or taxi in from the camping areas if you don't have a smaller vehicle available.

There are several small grocery stores in town for essential supplies. There are also some nice restaurants. Palenque is visited by a lot of tourists so it has developed more services than you would normally expect in such a small remote town. The square can be pleasant, especially in the evening and if you are not planning to drive farther into Chiapas you may wish to do some shopping for handicrafts here.

The Palenque Archeological Site is not to be missed. If you have been on the Yucatán Peninsula you may feel that you have maxed out on ruins. Palenque is different enough to renew your interest. It is in a moist, jungle environment. Plants than we are accustomed to seeing indoors in pots grow everywhere. The crowds of Chichén Itzá and Tulúm are not in evidence. Most importantly, the ruins themselves are extensive and very interesting. Many frescos and inscriptions are at least partially intact and can be viewed. This is also the site known for the crypt found in the largest pyramid, the Temple of Inscriptions. You can climb down a

PALACE COMPLEX AT PALENQUE

long steep set of stairs inside the pyramid and take a look.

One big recent improvement in the Palenque area is a brick walking path that follows the road all the way from Santo Domingo to the Museum just below the archeological site. This means that you can walk (or bike) in to town from either campground without fear of being run down by a taxi or bus.

Campground No. 1

MAYABELL CAMPGROUND
   Address: Carret Palenque-Ruinas Km. 5.5,
   Palenque, Chis., Mexico
   Telephone: (934) 5-07-67,
   (967) 5-07-98 (Res.)

   Price: Low

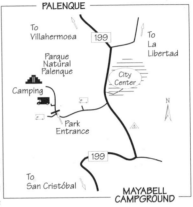

The Mayabell is the place to stay at Palenque, not because the facilities are great but because of the location. The campground is near the archeological site, right on the edge of the undeveloped forest. At night campers are almost always serenaded by howler monkeys, their call is an exotic sound you will long remember. The Mayabell tends to be a little funky, you'll see more Volkswagen campers here than you've seen in years. Larger rigs can get in and find room to park but there is a lot more room at Los Leones.

There are up to 35 full-service spaces with electricity, water, and sewer. The spaces are small but if you have a big rig you will just take up a bit more than one space. The hookups have recently been refurbished and there is even work underway on a new restroom. Some of the spaces are pull-throughs if the campground isn't crowded. There are cold water showers, some rental rooms, a small restaurant and a pool formed by damming a jungle stream.

The Mayabell also has a large area for tent campers on a small hill above the RV parking area that is complete with a number of palapas. When the campground is full there are a lot of people using just a few restrooms.

The Palenque site lower entrance is only a kilometer or so up the road. The walk to the upper entrance is about a mile and a half, you might take a bus up and then walk back to the Mayabell using the lower entrance when you come home. There are some nice pools in a stream near the bottom entrance, swimming is theoretically forbidden but the pools are extremely popular after a hot day climbing around the ruins above.

It is easy to find the Mayabell. The road to the ruins is well-marked, just follow the signs toward the archeological site from Mex. 199 near town. The Mayabell is on the left at 3.5 miles (5.6 km) from the cutoff from Mex. 199.

Campground No. 2

LOS LEONES HOTEL, RESTAURANT, AND TRAILER
PARK
   Address: Carret. Palenque-Ruinas Km 2.5,
   Palenque, Chis., Mexico
   Telephone: (934) 5-11-10
   Fax: (934) 5-11-40

Price: Moderate

Los Leones is a brand new campground
located behind a restaurant and motel on the
road to the ruins. There are at least 40 sites, all
with electricity, water, and sewer hookups. All are back-in sites and there are no
patios. This campground has been designed to give big rigs lots of room and will
probably be much better drained and dryer than the Mayabell during wet weather.
Unfortunately, there is absolutely no shrubbery and little grass at this time, perhaps
that will come later. The restrooms are very clean and nice, cold water showers
however. Out front there is a good restaurant.

To find the campground follow the signs toward the ruins. Los Leones is on the
right 1.4 miles (2.3 km) from the cutoff from Mex. 199.

Other Camping Possibilities

Without a doubt you will visit **Agua Azul**, you may also wish to camp here. The
Side Trips section describes the site. The entrance fee allows you to stay overnight.
There are designated camping areas requiring an extra fee but camping outside
them seems to be OK. There are no hookups but there are restrooms. Other
restrooms are provided outside the camping area. These require payment of a fee
and are usually extremely dirty. Theft can be a problem at Agua Azul, under no
circumstances leave your things unwatched. Camp where there are other people if
possible.

Many campground guides list the Maria del Mar and the Kin-Ha in the Palenque
area. They are both the same place and they no longer have camping sites.

On the road out of town toward San Cristóbal is the Nututun Hotel. It has camping
for tents and a great swimming hole out front but is not conveniently located and is
expensive.

Side Trips from Palenque

Thirty-five miles (57 km) up the road towards San Cristóbal de las Casas is one of
the most beautiful waterfalls in Mexico. It is known as **Agua Azul**. The pale blue
water flowing across the light colored rocks in a green jungle setting is just part of
the story. This is also a great place to swim. The water is a comfortable temperature
and there are lots of pools with a slower current and plenty of privacy.

The falls are located three miles (5 km) from the highway on a nice paved road that descends into the river valley. The area is formally known as the Parque Natural Turístico Cascadas de Agua Azul. It is run by a local ejido, the entry fee is low. There is plenty of room for larger rigs.

Don't expect much in the way of facilities. This is a regular stop for tour busses so there are vendor stalls and small rustic restaurants. There's also an airstrip. Several small restroom and changing rooms are available for a peso or two. Dirt paths lead up and down the river to viewing and swimming areas. Crosses placed next to the river mark the spots where you probably shouldn't swim. The river and falls are the attraction here, and they are more than enough.

SAN CRISTÓBAL DE LAS CASAS, CHIAPAS
(SAHN KREES-TOE-BALL DAY LAHS KAH-SAHS)
Population 90,000, Elevation 6,900 ft (2,150 m)

San Cristóbal de las Casas is another of those Mexican cities that has been designated a national historic monument. It is different, however, because it is far enough out of the way so that it is not overrun by holiday tourists. It does receive many visitors, many are from Europe. San Cristóbal is isolated and surrounded by Indian villages so the atmosphere here is unlike that in other small colonial towns like Guanajuato and San Miguel de Allende. This is a good place to shop for Indian

SAN CRISTÓBAL MARKET

crafts. It is also a good base for exploring the surrounding villages and countryside.

Most shopping, including groceries, will probably be done in the central area of the city. There are several small supermarkets located there.

Campground No. 1

HOTEL BONAMPAK TRAILER PARK
    Address: Calzada México No. 5, San
    Cristóbal de las Casas, Chiapas.
    Telehone: (967) 8 16 21

Price: Moderate

SAN CRISTÓBAL DE LAS CASAS

HOTEL BONAMPAK
TRAILER PARK

A very tidy park with 22 spaces, all with full utilities. The sites sit along the sides of a large grassy field surrounded by a wall, there is not much shade but at this altitude this isn't as much of a problem as it would be in the hot lowlands. All sites are back-in sites with no patios but since the campground is usually practically empty you can pretend they are pull-through sites. The campground has clean restrooms with hot water showers. The hotel out front has a good restaurant. It also has a tennis court.

This campground is easy to find. It is located on Mex. 190 about a mile west of the centro cutoff on the south side of the highway. Watch for the Best Western sign. Pull into the driveway on the right side of the motel and drive right through into the campground.

Campground No. 2

RANCHO SAN NICHOLÁS
    Telephone: (967) 8-00-57

Price: Moderate

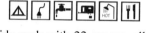

SAN CRISTÓBAL DE LAS CASAS

RANCHO SAN NICHOLÁS

The San Nicholas is in a pleasant area outside town. It is suitable for only smaller rigs because access is through the center of town. You don't want to try getting to the San Nicolas if you are longer than about 21 feet. There are 15 grassy spaces separated by trees, many with electricity and water. There are also tent spaces on the hillside above. The campground has restrooms and hot showers.

From Mex. 190 running south of the central part of town take the "Centro" cutoff. After turning towards Centro watch for a street called Francisco Leon (it is about the 8th intersecting street). Turn right on this street and follow it all the way to the end, about 2 miles (3.2 km). When you reach the arch and yard at the end of Leon you just passed the campground, it was on your right.

Other Camping Possibilities

The Lagunas de Montebello have a designated camping area. Drive straight (left fork) at the Y just inside the park entrance. At the end of the road is a paved parking area, this is it if you are in an RV. Tenters can camp below near the lake. There are restrooms but no hookups. This can be an active parking area with lots of traffic, it is one of those places where the local kids want a tip to guard your car. Tenters should be cautious about leaving valuables in their tent. There are many small lakes in this park, some have decent roads to their shore. We've talked with folks who have camped at locations other than the designated camping area with no problems.

Side Trips from San Cristóbal de las Casas

Seeing the Indians along the highways and in the town of San Cristóbal may inspire you to visit their villages. There are two major groups of Indians near San Cristóbal, the Tzotzil and the Tzeltal, but each village has it's own dress and customs. The two easiest villages to visit are **San Juan Chamula** and **Zinacantán**. Both of these villages are reached on paved roads. Frequent buses make the trip, they are almost San Cristóbal suburbs. The people speak Tzotzil. The unusual practices of worship in the San Juan Chamula church make it a popular visitor destination, you must ask for permission to enter at the village tourist office. Under no circumstances enter the church with a camera or without permission.

If you feel like going farther afield but don't have a high-clearance vehicle there are villages along the major highways that are easy to visit, these include **Huixtán** (Tzotzil), **Oxchuc** (Tzeltal) and **Abasolo** (Tzeltal) on Mex. 199 to Palenque and **Ixtapa** (Tzotzil), **Soyaló** (Tzotzil), and **Bochil** (Tzotzil) on Mex. 195 to Villahermosa.

The **Lagunas de Montebello** are an easy day's drive from San Cristóbal. They are located about 90 miles (145 km) south near the Guatemala border. They get mixed reviews. Some people say they are the prettiest part of Mexico, other consider them overrated and not nearly as attractive as some unimportant lakes in the Pacific Northwest. It probably depends upon what you are accustomed to. You can even camp at the lakes, see the Other Camping Possibilities section above.

TAMAZULAPÁN, OAXACA (TAHM-AH-ZOO-LAH-PAHN

This small town located along Mex. 190 between Oaxaca and Cuernavaca (and Puebla) makes a great place to spend the night. There is also a Pemex station. It is difficult to make the approximately 275 miles (450 km) trip along this free road from Oaxaca to Cuernavaca in one day. Tamazulapan is 94 miles (154 km) north of Oaxaca. If you elect not to take the toll route to Puebla you'll probably enjoy spending the night at this town's balneario. You may have to be persuasive with the young man in the entrance booth, but regardless of what he thinks, people do occasionally camp here. Hopefully you will prevail.

Campground

Balneario Atonaltzin

Price Moderate

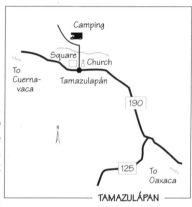

TAMAZULÁPAN

The Balneario Atonaltzin is not a formal campground, in fact few campers ever stop here. We heard about it from someone who had traveled the route with the Point South caravan company and found it an excellent place to overnight.

This small balneario has no hookups but there is a fairly large parking area near the pools and inside the fence. The large pool is beautiful with a large rock face along one side. The water at this balneario is cool, very refreshing after a long day on the road. Bathroom facilities are normal balneario quality, not great, and showers are cold. In the evening the gates are locked and you are left alone with only the night watchman for company.

The balneario is located about 1.2 miles (2 km) north of Mex. 190 on a road that soon becomes gravel. The road heads north from the center of Tamazulapan, it leaves Mex. 190 between the red-domed church and the central square.

Tehuantepec (teh-wan-teh-PECK)
Population 45,000 Elevation 330 ft.(100 m)

For RVers Tehuantepec is really just a good place to spend the night. It is conveniently located near La Ventosa, the crossroads where four important routes meet: Mex. 200 coming down the west coast, Mex. 190 from Oaxaca, Mex. 185 coming across the Isthmus of Tehuantepec from the Gulf Coast, and Mex. 190 from Chiapas.

The town's attractions are limited, you will enjoy a stroll around the square and market area in the morning before leaving town. Tehuantepec is known for its women, they have always played a much more important part in business and social life than women in other parts of the country. Their traditional costumes are elaborate with headdresses, huipiles, and lots of jewelry.

Campground No. 1

SANTA TERESA TRAILER PARK
  Address: Km. 6.5 Carr. a Mixtequilla
  (Ferrocarril #34 (Res.)), Tehuantepec,
  Oaxaca, Mexico
  Telephone: (971) 5-05-00, (971) 5-03-53
  Fax: (971) 5-02-12

Price: Low

The Santa Teresa has a pleasant country location, it was once a sugar hacienda. The campground is much-frequented by caravans. The friendly owners put on a fiesta for them with traditional costumes, music, and food.

There are 35 or so spaces scattered under big shade trees. Fluorescent fixtures are hung for light but there are no hookups. The campground has restroom facilities and cold showers.

The Santa Teresa is located down the road marked by the Hotel Calli, some 1.3 miles (2.1 km) toward the La Ventosa Junction from Tehuantepec. This is the Carretera a Mixtequilla. Zero your odometer as you pass the hotel. You will cross some railroad tracks at 1 mile (1.6 km). There is a campground sign at 1.5 miles (2.4 km) as the road curves left, it curves left again after 3.4 miles (5.5 km). Stay on the paved road until you have gone 3.8 miles (6.1 km), you will cross a tope and then see a sign for the campground pointing left down a small gravel road between typical rural Mexican houses. There will be one of the ubiquitous basketball courts on the right at 3.9 miles (6.3 km) and at 4.1 miles (6.6 km) you will reach the campground.

Campground No. 2

HOTEL CALLI
  Address: Carretera Cristóbal Colón Km 790,
  Tehuantepec, Oax., Mexico
  Telephone: (971) 5-00-85

Price: Moderate

The Calli is easy to find, and if you are arriving late and planning to leave early in the morning this is a good place to stay. Campers who are not fully self-contained won't like it. The Calli offers little in the way of amenities. It is a nice hotel, probably the best in town, but the campground facilities consist of a paved area behind the hotel. There is an electrical outlet that can be reached with a long cord, but that's about it. Security is provided by a night watchman. You'll have to make special arrangements with the management if you wish to use bathroom facilities or a shower.

The hotel is located right on Mex. 190 some 1.3 miles (2.6 km) east of Tehuantepec.

TUXTLA GUTIÉRREZ (TOOKS-TLAH GOO-TYEH-REHS)
Population 200,000, Elevation 1,722 ft (525 m)

Tuxtla is a modern commercial city. It has at least two attractions that make it an attractive stopping point.

The Sumidero Canyon with very tall steep cliffs falling to a narrow river can be seen two ways. You can catch a boat in Chiapa de Corzo to see the canyon from the bottom. This is not a white water trip, in the canyon the river is really a lake formed by the Chicoasén Dam. You can also see the cliffs from the top by driving up into· the Sumidero National Park which overlooks Tuxtla and the Canyon. The road is good but steep, the end is about 15 miles (25 km) from the Tuxtla northern bypass (Libramiento Norte). There are several *miradors* (overlooks) before you reach the main one at the end of the road.

Tuxtla also has a fine zoo filled with local animals in natural settings. It is well signed off the Libramiento Sur.

Campground No. 1

LA HACIENDA HOTEL TRAILER PARK
Address: Blvd. Dr. B. Dominguez 1197,
Tuxtla Gutiérrez, Chiapas, Mexico
Telephone: (961) 1-38-44
Fax: (965) 8-30-96

Price: Low

Tuxtla is difficult for larger rigs. The one good trailer park in town, La Hacienda, is a little tight. Take a look at the Other Camping Possibilities section for ideas if you are in a big rig.

La Hacienda is a motel-style hotel with a central well-shaded parking area that doubles for an RV park. There are 10 RV spaces. Five of these are normal car-size parking spaces only suitable for vans or pickup campers. The other five are longer, a couple of them large enough for a 36-footer. All parking slots have water and electricity. One of them has a dump station. La Hacienda sits on a busy intersection, the slots near the road (the big ones) will be noisy. There is a very small swimming pool in the middle of the parking area with lots of greenery, the hotel also has a restaurant. There are bathrooms for the trailer park, they are clean and have hot water showers. There is a large shopping center with a supermarket a ten-minute walk down the road towards Oaxaca. It is modern and flashy.

To find the campground when you are coming from the west on Mex. 190 just stay on the main highway until you come to the first glorieta. The hotel is located right next to the glorieta, go around 270 degrees to the third road, get in the center lane because you have to turn sharply right almost immediately into the entrance road which descends into the motel parking lot. The entrance is narrow so swing wide, the descent is gradual enough that it should cause no problems.

If you are coming into town from the east on Mex. 190 follow the southern bypass (Libramiento Sur) past the zoo. Watch carefully once you pass the zoo signs, in 2.8 miles (4.5 km) from the zoo cutoff at a tall monument the bypass turns right but another four-lane road which appears to be the main road continues straight. Turn right here, you will see a Pemex on your right in .6 miles (1 km) and immediately after that the glorieta. Go straight through, get as far left as possible, and almost immediately turn right into the La Hacienda.

Campground No. 2

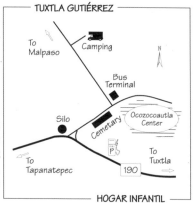

HOGAR INFANTIL
  Address: Ocozocoautla, Chiapas

Price: Donation

The Hogar Infantil is a boy's home located just outside the town of Ocozocoautla. This is some 34 miles (55 km) from Tuxtla Gutiérrez but really the best place around for larger RVs. It also makes an interesting place to spend the night.

There are just a few parking spaces. They have full hookups. There is a restroom available with showers. The price is up to you, it is a donation to the home. You may find yourself giving impromptu English lessons.

The campground is located near the west end of the bypass that passes south of Ocozocoautla. Take the road into town from here, you'll see grain storage silos nearby. You will pass a cemetery on the right and at .5 miles (.8 km), just before the bus terminal on the left, turn left. Drive .4 miles (.7 km) down the road, you'll see the Hogar Infantile entrance on the right.

Other Camping Possibilities

Some folks report that they have successfully free camped in the parking lot at the zoo. There is lots of room, there are watchmen on duty during the day and you might discuss it with them.

As you leave town toward the west you may see a sign for Trailer Park El Mangal on the right. This trailer park is associated with the Palma del Vijaro Hotel (telephone (961) 2-16-38). The low trees here make parking very difficult although there may be room for a larger rig or two toward the front of the property. Hookups and restrooms are questionable, check with the hotel if you are desperate. There may or may not be a caretaker on-site to let you in.

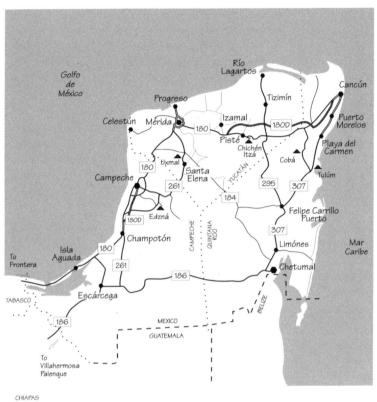

THE
YUCATÁN
PENINSULA

CHAPTER 10

THE YUCATÁN PENINSULA

INTRODUCTION

The Yucatán Peninsula is one of the most-visited regions of Mexico. Most visitors are bound for the east coast mega-resort, Cancún. It is no surprise that this relatively young destination, developed from nothing since 1974, is a big success. The Yucatán has lots to offer visitors: sun, sand, crystal clear waters, archeological ruins, the unique Mayan culture, crafts, wildlife (especially birds) and even several colonial cities.

When you visit the Yucatán today it is difficult to believe that forty years ago there was no road to the Yucatán, travelers had to take a train from Coatzacoalcos to Campeche. There was also no road to the Quintana Roo coast. Once the traveler reached Quintana Roo, not yet a state, the only non-Mayan population centers were Isla Mujeres, Cozumel, and Chetumal.

The Yucatán is a huge limestone plateau. Much of it is very dry, and what rain does fall quickly percolates into the ground. Cenotes, natural wells where the limestone has collapsed when the underground water undercut the surface, are one of the few sources of water. There are a few small ranges of hills near the west coast of the peninsula, but the remainder is very flat. Miles and miles of dry scrub cover everything including hundreds, if not thousands, of Mayan structures. Surrounding it all is warm tropical water, and particularly on the east coast, beaches and coral reefs for diving.

Politically the peninsula is divided into three states. In the east along the Gulf is Campeche with its colonial capital, also called Campeche. In the north is Yucatán, Mérida is the capital. Finally, along the east coast is the state of Quintana Roo. Most people think of Cancún as the major city in this state but in fact the capital is in the far south, the city of Chetumal.

Campgrounds are not plentiful in the Yucatán, but they are well-located. You can visit all the more interesting attractions and spend the night in full-service campgrounds. There are also good prospects for free camping along the coasts.

Probably the best time to visit the Yucatán is in the late fall or early winter beginning toward the first half of November. The rains have stopped and things are a little cooler. Later in the winter the weather is usually nice but occasionally there are spells of cool weather. These spells, which often last several days, make a good time to leave the beach and explore the usually hot interior of the peninsula. The rains start again in April. With rain, extreme heat, and the occasional hurricane, most campers give the Yucatán a wide berth in the summer.

ROAD SYSTEM

The majority of the visitors traveling to the Yucatán come by air. For automobile and RV visitors the region is remote. The driving distance from McAllen, Texas to Campeche is 1,240 miles (2,000 km). Today there are two routes into the peninsula from the west. Mex. 180 follows the coast from Villahermosa into the Campeche area, Mex. 186 runs inland and, although there are also good roads connecting it to the eastern and northern peninsula, it is the quickest and most direct route for those in a hurry to reach the eastern Quintana Roo coast and Cancún.

The nature of the peninsula, a flat limestone plateau, makes roads easy to build and there are many of them. The major ones are Mex. 180 running all the way across the peninsula through Campeche and Mérida to Cancún, Mex. 186 running across the southern Peninsula to Chetumal, and north-south Mex. 307 which connects the two along the east coast. Smaller highways connect these major roads making it easy to get from almost any location to any other location in a day of driving. The only thing to slow you down are the topes. They are very popular, most villages have a complete collection. Since the roads run through the villages you will see many of them.

There are few divided highways yet but they are coming. There is an expensive toll road, Mex. 180D from east of Mérida to Cancún and another, also labeled Mex. 180D that runs for a few miles south of Campeche. The coastal highway Mex. 307 is being four-laned from Cancún to Playa del Carmen. This will probably not be a toll road since there is no alternate road.

HIGHLIGHTS

For many visitors the first priority is sun and sand. For this you will probably be attracted to the Cancún area. Campers are not particularly well served here, however. The hotel zone beaches are nice but difficult to enjoy if you aren't staying in one of the hotels. After at least a week in the real Mexico on your drive south you will probably quickly tire of the Cancún tourist scene. Before you leave Cancún however, you should make a visit to laid-back Isla Mujeres and perhaps even a tour to Isla Contoy bird reserve.

From Cancún it is not far to beach destinations that are much more attractive to campers. All along the Cancún-Tulúm corridor running for 85 miles (139 km) south there are many campgrounds and quiet beaches.

The most popular archeological sites on the Yucatán are Chichén Itzá, Tulúm, Cobá and Uxmal. There are dozens more. An interesting and easy-to-reach lesser-known group is the Puuc Sites near Uxmal. Between Chetumal and Escárcega off Mex. 186 are the Río Bec Sites, popular with hikers and more eco-oriented travelers. Dzibilchaltún, north of Mérida has a famous cenote.

If you are interested in the Spanish culture in Mexico there are two cities you'll want to visit: Mérida and Campeche. You might also find the churches and monasteries in places like Izamal, Valladolid, Muna, and Ticul of interest. They're all located within easy driving distance of campgrounds in Mérida, Uxmal or Chichén Itzá.

Bird watchers will love the Yucatán. For flamingos the destinations are Celestún near Mérida and the Parque Natural Río Lagartos on the Yucatán north coast. Isla Contoy, north of Isla Mujeres, is uninhabited and home to 70 species. The Sian Ka´an Biosphere Reserve south of Tulúm also has possibilities. You can see both ruins and birds if you visit the Cobá archeological site which is mostly unexcavated and covered by jungle.

If you are a diver you'll be attracted by the Belize Barrier Reef, the fifth longest reef in the world that runs from just south of Cancún all the way to the Gulf of Honduras. The Isla de Cozumel is the real center for divers on the coast but there are plenty of dive shops on the mainland too. Experienced divers may want to try a unique Yucatán specialty, the cenote dive.

THE CAMPGROUNDS

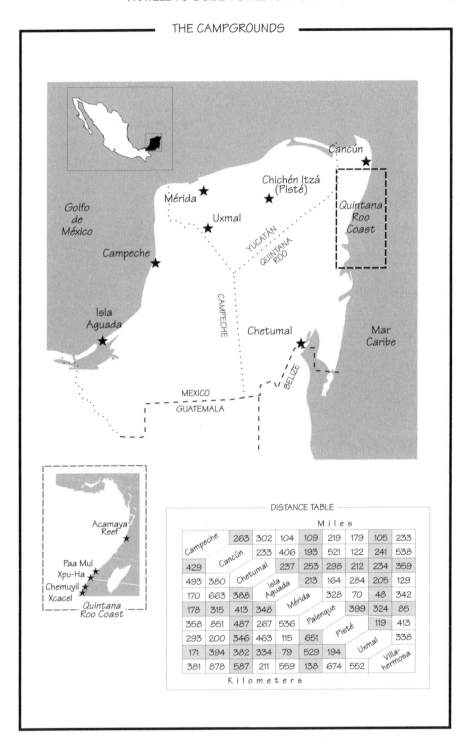

DISTANCE TABLE

			M i l e s						
Campeche	263	302	104	109	219	179	105	233
	Cancún	233	406	193	521	122	241	538
429		Chetumal	237	253	298	212	234	359
493	380		Isla Aguada	213	164	284	205	129
170	663	388		Mérida	328	70	48	342
178	315	413	348		Palenque	399	324	85
358	851	487	267	536		Pisté	119	413
293	200	346	463	115	651		Uxmal	338
171	394	382	334	79	529	194		Villa-hermosa
381	878	587	211	559	138	674	552	

K i l o m e t e r s

SELECTED CITIES AND THEIR CAMPGROUNDS

CAMPECHE, CAMPECHE (KAHM-PEH-CHEH)
Population 250,000, Elevation sea level

Few people stop at Campeche the first time they visit the Yucatán. Some are in a hurry to reach the ruins farther east, some just don't know about Campeche's attractions.

Campeche is an old city, it was founded in 1542. To protect it from pirates (who hid out near Isla Aguada) it was encircled by a wall in 1686. Much of the wall still remains with the guard towers or *baluartes* often housing small museums or government offices. The old city is a national historical monument and has a very Spanish atmosphere. It has a pleasant central plaza with a cathedral. The town's museum, the **Regional Museum of Campeche**, has both colonial and Mayan exhibits.

Campground

SAMULA TRAILER PARK
    Address: Calle 19, Camp., Campeche, Mexico

            Price: Low

The Samula Trailer Park is a favorite of veteran Yucatán campers. It sits in the Campeche suburb of Samula. The grounds are planted with orange trees, there's lots of greenery and shade. The owner speaks English and will make you feel right at home.

Campeche Campground has 30 level sites on grass, all with full hookups. There are two toilets and two showers with cold water. We've seen some pretty big rigs here but watch for the branches on the orange trees when maneuvering. They've been pruned and the soft-looking leaves hide some sharp branches.

The campground is a great base for exploring the city of Campeche. Like almost everywhere in Mexico bus service is available nearby, just walk out to Calle 12. Taxis are also inexpensive and easy to use. Don't be surprised if a student from the nearby University drops by in the afternoon. They like to practice their English with the campers. Some of them are quite knowledgeable about the nearby Mayan archeological sites.

There is a nice small supermarket less than a mile away from the campground. Head out again on the same route you used to get to the campground and you will see it on the right in about .9 mile as you reach Avenue Agustin Melgar.

The campground can be difficult to find. The easiest approach is from the waterfront south of the centro area. Coming into Campeche from the south along the water you will see a large statue in the middle of the road, it appears to be a man emerging from the ground with a torch. Zero your odometer there. The road then becomes a divided four-lane road.

At 1.2 miles (2.0 km) turn right just before a Pemex on the right. This is a major street called Avenue Agustin Melgar but is not signed. You'll soon pass the University on the right.

In .5 mile, at 1.7 miles (2.8 km) the road will bend to the left but you want to stay on the street that branches off and continues straight ahead. Go straight ahead for another .2 miles (.3 km) to a T at 1.9 miles (3.1 km), and turn right. You are now on Calle 12. In Campeche the even *calles* (streets) run one way and the odd calles run the other so it makes sense that you are now watching for Calle 19, where you are going to turn right. This section of the road seems narrow if you are in a big rig but the next turn is the only difficult part. We've done it in a 34-footer and have seen some huge fifth-wheels in the campground so most people will be able to make the turn. Carefully turn right on Calle 19 in .6 mile at 2.5 miles (4.1 km) and then proceed about .1 mile (.2 km) to just before the point where the road begins to climb a hill. The campground is now on your left.

Other Camping Possibilities

Caravans now often spend the night free camping near the boat harbor on a peninsula north of central Campeche. You might consider this location if the entrance to the Samula Trailer Park doesn't seem worth the effort.

The Si-Ho Hotel south of Campeche on the coast no longer takes campers. It continues to be listed in a few camping guides.

Side Trips from Campeche

Edzná is a nice ruin to visit before you get spoiled by Uxmal. The parking lot is large enough for large rigs to turn around in, although people pulling cars may have to unhook to do so if there are many cars in the lot. There is no parking charge. Edzná's location well to the south of the majority of the Puuc area sites means that you probably won't visit if you don't stop when en route to Uxmal.

CANCÚN, QUINTANA ROO (KAHN-KOON)
Population 175,000 (and rapidly growing), Elevation sea level

---

There are really two Cancúns. One is the **Hotel Zona**, a strip of hotels, restaurants, beaches, and expensive shopping malls located on a spit of land running for miles off the Quintana Roo coast. The other is the town of Ciudad Cancún located on the mainland nearby.

If you spend much time on the Quintana Roo coast you will probably visit Ciudad Cancún a few times to shop for the necessities of life. You won't find better stores for various types of supplies nearer than Mérida.

The tourist Cancún is also worth a visit, especially if you haven't seen it before. This is Mexico's premier fly-in international resort, truly world class. The hotels are fantastic and the shopping malls are first rate. If you don't watch yourself you could drop a wad here. You will also probably feel out of place. By now you're a true Mexico travel veteran with several weeks and 1,500 miles (2,500 km) under your belt, the tourists here hardly seem to know that they are in Mexico.

Campground

TRAILER PARK MECOLOCO
  Address: Km 3 Carretera Puerto Juárez a
  Punta Sam, Cancún, Q. Roo., Mexico
  Telephone (98) 7-41-474

Price: Low

This is really the best choice for a campground near Cancún. It is located north of town between Punta Sam and Puerto Juárez. These are the mainland terminals for the ferries to Isla de Mujeres, the park is ideal for those wishing to visit the island. It also has convenient bus service to Ciudad Cancún.

The sign says there are 150 spaces here, and there may be, this is a big place. Almost all of the spaces have full hookups. The entire area is paved and there is lots of room for large RVs. Unfortunately this park has little shade and even less charm. There are two thatched roof restroom buildings with hot showers. There is also a laundry and a small store associated with the campground. English is spoken.

Although the campground is close to the water beach access is limited. The beach across the street is not at all attractive, a city beach about a mile toward Cancún is probably a better choice for sunning and swimming. Better yet, take the half-hour ferry ride to Isla Mujeres which has some of the nicest beaches in Mexico.

Other Camping Possibilities

There is a campground near the airport called the Rainbow Trailer Park. We must warn you that there is some question about whether this trailer park is even open. We've stopped and talked with the caretaker several times. Each time he offers to let us stay (and we've talked to others who have done so), the facility is always neatly clipped but otherwise seems abandoned. The water has been on but not the electricity. Campgrounds can change rapidly, if the electricity were turned on, the water heater lit, and the bathrooms spiffed up this place would be ready for business. However, there is no real reason to stay here, it is near the airport so it is noisy, it is isolated, and the alternatives farther south along the coast are just too attractive. If you've been to Mérida you'll recognize the logo on the entrance sign, it's the same as the campground there. It is a large grassy field with about 35 sites, all with full hookups, although the place has seen better days and the equipment at some of the sites is not in good condition. There is little shade.

The Rainbow is located on Mex. 307 in the northwest quadrant of the intersection with the south branch of the new Cuota Mex. 180D south of Ciudad Cancún. It is 7.8 miles (12.7 km) south of the intersection of the Ciudad Cancún bypass and Mex. 307 with the big Pemex station. The campground has a very small sign and is on the right side of the highway as you drive south, just before the Mex. 180D overpass.

Some people take smaller RVs and vans to Isla Mujeres on the Punta Sam car ferry. They find a quiet spot and inconspicuously dry camp for the night. You might also try one of the balnearios on the west side of the island. Possibilities are very limited, however.

Side Trips from Cancún

Isla Mujeres is largely known as a day trip destination for people spending the week at nearby Cancún. There are also small hotels and restaurants for folks with a slightly different idea of the perfect Cancún-area vacation.

The island is located a few miles offshore just north of Cancún. You can reach it by taking a half-hour ferry from either Puerto Juárez or Punta Sam. The Punta Sam ferry is the automobile ferry. If you don't like small boats you might prefer this ferry. It runs six times daily each way. The smaller Puerto Juárez boats run at least hourly, they serve as marine busses for the island residents and visitors.

Day-trippers usually head for either the snorkeling at **El Garrafón park** or the beaches on the west and north edges of the town on the north end of the island. If you've already maxed out on diving and beaches you can wander around Isla Mujeres Town and have lunch at one of the restaurants. If you have a bicycle you should take it to the island, it is a good place to ride. Otherwise you might rent a mo-ped to tour the island. There are also lots of taxis.

Isla Contoy is a small uninhabited island that is a national park. It is located north of Isla Mujeres and day trips can be arranged from Isla Mujeres. It is a birders paradise but also a good place to snorkel and lie in the sun.

CHETUMAL, QUINTANA ROO (CHEH-TO-MAHL)
Population 95,000, Elevation sea level

This isolated Mexican town seems like it could easily be part of Belize rather than Mexico. You will be impressed by the wide boulevards running all over town, probably the result of the frequent rebuilding that this town gets after destruction by hurricanes. A lot of the economic activity here is related to trade with Belize, this is also a shallow water port requiring that lighters be used to load freighters.

The downtown area here is really not too inspired. A few blocks south is the waterfront with a nice walkway along the ocean. There is a new museum in Chetumal that is said to be well worth a visit. It is the *Museo de la Cultura Maya* **(Museum of Mayan Culture)** located two blocks east and four blocks north of the main square on Efraín Aguilar and Av. Héroes. The other attractions for visitors are the **Laguna Bacalar** area to the north, **Belize** to the south, and the ruins lining Mex. 186 to the east.

Campground No. 1

CENOTE AZUL TRAILER PARK
  Address: Kilometer 15 Mex. 307, Bacalar,
  Q. Roo, Mexico

Price: Low

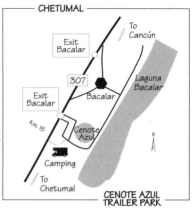

Located just south of Bacalar near the Cenote Azul, about 18 miles (29 km) north of Chetumal, this campground is a handy place to spend the night if you are traveling between Palenque and the coast of the Cancún-Tulúm corridor to the north. It is also a good destination in its own right. The nearby Laguna Bacalar and Cenote Azul are interesting attractions.

There is room for about 50 rigs or tent set-ups at Cenote Azul, depending upon their size, the campground is a grassy field with trees. Hookups are limited to a very few small electrical outlets on the light poles and in the shelter palapas (four that we could find). There is a dump station and water faucet. The restrooms are clean and have hot water. The campground has lots of shade.

The really important amenity at Cenote Azul Trailer Park is the cenote, located across the street and down the hill. It is quite large and very deep. Swimming is great, the water is warm. The best place to swim is next to the restaurant, they may let you jump off the roof. The restaurant is handy if you don't feel like cooking.

The entrance road to the campground is at the 15 kilometer post, about 1.7 miles (2.7 km) south of the south entrance to the town of Bacalar. There is a pictogram sign pointing to the east or left side of the road if you are driving south and also a Bacalar sign. Follow the second of two roads at the sign, drive about 100 yards and the campground is on the right. After passing the campground this road curves down to the laguna and then back along the shore to the town of Bacalar. If you miss the road off Mex. 307 there is a second entrance about 100 yards farther south leading directly into the campground from the main road.

Campground No. 2

R.V. PARK AND BUNGALOWS CALDERITAS (ALSO KNOWN AS SUNRISE ON THE CARIBBEAN)
  Address: Km. 8 Carr. Chetumal-Calderitas (Apdo. 1), Chetumal, C.P. 77000 Q. Roo, Mexico

Price: Inexpensive

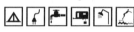

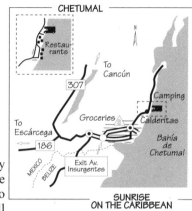

This campground is located on Calderitas Bay north of Chetumal. It sits in a beautiful grove of palm trees right on the water. There is no beach, the campground has a low rock wall boundary for defense from the waves. The ocean is very shallow here but popular for swimming.

Sunrise on the Caribbean has spaces for about 32 rigs in sites with electricity. About half have water faucets but you should only get drinking water from the faucet near the gate. There is a dump station drain, you'll probably have to have the attendant show it to you. The ground is covered with well-clipped grass making this a very pleasant spot. The grass-roofed restrooms have cold water showers.

People have a terrible time finding this campground. The entrance sign is small and very faded, if you don't know exactly where it is you will drive right on by and find yourself on a narrow road with no good places to turn if your vehicle is larger than a VW. Zero your odometer at the intersection of Mex. 307 and Mex. 186 west of Chetumal. Head east towards Chetumal. The road to Belize goes right at 6.6 miles (10.8 km), continue straight toward Chetumal. There is a Pemex on the left at 6.8 miles (11.2 km). Follow Ave. Insurgentes to the left at a Y at 7.7 miles (12.6 km). You'll see a zoo on the left at 11.3 miles (18.5 km), then a Pemex on the right at 12.2 miles (19.9 km). Directly across the street from the Pemex, on your left, is a handy supermarket that you might want to remember. You'll come to a glorieta at 12.3 miles (20.1 km). Go three-quarters of the way around it (about 270 degrees) and take the third exit, you may see a sign for Calderitas marking this road. At 15.1 miles (24.7 km) take the right fork as the road comes to a Y. When the road meets the water at 15.8 miles (25.8 km) go left, then left again at 16.0 miles (26.1 km). After a block there is a stop sign. Go right here and follow the waterfront, you'll pass a few small seafood restaurants and then come to the campground entrance at 16.4 miles (26.8 km). Do not pass any entrances without checking them carefully. At our last visit the owner had dressed up his almost-invisible sign by putting a few caravan stickers on it.

Other Camping Possibilities

There are several balnearios north of Chetumal near Laguna Bacalar that allow camping but have little in the way of hookups. Some are quite primitive, others are well-developed. Some, unfortunately, even have discos.

Adventure-camping aficionados will want to explore the beaches along the long deserted coast north of Chetumal and south of the Sian Ka´an Biosphere Reserve, especially the Xcalak Peninsula. Access is from Mex. 307 just south of the town of Limónes 28 miles (46 km) north of Bacalar. There's a paved road to the coast, a distance of 35 miles (56 km) and then sometimes paved roads running both north and south. You can arrange a camping spot with one of the diving and fishing resorts or free camp on your own. Far offshore is the Banco Chinchorro, a popular diving and fishing destination.

Side Trips from Chetumal

The town of **Bacalar** is located about 17 miles (38 km) north of Chetumal on the west shore of the **Laguna Bacalar** (Bacalar Lagoon). The town is old, it was the Spanish settlement here before Chetumal, and now is a small local resort with many nice homes along the lagoon. There is an old fort with a museum covering the history of the area. The Bacalar Lagoon, also known as Las Lagunas de Siete Colores (The Lagoons of Seven Colors) is now a landlocked lagoon, very shallow with a light-reflecting bottom, that changes colors depending upon the time of day and lighting conditions. Several balnearios along the shore provide a places to swim and perhaps to camp.

Just south of the town of Bacalar is **Cenote Azul**. It is separated from Lake Bacalar by only a narrow strip of land but is entirely different. Reported to be over 175 feet deep, this large circular cenote is very familiar to Yucatán campers, the popular Cenote Azul Trailer Park is just across the road.

East of Chetumal off roads on either side of Mex. 186 are many Mayan archeological sites. The easiest-to-visit and most well-known is **Kohunlich**, located 42 miles (67 km) west of Chetumal and 5 miles (8 km) south on a side road. Another cluster of Río Bec sites; **Becán**, **Xpujil**, and **Chicanná**; is two hours farther west, about 124 miles (200 km) from Chetumal.

CHICHÉN ITZÁ, YUCATÁN (CHEE-CHEN EET-SAH)

This is one of the top archeological sites in Mexico, a must-see attraction. The site covers many acres, has eighteen excavated structures including a huge pyramid, and two cenotes. Chichén Itzá has been largely restored.

Pisté is a small town next to the site which seems totally devoted to supporting the tourist attraction next door. The archeological site is located about a mile to the east. There are several hotels with restaurants in Pisté if you feel like giving them a try. The grocery shopping possibilities are limited, but there are a few small places where you can pick up basic things. Near the archeological site is a famous hotel, the **Mayaland**, which you might want to visit for dinner.

Campground

STARDUST INN
  Address: Carretera Mérida-Puerto Juárez
  Km. 118, Pisté, Yuc., Mexico
  Telephone: (985) 1-01-22

Price: Low

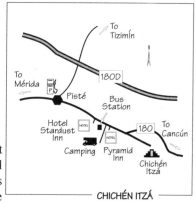

This campground is run by the Stardust Inn but the entrance is 50 yards or so east of the hotel between the Pyramid Inn and a small bus station. The caretaker lives at the rear of the campground and will probably greet you and collect the fee when you arrive.

There are 20 spaces in the small campground, all with electricity and water, most with sewer, arranged along two sides of a grassy lot enclosed with a rock wall. Flowering plants and banana trees grow along the wall, they don't create much shade but they are attractive.

There are restrooms with hot showers at the campground, and you can follow a trail to a back entrance to the Stardust Inn and use their pool for free, it is a nice pool.

The RV park is located at the edge of Pisté near the archeological site, the distance is about a mile and there is a sidewalk the entire distance. If you wish to drive there is plenty of parking, although you will have to pay. It is easy to find the campground since it is on the main road through town.

Side Trips from Chichén Itzá

The **Balankanche Caves** are only 4 miles (6 km) east of Chichén Itzá. They were discovered in 1959 and were a Maya ceremonial site. There's a restaurant, a museum, and each night a sound and light show.

Valladolid is just 27 miles (44 km) east of Chichén Itzá. It is a colonial town with many churches and an active central square. Largely ignored by visitors until recently it is being spruced up but still isn't full of tourists.

Izamal is located about 10 miles (16 km) north of the place where Mex. 180D begins on the road between Mérida and Chichén Itzá. It is, therefore, about 41 miles (70 km) from Pisté. The downtown area is almost all painted yellow, the Pope visited a few years ago and the town was spiffed up for the visit. The Convent of St. Anthony de Padua, built on top of a Mayan temple, is located here as are unrestored Mayan ruins. History buffs will be interested to know that John L. Stephens visited these ruins during his trip described in Incidents of Travel in Yucatán and also that the fanatic friar Diego de Landa, responsible for much of the destruction of Mayan culture, was originally posted to this convent. Just to the west of town is a reconstruction of a Mayan sacbe or "white road". A small sign points it out, otherwise you would drive right past and never see it, although it is less than 100 feet from the road.

Río Lagartos (Lizard River or Alligator River) **National Park** is another place to see flamingoes and water birds on the Yucatán. The flamingos are not at Celestún and Río Lagartos at the same time of the year. Here's the cycle. The birds come to Río Lagartos in April, lay eggs in June, and hatch and raise the chicks until November. Then they fly to outlying lagoons, including Celestún, to feed. They return again to Río Lagartos then in April. The Río Lagartos birds should only be visited during the pre-nesting period in April and May. To reach the Río Lagartos National Park drive east to Valladolid and then north on Mex. 295. The distance from Chichén Itzá is about 90 miles (150 km). You must rent a boat and guide to see the birds.

ISLA AGUADA, CAMPECHE (EES-LA AH-GWAH-DAH)
Population 2,900, Elevation sea level

Fishing is the main preoccupation in Isla Aguada. Each morning you'll hear the outboards as the fishermen head out to sea in skiffs. We walked out onto the toll bridge and watched some men fishing with hand lines and nets for fish to sell to the passing cars. Each time a net was thrown it came up with several fish, they must be thick down there. Shelling is pretty good on the outer coast almost everywhere in the vicinity of Isla Aguada.

You can walk to the center of town by following the streets east from the campground. The distance is about a mile. There are a few small grocery stores, a phone office, and you can watch the fish unloaded from the skiffs each day. Other than that not a lot happens in Isla Aguada.

Campground

HOTEL AND TRAILER PARK LA CABAÑA
    Address: Calle Marina S/N Centro, Isla
    Aguada, Camp., Mexico
    Telephone: (982) 5-90-18

        Price: Moderate

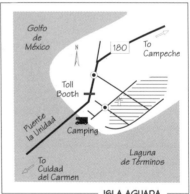

ISLA AGUADA

This is a sandy campground right on the beach of the inner lagoon near the toll bridge. Although called a hotel it is actually much more of an RV park, there are some rooms in the middle of the RV parking area. If you follow the beach around to the right and under the bridge you can walk for miles along the water and find tons of shells. The bridge is actually about a quarter mile away and there is little traffic so road noise is no problem at all.

The campground has at least 80 spaces with electricity and water, a few sites also

WATCH OUT FOR STOCK ON THE ROADS

have sewer drains. There is also a dump station. Pines and other trees of various sizes shade many of the sites, there are several very large ones near the water. Our favorite sites were under the big trees with the nose of the RV about 50 feet from the lagoon.

Five clean shower rooms, each with it's own toilet, have lots of hot water. The family running the campground speaks enough English to get by, but don't expect to be able to ask complicated questions.

You can drive right to the campground by taking the first possible right after leaving the bridge toll booth. Drive toward the lagoon, you'll see signs for the campground.

MÉRIDA, YUCATÁN (MEH-REE-DAH)
Population 525,000, Elevation 30 ft (9 m)

Mérida is the largest city on the Yucatán Peninsula and capital of the state of Yucatán. It is also one of Mexico's oldest cities and a designated national historic monument.

Mérida is very much a tourist city. When you tour the downtown area you'll see lots of Americans and Europeans. Many visitors to the Cancún area make side trips here for the nearby ruins and for the shopping. The real bargains are local products

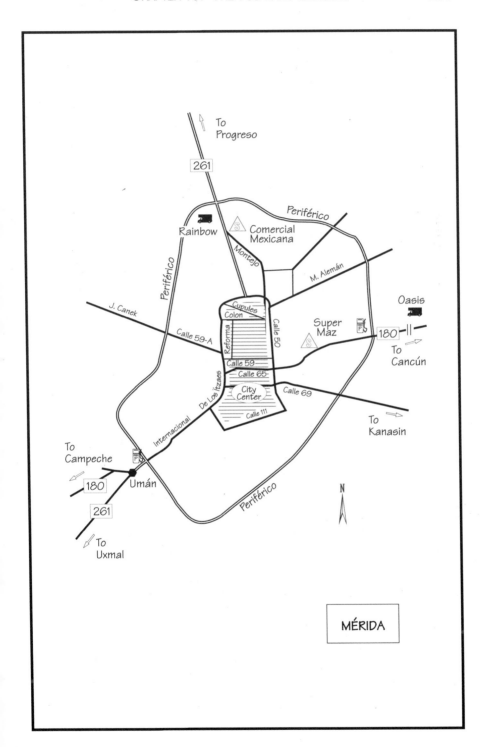

To
Progreso

261

Periférico

Rainbow

Comercial
Mexicana

Periférico

Montejo

M. Alemán

J. Canek

Oasis

Cupules

Colon

Calle 59-A

Reforma

Calle 50

Super
Maz

180

To
Cancún

Calle 59

Calle 65

De Los Itzaes

City
Center

Calle 69

Calle 111

To
Kanasin

Internacional

To
Campeche

180   Umán

261

Periférico

To
Uxmal

N

MÉRIDA

like hammocks, Panama hats, guayabera shirts and huipile dresses. Other items from all over Mexico are available, but unlike the other visitors here you will probably have an opportunity to buy these other things much nearer their point of creation, and you can get better prices. Be forewarned that Mérida's vendors are some of the pushiest around.

The central downtown area is well worth a visit for the shopping in the market and to tour the plaza, cathedral, and streets of the city. You can rent a horse-drawn buggy called a *calesa* if you wish. Do not take a large rig into town, the streets are narrow and crowded.

The best way to drive in to town is to drive around the ring road so that you enter the city on the road from Progreso. This is the road where the Rainbow Trailer Park is located so you can follow the directions given below to find it. As you continue in towards the centro area the road becomes the Paseo Montejo which is one of the city's tourist attractions. During the late 19th and early 20th century Mérida was a very rich town because of it's sisal fiber exports, the Paseo is lined with mansions, it is Mérida's version of a fashionable Paris-style boulevard.

The Paseo ends before it reaches the centro area. You should jog a block or so to the right and then turn left. The central area is bounded by Calle 57 on the north, Calle 69 on the south, Calle 66 on the west and Calle 54 on the east. You should be able to find street parking on the borders of this area for cars and smaller vehicles.

Campground No. 1

Rainbow RV Campground
　Address: Calle 61, No. 468, Mérida, C.P.
　97000-4 Yuc., Mexico
　Telephone: (99) 24-24-11
　Fax: (99) 24-77-84

　　　　Price: Low

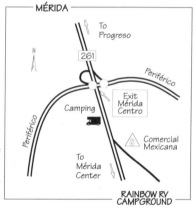

The Rainbow is the larger, older, and more convenient of the two Mérida campgrounds. There are about 100 sites, many with hookups for electricity, water, and sewer. Some sites have patios and some are pull-throughs. The entire campground is grassy and a few older sites have some shade.

There are two restroom buildings, one near the entrance and the other back near most of the sites. They are usually clean with hot showers..

Grocery shopping is convenient to this campground. Leave the campground and turn right towards town. You will see a large shopping center with a Comercial Mexicana on the left about 1 mile (1.6 km) from the campground.

The Rainbow is easy to find and has very good access that does not require driving through town. Just follow the ring road to the north side of Mérida. At the Progresso interchange drive toward town, almost immediately you'll see the Rainbow on the right or west side of the road.

Campground No. 2

OASIS RV CAMPGROUND
  Address: Carretera 180 Mérida a Valladolid
    Km. 10, Kanasin, C.P. 97370 Yuc., Mexico

  Price: Moderate

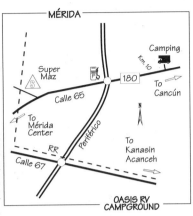

The Oasis is a relatively new campground. It will remind you very much of a campground in the U.S. or Canada. Pains have been taken to make sure that there is good electrical power, lots of room to maneuver big rigs, and that the water in the showers is hot. Unfortunately it may now be closed. Last time we passed by (winter 96-97) the gate was locked and a building was going up behind the restrooms.

There are 26 gravel parking areas, 17 with electrical power. All of the sites are back-in spots that are plenty long for big rigs and they are well separated by grassy areas. Trees have been planted but they aren't very big yet.

There are water spigots liberally sprinkled around the campground and there is a dump station. Everything is very clean.

The most convenient grocery shopping is about four miles away. To reach it turn right at the campground entrance and drive towards Mérida. Zero your odometer when you leave the campground. When you reach the ring road at odometer 2.5 continue straight across it towards town. In .8 miles (1.3 km) at odometer 3.3 miles (5.4 km) there is a stop light and the road bears left and merges with Quetzacóatle. The supermarket is .8 miles (1.3 km) ahead, at odometer 4.0 miles (6.5 km). It is in a shopping center on your right as you stop at the light. The shopping center is called Plaza Oriente and the supermarket is a Super Maz.

Other Camping Possibilities

Many people free camp on the beach near Celestún on the coast west of Mérida. Conditions can be windy and gritty.

Side Trips from Mérida

Located north of Mérida on the road to Progresso the **Dzibilchaltún Ruins** are unusual because they were in use for such a long time, from 2000 BC until the arrival of the Spanish. They are largely unexcavated. The Temple of the Seven Dolls has been restored and there is a Cenote where divers have recovered artifacts.

Celestún is located west of Mérida on the Gulf Coast in the Parque Natural del

Flamingo. This is one of the places on the Yucatán to see flamingos, you must rent a boat and guide to get close. The flamingo-watching season is from November to March.

Progreso is a beach resort on the coast north of Mérida. The distance is about 19 miles (30 km). The town has a malecón and good shallow-water beaches. It is a good side trip from town if you can't wait until you reach Cancún for a beach.

QUINTANA ROO COAST SOUTH OF CANCÚN, QUINTANA ROO
(KEEN-TAH-NUH ROW)

For purposes of this guide we define this area as starting near Puerto Morelos about 19 miles (31 km) south of Ciudad Cancún and running all the way south to Tulúm, which is about 75 miles (123 km) south of Ciudad Cancún. This coastal area is becoming increasingly popular as people discover that it offers a less crowded, less expensive, and much less developed alternative to Cancún.

The main town along the coast is **Playa del Carmen**. It is full of small hotels, good restaurants, small shops, and is the departure point for foot-passenger ferries to the Island of Cozumel. Playa del Carmen also has a Pemex station and a small supermarket so it is the supply center for campers not willing to trek north to Ciudad Cancún.

HAPPY CAMPERS!

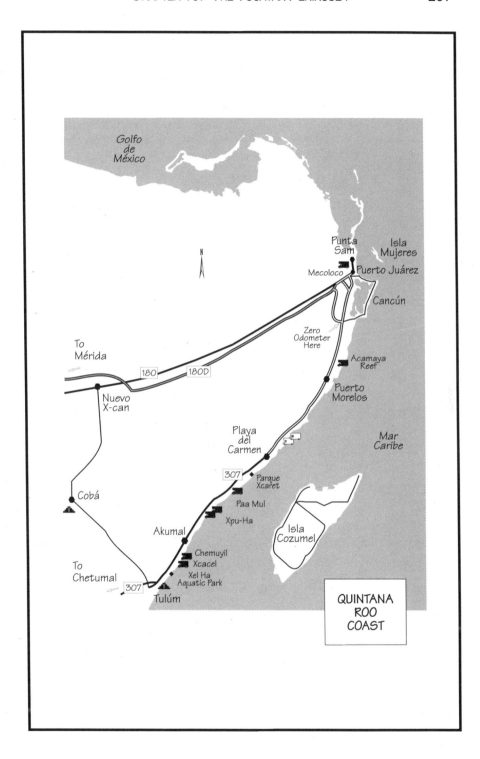

Golfo
de
México

Punta
Sam

Isla
Mujeres

Mecoloco   Puerto Juárez

Cancún

Zero
Odometer
Here

To
Mérida

Acamaya
Reef

180   180D

Puerto
Morelos

Nuevo
X-can

Playa
del
Carmen

Mar
Caribe

307   Parque
Xcaret

Cobá

Paa Mul

Xpu-Ha

Akumal

Isla
Cozumel

Chemuyil
Xcacel

To
Chetumal

Xel Ha
Aquatic Park

307

Tulúm

QUINTANA
ROO
COAST

Smaller **Puerto Morelos**, much nearer to Ciudad Cancún, is another ferry departure point for Cozumel, this one for automobiles. Puerto Morelos has a couple of good restaurants but shopping is limited.

Along the coast from Puerto Morelos to Tulúm there are many resort communities, all with beaches and many open to the public with restaurants and limited shopping. They range from luxurious to almost undeveloped. Some of the larger ones are **Punta Bete**, **Puerto Aventuras**, and **Akumal**. If you spend much time on the coast you'll probably explore them all.

Tulúm marks the south end of the developed section of coast. There's a Pemex and limited supplies here. If you head coastwards just south of the archeological site you'll find the **Boca Paila Road** which quickly becomes a gravel and sand track leading 35 miles (57 km) south to Punta Allen. You'll find simple cabaña resorts and free camping possibilities along this route.

CAMPGROUNDS

There are so many campgrounds, beaches, towns and sights on the Quintana Roo coast that it can be difficult to remember the location of them all. This listing of campgrounds will start with Paa Mul, probably the most popular campground along the coast. Then it will list the others, from north to south, along with their odometer readings from the intersection of the southern branch of Mex 180D and Mex. 307. Addresses along the north-south highway use a kilometer marking system that runs from north to south, unfortunately the markings now on the highway start far south and get larger as you go north. To make things even more difficult the road is being widened to four lanes as far south as Playa del Carmen. To avoid confusion you should probably just use our odometer readings although the campgrounds generally use one of the kilometer marks as their address.

Campground No. 1

CABAÑAS PAA MUL
    Address: Km 85 Carretera Cancún-Tulúm
    (Apdo. 83), Ciudad de Carmen, C.P. 77710
    Q. Roo, Mexico (See res. address and
    phone below)
    Telephone: (987) 4-13-87

Price: Moderate

This campground is located right on the water. The bay in front is beautiful, it is well known for good snorkeling and has a nice beach.

There are now about 130 spaces at Paa Mul, most with electricity, water and sewer. The best spaces, 30 of them along the water, are occupied by people who rent them on an annual basis. This phenomenon, common on the Baja Peninsula and the west coast, is unusual here on the Yucatán. The North American RVers build semi-permanent roofs, patios, and sometimes walls enclosing their RV's. With most of the conveniences of a permanent building, some are so elaborate that you would be hard pressed to tell that there is really an RV inside. There are also nice motel-style rental rooms along the beach.

The resort has two clean restroom buildings, each with several hot water showers. There is also an open-air restaurant and bar overlooking the beach and an active dive shop with charter boats. English is spoken, you just have to find the right people. Out on the main road there are two small stores. One sometimes carries the English language newspaper from Mexico City, *The News*.

Paa Mul is so self-contained that you may never need to leave it. It is popular with caravans because it has a combination of features not found at other parks on this coast. If you want to insure a spot you can make an advance reservation: Paa Mul Cabañas & RV Park, Depto. D-211, Av. Colon No. 501-C, Mérida, Yuc., Mexico (tel. (99) 25-94-22, fax. (99) 25-69-13). Many people stay for several months.

You can walk north along a small road behind the beach for about two miles (3 km) from the campground. If you are seeking a quiet beach this is the place to find it. It's also a great place for a daily constitutional.

Paa Mul is located 41.3 miles (67.4 km) south of our reference point, the intersection of the southern branch of Mex. 180D and Mex 307. It has hard-to-miss signage on the main road, turn toward the coast on a good paved road and drive for .4 miles (.7 km)

The down side of this park is that the RV's are crowded together in what is essentially a sandy parking lot with little shade (the trees are getting bigger, however). The nicer spaces are reserved for the permanent residents and transients are relegated to the space between the permanent resident's palapas and the jungle. If you must have all of the conveniences, though, this is the place for you. Otherwise, read on.

Campground No. 2

ACAMAYA REEF TRAILER-PARK
  Address: Km 29 Carratera Cancún-
  Chetumal, Q. Roo., Mexico
  Telephone (987) 1-01-32
  Fax: (987) 1-00-81

Price: Moderate

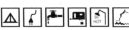

The Acamaya Reef is a small place sitting right next to a long, mostly deserted, open beach. It is relatively close to Cancún and within hiking distance (2 miles) of Puerto Morelos and its restaurants. An added benefit, especially for those with family joining them for the holidays, is that the Acamaya has a few clean, simple cabaña style rooms where the extra guests can comfortably be put up.

There are ten spaces, all with electricity, water and sewer. These are small spaces, to get 10 rigs in here they would all have to be van-size. All of the parking spots slope slightly so you'll have to work out an arrangement to level your vehicle.

There is a very clean restroom building with hot showers. A thatched shelter near the beach provides shade and there are scattered tables and chairs. A small restaurant is sometimes open.

The turn from Mex. 307 is next to the well-signed Croco Cun crocodile farm. It is 9.6 miles (15.7 km) south of the Mex. 180D and Mex. 307 intersection. This section of Mex. 307 is being widened to four lanes, you may have to go a few hundred yards south to a retorno if you are driving south from Cancún. From the highway drive 1.3 miles (2.1 km) toward the beach on a paved but potholed road. Then turn right at the sign and follow an even poorer but passable road for another .3 miles (.5 km) to the campground. Access on foot is also possible along a road running behind condos and hotels north along the beach from the little town of Puerto Morelos, located a couple miles to the south. This road is pretty bad, vehicles should use the road from the highway.

Campground No. 3

TRAILER PARK CAMPING MANATI XPU-HA (XPU-HA NORTH)

Price: Inexpensive

Located at 46.6 miles (76.1 km) south of the intersection of Mex. 307 and the southern branch of Mex. 180D. There are many entrance roads here. They are marked by hand-painted signs that mean nothing to the uninitiated (X-1, X-2, etc.). You can recognize the road to this trailer park by the power lines that it follows toward the beach. Drive .4 mile toward the beach, the road is rough and uneven, but big rigs negotiate it by taking it slow. This campground is right next to the Bonanza Xpu-Ha Campground which has its own entrance road.

The campground sits on a raised area overlooking the beach. This is one of the few places along the coast where you can park a large rig with an unobstructed view of the water. Unfortunately the camping area is almost treeless.

There is a restroom with cold showers. Electricity is available although the service is really long extension cords.

Campground No. 4

BONANZA XPU-HA CAMPGROUND (XPU-HA SOUTH)

Price: Inexpensive

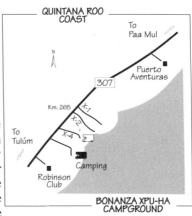

QUINTANA ROO COAST

To Paa Mul

To Tulúm

Puerto Aventuras

307

Km. 265

X-1

X-2

X-4

Camping

Robinson Club

BONANZA XPU-HA CAMPGROUND

Located at 46.8 miles (76.4 km) south of the intersection of Mex. 307 and the soutern branch of Mex. 180D. A small sandy campground with room for about 20 smaller rigs. The camping area spreads across a dune behind the beach with some shade. There are no utility hookups here and most of the campers seem to be glad that there aren't. There is a nice restroom with cold water showers and a beautiful beach.

Campground No. 5

PLAYA CHEMUYIL

Price: Inexpensive

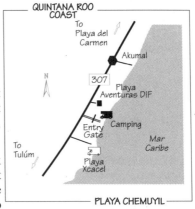

QUINTANA ROO COAST

To Playa del Carmen

Akumal

307

Playa Aventuras DIF

Entry Gate

Camping

Mar Caribe

To Tulúm

Playa Xcacel

PLAYA CHEMUYIL

The beach here is advertised as the most beautiful on the coast, it may be. It is a quiet cove with good snorkeling and a wide, clean, white-sand beach.

The camping area for vehicles sits just back from the beach, there is probably room for at least 50 good sized rigs here, but there are never that many because Chemuyil has no hookups of any kind. Some caravan companies stay here for several days even without hookups, that should give you an idea of how nice the place really is. A large percentage of the campers here use tents or vans with many of the tents set up right on the beach.

Although there are no hookups there are facilities. The beach is well-known and gets a lot of day use. There is a restaurant bar and large clean public restrooms and cold-water showers. Noise from the restaurant and day use areas never seems to be a problem, you will be impressed by the way this place is run.

Chemuyil has good signage. It is located 56.2 miles (91.8 km) south of the intersection of Mex. 307 and the southern branch of Mex. 180D. The entrance road might make you think you're entering a major resort, it seems very over-built. You'll be stopped at a gate and a camping or day-use fee collected.

Campground No. 6

PLAYA XCACEL

Price: Inexpensive

Just two miles (3.3 km) south of the Chemuyil campground, Xcacel is very similar and is just as nice. The campground here tends to attract smaller vehicles and younger people, it is sandy and has a little less room than the one at Chemuyil. The camp area sits behind the beach and is lower so there is not as much benefit from breezes as there might be. This beach also has a lot of visitors, there is a restaurant-bar and public restrooms with cold water showers.

The Xcacel beach is much longer and more exposed to waves than the one at Chemuyil. If you walk about a quarter mile to the right along the beach there is a short trail inland to a cenote. It contains beautiful clear turquoise water, you won't be able to resist a swim.

Walkers can make a somewhat strenuous hike north along the beach as far as Chemuyil. There is also an easy hike south on back roads to the water park at Xel-Ha.

The entrance to Xcacel is 57.8 miles (94.4 km) south of the intersection of Mex. 307 and the southern branch of Mex. 180D. It has a good sign.

Other Camping Possibilities

At Punta Beta or Xcalcoco there are several small resorts with cabañas, restaurants, and a beautiful beach. Some of them have room for a few small RV's or for tent campers. The road to the beach where these campgrounds are located is 27.2 miles (44.4 km) south of the intersection of Mex. 307 and the southern branch of Mex. 180D. The 1.3 mile long road is small and sometimes sandy with several Y's, each one with many signs pointing towards various establishments. You should find cold showers, no hookups, and a very relaxed ambiance.

Just south of the Tulúm archeological site there is a beachside cabaña city. It is known as Camping Santa Fe. There are dozens of thatched-roof huts and also room for some van and tent camping. No hookups but cold showers and several nearby restaurants. Access is from the side road that runs toward the beach just south of the Tulúm archeological site (the Boca Paila Road). From Mex. 307 drive east, at the T turn left and watch for the Don Armando Cabañas and Restaurant. Turn in here, bear left at the restaurant, the campground is just ahead.

Free campers often head farther south along the Boca Paila Road to camp along the beach.

Side Trips from the Quintana Roo Coast

If you are a scuba diver you are probably well aware of the Island of **Cozumel**. There are two Cozumel's just as there are two Cancúns. One is a world famous scuba diving destination making its living by catering to divers. The other is a port for cruise ships and everything that that implies. If you've never had the experience of traveling on a Caribbean cruise, you should know that the ports visited are generally tacky and expensive because they cater to the boatloads of passengers who come ashore for a few hours looking for souvenirs before moving on to another port. Cozumel is no exception. Don't plan on shopping here. Prices are actually quoted in U.S. dollars. If you want to dive, that's another story.

The easiest way to get to Cozumel is by ferry from Ciudad del Carmen. There are fast ferries running both ways every couple of hours, the trip takes about 45 minutes. The boat trip is a highlight for us, we've seen flying fish from the hydrofoil. To see them you should ride on deck, the fish launch themselves from the bow wave and fly for distances of over 50 yards before they splash in.

You'll want to visit **Xel-Ha**, it's not like anything you've seen elsewhere. It is a beautiful saltwater lagoon where you can actually watch tropical fish from the shore. It became so popular with snorkelers that it was declared a national park so that it wouldn't be destroyed. Extensive paved pathways have been built around the

TULÚM

lagoon so you can easily walk around and watch the fish. Swimming is also allowed, in fact most people come here to snorkel. The inner lagoon is closed to swimming but a large part of the outer lagoon is open. If you are uneasy swimming in open water you may find that Xel-Ha is your favorite snorkeling site ever. Xel-Ha is located off Mex. 307 just south of Chemuyil and Xcacel.

If you decide to visit **Xcaret** you had better set aside a whole day for it. Not only is there lots to keep you busy, it is so expensive that you will want to make them earn every cent. Here's what you can do. Float an underground river. Visit a wild bird breeding area. View a Mayan archeological site. Lie on the beach. Swim with a dolphin. Ride a horse. Tour a botanical garden. View tropical fish in an aquarium. Snorkel or scuba dive. Open from 8 A.M. to 5 P.M. Xcaret is located off Mex. 307 between Playa del Carmen and Paa Mul.

Tulúm archeological site is famous not for the quantity or quality of its buildings (no pyramids), it is famous for its setting. The site sits on a rocky bluff above the sea, it was one of the first Mayan cities discovered by the Spanish since they could actually see it from their ships when they sailed past. Probably the most common and beautiful photograph of Mexico is a shot of El Castillo (the watchtower) backed by dark blue Caribbean water.

Cobá is a very large site, actually covering more than 50 square miles, it is largely unrestored. There are miles of hiking trails through the brush so if you like to hike, this is the place. Two large Pyramids have been partially restored, stairs lead to the top. If you've come to like climbing pyramids you can visit both of them and not walk more than about 5 kilometers. After the crowds at Tulúm these ruins will seem empty, kind of nice.

A huge area just south of the Cancún-Tulúm corridor has been set aside as a wildlife refuge called the **Sian Ka´an Biosphere Reserve**. Access is a little difficult but rewarding, especially for nature lovers. The rough unsurfaced Boca Paila Rd. running south from Tulúm to Punta Allen, a distance of 35 miles (57 km) is the best access. There's no gas so be sure to fill up before leaving, this road is slow going. This is a terrain of sand dunes, scrub jungle, and swampy lagoons. It is home to lots of birds and lots of mosquitoes. Also visit **Chunyaxché archeological site** on the main road (Mex. 307) 27 miles (43 km) south of Tulúm. It sits at the edge of a lagoon and is surrounded by jungle.

UXMAL, YUCATÁN (OOSH-MAHL)

Uxmal is one of what we call the "big 4" archeological destinations in this part of Mexico. The others would be Chichén Itzá, Tulúm, and Palenque. They are included in the big 4 because they are important and interesting. They are also well-promoted and are visited by lots of tourists. This doesn't make them places to be avoided, just expect to see a lot more tourists than you have so far on this trip.

Almost everyone who visits Uxmal wants to see the "sound and light" show which is given in English every night at 9 P.M. For this reason many people think that they should camp at the ruins so they don't have to drive at night. See the camping

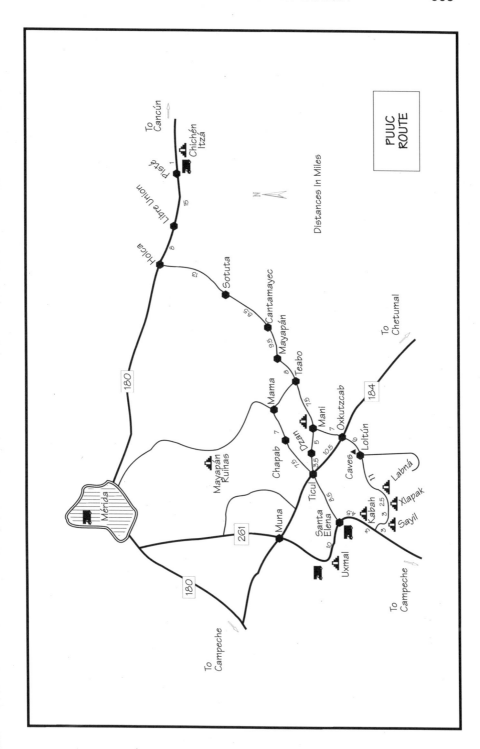

PUUC ROUTE

Distances In Miles

To Cancún

Chichén Itzá

Pisté

1

Libre Unión

15

Holca

8

13

Sotuta

8.5

Cantamayec

9.5

Mayapán

8

Teabo

180

7.5

Mama

Mani

7

Oxkutzcab

184

To Chetumal

Mayapán Ruinas

Chapab

7

Dzan

5

10.5

3.5

Loltún

6

Caves

11

Labná

Ticul

1.5

Xlapak

2.5

Santa Elena

8.5

Kabah

4.5

Sayil

3

Muna

10

261

Mérida

180

Uxmal

To Campeche

To Campeche

section about this. We prefer to camp nearby and drive a small vehicle. We don't often break our no night driving rule, but this is one time we think it's OK.

Uxmal is in the center of a number of archeological sites, you will be missing a lot if you limit yourself to Uxmal only. Many people spend several days here and don't see all that they wish to. This is also a good area to do some bicycle touring.

Services at Uxmal are limited but several hotels in the area do have decent restaurants. If you are staying at Camping Sacbe you might want to visit the little government-run Conasupo store in Santa Elena just to see what they are like.

Campground

CAMPING SACBE
   Address: Fam. Portillo, Apdo. 5, Ticul, C.P.
   97860 Yucatán, Mexico

Price: Low

This small family-run campground has a lot going for it. It is located 9 miles (14.5 km) south of Uxmal on Mex. 261. This places it conveniently close to many of the other archeological sites that you will probably wish to visit while you are in the area.

Sacbe has 9 RV sites, six of them with electrical hookups. Water and sewer are not available, nor is there a dump station. There are three toilet areas and three showers, cold water only. The facilities are exceptionally clean and well maintained, as are the grounds. This campground is only about three years old and the facilities are in good condition.

The campground also has a very nice tent area with concrete picnic tables and fiberglass-roofed palapas. There is a bulletin board with information about the bus service to the various sites including evening service to the sound and light show at Uxmal. There are also maps and even a listing of birds that can be seen in the area. English is spoken here.

Other Camping Possibilities

Many people dry camp in the parking lot at the Uxmal archeological site. The advantage of this is that you can walk to the sound and light show in the evening. You probably won't want to stay here if you are planning on spending more than one night in the area, this parking lot is busy during the day.

The Parador Touristico Cana-Nah is located 2.6 miles (4.2 km) north of Uxmal on the main road to Mérida. This restaurant and motel has room for about ten rigs in an area next to the restaurant. There are restrooms and cold showers in a building adjacent to the parking area. The manager says that electricity is available but the two hookups look rather jury-rigged to us.

Next to the Cana-Nah is Rancho Uxmal. This restaurant and hotel has offered camping in the past but now has pretty much covered the available space with buildings. They'll still let you park and hook up to electricity but you'll be right in the middle of their crowded parking lot.

Many of the archeological sites on the Yucatán will allow campers to spend the night in or just outside their parking lots. Some of these lots are fenced and some are not. All are dry camps. If the place looks good to you ask the manager if overnight camping is OK. There may be a fee.

Side Trips from Uxmal

There are several smaller archeological sites located near Uxmal, a tour of them is known as the **Puuc Route**. They include **Kabah, Sayil, Xlapak,** and **Labná.** The roads to these sites are good and parking is uncrowded and fine for RV's so if you don't have a tow car or scooter you can easily use your RV for transportation.

Ticul, 18 miles (29 km) from Uxmal and 9 miles (14.7 km) from Camping Sacbe in Santa Elena is the place to go to buy shoes and replicas of Mayan artwork.

The **Loltún Caves**, 37 miles (60 km) from Uxmal and 27 miles (44 km) from Camping Sacbe in Santa Elena are the most impressive caves on the Yucatán. They have huge limestone chambers complete with stalagmites and stalactites and a Mayan wall carving. You are required to tour with one of the guides you will find there.

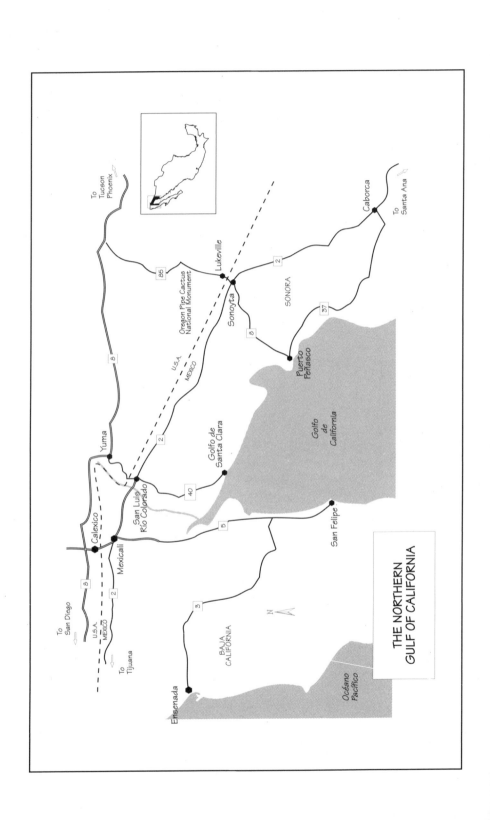

THE NORTHERN
GULF OF CALIFORNIA

CHAPTER II

THE NORTHERN GULF OF CALIFORNIA

INTRODUCTION

The northern Gulf of California destinations: Puerto Peñasco, San Felipe, and Golfo de Santa Clara; are so close to the border, so easy to reach, and so full of Americans that you can almost consider them to be part of the U.S. Each of them can be reached by driving only a few hours south of the border on decent and mostly uncrowded two-lane roads.

Another great feature of these destinations is that they all fall within special zones in Mexico. Paperwork formalities are minimized, particularly regulations limiting the number of vehicles that you can bring south of the border. Off-roaders appreciate these special rules. For details see the Vehicle Documentation heading in our Crossing the Border chapter.

The Sea of Cortez or Gulf of California is a long narrow body of water extending 700 miles (1,125 km) northward from the Tropic of Cancer which almost exactly traces a line between Cabo San Lucas and Mazatlán. The waters of the Sea or Gulf teem with fish and have some of the highest tides in the world. The northern reaches including the three towns featured in this chapter have a tidal range exceeding 20 feet between high and low water. This can be an interesting place to operate a boat.

Winter is probably the most pleasant time to visit this area because it has a desert climate with extremely high temperatures during the summer, even along the water. Many people do visit in the summer, however, because that's when the fishing is best.

ROAD SYSTEM

All of these towns are within 110 miles (175 km) of each other as the crow flies, driving between them is another matter.

Puerto Peñasco is arguably the easiest of the three to reach. There is an excellent 61 mile (100 km) two-lane paved road running south from the Lukeville/Sonoyta border crossing. The crossing itself is excellent. It is uncrowded, has lots of room for RVs, and generally takes only a few minutes to negotiate. On the U.S. side of the border the roads are also pretty good, Hwy. 85 south from Interstate 8 is 80 miles (129 km) long and there are conveniently located campgrounds in the town of Lukeville and in the Organ Pipe Cactus National Monument. Mexican insurance is available in Lukeville. Neither tourist cards nor vehicle-import permits are necessary for a visit to Puerto Peñasco.

Golfo de Santa Clara access is also easy. The closest crossing is at San Luis Río Colorado just south of Yuma, Arizona. Follow signs south and then southwest for Golfo de Santa Clara. The distance between the two towns is 70 miles (114 km). Like Puerto Peñasco, a visit to Golfo de Santa Clara requires no tourist cards or vehicle-import permits.

The closest crossing point for San Felipe is Calexico/Mexicali. This is a large town, the population approaches a million people, but it is not difficult to drive through. It has wide boulevards that make driving southeast from the central border crossing quite easy. You can get a vehicle-import permit here but you don't need it if you are heading south for San Felipe and the Baja. A tourist card, however, is necessary and should be picked up at the border crossing. Many people do not do this and occasionally fines are levied during surprise inspections of San Felipe RV parks. The road south from Mexicali to San Felipe is 122 miles (200 km) long and takes about 3 hours to drive. Most of it is decent two-lane paved highway, some of the northern portion has four-lanes. Many folks from southern California whip over to Mexicali on Interstate 8 for a quick weekend visit to San Felipe.

There are few additional roads in this region. Mex. 2 runs just south of the U.S. border across the entire area, and is fine for local access, but it is generally two-lane and the heavy Mexican truck use that it receives has ruined the surface and makes driving some sections of it less than fun.

There is a newly-paved road that runs east from Puerto Peñasco to Caborca, if you are approaching the area from the east you may want to give it a try rather than following Mex. 2 all the way up to Sonoyta and then back down to Puerto Peñasco. Heading east you might want to have your visa and vehicle permit in hand since they are required farther east.

HIGHLIGHTS

For folks accustomed to spending their winters in arid Arizona and New Mexico the highlights of this area are obvious, this is the closest salt water with its accompanying beaches and water sports. Californians can find warmer winter weather and much better access to beaches and many water sports than they have back home. Fishing, sailing, and sail-boarding are extremely popular. Added to that are huge areas to explore in off-road vehicles.

WATCHING THE MOON RISE OVER SAN FELIPE

THE CAMPGROUNDS

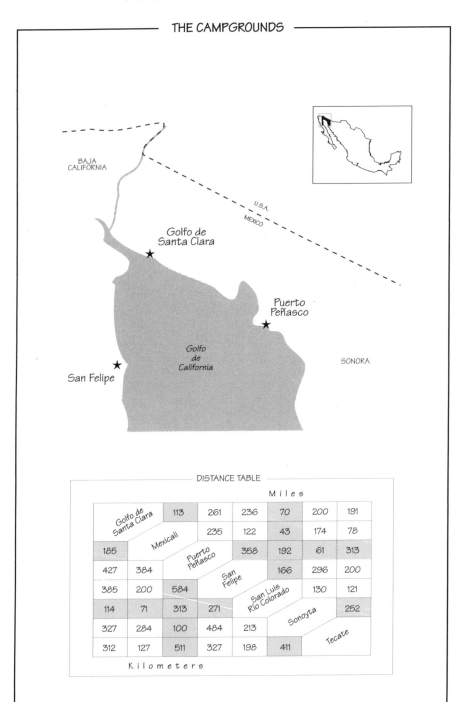

DISTANCE TABLE

Miles

Golfo de Santa Clara	113	261	236	70	200	191
	Mexicali	235	122	43	174	78
185		Puerto Peñasco	358	192	61	313
427	384		San Felipe	166	296	200
385	200	584		San Luis Río Colorado	130	121
114	71	313	271		Sonoyta	252
327	284	100	484	213		Tecate
312	127	511	327	198	411	

Kilometers

SELECTED CITIES AND THEIR CAMPGROUNDS

GOLFO DE SANTA CLARA, SONORA (GOLF-OH day SAHN-TAW claw-RAH)
Population 1,500, Elevation sea level

If you are looking for a piece of the real outback Mexico with no tourist glitz Golfo de Santa Clara is the place for you. This is a small fishing village surrounded by miles and miles of sand. Most tourist guides don't even mention the town but it is becoming something of a popular camping destination. We even hear that KOA has been taking a look at Golfo de Santa Clara. The beach south of town stretches for miles and ATVs are welcome.

Golfo de Santa Clara is built entirely on sand. This means that driving can be challenging. The streets in town aren't much of a problem, they are packed and if you are careful you aren't likely to get stuck, even with a big rig. The road out of town toward the cluster of campgrounds located a mile east on the beach is another story. This road is usually passable and big rigs, even fifth-wheels and 40-foot motorhomes can make it to the Pionero if they do not slow and stop in the loose sand. Momentum is everything so stay to the part of the road that seems best and forge ahead! You might be smart to stop before starting down this road and see if other traffic is having problems, you can see almost the entire mile of soft sandy road straight ahead.

Campground No. 1

NUEVO MOTEL DEL GOLFO
 Address: Av. Almejas y 1ra., Golfo de Santa
 Clara, Son. Mexico
 Telephone: (653) 8-02-21

Price: Low

GPS Location: N 31° 41' 225", W 114° 30' 15.2"

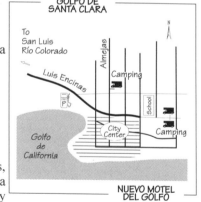

This new motel actually has two RV parks, and they are welcome additions to the Santa Clara area. One, with three spaces, is directly behind the hotel. A second, with 17 spaces, is a few blocks away and is near completion (planned for spring 1997). These campgrounds have a big advantage, they are in town and can be reached without driving the sand road a mile east to where the other Santa Clara campgrounds are located.

All 20 slots are back-in with 30-amp. electricity, sewer, and water on a gravel base. The motel has toilets built for the camping area but no showers. They may let you use one of the rooms for a shower if one is empty. The second campground has no toilet or shower building yet, both are planned for the near future. There is an open-air restaurant here and one of the owners, Raul Agraz, can fill you in on recreation possibilities. He speaks excellent English.

The motel is well signed. Zero your odometer at the Pemex as you enter town. The left turn for the motel is at .1 mile (.2 km) on Almejas. For the 17 space RV park continue straight on the pavement for .2 miles (.3 km) from the Pemex, the park is on both sides of the road and is just after you reach the end of the pavement but before you reach loose sand.

Campground No. 2

PIONERO R.V.
   Address: Domocilio Conocido, El Golfo de
   Santa Clara, Son., Mexico

  Price: Moderate, Low without hookups

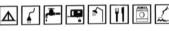

GPS Location: N 31° 40' 45.1", W 114° 29" 34.1"

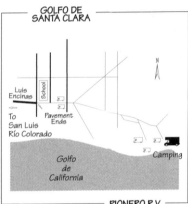

This is a huge RV park that had excellent facilities at one time, unfortunately it is presently somewhat run-down. A little maintenance could really make this place shine. It is right on a beautiful beach that goes south and east for uncounted miles. ATV heaven.

There are 100 spaces, all with 50-amp. and 30-amp. electricity, sewer, and water. All of the spaces have patios and the gravel driving and parking surfaces are solid. The spaces near the beach have been damaged by storms and the electricity doesn't work, some people get around this by stringing long electric cords. Restrooms have flush toilets and cold water showers, cleaning is spotty. There is a pool (empty when we visited in February) and a restaurant (closed when we visited). There is also a laundry with coin-operated machines but no hot water.

To reach the Pionero drive straight through town, past the end of the pavement, and along the loose sandy road that is the continuation of the main highway. About .9 mile (1.5 km) after the end of the pavement the road reaches a T, turn right and you'll see the campground immediately ahead. You might check in town to see if the campground is open before venturing out there. See the section about driving this sandy road above.

Other Camping Possibilities

There are three other camping areas near the Pionero. Just next door is Las Cabañas. There is a restaurant here and some older motel units. There are also about 20 spaces for camping, they are small, on sand, covered, and have lights and a few very low amperage electrical outlets. This area is really designed for tent campers during the big Mexican holidays but is certainly useable. The price is low and the restaurant has bathroom with cold showers.

About a tenth of a mile before you reach the Pionero T there is a road to the right that goes to the El Capitán Restaurant. They also have campsites similar to those at Las Cabañas but without any electricity. This restaurant also has bathrooms with cold showers.

About a hundred yards in front of the El Capitán on the beach is a government-owned recreation area. There are palapas but no services, people use those at the El Capitán. The sand is soft and you should take a close look before driving down there.

PUERTO PEÑASCO, SONORA (PWEHR-TOE PEN-YAHS-KOE)
Population 13,000, Elevation sea level

Many Mexico travel guides ignore Puerto Peñasco, as if it weren't even part of Mexico. This attitude is understandable, the town really does have a great deal of American influence. To ignore Puerto Peñasco in a camping guide to Mexico would be something of a crime, however. RVers virtually own this town, hordes of them fill RV parks and free camp in the vicinity. On weekends and holidays Puerto Peñasco is even more popular. After all, it is only 60 miles (98 km) south of the Arizona border, it is located in a free zone requiring no governmental paperwork, and there are beaches, desert, fishing, and Mexican crafts and food. Don't forget to pick up Mexican auto insurance, however.

Americans often call the town Rocky Point, you'll see why when you see the location of the old town. The road to Rocky Point was built by the American government during World War II when it was thought that it might be necessary to bring in supplies this way if the west coast was blockaded by Japanese submarines. That never happened, but the good road, now paved and in good shape, makes the town easy to reach. Puerto Peñasco is also a fishing port, not everything here is tourist oriented. Campgrounds are located in two areas: most are along the beach to the east of the old town, two others are along the beach to the northwest. Free campers congregate farther west toward La Choya. The road along which most of the campgrounds in the first area are strung has just been paved, Rocky Point is going upscale. In fact there is lots of talk of major tourist developments here in the next few years. Supplies of all kinds are available, there are some small supermarkets.

Campground No. 1

PLAYA ELEGANTE R.V. PARK
   Address: Apdo. 101, Puerto Peñasco, C.P. 83550 Son., Mexico
   Telephone: (638) 3-37-12
   Fax: (638) 3-60-71

Price: Moderate

GPS Location: N 31° 17' 46.4", W 113° 31' 55.5"

Open Oct. 1 to May 31.

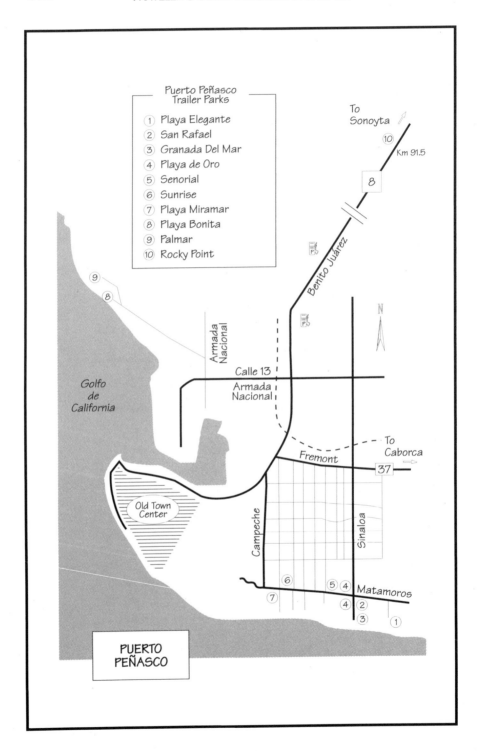

Puerto Peñasco Trailer Parks

1. Playa Elegante
2. San Rafael
3. Granada Del Mar
4. Playa de Oro
5. Senorial
6. Sunrise
7. Playa Miramar
8. Playa Bonita
9. Palmar
10. Rocky Point

To Sonoyta

Km 91.5

Benito Juárez

Armada Nacional

Calle 13

Armada Nacional

Golfo de California

Fremont

To Caborca

37

Old Town Center

Campeche

Sinaloa

Matamoros

PUERTO PEÑASCO

The Playa Elegante is the farthest east trailer park in the look-alike group clustered along Calle Matamoros on the oceanfront east of the old town. It is a large beach-fronting campground with easy access.

The campground has 200 spaces. They are all back-in slots with 30-amp. electricity, sewer, water, and satellite TV hookups. None of the spaces has a patio or shade, they all have a gravel parking surface. The bathrooms are in the main building which also houses a self-service laundry and meeting room. The bathrooms are modern and clean and have hot showers. There is a sun deck on the top of the main building, the beach is better for sun but the deck offers a good view. English is spoken.

To reach the campground when approaching Puerto Peñasco from the north on Mex. 8 zero your odometer as you pass the airport. At 1.3 miles (2.1 km) you'll enter Puerto Peñasco, at 2 miles (3.2 km) you'll see the town square on the left, at 3.1 miles (5 km) you'll cross Armada Nacional Avenue/Hidalgo which is marked with a cluster of green overhead signs. At a stoplight at 3.5 miles (5.6 km) Fremont Boulevard cuts off to the left, this is Son. 37 to Caborca. Continuing straight and bear left at the Y at 3.6 miles (5.8 km) and at 4.1 miles (6.6 km) you'll reach Calle Matamoros which runs east and west along the beach. Turn left here and pass a series of campgrounds and finally reach the right turn for the Playa Elegante at 4.7 miles (7.6 km). The campground is just down the road toward the water and to the left, the entrance is obvious.

If you are approaching from Caborca on Son. 37 watch carefully as you enter town. You'll see a paved road with wide shoulders on the left that is well marked with campground signs. This is Sinaloa, if you turn here you'll soon reach the beach and can make a left and then a right to reach the Playa Elegante. The other Calle Matamoros campgrounds are to the right.

Campground No. 2

SAN RAFAEL R.V. PARK
  Address: Apdo. 58, Puerto Peñasco, C.P. 83550 Son., Mexico
  Telephone: (638) 3-50-44, (638) 3-26-81

Price: Moderate

GPS Location: N 31° 17' 51.1", W 113° 31' 59.6"

This is a smaller campground with no beachfront sites even though it is south of Calle Matamoros. For this reason it is slightly less expensive than the other campgrounds on the south side of the street.

The campground has 53 slots, all have 30-amp. electricity, sewer, and water. These are gravel-surfaced back-in spaces without patios or shade. The campground has clean modern restrooms with hot showers, a TV room, a self-service laundry, and English is spoken.

To find the campground follow the instructions given for the Playa Elegante above.

After turning left onto Calle Matamoros proceed .5 miles (.8 km), you'll see the San Rafael entrance on the right.

Campground No. 3

HOTEL AND R.V. PARK GRANADA DEL MAR
   Address: P.O. Box 30806, Tucson, AZ 85751 U.S.A.
   Telephone: (638) 3-27-42

Price: Moderate

GPS Location: N 31° 17'46.7", W 113° 32' 02.6"

The Granada is a new trailer park in Puerto Peñasco, it occupies the beach in front of the San Rafael and also some of the beach in front of the Playa de Oro. The trailer park is an addition to a motel-style hotel that has occupied the site for some time.

The campground has 48 back-in spaces, they all have 30-amp. electricity, sewer, and water. These spaces have the customary Puerto Peñasco gravel surface with no patio or shade. About a third are beachfront sites. The small bathroom cubicles are new and clean and have hot water. There is a bar/disco on the water to the west of the hotel building that serves some food and is popular with the folks from this park and also the Playa de Oro next door.

To find the campground follow the instructions given for the Playa Elegante above. After turning left onto Calle Matamoros proceed .5 miles (.8 km), you'll see the San Rafael entrance on the right. Turn right down the street just before the San Rafael, the Granada is at the end of the street next to the water.

Campground No. 4

PLAYA DE ORO R.V. PARK
   Address: Apdo. 76, Puerto Peñasco, C.P. 83550 Son., Mexico
   Telephone: (638) 3-26-68

Price: Moderate

GPS Location: N 31° 17' 49.8", W 113° 32' 05.6'

This huge campground is one of the oldest ones in Puerto Peñasco. It bills itself as the only full service RV park in Rocky Point. This is somewhat true, the campground does have many amenities, but is also is showing it's age in some ways.

There are now 350 spaces at the Play de Oro. They are located south of Calle Matamoros along and back from the beach and also extending well inland to the north of Calle Matamoros. The sites have 30-amp electricity, sewer, water, and satellite TV. They have gravel surfaces, no shade, and no patios. The bathrooms are older but clean, the showers require a quarter for 4 to 5 minutes and the hot water was intermittent in the one I used. The campground has a small, simple restaurant, a mini-mart, a self-service laundry, and a boat ramp. There is also a large long-term storage yard for those wishing to leave a trailer or boat when they go back north.

To find the campground follow the instructions given for the Playa Elegante above. After turning left onto Calle Matamoros proceed .4 miles (.6 km), you'll see the Playa de Oro entrance on the right.

Campground No. 5

TRAILER PARK SENORIAL
   Address: Apdo. 76, Puerto Peñasco, C.P. 83550 Son., Mexico (same as Playa de
      Oro)
   Telephone: (638) 3-35-30

Price: Moderate

GPS Location: N 31° 17' 50.4", W 113° 32' 05.6"

The Trailer Park Senorial is located just across the street and slightly west of the Playa de Oro and has the same owners. It is a smaller park and has a swimming pool to make up for the fact that it is not on the beach.

The campground has 65 spaces. All are back-in slots with electricity, water, and sewer. The parking pads are cement but there are no patios or shade. The bathrooms are clean and in good repair, the showers are hot and require a $.25 payment. The swimming pool sits at the upper end of the campground and is quite nice.

To find the campground follow the instructions given for the Playa Elegante above. After turning left onto Calle Matamoros proceed .3 miles (.5 km), you'll see the Trailer Park Senorial entrance on the left.

Campground No. 6

SUNRISE EXECUTIVE R.V. PARK
   Address: P.O. Box 625, Lukeville, AZ 85341 U.S.A.
   Telephone: (638) 3-44-50

Price: Moderate

GPS Location: N 31° 17' 51.1", W 113° 32' 23.1"

The Sunrise is small but is one of the nicest trailer parks in town. It is not on the beach but you probably won't even notice. There are 16 spaces, all are back-in with 30-amp. electricity, sewer, water, satellite TV, patio, and barbecue grill. The restrooms are clean and nice, they have hot water showers. There is a swimming pool and jacuzzi, a recreation room, and a laundry room with free self-service machines.

To find the campground follow the instructions given for the Playa Elegante above. After turning left onto Ave. Matamoros (Calle 1) proceed .1 miles (.2 km), you'll see the Sunrise entrance on the left. It is on the corner of Matamoros and Coahuila.

Campground No. 7

PLAYA MIRAMAR R.V. PARK
  Address: Apdo. 2, Puerto Peñasco, C.P. 83550 Son., Mexico
  Telephone: (638) 3-25-87
  Fax: (638) 3-23-51

Price: Moderate

GPS Location: N 31° 17' 50.4", W 113° 32' 25.0"

This is the last (or first) of the three big RV parks between Ave. Matamoros (Calle 1) and the beach. The Playa Miramar has 146 spaces, all are back-in with 30-amp. electricity, sewer, water and satellite TV. The restrooms are very clean and have hot water for showers that are metered and cost a quarter. There is a recreation room and a laundry.

If you follow the instructions given above for reaching the Playa Elegante Trailer Park the Playa Miramar is the first trailer park you'll see after turning onto Matamoros. It is on the right.

Campground No. 8

PLAYA BONITA R.V. PARK
  Address: Apdo. 34, Puerto Peñasco, Son. Mexico
  Telephone: (638) 3-25-96

Price: Moderate

GPS Location: N 31° 19' 08.1", W 113° 33' 25.3"

This is the larger of two trailer parks located northwest of town on Playa Bonita. The Playa Bonita R.V. Park is affiliated with a nice hotel next door.

There are 300 spaces in this huge campground. All are back-in slots with 30-amp. electricity, sewer, water, and satellite TV connection. Restrooms are modern and clean and have hot water. The campground has a small recreation room with a TV, a self-service laundry, and the hotel next door has a restaurant. The beach out front is beautiful and there are pits constructed on it for fires.

As you enter town you will pass two Pemexes, the first on the left and then one on the right. A half mile (.8 km) after the second Pemex is a cross road marked with many large green signs over the road. Turn right here on Calle 13. Proceed across the railroad tracks and drive for .3 mile (.5 km), turn right on sandy Armada Nacional. The turn is marked with a sign for the campground. Drive up this road for .9 miles (1.5 km) to the gate of the trailer park.

Campground No. 9

PALMAR R.V. PARK
Address: Apdo. 24, Puerto Peñasco, Son. Mexico
Telephone: (638) 3-58-77

Price: Moderate

GPS Location: N 31° 19' 15.6", W 113° 33' 46.2"

This is the second trailer park on Playa Bonita. It's a large, well-run park with only one disadvantage, no electricity.

The campground has about 150 generously-sized spaces, 100 of these have sewer and water hookups. The restrooms are modern and clean, they have hot water showers that cost a dollar. There is also a meeting room. The beach in front is very nice.

To reach the campground follow the instructions for finding the Playa Bonita given above. Just before you reach the Playa Bonita gate you will see a sign pointing right to a road running around the Playa Bonita. Follow this another .5 mile (.8 km) to the Palmar.

Campground No. 10

ROCKY POINT R.V. AND GOLF RESORT
Address: Carr. Sonoyta-Peñasco Km. 91.5, Puerto Peñasco, Son., Mexico
Telephone: (800) 762-5956 (Res. in U.S.A.)

Price: Low

GPS Location: N 31° 22' 05.7", W113° 30' 26.7"

Yes a 9 hole golf course! It isn't finished yet, and it will be sand with carpet greens, but the manager here says he'll have it finished next year (1998).

The campground is located right in the middle of barren desert north of Puerto Peñasco. There are 28 large pull-through spaces, each with 20-amp. electricity, sewer, water and satellite TV hookups. The restrooms are clean with hot showers. There is a recreation room and a self-service laundry. The campground is fenced and there is 24-hour security.

You'll find the campground on the west side of Mex. 8 some 2.7 miles (4.4 km) north of Puerto Peñasco.

Other Camping Possibilities

About 4 miles (6 km) east of town on the road to Cholla Bay is **Sandy Beach**, a popular free camping area, especially for ATV owners.

SAN FELIPE, BAJA CALIFORNIA (SAHN FAY-LEE-PAY)
Population 15,000, Elevation sea level

Although San Felipe is a Baja town its location in the far northeast portion of the peninsula means that it is not normally part of a visit to the peninsula's destinations farther south. That doesn't mean that this isn't a popular place, like Puerto Peñasco this town is full of Americans looking for easily accessible sun and sand.

While there are many similarities between Puerto Peñasco and San Felipe there are also important differences. San Felipe is a more attractive town than Puerto Peñasco, it has more hotels and restaurants, and also, amazingly, more RV parks. Not only are there many parks in the town itself, the beaches north and south, particularly north, are filled with places to set up your RV along the water. Many of these out-of-town parks do not have hookups and are not individually covered in this guide.

Most of the important streets in town are paved and the rest present no driving problems. Watch for stop signs, however. They are in unexpected places. Sometimes the smallest dusty side street has priority over a main arterial. There are small supermarkets and Pemex stations in San Felipe. Many people spend the entire winter here and never visit larger towns for supplies. If you would like to visit a larger store you can go to Mexicali which has plenty of them.

Campground No. 1

SAN FELIPE MARINA RESORT RV PARK
   Address: Km. 4.5 Carr. San Felipe-Aeropuerto, San Felipe, B.C., Mexico
   Telephone: (619) 558-0295, (800) 291-5397 (U.S. Reservations)

Price: Expensive

GPS Location: N 30° 59' 21.5", W 114° 49' 43.1"

This campground may have the nicest facilities you will find in Mexico. It is only a few years old and is affiliated with a resort hotel below the campground on the beach. The campground itself is not next to the beach, it is set on a hillside above and has a great view.

There are 143 large back-in spaces with lots of room for bigger rigs. They have 50-amp. and 30-amp. electricity, sewer, water, and satellite TV. The slots are all paved and have patios but no shade. The central facilities building has clean modern restrooms (an understatement) with hot showers, a beautiful pool and a lounge area. There is also a laundry in the building. The affiliated hotel has another pool and a restaurant. The campground and hotel are gated and have tight 24-hour security.

To find the San Felipe zero your odometer as you reach the glorieta at the entrance to town. Turn 90 degrees right toward the airport and head south. At 2.9 miles (4.7 km) you'll see the campground on the left.

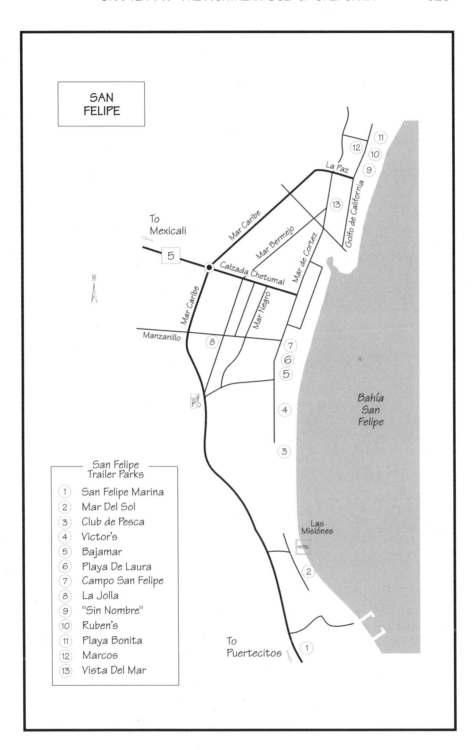

SAN
FELIPE

To
Mexicali

5

Calzada Chetumal

Mar Caribe

Mar Bermejo

Mar de Cortez

Mar Negro

Mar Caribe

La Paz

Golfo de California

N

Manzanillo

Bahía
San
Felipe

Las
Misiónes

HOTEL

To
Puertecitos

San Felipe
Trailer Parks

1   San Felipe Marina
2   Mar Del Sol
3   Club de Pesca
4   Victor's
5   Bajamar
6   Playa De Laura
7   Campo San Felipe
8   La Jolla
9   "Sin Nombre"
10 Ruben's
11 Playa Bonita
12 Marcos
13 Vista Del Mar

Campground No. 2

R.V. PARK MAR DEL SOL
Address: Av. Misión de Loreto No. 130, San Felipe, B.C., Mexico (Res. info. below)
Telephone: (657) 7-10-88

Price: Front with util. - Expensive, No util. - Moderate

GPS Location: N 30° 59' 50.3", W 114° 49' 57.7"

The Mar del Sol is another very nice but rather expensive trailer park located a short distance south of San Felipe. It is affiliated with the very nice Hotel Las Misiónes next door. The beachside location is a plus.

The campground has 85 spaces with 30-amp. electricity, sewer and water. These are back-in sites but are large with lots of room for bigger rigs. There are another 30 spaces with no utility hookups, these cost a lot less. The restrooms are individual cubicles for toilets and showers, they are tiled, clean, and in good repair. The showers have hot water. The campground has a swimming pool overlooking the beach, a palapa and meeting room for get-togethers, and a laundry. The nearest restaurant is in the Hotel Las Misiónes. The U.S. reservation address is Mexico Resorts International, 664 Broadway, Suite G, Chula Vista, CA 92010 (619) 422-6900.

To find the Mar del Sol zero your odometer as you reach the glorieta at the entrance to town. Turn 90 degrees right toward the airport and head south. At 2 miles (3.2 km) turn left on the well-marked road to the Hotel Las Misiónes and the RV Park Mar del Sol. The road winds down a short hill to a T, turn right and you will find the campground at the end of the street.

Campground No. 3

CLUB DE PESCA R.V. PARK
Address: Apdo. 90, San Felipe, C.P. 21850 B.C., Mexico
Telephone: (657) 7-11-80
Fax: (657) 7-18-88

Price: Along beach - Expensive, Off beach - Moderate

GPS Location: N 31° 00' 46.4", W 114° 50' 10.4"

This is an old San Felipe favorite. The campground has many permanents, but also some choice slots for smaller rigs along the ocean and others toward the rear of the park.

There are 32 short slots along the beach with 30-amp. electricity (but small plugs) and water but no sewer hookups. These spaces are paved and have palapas. At the rear of the park are 22 larger slots with 30-amp. electricity, sewer, and water. Restrooms are neat and clean and have hot water showers. There is a small grocery store and a meeting room next to the beach dividing the beachside sites.

As you enter town zero your odometer at the glorieta. Turn right toward the airport and drive .8 miles (1.3 km) to the Pemex. Turn left here and drive down the hill toward the beach. You'll come to a T at 1.2 miles (1.9 km). Turn right and you'll find the Club de Pesca at the end of the road.

Campground No. 4

VICTOR'S R.V. PARK
  Address: El Cortez Motel, P.O. Box 1227, Calexico, CA, U.S.A. (Res.)
  Telephone: (657) 7-10-56

Price: Moderate

GPS Location: N 31° 00' 46.5", W 114° 50' 09.3"

This 50-space campground is older with a lot of permanently located rigs. There are a couple of slots near the beach and quite a few at the back of the park available for daily rent. It is jointly run with the El Cortez Motel located just next door so the facilities are really pretty good for such a small park.

Victor's parking slots have electricity, sewer, and water. Each space has a covered patio. The restrooms are clean and showers have hot water. The campground has a meeting room near the front next to the beach and the motel next door has a swimming pool and restaurant for the use of campground residents. There is also a laundry. This campground is fully fenced, even along the beach, and has an attendant.

As you enter town zero your odometer at the glorieta. Turn right toward the airport and drive .8 miles (1.3 km) to the Pemex. Turn left here and drive down the hill toward the beach. You'll come to a T at 1.2 miles (1.9 km). Turn right and almost immediately you'll see Victor's on your left.

Campground No. 5

BAJAMAR R.V. PARK
  Address: Av. Mar de Cortez s/n, San Felipe, B.C., Mexico
  Telephone: (65) 53-23-63 (Res.)
  Fax: (65) 63-13-60 (Res.)

Price: Along beach - Expensive, Center and back- Moderate

GPS Location: N 31° 01' 04.6", W 114° 50' 09.0"

The Bajamar is the newest of the downtown San Felipe campgrounds. You'll find all of the nearby campgrounds to be very similar, they're just not quite as new. They're all on a nice beach and have convenient strolling access to central San Felipe.

There are 60 full-service spaces with 30-amp. electricity (small plugs however), sewer, and water. The central access roads are paved with curbs and the parking pads are gravel with covered patios. This campground has left the waterfront open so that it can be enjoyed by all of the residents, there is a large patio with a palapa there and some small tables with umbrellas on the sand. The campground has no apparent permanents yet. Restrooms are new and clean and have hot water showers. There is a small restaurant, a self-service laundry, and a playground. English is spoken.

As you enter town zero your odometer at the glorieta. Turn right toward the airport and drive .8 miles (1.3 km) to the Pemex. Turn left here and drive down the hill toward the beach. You'll come to a T at 1.2 miles (1.9 km). Turn left and almost immediately you'll see the Bajamar on the right.

Campground No. 6

PLAYA DE LAURA
   Address: P.O. Box 130, Calexico, CA 92231 U.S.A. (Res.)
       Price: Along beach - Expensive, Back rows - Moderate

GPS Location: N 31° 01' 07.1", W 114° 50' 07.5"

This older RV park doesn't seem to have been kept up to quite the same standards as the ones on either side. Still, it has a good location and is quite popular.

43 campsites are arranged in rows running parallel to the beach. The front row is really packed and limits beach access by campers in the rows farther from the beach. Pricing varies with beach slots much more expensive than those farther back. Each camping space has electricity, sewer, water and covered patios with tables and barbecues. Most of the spaces are pull-throughs. Restrooms are older and need maintenance, they have hot water showers.

As you enter town zero your odometer at the glorieta. Turn right toward the airport and drive .8 miles (1.3 km) to the Pemex. Turn left here and drive down the hill toward the beach. You'll come to a T at 1.2 miles (1.9 km). Turn left and almost immediately you'll see the Playa de Laura on the right in .2 miles (.3 km).

Campground No. 7

R.V. PARK CAMPO SAN FELIPE
   Address: P.O. Box 952, Calexico, CA 92232 U.S.A. (Reservations and mail)
   Telephone: (657) 7-10-12
       Price: First row - Expensive, Second and third row - Moderate

GPS Location: N 31° 01' 13.6", W 114° 50' 07.1"

You'll find the San Felipe to be very much like the Playa de Laura next door but in much better condition. It has the distinction of being the closest campground to central San Felipe. The campground also maintains a mailbox in the U.S. so you can get your mail much more quickly here than if it has to come into Mexico.

The campsites are arranged in several rows parallel to the beach, the closer to the beach you are the more you pay. 34 sites have electricity, sewer, water, and covered patios. Most are pull-throughs. Another 5 are small and have sewer and water only. The restrooms are clean and in good repair, they have hot water showers. English is spoken.

As you enter town zero your odometer at the glorieta. Turn right toward the airport and drive .8 miles (1.3 km) to the Pemex. Turn left here and drive down the hill toward the beach. You'll come to a T at 1.2 miles (1.9 km). Turn left and almost immediately you'll see the Campo San Felipe on the right in .2 miles (.4 km).

Campground No. 8

LA JOLLA R.V. PARK
    Address: P.O. Box 978, El Centro, CA 92243 U.S.A. (Res.)
    Telephone: (657) 7-12-22

Price: Moderate

GPS Location: N 31° 01' 08.9", W 114° 50' 26.2"

The La Jolla isn't on the beach and suffers as a result. It is a friendly, well-run place and has spaces available when the places on the beach are full. If you want a quieter atmosphere you might give this place a try.

There are 55 camp sites, each with electricity, sewer, water, and covered patios. These are back-in spaces. The restrooms are in a simple cement block building with an unfinished interior but are in good condition and have hot water showers that are metered and cost a quarter. The La Jolla has a nice new swimming pool. English is spoken.

As you enter town zero your odometer at the glorieta. Turn right toward the airport and drive .4 miles (6 km) to a stop sign at Manzanillo. Turn left and drive about .2 miles (.3 km) and you'll see the La Jolla on the right.

Campground No. 9

TRAILER PARK "SIN NOMBRE" (TRAILER PARK WITHOUT A NAME)
Price: Big rigs - Moderate, Small rigs - Low

GPS Location: N 31° 01' 59.4", W 114° 49' 43.1"

This little trailer park is located right next to the much better known Ruben's. At first glance it even looks like Rubens, it has Ruben's trademark two-story palapas.

There are 22 spaces in this park. Six are along the front next to the beach. Most spaces are really van-size or short-trailer-size but a few will take large motorhomes. The camping slots have electricity, sewer, water, and paved patios with a roof serviced by a ladder. You can use them for the view or pitch a tent up there. The bathrooms are old and need maintenance, they have hot water showers. The manager only appears occasionally, park and he'll show up to collect.

From the glorieta at the entrance to town take the road that leads northeast. This is Mar Caribe Norte and is the road to the left as you come from Mexicali. It will curve to the right at .8 miles (1.3 km) and come to a T at 1 mile (1.6 km). Turn left and Trailer Park "Sin Nombre" is on the right almost immediately.

Campground No. 10

RUBEN'S R.V. TRAILER PARK
  Address: Apdo. 59, San Felipe, C.P. 21850 B.C., Mexico
  Telephone: (657) 7-10-91

Price: Moderate

GPS Location: N 31° 02' 01.7", W 114° 49' 43.0"

Ruben's is well known in San Felipe for its two story patios. These are very popular with tenters during the Mexican holidays, it is easy to enclose the patio below and use the roof for added room. Some people think the two-story patios give the crowded campground the atmosphere of a parking garage but Ruben's remains a popular beach-front campground.

There are 45 camping spaces, all with 30-amp. electricity, sewer and water. Most spaces are small and maneuvering room is scarce. The restrooms are adequate and have hot water showers. There is also a well-liked bar/restaurant and a boat launch ramp and service. Ruben's doesn't take reservations. English is spoken.

From the glorieta at the entrance to town take the road that leads northeast. This is Mar Caribe Norte and is the road to the left as you come from Mexicali. It will curve to the right at .8 miles (1.3 km) and come to a T at 1 mile (1.6 km). Turn left and you'll pass the entrance to Trailer Park Sin Nombre and come to the two Ruben's entrances on the right.

Campground No. 11

CONDO SUITES AND R.V. PARK PLAYA BONITA
  Address: 475 E. Badillo Street, Covina, Cal. 91723 U.S.A. (Res.)
  Telephone: (657) 7-12-15, (818) 967-8977 (USA)

Price: Moderate

GPS Location: N 31° 02' 04.5", W 114° 49' 42.6"

This is another beachfront campground at the north end of town. Some day the campground may be replaced by condo suites, but so far only one building has been completed and it cohabits peacefully with the RVs and trailers.

There are 28 camping spaces in this campground. Ten are large back-in spaces with

30-amp. electricity, sewer and water. Another 18 spaces are suitable only for vans, tents or small trailers. Most of these smaller spaces have electricity, sewer, and water. All spaces have paved patios with palapa-style roofs and picnic tables. The restrooms are older and rustic, the showers were barely warm when we visited.

From the glorieta at the entrance to town take the road that leads northeast. This is Mar Caribe Norte and is the road to the left as you come from Mexicali. It will curve to the right at .8 miles (1.3 km) and come to a T at 1 mile (1.6 km). Turn left and you'll come to the entrance on the right at 1.1 miles (1.8 km).

Campground No. 12

MARCOS TRAILER PARK
   Address: Av. Golfo de California 788, San Felipe, B. C., Mexico
   Telephone: (657) 7-18-75

Price: Low

GPS Location: N 31° 02' 04.5", W 114° 49' 42.4"

Marcos isn't on the water and all San Felipe campers seem to want to be in a campground next to the beach, even if they're parked so far back that they never see the water. Nonetheless Marcos succeeds in staying relatively full, perhaps because it is *almost* next to the beach.

There are 20 back-in spaces arranged around the perimeter of the campground. There is lots of room in the middle of the campground but large rigs have trouble parking because the lot slopes and the leveled parking pads aren't very long. Each space has electricity, sewer, water, and a covered patio. There is even a little shrubbery to separate the sites, unusual in San Felipe. The restrooms are old but clean and in good repair, they have hot water showers. There is a small meeting room with a library and a sun deck on top.

From the glorieta at the entrance to town take the road that leads northeast. This is Mar Caribe Norte and is the road to the left as you come from Mexicali. It will curve to the right at .8 miles (1.3 km) and come to a T at 1 mile (1.6 km). Turn left and you'll see the entrance to the campground on the left at 1.1 miles (1.8 km).

Campground No. 13

VISTA DEL MAR
   Address: 601 Ave. de Cortez, San Felipe, B.C., Mexico

Price: Moderate

GPS Location: N 31° 01' 54.9", W 114° 49' 52.7"

The Vista del Mar is another campground suffering from a location far from the water. The facility is really very good, but often virtually empty.

There are 21 back-in spaces arranged on both sides of a sloping lot with a view of the ocean and hills to the north of town. Each space has 20-amp. electricity, sewer, and water. Large rigs will have trouble parking because the level parking pad is not very long. The entire campground is paved, much of it with attractive reddish bricks. Each campsite has a tile-roofed patio with a table and barbecue. The restrooms are spic-and-span and have hot water showers. At the upper end of the campground is a group barbecue area.

From the glorieta at the entrance to town take the road that leads northeast. This is Mar Caribe Norte and is the road to the left as you come from Mexicali. It will curve to the right at .8 miles (1.3 km). You must take the turn to the right at .9 miles (1.4 km) just before the fenced sports field, the campground is a short way up the hill on the left.

Campground No. 14

EL DORADO RANCH
   Address: P.O. Box 3809, Calexico, CA
   92232 (Res.)
   Telephone: (303) 790-1749 (U.S.A.)
   Fax: (657) 7-17-79

   Price: Very Expensive

GPS Location: N 30° 59' 21.5", W 114° 49' 43.1"

The El Dorado Ranch is a land development a few miles north of San Felipe along the coast. The area to be developed is huge, the project complex, and the promotion frenetic. Most importantly, to us anyway, there is a nice new RV park incorporated into the project.

There are 100 sites with electricity, sewer, and water. All are on packed sand and separated by rows of painted white rocks. There are no patios and no shade but lots of room for large rigs. There is a very nice swimming pool pavilion with bar, a pool that is kept at bath temperature, and Jacuzzis that are even hotter. There's also a restaurant, a store, beautiful tennis courts, horse-back riding, desert tours, and lifestyle (sales) presentations. Amazingly enough there are only cold water showers.

The El Dorado Ranch is located about 8 miles (13 km) north of San Felipe. Take the well-marked road toward the beach near the 177 Km. marker. There's also a second campground that has been developed as part of this project. It is located on the mountain side of the highway about 1.5 miles (2.4 km) closer to town.

You should be warned that while this is a great RV park it is also a membership-type real estate development. They have a friendly but active sales force.

Campground No. 15

EL FARO BEACH R.V. PARK
   Address: Apdo. 107, San Felipe, B.C.,
   Mexico

   Price: Very expensive

GPS Location: N 30° 55' 53.4", W 114° 43' 41.8"

The El Faro is worth a visit even if you don't stay there. This huge and at one time well-equipped campground flows down a steep hill toward the ocean. There is apparently a constant battle to keep drifting sand from covering the whole thing, when we visited the sand was winning. The manager tells us that the summer is the busy season for this campground, in the winter the beautiful pool is empty, the bars closed, and the campground virtually deserted.

The El Faro has 135 spaces, all have 30-amp. electricity, sewer, and water. Most, or maybe all, have patios, we couldn't tell because of the sand. All have ocean views. Brick roads, steep enough in places to cause access problems, connect the sites. The bathrooms needed maintenance when we visited. There is a beautiful pool complex with bar toward the bottom of the campground and tennis courts above.

To find the El Faro drive south toward the airport. Zero your odometer as you pass the San Felipe Marina R.V. Park. At 3.4 miles (5.5 km) take the paved road to the left. Finally, at 7.5 miles (12.1 km) you'll see the paved entrance road to the El Faro Beach R.V. Park.

Other Camping Possibilities

The campgrounds listed above only scratch the surface in San Felipe. Starting about 10 miles (16 km) north of town you will see many roads heading for the beach. Most of these roads end at small campgrounds with few services and facilities. If you don't need hookups you can explore some of them and find a place that suits you.

Side Trips from San Felipe

South of San Felipe the road is paved another 56 miles (91 km) to **Puertecitos**. There are many campgrounds along the beach north of Puertecitos and one in town. The one in town has electricity for a few hours each day. Puertecitos also has a restaurant, a small store and a Pemex. The road continues for 87 more miles (123 km) to connect with Mex. 1 near the Laguna Chapala lake bed at the 223 Km. mark. There have been rumors for several years that this stretch of road is about to be paved, until it is the road is said to be suitable for all sturdy rigs but has many miles of washboard bumps and lots of dust. Check road conditions before heading down it yourself and be prepared for many miles of road with no services.

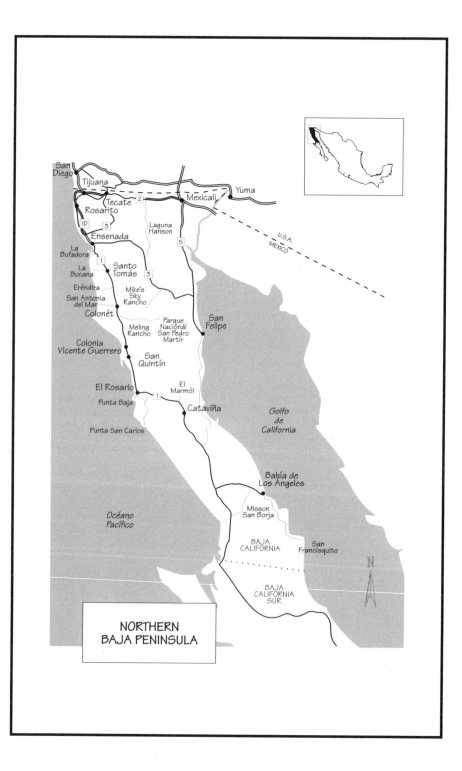

CHAPTER 12

NORTHERN
BAJA PENINSULA

NORTHERN BAJA PENINSULA

INTRODUCTION

The Baja Peninsula is an extremely popular camping destination. There are so many people living so close by in California that the peninsula, especially the northern part, seems almost an extension of that state. There are many campgrounds on the Baja, fully a third of all formal Mexican campgrounds are located there. Additionally, this is without a doubt the most popular area of Mexico for free camping outside formal campgrounds. There is much more information available about the Baja than about the remainder of the country. Take a look at our section entitled Travel Library in the Details, Details, Details chapter for some of the many guidebooks covering only the Baja.

One good reason for the Baja's popularity is the lack of bureaucratic nonsense required for a visit. Only if you plan to stay for more than three days or continue south of Maneadero (on Mex. 1 about 10 miles (16 km) south of Ensenada) do you need a tourist card. Vehicle permits are not necessary at all.

The Baja Peninsula extends for approximately 1,000 miles (1,600 km) from the California border of the U.S. to its tip near Cabo San Lucas. For most of its length the peninsula's eastern portion is made up of rugged mountains. Bordering the Baja on the west is an often harsh Pacific Ocean coastline. On the east is the Gulf of California, also called the Sea of Cortez (Mar de Cortés in Spanish). The fascinating gulf coast is by far the more accessible to visitors, particularly if they hesitate to use the many rough unpaved roads that are often the only way to reach long stretches of the west coast.

The Baja has an arid climate. Much of the peninsula is desert. Throughout most of the region the only relief from the dry climate is the occasional oasis, irrigated farm area, or seashore. There is a lot of seashore, about 2,000 miles (3,250 km) of it, no location on the peninsula is really far from the ocean.

A lot of people visit the Baja Peninsula during the winter because they are traveling to avoid the harsh weather in the north. This is not the best time for weather on the peninsula either, many northern sections are cool, especially on the Pacific coast. The southern Baja is more comfortable, but still not overly hot. The spring after Easter brings much better weather. It is not yet extremely hot but many of the tourists have gone home. During the summer both the air and water are very warm. It is still possible to stay comfortable along the coast however, and this is the best time of the year for fishing and water sports.

For the sake of convenience we have broken the Baja Peninsula into three areas in this book. The eastern portion of the northern peninsula is included in Chapter 11 covering the Northern Gulf of California. The easiest access to this part of the peninsula is by Mex. 5 south from Mexicali and it has much in common with Puerto Peñasco and Gulfo de Santa Clara in the state of Sonora. This chapter will cover the remainder of the northern state of Baja California which stretches from the U.S. border south to the 28th parallel, a distance of about 350 miles (570 km) as the bird flies. Chapter 12 covers the southern portion of the peninsula, that part that comprises the state of Baja California Sur. From the 28th parallel to the tip of the peninsula the distance is about 425 air miles (690 km).

ROAD SYSTEM

The most important road on the Baja is Mex. 1. This mostly two-lane paved road runs from the border crossing at Tijuana for 1,061 miles (1,711 km) south to the very tip of the Baja Peninsula at Cabo San Lucas. This highway was finished in 1973 and completely changed the character of the peninsula because it provided easy access for tourists and for commercial haulers.

Mex. 1 is well supplied with kilometer markers and they make a convenient way to keep track of both your progress and the location of campgrounds. They do not progress in a uniform manner, however. In the state of Baja California there are four different segments of signed road. Kilometer markers in each section count from north to south: Tijuana to Ensenada, 109 kilometers; Ensenada to San Quintín, 196 kilometers; San Quintín to the junction of the road to Bahía de Los Ángeles, 280 kilometers; and Bahía de los Ángeles junction to the Baja Sur border, 128 kilometers. This is a total distance of 713 kilometers or 436 miles.

Mex. 1 begins in Tijuana. From Tijuana to Ensenada there are actually two different segments, one is the free road, Mex. 1 Libre, the other is a toll road Mex. 1D. The toll road is by far the best road, it is four lanes wide and for most of its length a limited access highway. There are three toll booths along the 65-mile road, an automobile or van was being charged about $5 U.S. during the late winter of 96/97 to cover the entire distance. A four-axle rig would pay about $17 for the same section of road. For more information about Mexican toll roads see our section titled Toll Roads in the Details, Details, Details chapter of this book. This is the only section of toll road on all of Mex. 1.

From Ensenada south Mex. 1 is a two-lane road except for short sections of boulevard through some towns and a section of four-lane highway near San Jose del Cabo. All of the highway is paved but much of it is relatively narrow and the surface in some places is potholed or rough. The key to a successful trip down this highway is to keep your speed down and, especially if you are in a big rig, slow down and exercise extreme caution when meeting large vehicles coming from the opposite direction. There is always enough room to pass but often not much more than that. Inexperienced drivers sometimes tend to crowd the center line because they fear the often shoulder-less outside pavement edge. We have met a surprising number of people who have had unnecessary problems because they weren't careful enough while passing traffic traveling the opposite direction.

Mex. 1 follows a route that crosses back and forth across the peninsula. In the northern state of Baja California the highway never does reach the Gulf of California after leaving Ensenada. It heads south slightly inland until reaching El Rosario just south of San Quintín, then turns inland to pass through the mountainous interior before coming back toward the Pacific near Guerrero Negro and the border with Baja California Sur. It is important to gas up at El Rosario because gas stations are unreliable from there almost to Guerrero Negro, about 216 miles (353 km) south.

In the north there is a good alternate to Mex. 1 as far south as Ensenada. This is Mex. 3 which runs from Tecate on the border to Ensenada. Actually this is a very useful highway if you are headed north since the Tecate border crossing usually has much shorter waits while traveling north than the Tijuana crossings. See the Chapter 3 for more information about crossing the border.

Most Baja visitors probably never have a chance to drive Mex. 2, an east/west route that actually crosses all the way across Mexico from Tijuana to Matamoros on the east coast. The northern Baja section of this trans-continental highway is a decent route, often with four lanes. The section crossing the mountains east of Tecate and then dropping into the Central Valley near Mexicali is called the Cantu Grade. It is especially spectacular, although if you are traveling from east to west it can be a long hot climb up the grade.

Mex. 3 also continues from Ensenada to meet with Mex. 5 about 31 miles (51 km) north of San Felipe on the Gulf of California. This 123 mile (201 km) two-lane paved highway offers an alternative to Mex. 5 south from Mexicali for San Felipe-bound travelers and is one of only two paved routes across the peninsula in Baja Norte other than the Mex. 2 border route. The other is a good two-lane paved road that goes east from Mex. 1 to Bahía de Los Ángles from a point 364 miles (594 km) south of Tijuana. This road is 42 miles (68 km) long and is the only paved access to the Gulf of California south of San Felipe.

Most RVers will probably want to stay pretty close to paved roads but there are several routes that will accommodate smaller carefully driven RVs if drivers are willing to put up with lots of dust and the occasional washboard surface. From Mex. 3 there is a road north to Laguna Hanson, see Ensenada Side Trips for this trip. The road to La Bufadora just south of Ensenada is paved and easy to negotiate, see the Punta Banda description section. Roads lead to the Pacific coast at La Bocana and Ejido Eréndira from Mex. 1, see Santo Tomás Side Trips. There is a road from Colonét to San Antonio del Mar on the Pacific Coast, see San Quintín Side Trips for this. There is also a road east from the same area to the Meling Rancho, see San Quintín Side Trips. El Marmól quarry is accessible from Mex. 1 north of Cataviña, see Cataviña Side Trips for this road. Finally, there is a road south from San Felipe that eventually connects with Mex. 1 some 34 miles (56 km) south of Cataviña near Km. 229, see the San Felipe Side Trips section in Chapter 11 for a description of this road.

Smaller rigs with good clearance will find it possible to do some exploring. The following roads are reported to be fine for pickups and small sturdy vans, you need decent clearance but not necessarily four-wheel drive. You should make sure that your rig is in good mechanical condition and that you are well supplied before attempting these roads because help is scarce. You should also avoid these tracks in wet weather since many of them become virtually impassable when wet. Check with the locals before attempting them to make sure they are passable. The road connecting Laguna Hanson with Mex. 2 to the north is covered in Tecate Side Trips. For the road from Meling Rancho to the Astronomical Observatory in the Parque Nacionál Sierra San Pedro Martír see San Quintín Side Trips. The road from Mex. 3 to Mike's Sky Rancho is in the Ensenada Side Trips section of this book. There is a road south from Bahía de Los Ángeles to San Francisquito, see the Bahía de Los Ángeles Side Trips. Misión San Borja is accessible from near a small town called Rosarito, see Side Trips from Cataviña. El Rosario Side Trips covers roads to Punta Baja and Punta San Carlos.

HIGHLIGHTS

The Northern Baja Peninsula covered in this chapter, like the Southern Baja, has few large towns. In fact, other than those along the border and Ensenada there are really only small settlements. Popular San Felipe is covered in Chapter 11 in this book.

The Baja Peninsula is a paradise for outdoors enthusiasts. It offers unequaled opportunities for off-road exploration, hiking, fishing, kayaking, whale watching, sailing, surfing, wind surfing, clam digging, and even bicycling.

The area surrounding Ensenada and north to Tijuana is full of campgrounds and very easy to visit. It is virtually an extension of the U.S. and is very popular with California residents for short visits. Visitors staying for less than 72 hours are not even required to get a tourist card. People come down for the shopping, the restaurants, and the oceanside campgrounds. During the summer this coastal area has pleasant California-like weather but in the winter it is cool. Tijuana is probably best visited on day trips from north of the border but Ensenada is a good camping destination. Probably the only other interesting city of any size in the area covered by this chapter is Tecate, one of the nicest border towns in Mexico.

As you head south down the peninsula there are two major regions offering fishing and water sports, on the Pacific side is San Quintín and on the Gulf side is Bahía de Los Ángeles. Both of these regions are easily accessible and provide lots of opportunities for anglers and boaters of all kinds.

There are two mountain regions in the northern Baja that make good destinations for hikers and campers. One of these is the Laguna Hanson area between Mex. 2 and Mex. 3. The formal name for this area is Parque Nacional Constitución de 1857, see the Ensenada Side Trips section below. The other is the Parque Nacionál Sierra San Pedro Martír which is located east of San Quintín, see the San Quintín Side Trips section.

Many of the communities on the Baja Peninsula grew up around missions founded by Jesuit, Franciscan, and Dominican missionaries. About 30 were built beginning in 1696 in Loreto. These missions were an important part of the peninsula's history and many can be visited today. Some are ruins, some are restored, some are in use, some are remote, and a few are lost. Some of those you might want to visit in North Baja are the Misión Santo Tomás ruins (Santo Tómas section), the Misión Rosario ruins (El Rosario section), Misión Santa Maria ruins (Cataviña Side Trip section) and Misión San Borja ruins (Cataviña Side Trip section).

Fishing along both coasts of the peninsula is excellent. In the Northern Baja favorite destinations accessible on good roads include Bahía de Los Ángeles and San Quintín. Fishing is generally considered to be better in the late summer and early fall but there is what would be considered decent fishing by most standards available almost everywhere all year long.

Kayaking is extremely popular along the Sea of Cortez. The Bahía de Los Ángeles is often used as a departure point for coastwise trips to the south all the way to La Paz.

Surfing is a west coast activity since the Gulf of California offers little in the way of surf except at the far south end. Remote beaches all along the coast are popular. Easily accessible surfing opportunities in the northern Baja include the coast between Tijuana and Ensenada, south from Ensenada to El Rosario, and some spots north of Guerrero Negro.

THE CAMPGROUNDS

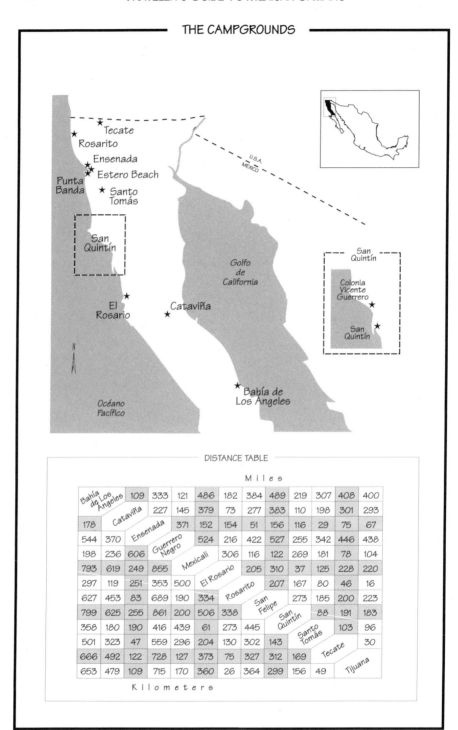

SELECTED CITIES AND THEIR CAMPGROUNDS

BAHÍA DE LOS ÁNGELES, BAJA CALIFORNIA
(BAH-HEE-AH LOES AHN-HAIL-ACE)
Population 500, Elevation sea level

The Bahía de Los Ángeles (Bay of the Angels) is one of the most scenic spots in Baja California with blue waters and barren desert shoreline backed by rocky mountains. The huge bay is protected by a chain of islands, the largest is Isla Angel de la Guarda which is 45 miles (75 km) long. Even with this protection boating is often dangerous because of strong winds from the north or west. Fishing, boating, diving, and kayaking are good in the bay, among the islands, and offshore and there are several launch ramps in town. There is a turtle hatchery in Bahía de Los Ángeles near the Las Brisas Marina Trailer Park where you can see some of these endangered animals. The village itself doesn't offer much except a Pemex, a couple of motels, several RV parks and a few small stores including a Conasupo.

Campground No. 1

VILLA VITTA HOTEL AND RV PARK
   Address: 509 Ross Drive, Escondido, CA
   92029 U.S.A. (Res.)
   Telephone: (619) 741-9583 (Res. in U.S.A.)

   Price: Low

The Villa Vitta RV Park is located across the street from the hotel of the same name. This is a flat dirt lot with no landscaping. There are 46 pull-through slots with electricity, many have patios. There is also a lot of room for rigs and tents not needing hookups. The campground also has a dump station and water is available. Bathrooms and hot showers are available at the hotel, so is a restaurant, bar, and swimming pool. This motel/campground has a good launch ramp, available for an extra fee.

You'll find that the Villa Vitta is hard to miss, you'll see the hotel on the right and the RV park on the left soon after entering town.

Campground No. 2

GUILLERMO'S HOTEL AND RV PARK
   Address: Bahía de Los Ángeles
   Telephone: (665) 0-32-06,
   (617) 6-49-46 (Ensenada)

Price: Inexpensive

This campground has 40 camping spaces with
full hookups. Some have patios and some
palapas. This is a dirt and gravel lot next to the
beach with a few small trees to provide a little
shade, permanents here block any view of the water. The restrooms have hot
showers. There is a restaurant, bar, store and also a launch ramp.

To find Guillermo's drive into town, pass the Villa Vitta, and you'll soon see the
campground on the left.

Campground No. 3

CAMP GECKO

Price: Inexpensive

This waterside campground has an idyllic
location on a long sandy beach with a few
rocks. Unfortunately you must drive almost
four miles of washboard gravel road to reach it.

Camp Gecko has about 10 camping spaces
with palapas. There are no hookups but the
camping area does have flush toilets and hot
water showers. There are also cabins for rent and a small boat ramp.

As you head south through Bahía de los Ángeles village you will come to a rock
wall and the entrance to Diaz RV park. Go to the right around it and follow a
washboard gravel road south. At 4.0 miles (6.5 km) take the sandy road left toward
the beach and Camp Gecko. Even bigger rigs should have no access problems.

Other Camping Possibilities

There is an old government-built campground like the others you've seen on the
peninsula which is located just north of town, follow signs for Brisa Marina RV
Park. There are about 50 spaces but none of the hookups work. Most people camp
nearby at some turtle ponds. There is a small fee and no facilities.

At the south end of the village is the old Diaz RV Park which is associated with the

Casa Diaz Motel with the same management. There are 6 poorly maintained sites with electricity, sewer, water and cement palapas. The bathrooms are basic and none too clean when we visited. The location across the street from the beach offers no views. There are also a restaurant, store and boat launching ramp.

North of town along the beach there are several places with beachside camping, no facilities, and small fees. The one at the end of the road (about 6 miles (10 km)) is known as Playa La Gringa. The lack of facilities is more than compensated for by the isolated beachfront location.

Side Trips from Bahía de Los Ángeles

You can drive to **Bahía (bay) or Cala (inlet) San Francisquito**, about 85 road miles (139 km) south of Bahía de Los Ángeles. The road south from town is obvious, it is usually suitable for small RVs and trucks with boat trailers. This is a long drive through empty country so make sure you have supplies and a vehicle in good condition, ask about the road in Bahía de Los Ángeles before leaving because it occasionally gets washed out. Primitive campsites are available in San Francisquito for a small fee. Nearby Punta San Francisquito Resort also has some facilities including cabins and a restaurant. Bahía San Francisquito can also be accessed from El Arco by a road suitable only for rugged vehicles, see Side Trips under Guerrero Negro in the next chapter.

CATAVIÑA, BAJA CALIFORNIA (KAT-AH-VEEN-YAH)
Population 200, Elevation 1,900 ft. (580 m)

You can't really call Cataviña a town. There is little more here than a Hotel La Pinta, a Pemex, an old government-built campground, and a few shacks and restaurants. The area, however, is one of the most interesting on the Baja. The Cataviña boulder fields (formal name is Las Virgines - the Virgins) are striking. The road threads its way for several miles through a jumble of huge granite boulders sprinkled liberally with attractive cacti and desert plants. It is a photographer's paradise.

Campground

CATAVIÑA TRAILER PARK

Price: Low

⚠️

GPS Location: N 29° 43' 43.7", W 114° 42' 53.1"

This is one of the fenced compounds that were built by the government soon after the road south was finished. None of the hookups work any more, but this is still a very attractive campground. The landscaping has boulders and cactus, just like the surrounding area. There are bathrooms but no showers. Many people use this campground, there aren't a lot of other choices on this stretch of road.

The campground is located in Cataviña just west of the La Pinta motel and the Pemex on the south side of the road.

Other Camping Possibilities

Many people park in the lot at the Rancho Santa Inés, it is located about a mile off the highway. The access road is about .8 miles south of Cataviña.

Other folks just follow one of the many roads into the boulder field north of Cataviña and set up camp. This might be fine for a group of several rigs but there have been reports of robberies in the area so think twice before doing this.

CATAVIÑA CACTUS GARDEN

Side Trips from Cataviña

The virtually abandoned onyx mining area called **El Marmól** makes an interesting day trip. The access road is near the 143 Km. marker about 19 miles (31 km) north of Cataviña. This is a graded road that is about 10 miles long. Take a look at the old school house built entirely of onyx. This mine was very active in the early part of the century, the quarried onyx slabs were shipped by water from Puerto Santa Catarina about 50 miles west on the Pacific coast. You might also want to make the 3-mile hike (6 miles round trip) to El Volcán where you can see a small seep forming new onyx.

If you have a good off-road vehicle or the desire to make a desert hike you might want to visit the last-built of the Jesuit missions on the Baja, **Misión Santa Maria**. It is located about 17 miles (27 km) east of Mex. 1 with a rough access track from Rancho Santa Inés. You may be able to arrange a guided excursion through the Rancho. The mission was founded in 1767 and the walls are still standing.

Another mission, **Misión San Borja** is also accessible if you have four-wheel drive or a lightly loaded pickup with good ground clearance. From Rosarito, located about 97 miles (158 km) south of Cataviña on Mex. 1, drive east, roads leave the highway both north and south of the bridge over the arroyo. At about 15 miles (24 km) the road reaches Rancho San Ignacio, the mission is beyond at about 22 miles (36 km). Misión San Francisco de Borja was built in 1759 and has been restored by the government.

EL ROSARIO, BAJA CALIFORNIA (EL ROE-SAHR-EEH-OH)

For many years El Rosario was as far south as you could drive unless you were an off-roader. Today's road turns inland here and heads for the center of the peninsula, it won't return to the west coast until it cuts back to Guerrero Negro, and even there it won't stay for long. Espinosa's Place, a local restaurant, has been famous for years for its seafood burritos (lobster and crab meat). During the old Baja 1000 off road races this place was a favorite stop, it is reportedly not as good now but still worth a visit. The town of El Rosario is actually in two places, El Rosario da Arriba is on the main highway, El Rosario de Abajo is a 1.5 miles (2.4 km) away down and across the arroyo (river bed). Each has the ruins of an old mission, the first was in El Rosario de Arriba, it was later abandoned and moved to El Rosario de Abajo. Little remains of the first except the foundations, there are still standing walls at the second, which was abandoned in 1832.

Campground

MOTEL SINAI R.V. PARK
  Address: Carret. Transp. Km 56.5, El
  Rosario, B.C., Mexico
  Telephone: (616) 5-88-18

    Price: Small rigs - Low, Large rigs -
    Moderate

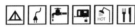

GPS Location: N 30° 04' 00.6", W 115° 42' 55.0"

EL ROSARIO

In the last few years this little hotel has installed RV spaces on the hillside behind. This is a welcome addition to the peninsula campgrounds because it reduces the longest gap between campgrounds with utilities by about 30 miles (49 km). It is 216 miles (353 km) between El Rosario and the next ones to the south in Guerrero Negro (unless you make a side trip to Bahía de Los Ángeles).

There are 12 paved pads for RVs, but they are so close together that there will probably be room for fewer campers most of the time. All sites have electricity and

VADOS ARE USUALLY EMPTY

water, sewer drains are available to most of them. There is a very nice toilet cubicle and two nice little shower rooms with hot water. There is plenty of room for big rigs to maneuver. The motel also has a little restaurant. Limited English is spoken.

The Motel Sinai is near the eastern outskirts of El Rosario on the north side of the highway. It is exactly .9 miles (1.5 km) east of the 90 degree turn in the middle of town.

Side Trips from El Rosario

You can drive 10.5 miles (17 km) west on a decent road to **Punta Baja**, a fish camp and beach hangout where free camping is possible. Surfing here is said to be excellent. This road is suitable for pickups and sturdy vans, but probably not RVs.

It is also possible for similar vehicles to drive about 48 miles (74 km) southwest to **Punta San Carlos** for primitive camping and wind surfing. Roads are dirt but generally not too bad by Baja standards.

ENSENADA, BAJA CALIFORNIA (EHN-SEH-NAH-DAH)
Population 400,000, Elevation sea level

Ensenada is the Baja's third most populous town and one of the most pleasant to visit. It is an important port and is more than ready for the tourist hordes that make the short-and-easy 67 mile (109 km) drive south from the border crossing at Tijuana or disembark from the cruise ships that anchor in Todos Santos Bay. There are many, many restaurants and handicrafts stores in the central area of town, English is often spoken so this is not a bad place to get your feet wet if you have not visited a Mexican city before. There are also many supermarkets and Pemex stations so Ensenada is the place to stock up on supplies before heading down the peninsula. Many banks have ATM machines so you can easily acquire some pesos.

When you tire of shopping and eating, Ensenada has a few other attractions. The best beach is at Estero Beach which also has many campgrounds, they are discussed below. The fishing in Ensenada is good, charters for yellowtail, albacore, sea bass, halibut and bonito can be arranged at the fishing piers. Ensenada has the largest fish market on the Baja, it is called the Mercado Negro (black market) and is located near the sport fishing piers. The waterspout at La Bufadora, located 10 miles beyond Punta Banda (see below) is a popular day trip. Whale watching trips are a possibility from December to March, check at the Museo de Ciencias de Ensenada (Science Museum).

Important fiestas here are Mardi gras or Carnaval in February, a wine festival in August, Day of the Dead on November 1 and 2, and Día de Nuestra Señora de Guadalupe on Dec. 12.

If you did not get a tourist card when you crossed the border in Tijuana you can obtain one and get it validated at the immigration office in Ensenada. It has recently moved, now it is located on the north side of the road soon after you cross the speed bumps when entering town from the north on Mex. 1. Vehicle permits, when needed, are more easily obtained at the border.

We have listed only four campgrounds in the Ensenada area. There are really several more. Some are very poor and really not very good choices. Others are located in outlying locations that are really destinations in their own right, see the Estero Beach and Punta Banda listings below for some of these. Finally, we've not listed others because we just don't have room in this book for them all. We hope, however, that we have included the best of them here.

Campground No. 1

CAMPO PLAYA R.V. PARK
    Blvd. Las Dunas & Delante St. (Apdo. 789),
    Ensenada, B.C., Mexico
    Telephone: (617) 6-29-18

Price: Moderate

GPS Location: N 31° 51' 00.6", W 116° 36' 46.7"

The Campo Playa is the only R.V. park actually in Ensenada and is the best place to stay if you want to explore the town. The downtown area is about a mile away and there is a large Gigante supermarket just up the street.

There are about 50 spaces in the park set among palm trees. Most are pull-throughs that will accept a big rig with slide-outs. The spaces have 20-amp. electricity, sewer, water and patios. There are also some smaller spaces, some with only partial utilities availability. The restrooms are showing their age but are clean and have hot showers. The campground is fenced but the urban location suggests that belongings not be left unattended. Credit cards and reservations are accepted.

The campground lies right on the most popular route through Ensenada. Entering town from the north on Mex. 1 zero your odometer as you cross the obnoxious topes (speed bumps) next to the harbor. You'll pass a shipyard on your right with huge fishing boats almost overhanging the highway. Take the first major right in .5 miles (.8 km) following signs for La Bufadora, this is Blvd. Lázaro Cárdenas. You'll pass a Sanborn's coffee shop on the right and also a plaza with a statue of three heads. At 1.8 miles (2.9 km) turn left onto Calle General Agustin, drive one block and turn left. The trailer park will be on your right.

Campground No. 2

BAJA SEASONS BEACH RESORT, VILLAS & RVS
    Address: 1177 Broadway Ave., Suite 2,
    Chula Vista, CA 91911 U.S.A. (Res.)
    Telephone: (800) 962-BAJA (Calif. Res.),
        (800) 356-BAJA (U.S. Res.)

Price: Very Expensive

GPS Location: N 32° 03' 50.6", W 116° 52' 38.8"

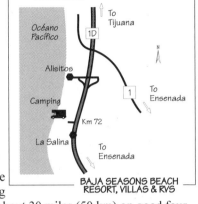

BAJA SEASONS BEACH
RESORT, VILLAS & RVS

The Baja Seasons is a large and very nice beachside RV park within reasonable driving distance of Ensenada. The drive into town is about 30 miles (50 km) on good four-lane highway, complicated only by a fascinating area where there seems to be an unending construction project to stabilize the road and keep it from sliding into the ocean.

The campground has about 140 very nice camping spaces with electricity (some 50-amp., the rest 30-amp.), sewer, water, TV, paved parking pad, patios and landscaping. The streets are paved, they even have curbs. There's a huge central complex with a restaurant and bar, swimming pool, jacuzzi, small store, tennis courts, sauna and steam baths, game room and library. There are also restrooms with hot showers. The entire set-up is on a wide, beautiful beach. English is spoken and reservations are accepted.

The campground is right next to Mex. 1D just south of the Km. 72 marker. Going south watch the kilometer markers and turn directly off the highway. Going north you will see the campground on your left but cannot turn because of the central divider. Continue north 4.1 miles (6.6 km) to the Alisitos exit to return.

Campground No. 3

RANCHO SORDO MUDO (DEAF-MUTE RANCH)
    Address: P.O. Box 1376, Chula Vista, CA
    91912 U.S.A. (Res.)

Price: Donation

GPS Location: N 32° 06' 38.1", W 116° 32' 53.8"

RANCHO
SORDO MUDO

If you decide to follow the inland route on Mex. 3 south from Tecate to Ensenada you might decide to spend the night at Rancho Sordo Mudo, about 24 miles (39 km) north of Ensenada. The ranch is actually a school for deaf and mute children, the campground was originally constructed for the use of visitors helping at the school. The income from the RV park goes to a good cause and the surroundings are very pleasant.

There are 10 spaces in a grassy field with full hookups including 50-amp. electricity. 30 more spaces offer electricity and water only. Many spaces are pull-throughs making this a good place for a one-night stop. The bathrooms are modern and clean and have hot water. The campground is likely to be deserted when you stop, just pull in and park and someone will eventually come across from the school to welcome you. The campground is located in a beautiful valley, the Domecq winery is just up the road and offers tours.

The campground is well-signed on Mex. 3. Driving south start watching as you pass the Domecq winery, it will be on your left right next to the highway just after the Km. 74 marker. Heading north it is even easier to spot just north of Francisco Zarco.

Campground No. 4

HOTEL JOKER
   Address: Carretera Transpeninsular Km.
   12.5, Ensenada, B.C., Mexico
   Telephone: (617) 6-72-01
   Fax: (617) 7-44-60

   Price: Moderate

   GPS Location: N 31° 48' 14.3", W 116° 35' 42.7"

Just south of Ensenada, right on Mex. 1, is a little motel with a few RV slots. Once you enter the gates you'll probably find you like the place. The hotel specializes in special-event parties, there are play areas with castle-like crenelations, a piñata party plaza, a barbecue area and a general atmosphere of good clean family fun.

The Joker has about 11 spaces, although most are pull-throughs they are small, rigs larger than 24 feet or so will have difficulty maneuvering and parking. The slots have electricity, sewer, water, and patios with shade, flowers, and barbecues. There's also a large grass area that is perfect for tents. The restrooms are older but clean and in good repair and have hot water. The hotel also has a restaurant and a swimming pool.

The Joker is on the east side of Mex. 1 just north of the Km. 13 marker. Heading north watch for it after you pass the airport, about 1.4 miles (2.2 km) north of the Estero Beach road. Heading south there are really no good markers, just watch for the hotel on your left.

Ensenada Side Trips

If you want to hike and tent camp you may want to visit **Sierra San Pedro Martír National Park**. This alpine park may seem completely out of character for the Baja, it has pines, mountain meadows and streams. This park is accessed from Mex. 1 north of San Quintín and about 83 miles (136 km) south of Ensenada, see the Side Trip section there for a description of the road. Access may also be possible on a poor road from Mex. 5 about 79 miles (129 km) from Ensenada near the 138 Km. marker. This road leads about 21 miles (34 km) to **Mike's Sky Rancho**, which is a small motel with an airstrip. Beyond Mike's the road is even worse but access to the park may be possible for four-wheel-drive rigs. The park is undeveloped and a fee is charged at the gate. There is also an astronomical observatory located at the park. The hiking is quite good.

Another national park, **Parque Nacional Constitución**, is accessible from Mex. 3 east of Ensenada. Near the Km. 55 marker a road goes north to the shallow Laguna Hanson, the distance to the lake is 22 miles (36 km). There are primitive campsites at the lake. This lake is also accessible from Mex. 2 to the north but the road is much worse and not suitable for small RV's like this one from the south.

ESTERO BEACH

The Estero Beach area is really a suburb of Ensenada. The road to Estero beach leads west from near the Km. 15 marker of Mex. 1 about 7 miles (11 km) south of Ensenada. There's not much here other than beaches, the resorts, and vacation homes.

Campground No. 1

ESTERO BEACH HOTEL/RESORT
    Address: Apdo. 86, Ensenada, B.C., Mexico
    Telephone: (617) 6-62-30
    Fax: (617) 6-69-25

        Price: Expensive

GPS Location: N 31° 46' 43.9", W 116° 36' 50.1"

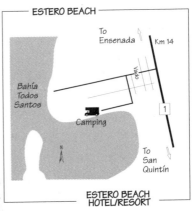

The Estero Beach Hotel has one of Mexico's finest RV parks, comparable in many ways with the more expensive places on the road between Tijuana and Ensenada. For some reason, perhaps because it is slightly off the main road, it doesn't get nearly as much traffic as they do. This is really a huge complex with a hotel as the centerpiece and many permanent RVs in a separate area from the current RV park.

The modern RV park has 30 big back-in spaces with 30-amp. electricity, sewer, and water. There is also a very large area for parking if you don't want utilities. There is grass under trees for tenters. The parked RVs look across an estuary (excellent birding) toward the hotel about a quarter-mile away. There's a paved walkway along the border of the estuary to the hotel. The restrooms are first class and have hot-water showers.

There is also a second RV parking area for use if the main one is full. This one has 33 back-in spaces with electricity, sewer, and water on a packed gravel surface. It is less attractive but OK. There is a separate set of restrooms which are older but in good condition with hot water showers.

The resort also has a restaurant, bar, several upscale shops, boat launching ramp, tennis courts, and playground. A swimming pool is under construction (spring 97).

To reach the Estero Beach Hotel take the Estero Beach road west from Mex. 1 some 5.2 miles (8.4 km) south of the Gigante on the corner of Ave. Reforma (Mex. 1) and Calle General Agustin. Drive 1 mile (1.6 km) west and turn left at the sign for the Estero Beach Hotel. You'll soon come to a gate. There is a very long entrance drive and then a reception office where they'll sign you up and direct you to a campsite.

Campground No. 2

EL FARO BEACH MOTEL AND TRAILER PARK
  Address: Apdo. 1008, Ensenada, B.C.,
    Mexico
  Telephone: (617) 7-46-30
  Fax: (617) 7-46-20

Price: Moderate

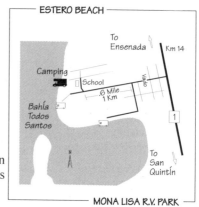

GPS Location: N 31° 46' 46.2", W 116° 37' 07.5"

This is a simple place, parking is right next to the beach on a sandy lot surrounded by a low concrete curb. There is room for about 20 rigs to back in with electricity and water. The campground has a dump station. There's also more space for more rigs not needing hookups. Showers are old, in poor repair, and cold. The El Faro has a restaurant from April to September.

To reach the El Faro take the Estero Beach road west from Mex. 1 5.2 miles (8.4 km) south of the Gigante on the corner of Ave. Reforma (Mex. 1) and Calle General Agustin. Drive 1.9 mile (3.1 km) west, taking the left fork of the Y at 1.6 miles (2.6 km). The El Faro is at the end of the road.

Campground No. 3

MONA LISA R.V. PARK
  Address: Apdo. 200, Chapultepec, B.C.,
    Mexico
  Telephone: (617) 7-49-20

Price: Moderate

GPS Location: N 31° 47' 04.5", W 116° 37' 02.4"

This is a quirky family-run campground, a fun place to visit. The name apparently comes from the murals painted on every available wall. They depict scenes from Mexico's history and are themselves worth a special trip to the Mona Lisa.

The campground has 13 fairly large back-in spaces. All are paved and have a palapa shaded table. All also have 50-amp. electricity, sewer, and water. The restrooms are old but clean and have hot water. There is also a restaurant, bar, and motel on the property. The Mona Lisa is next to a small beach but rock rip-rap fronts the actual RV park property, the current RV sites don't overlook the water. Plans are afoot to install a few dry-camping sites nearer the water. English is spoken and reservations are accepted.

To reach the Mona Lisa take the Estero Beach road west from Mex. 1 5.2 miles (8.4 km) south of the Gigante on the corner of Ave. Reforma (Mex. 1) and Calle General Agustin. Drive west and then north, taking the right fork of the Y at 1.6 miles (2.6 km). At 1.8 miles (2.9 km) turn left and you'll see the Mona Lisa ahead.

Campground No. 4

CORONA BEACH PARK
    Address: Apdo. 1149, Ensenada, Mexico

Price: Low

GPS Location: N 31° 47' 23.4", W 116° 36' 51.4"

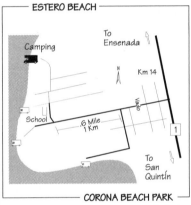

This is a simple campground with parking in a large flat area with no view of the nearby beach. There is parking for 30 rigs with electricity and water. There is also a dump station. The restrooms are clean and have cold water showers. A small grocery store sits next to the camping area. English is spoken.

To reach the Corona Beach take the Estero Beach road west from Mex. 1 5.2 miles (8.4 km) south of the Gigante on the corner of Ave. Reforma (Mex. 1) and Calle General Agustin. Drive west and then north, taking the right fork of the Y at 1.6 miles (2.6 km). At 1.9 miles (3.1 km) the road makes a quick right and then left to continue straight. You'll reach the campground at 2.1 miles (3.4 km).

PUNTA BANDA

Punta Banda is another small area that is virtually a suburb of Ensenada. To get there follow the road west from near the center of Maneadero near the 21 Km. marker, about 11 miles (18 km) south of Ensenada on Mex. 1. It is then another 8 miles (13 km) out to Punta Banda. Punta Banda has grown up around the large RV parks here. The beach is known for its hot springs, you can dig a hole and make your own bath tub. The springs are there because this area sits right on top of the Agua Blanca fault. A few miles beyond Punta Banda is the La Bufadora blow hole. There are several small campgrounds without hookups or much in the way of services near La Bufadora.

Campground No. 1

VILLARINO CAMPAMENTO TURISTICO
   Address: Km. 13 Carr. a la Bufadora (Apdo.
   1), Punta Banda, B.C., Mexico
   Telephone: (617) 6-42-46
   Fax: (617) 6-13-09

   Price: Low

GPS Location: N 31° 43' 01.6", W 116° 39' 57.5"

This campground with lots of permanents also has a good-size transient area. It's close to Ensenada, on the beach, and a little off the beaten path.

Behind a glass-fronted terrace is a large packed dirt area with some trees and about 20 larger sites. Some sites have electricity, sewer, and water and some have only electricity. The restrooms are very clean and well maintained, they have hot showers. In front of the campground is a restaurant, a small store, and a post office.

Take the road toward La Bufadora from Mex. 1 about 9.1 miles (14.7 km) south from the Gigante on the corner of Ave. Reforma (Mex. 1) and Calle General Agustin in Ensenada. You will see the Villarino on the right 7.8 miles (12.7 km) from the cutoff.

Campground No. 2

LA JOLLA BEACH CAMP
   Address: Apdo. 102, Punta Banda, C.P.
   22791 Ensenada, B.C., Mexico
   Telephone: (615) 4-20-05
   Fax: (615) 4-20-04

   Price: Low

GPS Location: N 31° 43' 00.1", W 116° 39' 52.2"

The La Jolla Beach Camp is a huge place. There are a lot of permanently located trailers here but most of the transient trade is summer and holiday visitors using tents and RVs. Several big empty dirt lots, both on the waterfront and on the south side of the highway, have room for about 400 groups. During the winter these areas are practically empty. You can park on the waterfront and run a long cord for electricity from a few plugs near the restroom buildings. Water is available and there's a dump station. Restrooms are very basic, like what you'd expect next to a public beach, and the showers are cold. There is a small grocery store and English is spoken.

Take the road toward La Bufadora from Mex. 1 about 9.1 miles (14.7 km) south from the Gigante on the corner of Ave. Reforma (Mex. 1) and Calle General Agustin in Ensenada. You will see the La Jolla on the right 7.7 miles (12.6 km) from the cutoff.

ROSARITO, BAJA CALIFORNIA (ROE-SAH-REE-TOE)
Population 40,000, Elevation sea level

You can't find a campground much closer to the border than those in Rosarito. This resort town depends upon visitors from California and Tijuana for its living. Mex. 1 (Libre) runs right through town about a block from the beach and many hotels are now located between the two. You will find restaurants and supplies readily available. The beach in front of town is nice, unfortunately it is heavily polluted. Neither of the two campgrounds listed below are actually in Rosarito, but they are close by.

Campground No. 1

ROSARITO KOA
    Address: Box 430513, San Ysidro, CA
    92143 (Res.)
    Telephone: (661) 3-33-05

        Price: Moderate

GPS Location: N 32° 25' 32.0", W 117° 05' 29.0"

KOA has actually been in Mexico for many years. Their current foray into Mexico isn't the first. The Rosarito KOA apparently is no longer fully affiliated with the company, although it is listed in their catalog. The location shown on their map is wrong, however, the campground is on the east side of the highway. The Rosarita KOA makes a good first stop if you enter Mexico late in the day at Tijuana. It's exactly 14.2 miles (22.9 km) from the border crossing.

The campground has about 200 grass-covered campsites. Most are pull-throughs and have electricity, sewer, and water. They also have good views of the coast far below. Unfortunately almost all of the spaces are filled with trailers that have been there for years. Traveler's will have a choice of perhaps 30 spaces. While the campground is virtually full there aren't usually many people around, the facilities won't be crowded. The bathrooms are old but reasonably clean and have hot water showers. There is a laundry and a small store. You can find groceries in Rosarito, a short drive away but if you're heading south wait for the big stores in Ensenada to stock up.

The campground is just off the toll highway Mex. 1D. If you are headed south follow the signs from the border for Rosarito, Ensenada and *cuota* (toll) highway Mex. 1D. If you zero your odometer at the border you will reach the first toll station at 6.6 miles (10.6 km). Take the San Antonio exit 7.6 miles (12.2 km) south of the toll station. Use the overpass to cross the road and then follow the cobblestone driveway up the hill for .2 miles (.3 km). If you are coming from the south or if you have taken the free road to Rosarita you should take the toll road north and exit at the San Antonio exit at the 22 Km. marker. There is no toll booth between the intersection of the free road and toll road in Rosarito and the KOA so free road users won't have to pay to get to the campground if they use this route.

Campground No. 2

OASIS BEACH RESORT
   Address: Km. 25 Carretera Escénica
   Tijuana-Ensenada, B.C., Mexico.
   Reservations: P.O. Box 158, Imperial
   Beach, CA 91933
   Telephone: (66) 31-32-50,
   (888) 709-9985 (U.S. Res.)

   Price: Expensive

GPS Location: N 32° 23' 49.6.", W 117° 05' 19.6"

This is the most expensive campground we've found in Mexico, reason enough to spend a night here just for the novelty. You won't spend much more than you would for a motel in the states and the facilities are great! In the winter the rates are $31 per day during the week and $37 per day on weekends. Summer rates are higher in this part of Mexico.

There are 78 back-in campsites available for visitors. Several others have big fifth-wheels permanently installed that the hotel rents as rooms. Each slot has a paved parking area, a patio, 50-amp. electricity, sewer, water, TV hookup, and barbecue. The whole place is beautifully landscaped, this is a posh place. Before accepting a campsite check it to make sure that you can level your rig, many have an extreme slope. There are very nice restrooms with hot showers, a swimming pool with a geyser-like fountain in the middle, a hot Jacuzzi next to the pool, a weight room and sauna with ocean view, a tennis court, a putting course, a laundry, and a very nice restaurant. There is also a convention center for groups of up to 1,200, if you need one of those. The campground is next to the beach and has beach access. Security is tight and English is spoken. Don't be run off by this description, the place really isn't as big or threatening as it sounds.

Heading south on the toll road Mex. 1D the exit for the Oasis is labeled El Oasis, it is at Km. 25 and is 9.4 miles (15.1 km) south of the northern-most toll booth. Heading north there is also an exit, it is labeled Rancho del Mar.

Other Camping Possibilities

There are quite a few campgrounds along the beach south of Rosarito. If you want to check them out just follow the free road south from Rosarito, most are full of permanents or are very basic and aimed at the surfing trade.

Side Trips from Rosarito

Mex. 1 (Libre) meets the toll highway Mex. 1D at the north end of Rosarito. The free highway runs through town while the toll road bypasses it, then they meet and run side by side for about 25 miles (41 km) south. There are lots of developments of various types along this double road, one of the most interesting is **Puerto Nuevo**, about 13 miles (21 km) south of Rosarito. This has become the place to go to get a lobster dinner, there are about 30 restaurants in the small town, they cover the spectrum in price and quality.

SAN QUINTÍN, BAJA CALIFORNIA (SAHN KWEEN-TEEN)

San Quintín is an interesting place, both geological and historically. The area is a large salt water lagoon system which fronts a fertile plain. Long sandy beaches stretch north and south. The lagoon and plain probably would have eroded away long ago except that there are eight small volcanoes (seven onshore and one an island offshore) that shelter the area from the sea. For the last few decades the plain has been heavily farmed, unfortunately there is not enough fresh water in the aquifer and salt water has started to displace the fresh water. Farming has gradually retreated to the east side of Mex. 1.

Farming is also responsible for the interesting history of the area. During the late 19th century the area was the focus of a settlement scheme by an English company called the Mexican Land and Colonization Company. The plan was to grow wheat but it turned out that there wasn't enough rainfall. Today there are several ruined structures to remind visitors of the colony, they include the Molino Viejo (old mill), the Muelle Viejo (old pier), and the English cemetery.

Outdoorsmen love the area. Duck hunting is good, fishing in both the estuary and offshore are excellent, and there are lots of clams on the sandy beaches along the ocean. The protected waters are a good place to launch a trailer boat if you've pulled one south.

In the interests of simplicity we've included several campgrounds in this section that are not properly in the San Quintín area. The two farthest north are 13 miles (21 km) north in the town of Colonia Guerrero, the farthest south are 10 miles (16 km) away from San Quintín. None of the campgrounds in this section, in fact, are actually in the town of San Quintín.

Campground No. 1

DON PEPE
  Address: Calle del Turista #102, Col.
  Vicente Guerrero, B.C, Mexico
  Telephone: (666) 6-22-16

Price: Low

GPS Location: N 30° 42' 59.2", W 115° 59' 20.1"

While we've listed the Don Pepe and the
following Posada Don Diego as San Quintín
trailer parks, long-time Baja travelers will
know that they are really about 13 miles (21 km) north of San Quintín in the town
of Vicente Guerrero. Both of these parks have been popular for a long time with
traveler's heading south or north, they are a comfortable day's drive from the
border. Both are located on the same entrance road, they're within a half-mile of
each other. The Don Pepe is the one on the highway and the first one the visitor
reaches, it is also the smaller of the two.

There are really two transient camping areas at this park. Just below the restaurant
is a grassy area with electrical outlets and water that is set aside for about 10 tent
and van campers. Farther from the restaurant on the far side of a few permanents is
the RV camping with about 20 pull-through spaces with electricity, sewer, and
water. Both camping areas have restrooms, they are older but clean and have hot
water showers. The restaurant at the Don Pepe is well-known and considered to be
pretty good.

The entrance to the trailer park is on the west side of Mex. 1 just south of Col.
Vicente Guerrero where the road starts to climb a small hill at the Km. 173 marker.
There are actually two entrances, the farthest north is well signed and will lead you
into the RV parking areas. The second is near the top of the hill, just north of the
propane plant, this will take you to the restaurant/office. After checking in there is
a road around the back of the trailer park to lead you back down to the camping
areas.

Campground No. 2

POSADA DON DIEGO T.P.
  Address: Apdo.   126,   Col.   Vicente
Guerrero,
  B.C., Mexico
  Telephone: (666) 6-21-81

Price: Moderate

GPS Location: N 30° 42' 56.0", W 115° 59' 31.9"

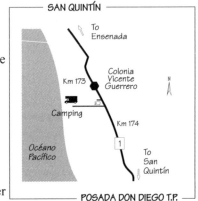

This second Col. Vicente Guerrero trailer

park is very popular with caravans, it is roomy and has lots of spaces, in fact it is the only large campground with full hookups in this area.

The campground has 100 spaces, almost 50 of these are usually occupied by permanents. Most of the available slots are large enough for big rigs with pull-outs, they have electricity, water, and patios. About half also have sewer. There is also a dump station available. The restrooms are in good repair and clean, they have hot water showers. The campground also has a restaurant/bar, a store, and a meeting room.

To reach the Posada Don Diego follow the road going west from just north of the propane plant at Km 173. This is just south of Col. Vicente Guerrero. The same road runs right past the restaurant at the Don Pepe, described above. The campground is about .5 miles (.8 km) down this sometimes rough gravel road.

Campground No. 3

OLD MILL TRAILER PARK
   Address: 858 Third Ave, Suite 456, Chula
   Vista, CA 91911-1305 U.S.A. (U.S. Res.)
   Telephone: 1-800-995-8482 (U.S.
   Reservations) or (619) 479-3467 (U.S.
   Reservations)

   Price: Expensive

GPS Location: N 30° 29' 08.6" W 115° 58' 32.9"

The Old Mill Trailer Park is becoming more and more popular both as an overnight stop and a fishing destination. It is located some 3 miles (5 km) off Mex. 1 on a washboard but otherwise fine dirt road. Big rigs don't hesitate to come here.

The campground has 20 spaces. They all have paved parking pads, patios, electricity, sewer, and water. Fifteen are in the front row with a good view of the estuary. There is also an area set aside for dry or tent campers. The bathrooms are only a few years old, they have hot water showers. The trailer park has the same owners as the nearby restaurant, check in at the bait shop across the driveway from the restaurant or, if it is closed, at the bar. Fishing is good here. There's a boat launch if you've brought your own or you can hire a boat and guide.

The access road to the Old Mill leads west from Mex. 1 south of Col. Lázaro Cárdenas. It is well-signed at the 1 Km. marker. The wide dirt road leads west for 3.3 miles (5.3 km), then you'll see a sign pointing left to the restaurant and RV park. Don't follow signs for Muelle Viejo, that is a different place.

Campground No. 4

CIELITO LINDO MOTEL AND R.V. PARK
  Address: Apdo. 7, San Quintín, B.C.,
  Mexico
  Telephone: (619) 222-8955 U.S. Res.),
  (619) 593-2252 (Voice mail in the U.S.)

Price: Low

GPS Location: N 30° 24' 31.6", W 115° 55' 25.7"

The Cielito Lindo Motel has been around for a long time. It actually has two camping areas. One is large and near the beach. Now called "The Dunes", it had full utility hookups at one time but now is for dry camping only. Frequent flooding was causing too many maintenance headaches. The other area is smaller and located near the hotel about a half-mile from the beach, it has full hookups.

The hotel camping area has 8 back-in slots, they have electricity, water and sewer. There is a row of pine trees to provide shade and some shelter from the frequent wind in this area. Electricity is produced by an on-site generator so it is available from 7 A.M. to 11 A.M. and from 3 P.M. until the bar closes. The bar also serves as a restaurant. There is also a small area set aside for tent and van campers not needing hookups. It has room for about 7 tents or vans and has water.

The Cielito Lindo is located near the San Quintín La Pinta Motel. The paved road with lots of potholes leads west from Mex. 1 near the Km. 11 marker. It is signed for both the La Pinta and the Cielito Lindo. Follow the road west for 2.8 miles (4.5 km) past the La Pinta entrance to the Cielito Lindo entrance, stop at the motel and check in for either campground.

Campground No. 5

EL PABELLÓN RV PARK

Price: Low

GPS Location: N 30° 22' 26.8" W 115° 52' 06.6"

Miles of sand dunes and ocean. That's El Pabellón RV park. There really isn't much else. This is a large graded area set in sand dunes close to the ocean. It is being gradually improved. There have been flush toilets and hot showers for some time. There are also six pull through spaces with sewer drains and water. Recently a long line of interesting table-like structures with sinks and barbecues have been built, these will apparently someday be pull-through campsites. Everyone just ignores the campsites anyway and parks where they want. Caravans often stop here and circle wagon-train style. Tenters pitch in the dunes in front of the campground. There is usually an attendant at the entrance gate.

The turn for El Pabellón is between Km. 15 and 16 south of San Quintín. Turn south at the sign and follow the 1.2 mile gravel road to the campground.

Other Camping Possibilities

If you drive the roads around the north side of the Puerto San Quintín estuary you will find primitive camping areas along the bay and on the coast.

At San Antonio del Mar, see Side Trips below, there are some primitive camping possibilities.

South of the San Quintín area and about 5.5 miles (9 km) south of the El Pabellón RV park cutoff is a road to El Socorro beach where free camping is possible.

Side Trips from San Quintín

About 34 miles (55.5 km) north of San Quintín near the Km. 141 marker a road goes east to San Telmo, the **Meling Rancho**, and the **Parque Nacionál Sierra San Pedro Martír**. The road as far as the Meling Rancho at about 32 miles (52 km) is reasonably good and usually OK for smaller RVs. The ranch is about a half-mile off the main road, it has an airstrip and offers overnight accommodations. Beyond the ranch to the park entrance gate at about 51 miles (83 km) the road may not be as good and is sometimes only suitable for pickups and sturdy vans. The road continues to an astronomical observatory at 65 miles (106 km). There are undeveloped campsites in the park and lots of hiking and other mountain climbing possibilities.

A road leads 7 miles (11 km) to the beach at **San Antonio del Mar** from north of Colonét near Km. 126. There is a long sandy beach backed by dunes, it has clams and offers good surf fishing.

SANTO TOMÁS (SAHN-TOE TOE-MAHS)
Population 200, Elevation 350 ft (105 m)

Tiny Santo Tomás is located in the Santo Tomás Valley some 28 miles (46 km) south of Ensenada. Grapes (for wine) and olives are grown in the valley. The El Palomar resort and balneario is the major attraction of the town. This was a mission village, the grape plantings were by the Dominicans. Today there isn't much left of the mission ruins which are just north of El Palomar's RV park.

Campground

Balneario El Palomar
   Address: Apdo. 1103, Santo Tomás, B.C.,
   Mexico. U.S. Res. - P.O. Box 4492 Camino
   de la Plaza #232, San Ysidro, CA 92173
   Telephone: (615) 3-80-02 (Campground)
   (617) 8-80-02 (Reservations in Ensenada)

Price: Moderate

GPS Location: N 31° 33' 21.9", W 116° 24' 45.4"

Balnearios (bathing resorts) are very popular in Mexico, they often make a good place to camp. This is the best example on the Baja. In 1997 it will be celebrating it's fiftieth anniversary.

The El Palomar has six pull-throughs large enough for big rigs and about 20 very small back-in spaces. All have 20-amp. electricity, sewer, water, patios and barbecues. Two restroom buildings are clean and in good repair, they have hot water for showers. There are two swimming pools near the camping area and a small lake and water slide about a half-mile away. There's also a small zoo and large areas for picnicking. Across the street in the main building there is a store, a restaurant, and a small gas station. Two words of warning are in order. Take a look at the steep entrance before entering and be aware that this is a very popular place on weekends during the summer and on holidays. Reservations are taken and English is spoken.

The El Palomar is at the north entrance to the town of Santo Tomás about 29 miles (47 km) south of Ensenada on Mex. 1. The office is on the west side of the road and the campground on the east.

Other Camping Possibilities

The coast near La Bocana and Puerto Santo Tomás has several sites suitable for primitive camping. There is also reported to be a formal campground near La Bocana. See the Side Trips section below for directions to these spots.

Camping without hookups has been available near San Isidro for some time. There is now a sign on Mex. 1 advertising the Malibu Beach RV park with full hookups at 12 miles (20 km). We have not visited but it sounds like this would be in Eréndira, which is just south of San Isidro. See Side Trips below.

About four miles (6 km) north of Santo Tomás on the main highway is a small picnic and possible camping area. It is associated with the Ejido Uruapan and there is a use fee.

Side Trips from Santo Tomás

There are a couple of roads that lead east to the coast from the vicinity of Santo Tomás. 1.9 miles (3.1 km) north of the El Palomar a gravel road goes along the

Santo Tomás valley to **La Bocana** and then north along the coast to **Puerto Santo Tomás**. La Bocana is at the mouth of the Santo Tomás River and is 17.6 miles (28.7 km) from Mex. 1. Puerto Santo Tomás is about three miles (5 km) to the north.

South of Santo Tomás near Km. 78 (a distance of 16 miles (26 km)) there is a paved road to the coastal town of **Eréndira** at 12 miles (20 km). A smaller road heads north another mile or so to **San Isidro**.

TECATE, BAJA CALIFORNIA (TEH-KAW-TAY)
Population 100,000, Elevation 1,850 ft. (560 m)

Tecate is probably the most relaxed and pleasant border town in Mexico. Besides being a great place to cross into Baja (there is a good road south to Ensenada and a very scenic one east to Mexicali) the town is well worth a short visit.

Tecate is an agricultural center that is gradually turning industrial as the maquiladora industries arrive. The center of town is dominated by the park-like square which is just a couple of blocks from the laid-back border crossing. Probably the most famous tourist attraction here is the brewery.

Campground No. 1

RANCHO OJAI R.V. PARK
    Address: P.O. Box 280, Tecate, CA 91980
    U.S.A. (Reservations)
    Telephone: (665) 4-47-72
            Price: Low

GPS Location: N 32° 33' 31.4", W 116° 26' 05.4"

Rancho Ojai is something a little different in Baja campgrounds. This is a working ranch located in the rolling hills just east of Tecate off Mex. 2. The facilities are brand-new and nicely done. This is normally a summer destination, the area is known for its mild summer weather, but winters have an occasional frost.

There are 75 campsites, 41 have full hookups with 30-amp. electricity, sewer, and water. The tiled restrooms are brand new and clean with hot water showers. The ranch offers a ranch-style clubhouse, a barbecue area, grocery shop, sports areas for volley ball and horseshoes, and a children's playground with small pool. The campground is fenced and the manager lives in a trailer near the gate so there is 24-hour security.

The Rancho is located about 13 miles (21 km) east of Tecate on the north side of the highway near the Km. 112 marker. There is a stone arch entrance near the highway and you can see the camping area across the valley.

Campground No. 2

HACIENDA SANTA VERONICA
 Address: Jim or Joan Ellis, 2272 Iris
 Avenue, San Diego 92154 (Reservations)
 Telephone: (619) 423-3830
 (U.S. Reservations)

Price: Moderate

GPS Location: N 32° 32' 13.8", W 116° 22' 28.2"
(Entrance Road)

Slightly farther east of Tecate than the Ojai Ranch is Hacienda Santa Veronica. To get there you must negotiate a six-mile dirt road but once you've reached the campground you're likely to want to spend some time. This is a 5,000 acre rancho. It is described in its own brochures as rustic, but other than the no-hookup campground it is really surprisingly polished. The rancho is very popular with off-road motorcycle riders and also offers quite a few amenities: rental rooms, a huge swimming pool with a bar in the middle, good tennis courts, a nice restaurant and bar, horseback riding, and occasionally even a bullfight. This is a popular summer destination, in the winter things are pretty quiet except on week-ends.

The camping area is a grassy meadow with big oak trees for shade. Spaces are unmarked, you camp where you want to. The restrooms are near the pool, not far from the camping area. In the summer when the pool is in use they have hot water showers. The Santa Veronica also has a nice full-hookup campground that has been closed down because it wasn't getting enough use. Perhaps they'll open it again if enough of us visit!

To find the hacienda head east on Mex. 2 from the Rancho Ojai R.V. Park. At 3.5 miles (5.6 km) start looking for their sign, it points down a dirt road to the south. The new toll highway is being built about a half-mile south of this point so the entrance road arrangement may change soon. Follow the signs on dirt roads for 6.4 miles (10.3 km) to the hacienda.

Side Trips from Tecate

Laguna Hanson is accessible from the north off Mex. 2 but the road is not as good as the one from the south off Mex. 3 which is discussed in the Side Trips from Ensenada section above. From Tecate go east to Km. 72 which is about 36 miles (58.8 km) distant. The road south is not suitable for RVs but OK for smaller rigs with good clearance. The distance to Laguna Hanson is about 40 miles (65 km).

A COMMON BAJA SCENE

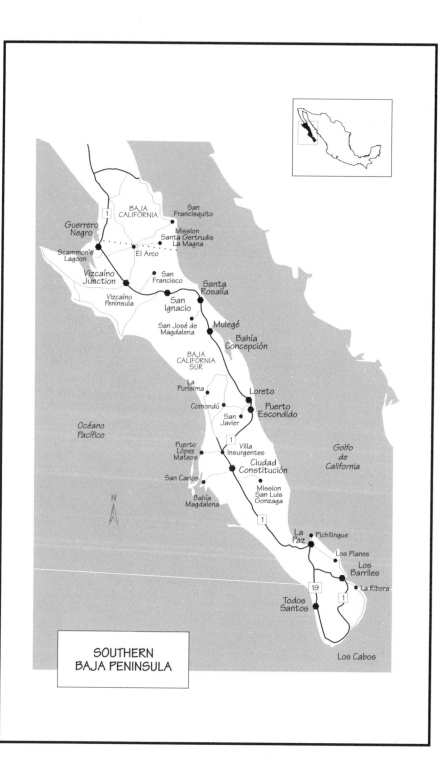

SOUTHERN
BAJA PENINSULA

CHAPTER 13

SOUTHERN BAJA PENINSULA

INTRODUCTION

The southern Baja Peninsula, the state of Baja California Sur, extends from the 28th parallel in the north to the tip of the peninsula near Cabo San Lucas, a distance of about 425 air miles (700 km). A range of mountains extends along much of the length of this section of Baja near the east coast, just as it does in the north. To the west the land is flat. Often there are large swampy estuaries along the flat west coast while the eastern Gulf Coast is generally rocky. Large areas of desert land have few inhabitants but there are major population centers at La Paz and near the southern tip of the state at San José del Cabo and Cabo San Lucas. The east coast between Santa Rosalía and Loreto has several interesting small towns, often tourist oriented, and farming regions center around Ciudad Constitución and Todos Santos.

ROAD SYSTEM

Just like in the Northern Baja there is one road, Mex. 1, that forms the backbone of the transportation system. From the north Mex. 1 crosses the 28th parallel near Guerrero Negro on the west coast. Then it turns inland and crosses the peninsula to Santa Rosalía on the east coast. Turning south the highway passes Mulegé, Bahía Concepción, Loreto, and Bahía Escondido before climbing into the Sierra de la Giganta and heading southwest for the farming center of Ciudad Constitución. La Paz appears as the highway once again reaches the Sea of Cortez after another desert crossing, then the road circles down the east side of the peninsula to San José del Cabo and Cabo San Lucas. There's also a short cut between La Paz and San Lucas, a west coast highway called Mex. 19.

Mex. 1 is well marked with kilometer signs. In Baja California Sur the signs count from south to north, an order exactly opposite that of the signs in Baja California to the north. In each section the signs begin at zero. The sections, from south to north, are as follows: Cabo San Lucas to La Paz, 137 miles (224 km); La Paz to Ciudad Insurgentes, 149 miles (243 km); Ciudad Insurgentes to Loreto, 74 miles (121 km);

Loreto to Santa Rosalía 122 miles (199 km); Santa Rosalía to Guerrero Negro, 137 miles (224 km).

Opportunities for RVers in larger rigs to get off the main road are limited but available. If you wish to stick to paved roads you can follow the road to the farming area of Los Planes south of La Paz (see La Paz Side Trips), drive along the coast to the northeast of La Paz to Pichilingue and the ferry dock (see La Paz Side Trips), drive west from Ciudad Constitución to San Carlos on the Bahía Magdalena or east from Villa Insurgentes to Puerto López Mateos (see Ciudad Constitución Side Trips).

RVers with smaller rigs have a wider selection of exploration options. A few of them include the road to Scammon's Lagoon from south of Guerrero Negro (see Guerrero Negro Side Trips), the road to El Arco (see Guerrero Negro Side Trips), portions of the road system on the Vizcaíno Peninsula east of Vizcaíno and south of Guerrero Negro (see Vizacíno Junction Side Trips), and soon perhaps even the road along the east coast of the peninsula between La Ribera and San José del Cabo if it gets completed as planned (see Los Barriles Side Trips).

Travelers with high-clearance vehicles who do not mind a lot of washboard surfaces may want to consider the roads east to the coast from El Arco (see Guerrero Negro Side Trips), the poorer roads on the Vizcaíno Peninsula (see Vizcaíno Junction Side Trips), the road from Mex. 1 near San Ignacio to San Francisco de la Sierra and the nearby cave paintings (see San Ignacio Side Trips), roads across the Sierra de la Giganta to Ciudad Insurgentes through La Purísima and Comondú (see Loreto Side Trips), the road east from Mex. 1 south of Ciudad Constitución to Mission San Luis Gonzaga (see Ciudad Constitución Side Trips), the road north along the coast from Los Barriles to connect with the paved road from La Paz at Los Planes (see Los Barriles Side Trips), or the road along the east coast of the peninsula between La Ribera and San José del Cabo if it doesn't get improved as planned (see Los Barriles Side Trips).

Before the completion of Mex. 1 south of Rosario the easiest access to the southern peninsula was by ferry from the mainland. There continue to be three ferry routes from the peninsula to the mainland in operation: Santa Rosalía - Guaymas, Pichilingue (La Paz) - Topolobampo (near Los Mochis), and Pichilingue - Mazatlán. It is possible to make reservations for these ferries and this is recommended but not always necessary. The phone number for reservations is 91-800-6-96-96 which is a toll-free Mexico number. The Santa Rosalía ferry runs twice weekly and the Pichilingue ones run daily. One inconvenience is that it is usually necessary to pick up your ticket at the local office on the day before sailing. If you are considering using the ferries to reach the mainland remember that you must have your paperwork in order including a vehicle permit for your rig. These are available in La Paz but you should consider getting them at the border when entering Mexico to make sure that you have everything in order before making the long drive south. See the Ferries section of Chapter 2 for more infomation.

HIGHLIGHTS

Fly-in tourists generally head for the cape area and the two towns there: San José del Cabo and Cabo San Lucas. These are also exciting destinations for the camping traveler with every sort of tourist attraction including golf, fishing, beaches, restaurants and many RV parks. The large city of La Paz, about 98 miles (160 km) north, is also an interesting destination because it has tourist facilities but retains a charm reminiscent of the older cities on the mainland.

La Paz, San José del Cabo, and Cabo San Lucas are really the only sizable destination cities on the southern peninsula but there are several smaller towns that make interesting stops because of their general ambiance or attractions. These include Todos Santos, Los Barriles, Loreto, Mulegé, Santa Rosalía, San Ignacio, and Guerrero Negro. Each of these towns has at least one RV park and is covered in more detail in this chapter.

One of the most popular attractions offered in the southern Baja is whale watching. Each winter thousands of gray whales visit the large shallow lagoons on the west side of the peninsula. From January until April they remain in these nursery lagoons where the young are born and grow until they are strong enough for a long migration north to the Arctic Ocean. Probably the best place to see them is Scammon's Lagoon near Guerrero Negro, but they are also present in San Ignacio Lagoon and Magdalena Bay. See the Guerrero Negro and San Ignacio sections of this chapter for information about visiting the whales.

The Baja Peninsula offers something available almost nowhere else in North America, lots of primitive or free camping right on the beach. The easiest access to this type of camping, especially for large RVs, is on Bahía Concepción which has a special section in this chapter. There are plenty of other much more remote camping locations. Most require several hours and many miles of driving on rough unimproved roads, but if you have the right rig Baja has some unique offerings. It's hard to think of another place in the world with so many miles of beautiful deserted beaches, and these beaches are in a sunny, warm climate.

Fishermen will find some excellent sport on the southern Baja. Deep sea fishing is popular out of Cabo San Lucas. Panga charters are available from Mulegé, Loreto, La Paz, and Los Barriles. Campers with their own boats should bring them along, there will be lots of opportunities to use them.

Hikers and tent-campers looking for high pine country like that in the two national parks in the northern Baja have a southern Baja option also. This is the Sierra La Laguna. Located in the middle of the loop that Mex. 1 and Mex. 19 make between La Paz and Cabo San Lucas these granite mountains rise to 7,000 feet and are accessible only on foot. The easiest-to-find route in is from the west near Todos Santos so you'll find further information in this book under Side Trips from Todos Santos.

As you drive along Mex. 1 there are several places where you may see government signs pointing down gravel roads where you can find *pinturas rupestres*. These are cave paintings, paintings on the rocks done by Indians long ago. The actual age of most of these paintings is unknown. A side trip to view cave paintings is included in the San Ignacio section.

THE CAMPGROUNDS

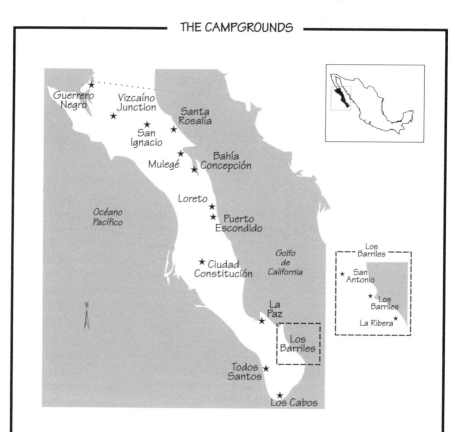

DISTANCE TABLE

Miles

Cabo San Lucas	719	228	576	98	320	81	407	303	486	440	1012	50	532
	Cataviña	489	145	619	399	682	316	416	233	279	293	669	188
1174		Ciudad Constitución	344	130	89	194	173	73	255	210	782	179	301
373	798		Guerrero Negro	475	255	538	171	271	89	134	438	526	43
940	236	562		La Paz	220	63	303	203	386	340	912	48	431
160	1011	213	775		Loreto	283	83	17	166	121	693	270	211
522	652	146	416	359		Los Barriles	366	266	449	404	976	80	494
133	1114	316	878	103	462		Mulegé	100	83	37	609	357	128
664	516	282	280	495	136	598		Puerto Escondido	182	137	709	254	228
495	679	119	443	332	27	435	163		San Ignacio	45	527	436	45
793	381	417	145	630	271	733	135	298		Santa Rosalía	572	391	91
719	455	343	219	556	197	659	61	224	74		Tijuana	963	481
1653	479	1277	715	1490	1131	1593	995	1158	860	934		Todos Santos	483
81	1093	292	859	79	441	131	583	414	712	638	1572		Vizcaíno Junction
869	307	491	71	704	345	807	209	372	74	148	786	788	

Kilometers

SELECTED CITIES AND THEIR CAMPGROUNDS

BAHÍA CONCEPCIÓN, BAJA CALIFORNIA SUR
(BAH-HEE-AH KOHN-SEP-SEE-OHN)

For many people, especially RVers, the Bahía Concepción is the ultimate Baja destination. This huge shallow bay offers many beaches where you can park your camping vehicle just feet from the water and spend the winter months soaking in the sunshine. Mex. 1 parallels the western shore of the bay for about 20 miles (33 km), you'll see many very attractive spots and undoubtedly decide to stop. The many beaches offer different levels of services. Full hookups are not available at any of them, but many have toilets, showers, water, and restaurants. Information about the most popular beaches is offered below. While many of these places seem to have no formal organization do not be surprised if someone comes by in the evening to collect a small fee. This usually covers keeping the area picked up, trash removal and pit toilets. Ask one of your fellow campers about arrangements if you have questions. The closest place to get supplies is Mulegé, about 12 miles (20 km) north.

Beach No. 1

PUNTA ARENA

Price: Inexpensive

GPS Location: N 26° 46' 42.2", W 111° 52' 22.6"

There are actually two different camping area on this large beach: Playa las Naranyos to the north and Playa Punta Arena to the south. The entry road branches not far from the highway and you make your decision there. In the past it has been possible to drive from one to the other along the beach but now the campground down the left fork is fenced.

The beach at Punta Arena is long and not nearly as crowded as the beaches to the south. It is quite easy to find a place along the water most of the time. There are pit toilets and Playa las Naranyos has cold showers. Small palapas are available. The beach here is not nearly as sheltered as those in Bahía Coyote to the south but the southern-most beach (Playa Punta Arena) is somewhat sheltered from north winds. In the scrub behind the beach the residents have set up a small sand golf course.

The entrance to Punta Arena is near the Km. 119 marker. The road in to the beach is rough but should be negotiable by any RV. It is two miles (3 km) long, at .4 miles (.7 km) there is a Y where you go left for Playa las Naranyos and right for Playa Punta Arena.

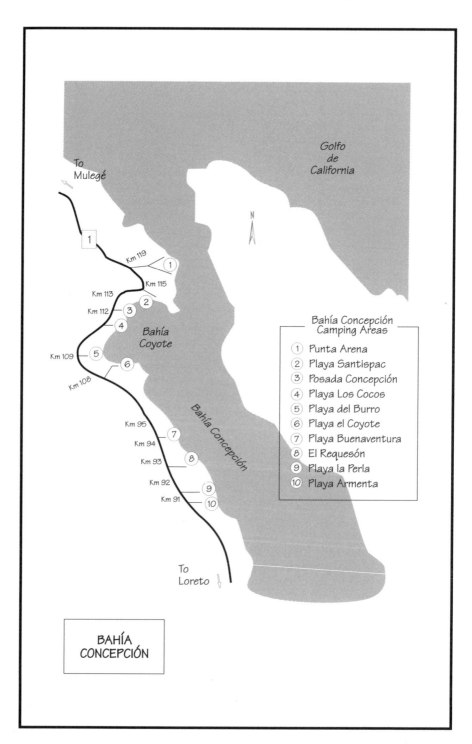

Beach No. 2

PLAYA SANTISPAC

Price: Inexpensive

GPS Location: N 26° 45' 58.4", W 111° 53' 19.5"

The farthest north beach on sheltered Bahía Coyote is very popular, partly because the entrance road is so short and easy.

The long beach offers beachside parking for many, but you will find that the beach sites are often very crowded together and full. There are flush toilets, a dump station, sometimes cold showers, a couple of restaurants, kayak rentals and even a Rotary Club sign. There is also a hot spring located a short walk along the water to the west.

The entrance to Playa Santispac is midway between the Km. 115 and Km. 114 markers. The beach is visible from the road. While short and in good shape the entrance road is a little steep, exercise care when leaving the highway.

Beach No. 3

POSADA CONCEPCIÓN/BAHÍA TORDILLO

Price: Low

GPS Location: N 26° 45' 14.7", W 111° 53' 51.9"

Posada Concepción is really more subdivision than beachfront camping area, most of the people here live in houses or permanently-installed trailers. There are a few spaces for transients but they are nowhere near the water.

There are eight slots here with full hookups. Restrooms have flush toilets and hot showers. This beach is also near the hot springs mentioned in the description of Playa Santispac.

The entrance to Posada Concepción is near the Km. 112 marker.

Beach No. 4

PLAYA LOS COCOS

Price: Inexpensive

GPS Location: N 26° 44' 31.5", W 111° 54' 05.7"

Playa los Cocos is another beautiful beach with minimal facilities. There are palapas, pit toilets, and a dump station.

The entrance is near the Km. 111 marker. There is no sign and the entrance road is about .3 miles (.5 km) long.

Beach No. 5

PLAYA DEL BURRO

Price: Inexpensive

GPS Location: N 26° 43' 57.8", W 111° 54' 25.5"

This beach offers the standard pit toilets and dump station but also has a restaurant. Parking is along the water. Caravans often stay here.

The entrance to Playa Del Burro is at the Km. 109 marker.

Beach No. 6

PLAYA EL COYOTE

Price: Inexpensive

GPS Location: N 26° 42' 58.5", W 111° 54' 26.7"

Another good beach with few facilities, just pit toilets. A tree or two provide shade on this beach and it is not quite as crowded as the spots farther north, perhaps because the road is slightly more difficult. There is a hot spring along the beach to the east. There is also an RV park on the inland side of the highway near the entrance road to the beach.

The entrance road to El Coyote is signed on the highway, it is near the Km. 108 marker. After leaving the highway and driving down to the water turn right and proceed .5 miles (.8 km) along the water to the camping area.

Beach No. 7

PLAYA BUENAVENTURA
   Address: P.O. Box 90139, San Diego, CA 92169 (U.S. Res.)
   Telephone: (115) 3-04-08

Price: Low

GPS Location: N 26° 38' 36.5", W 111° 50' 39.7"

Playa Buenaventura has a very nice little hotel, restaurant/sports bar and trailer park, all under the same ownership. English is spoken. The trailer park has 15 slots along the beach with palapas but no hookups. Actually even a few more rigs can be accommodated. There is a flush toilet, a launch ramp, and security with lights at night. Some caravans like this spot but individual campers seem to think the place is too expensive considering the wealth of nearby primitive camping beaches. This well-run operation necessarily has higher overhead than some of the shoestring camping areas on other beaches.

The entrance to Playa Buenaventura is near Km. 94 on Mex. 1. The main road is almost at beach level here. There's quite a bit of room out front making this a good turn-around spot.

Beach No. 8

El Requesón

Price: Inexpensive

GPS Location: N 26° 38' 16.9", W 111° 49' 55.7"

This is the most picturesque of the Bahía Concepción beaches. The beach is a short sand spit which connects a small island to the mainland at low tide. Small, shallow bays border both sides of the spit. There are pit toilets but no other amenities. You can hike along the water to the south as far as Playa La Perla. Someone will come by to collect a small fee each evening.

The entrance to El Requesón is near the Km. 93 marker and is signed. The entrance road is rough but should present no problems for most RVs, it is about .2 miles (.3 km) long. You may find that it is easier to enter the road if you are approaching from the north so northbound travelers may drive on less than a mile and turn around in front of Playa Buenaventura.

EL REQUESÓN BEACH ON BAHÍA CONCEPCIÓN

Beach No. 9

PLAYA LA PERLA

Price: Inexpensive

GPS Location: N 26° 37' 44.1", W 111° 49' 23.3"

This beachside camping area offers only pit toilets and palapas. It is usually virtually empty. The entrance road is between Km. 91 and 92.

Beach No. 10

PLAYA ARMENTA

Price: Inexpensive

GPS Location: N 26° 37' 36.4", W 111° 49' 07.9"

This is an exposed location without a great beach, but it has palapas and pit toilet. The entrance road is near Km. 91.

Other Camping Possibilities

While the most popular beaches are mentioned above you will find that there are others, particularly between Km. 89 and 80. The southern shore of the Bahía Concepción is accessible from a road between the Km. 76 and 77 markers. There is one of the old government-built RV parks along this road but it is no longer used. There are many campsites along the southern shore of the bay but this area is exposed to weather and not as attractive as the western shore of the Bahía.

CIUDAD CONSTITUCIÓN, BAJA CALIFORNIA SUR
(SEE-OOH-DAHD KOHN-STIH-TOO-SEE-OHN)
Population 45,000

This burgeoning farm town isn't found in most tourist guides. It has little to offer other than a few services. It does have both RV parks and supermarkets. Ciudad Constitución's location makes it a handy stop if you're headed north from beyond La Paz (only 130 easy miles (213 km) southeast) or need a base for whale watching in Bahía Magdalena to the west.

Campground No. 1

MANFRED'S RV TRAILER PARK
   Address: Apdo. 120, Cd. Constitución,
   B.C.S., Mexico
   Telephone: (113) 2-11-03

Price: Moderate

GPS Location: N 25° 02' 54.4", W 111° 40' 48.9"

This is a trailer park you'll just have to appreciate. The Austria-born owners are turning a dusty lot into a garden, at last count they had planted 1,600 shrubs and trees.

The campground is only a few years old and has just been expanded. There are now 34 large pull-throughs with electricity, sewer, and water and at least that many smaller back-in spaces with electricity and water. Two spotless restroom buildings have hot showers. There is a small swimming pool and even an Austrian restaurant.

The campground is very near the northwestern border of Ciudad Constitución and right on Mex. 1 at about Km. 212.5.

Campground No. 2

CAMPESTRE LA PILA BALNEARIO AND TRAILER
   PARK
   Address: Apdo. 261, Ciudad Constitución,
   B.C.S., Mexico
   Telephone: (113) 2-05-82

Price: Low

GPS Location: N 25° 01' 03.7", W 111° 40' 39.4"

The La Pila is another of the balneario trailer parks. Winter travelers will probably not appreciate the pool quite as much as those passing this way during the really hot months.

There are 18 back-in spaces with electricity, sewer, and water. As a practical matter this really translates into 9 pull-throughs, there are rarely enough visitors to fill even 9 spaces except on Mexican holidays. The parking surface is the very fine sand common to this area and the camping area is a very large lot surrounded by palm trees. The pool area next to the camping area has the bathrooms, there are hot water showers. The balneario has two large pools and a covered picnic area.

The turn-off from Mex. 1 to the campground is near the south end of Ciudad

Constitución at the point where the lateral streets begin. Turn west and follow the high tension electrical lines for .7 miles (1.1 km) and turn left into the campground at the sign. The campground is around to the left near the pools, the office is in the large building on the right. There is plenty of room to maneuver.

Other Camping Possibilities

Puerto San Carlos (see Side Trips below) has several location suitable for primitive camping. The town is located on an island accessible by bridge and there are primitive campsites north of town along the water and also through town and near the southeast point of the island where many people camp along the shore near what used to be an RV park called Las Palapas.

Side Trips from Ciudad Constitución

There are two good spots to access the gray whale breeding waters of the **Bahía Magdalena**. One is **Puerto San Carlos** which is accessible on a good, paved 36-mile (50-km) highway that heads west from Ciudad Constitución. The other is **Puerto López Mateos**, also accessible by good paved highway. Drive north on Mex. 1 from Ciudad Constitución to Villa Insurgentes and then west to Puerto López Mateos. The distance is 35 miles (56 km). The whales are in the Bahía from January to March, you can arrange tours in both towns. The waters of the Bahía Magdalena are great for small boats, you can easily find isolated beaches for camping if you have one.

Nine miles (15 km) south of Ciudad Constitución on Mex. 1 at Km. marker 191 a road goes east to **Mission San Luis Gonzaga**. The road is marked for Presa Iguajil and the palms of the San Luis Gonzaga oasis are 25 miles (40 km) down the road which is suitable for small RVs. The mission church has been restored by the Mexican government.

Guerrero Negro, Baja California Sur (GEH-REH-row NEH-grow)
Population 8,000, Elevation sea level

The 28th parallel is the dividing line between the states of Baja North and Baja South. You'll know when you pass over the line because it is marked by a huge statue of a stylized Eagle, most people think it looks like a huge tuning fork and it is visible for miles. Two miles (3 km) south of the Eagle the road to Guerrero Negro goes west.

Guerrero Negro is one of the newest towns on the Baja, and it's a company town. Founded in 1955 the town owes its existence to the Exportadora de Sal (ESSA) salt works. Large flats near the town are flooded with sea water which quickly evaporates leaving salt. This is gathered up and shipped to Isla Cedros offshore where there is enough water to allow cargo ships to dock.

More recently the town has gained fame for the gray whales that congregate each winter in the nearby Ojo de Liebre or Scammon's Lagoon. There is now a lively tourist industry devoted to catering to the many people who come here to visit the whales.

The town itself is small and the places of interest, restaurants and stores, are almost all arranged along the main street. Guerrero Negro has a small supermarket and also a Pemex.

Campground No. 1

GUERRERO NEGRO

MALARRIMO R.V. PARK
Address: Guerrero Negro, B.C.S., Mexico
Telephone: (115) 7-01-00

Price: Moderate

GPS Location: N 27° 58' 04.4", W 114° 01' 45.8"

The Malarrimo is generally considered the best place to stay in Guerrero Negro. Not only are the campground facilities pretty good, the restaurant is the best in this section of Baja.

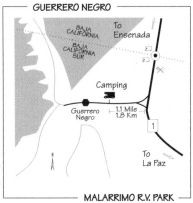

MALARRIMO R.V. PARK

There are 33 RV spaces with electricity, sewer, and water located behind the restaurant. Restrooms are modern and clean and have hot water showers. This is a well-run place and English is spoken. They run tours to see the gray whales and even have a gift shop. Many people make a special point to overnight in Guerrero Negro so they can eat at the restaurant.

Recently they began work on a second camping area across the street from the motel so there should always be room for unexpected travelers.

To find the campground drive in to Guerrero Negro from the east. Almost immediately after entering town you will see the Malarrimo on the right.

Campground No. 2

BENITO JUÁREZ TRAILER PARK
Address: Asunción Morian Canales, Apdo
188, Guerrero Negro, B.C.S., Mexico

Price: Low

GPS Location: N 27° 59' 54.5", W 114° 00' 50.8"

The Benito Juárez is another of the government-built trailer parks. This one is run by the Ejido Benito Juárez. We had about written this place off, but the last time we were in Guerrero Negro (spring 1997) there it was,

BENITO JUÁREZ TRAILER PARK

full of RV's and with full services, including electricity and hot showers. Let's hope they keep up the good work, full-service campgrounds can fill up in Guerrero Negro during the whale-watching season.

This is a large campground. The spaces are pull-throughs with electricity, sewer, and water. Cactus are planted throughout for landscaping, there's a pretty complete collection of the different types you've been seeing along the road on the way south, including boojums. The restrooms are old but work, there are hot showers. The campground is fully fenced and has a full-time manager who speaks some English.

This is an easy campground to find. Just watch for the huge eagle monument at the border between North and South Baja. The campground is just to the west.

Other Camping Possibilities

A restaurant along the highway just north of the border called La Espinita has a big parking lot next to it. There are usually a few RVs camped here with the permission of the restaurant. The restaurant has a restroom. It would be diplomatic to have dinner at the restaurant if you overnight here.

As mentioned in the Side Trip section below there is primitive camping at Scammon's Lagoon. A small fee is charged.

Side Trips from Guerrero Negro

The number-one side trip from Guerrero Negro is a visit to see the gray whales at the **Parque Natural de la Ballena Gris** which encompasses **Scammon's Lagoon** or **Laguna Ojo de Liebre** as it is known in Mexico. There are really two ways to do it. You can make arrangements for a tour from town with an operator there, one of the best is offered by the owners of the Malarrimo, also site of a great restaurant and the best RV park in town. Alternately, you can visit the whales in your own vehicle. If you head south on Mex. 1 from the Guerrero Negro cutoff for 5.7 miles (9.3 km) you will find a road heading toward the ocean near the Km. 208 marker. Follow the road for about 15 miles (24 km) and you will come to the lagoon. You can camp here for a small fee, no hookups. The whales aren't easy to see from the beach, you'll want to take a boat tour from here. Private boats aren't allowed on the lagoon during whale season.

Before the completion of the new highway the old mining town of **El Arco** was an important waypoint on the old road. This may explain why there was a decent paved road built in to the town from Mex. 1 soon after its completion. There seems to be no other reason for a good road to this small place. Today the road is a mess with only shreds of the original surface remaining but if you take it slowly the 26 mile (42 km) drive into El Arco can even be made in an RV. This road leaves Mex. 1 near the 190 Km. marker, about 16.4 miles (26.8 km) southeast of the Guerrero Negro cutoff from Mex. 1.

From El Arco you can drive on another 23 miles (38 km) east to **Misión Santa Gertrudis La Magna** on a recently improved road suitable for small sturdy RVs and other more maneuverable vehicles. Once San Gertrudis served as the headquarters for Jesuit work in the north. The mission was founded in 1751 and abandoned in 1822, a small chapel continues to be used and is visited by pilgrims, especially on November 16 for the Fiesta de Santa Gertrudis. There is a museum and restoration work underway.

From El Arco it is also possible to reach the coast at **San Francisquito** and then drive on north to **Bahía de Los Ángeles**. The distance to San Francisquito is 48 miles (78 km), it is another 81 miles (132 km) on to Bahía de Los Ángeles. The road to San Francisquito is poor and really only suitable for high clearance vehicles, preferably with four-wheel-drive. It passes through rugged, empty country and extra caution is advised. See the Side Trips from Bahía de Los Ángeles section for information about the better road from there to San Francisquito.

LA PAZ, BAJA CALIFORNIA SUR (LAW PAHS)
Population 170,000, Elevation sea level

A favorite city on the Baja Peninsula, La Paz has lots of stores for supplies and a number of good campgrounds. Good, not fancy! La Paz has been continuously occupied only since 1811, earlier settlement attempts, including one by Cortés in person were not successful. The city feels more like a colonial mainland city than any other on the Baja. The waterfront malecón is good for strolling and you'll enjoy exploring the older part of town a few blocks back from the water. La Paz's best beaches are outside of town toward and past Pichilingue and are virtually empty except on weekends. There's a decent museum, the **Museum of Anthropology**, covering the area's early inhabitants. Ferries to the mainland cities of Topolobampo and Mazatlán dock at Pichilingue, see the section about ferries in the introduction to this chapter.

Campground No. 1

AGUAMARINA RV PARK
  Address: Nayarit Street # 10 (Apdo. 133), La
  Paz, B.C.S, Mexico
  Telephone: (112) 2-37-61
  Fax: (112) 5-62-28

Price: Expensive

GPS Location: N 24° 09' 01.9", W 110° 20' 07.2"

We think this little campground is La Paz's nicest trailer park but you can make up your own mind. This is a well-kept park with flowering plants and lots of shade.

There are 19 back-in slots, all have 30-amp. electricity, sewer, water, a patio and shade. Really big rigs might find this campground a little cramped. In the center of the park is a swimming pool and covered patio. Restrooms are well maintained and clean, they have hot water showers. The same owners have a dock in front of the campground where larger yachts tie up, there is a coin-operated laundry in the building they use as an office for both operations. English is spoken and reservations are recommended. This is the La Paz campground most likely to fill up.

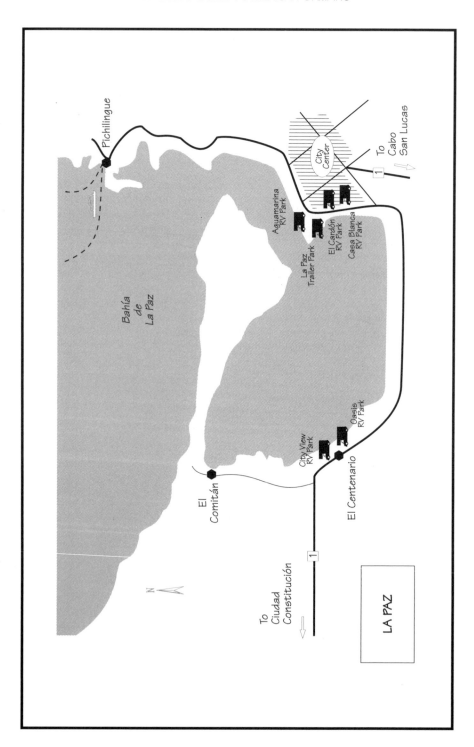

The campground is located at the ocean end of Av. Nayarit, which is a hard-to-find dirt street off Mex. 1 as it comes into La Paz. If you zero your odometer at the dove statue (some people see a whale's tail instead) Nayarit goes to the left at 2.5 miles (4 km). There is a small trailer pictogram sign marking the street and a four-story white building with balconies on the right opposite the turn. Follow Nayarit to the end, about .4 mile (.6 km) and you'll find the gate on your right at the beach. You'll pass another gate before reaching this one, it is the night gate and you won't be able to enter here during the day.

Campground No. 2

LA PAZ TRAILER PARK
    Address: Brecha California #1010, La Paz,
    B.C.S., Mexico
    Telephone: (112) 2-87-87
    Fax: (112) 2-99-38

        Price: Expensive

GPS Location: N 24° 08' 41.6", W 110° 20' 27.7"

This large park is a little off the beaten path which is good, less road noise. Unless it is filled by a caravan you can usually find a place to camp here even without reservations.

There are 44 campsites, both pull-through and back-in. They have 30-amp. electricity, sewer, and water. The sites are completely paved over and the few palms provide little shade but many are wide enough for pop-outs. The tiled restrooms are clean and modern and have hot showers. There is a swimming pool with jacuzzi (it wasn't working when we visited) and a coin-operated laundry. English is spoken and reservations are accepted.

As you enter La Paz zero your odometer at the dove statue (whale's tail). At 1.7 miles (2.8 km) turn left on the first paved road after you pass the El Cardón R.V. Park. This is Instituto Politecnico Nacional. Drive straight to the water ignoring the left turn that the pavement makes at .6 miles (1 km). Turn right on the last road before the water and drive .2 miles (.3 km) north to the campground.

Campground No. 3

EL CARDÓN R.V. PARK
Address: Apdo. 104, La Paz, B.C.S., Mexico
Telephone: (112) 4-00-78
Fax: (112) 4-02-61

Price: Moderate

GPS Location: N 24° 08' 09.5", W 110° 20' 17.4"

The El Cardón is an older trailer park. They store some older RV's and boats at the front of the campground which may give a bad impression when you enter. The watchman says he can keep a better eye on them there.

There are about 60 useable spaces, most with electricity, sewer, and water. Some also have patios and palapas for shade. There are also quite a few pull-throughs. The campground has two restroom blocks, one is fine with tile and hot water, the other is best ignored. Water at this campground is slightly salty but they do have a city water tap, ask about the location. This campground also has a swimming pool and a coin-operated laundry. There is a fence around the campground and a night watchman.

The El Cardón is right off Mex. 1. Zero your odometer at the dove (whale's tail) statue and you'll see the campground on the right at 1.6 miles (2.6 km).

Campground No. 4

CASA BLANCA RV PARK
Address: Carret. Al Norte Km. 4.5, Esq.
Av. Delfines (Apdo. 681), Fracc. Fidepaz,
C.P. 23094 La Paz, B.C.S., Mexico
Telephone: (112) 4-00-09
Fax: (112) 5-11-42

Price: Expensive

GPS Location: N 24° 07' 51.7", W 110° 20' 29.1"

The Casa Blanca is quite nice, very tidy, easy to find, and usually has lots of room.

There are 43 slots with 50-amp. electricity, sewer, and water. One is a pull-through, the others are all back-in spaces. The entire area is hard-packed sand and spaces are separated with low concrete curbs. The restrooms are plain but clean and have hot showers. The entire campground is surrounded by a high white concrete wall. It is good for security but seems to keep the temperature in the campground about 5 degrees higher than anywhere else in town. There is a swimming pool, a decent tennis court, and a palapa meeting/party room. The office is in a large laundromat out front. There is often no one around to collect the fees, a siesta is taken from one to four in the afternoon, just pull in and park and someone will eventually show up. The gate is locked at night so security isn't bad.

The Casa Blanca is right off Mex. 1. Zero your odometer at the dove statue (whale's tale) as you come into town, the campground is on the right at 1.2 miles (1.9 km).

Campground No. 5

OASIS R.V. PARK
  Address: Km. 15 Carr. Transp. al Norte, La
  Paz, B.C.S, Mexico
  Telephone: (112) 4-60-90

  Price: Moderate

GPS Location: N 24° 06' 31.2", W 110° 24' 57.3"

This is a very small park located west of La Paz. It is one of two RV parks in the small town of El Centenario and is located right on a rather marshy beach.

There are 24 back-in spaces, all with electricity, sewer, and water. The restrooms are old but clean, they have tiled floors, white painted walls, and hot water showers. There is a swimming pool, a coin-operated laundry, and a restaurant/bar overlooking the beach. Some English is spoken and reservations are taken.

The campground is on the water side of Mex. 1 half way between the Km. 14 and Km. 15 markers. It is in the town of El Centenario which is just west of La Paz.

Campground No. 6

CITY VIEW R.V. PARK
  Address: Km. 15 Carretera al Norte (Apdo.
  680), El Centenario, La Paz, B.C.S.,
  Mexico
  Telephone: (112) 4-60-88

  Price: Low

GPS Location: N 24° 06' 51.1", W 110° 25' 24.0"

This is another campground located in the small town of El Centenario to the west of La Paz. It is one of the old government campgrounds, but in much better condition than most. The name refers to the view of La Paz across the water. The campground is operated as part of a maquiladora with a U.S. company, unfortunately there are rumors that it may close soon. Many loyal customers hope the rumor isn't true.

There are 30 pull-through spaces with electricity, sewer, and water and many more without hookups. When the government campgrounds were built someone must have used their crystal ball to see big rigs in the future because there is plenty of room for big rigs and pop-outs. The small cement restroom has an unpainted cement floor and isn't too impressive but does have a flush toilet and hot shower, it isn't in the original plywood services building installed when the campground was built.

The campground is on the water side of Mex. 1 near the Km. 15 marker. It is in the town of El Centenario which is west of La Paz.

Other Camping Possibilities

There are primitive campsites along the beach at Tecolote and near San Juan de los Planes. See the Side Trips section below.

Side Trips From La Paz

Ferries from La Paz to the mainland leave from **Pichilingue** which is 14 miles (23 km) northeast of the city along the coast. There are also several beaches up this road, some suitable for primitive camping. The road is paved, after Pichilingue you pass a beach called **Puerto Balandra** and reach **Tecolote** beach in another 4 miles (6.5 km). Tecolote is wide and sandy and has many spots for primitive camping. Unfortunately campers here are often hassled by drunks from town and the tourist department does not consider camping on Tecolote to be safe.

Highway 286 runs south from a junction with Mex. 1 in the southern section of La Paz. It leads about 40 miles (65.3 km) southeast to the farming town of **San Juan de los Planes** and nearby beachside villages of El Sargento and La Ventana. There are primitive campsites available on the beach near La Ventana and also beyond San Juan de los Planes at **Bahía de los Muertos**. The road as far as San Juan de los Planes and some distance beyond is paved, access to Bahía de los Muertos is OK for smaller RVs. There is a road along the ocean that leads to Los Barriles but it is only suitable for 4-wheel-drive vehicles due to a bad section called Cuesta de los Muertos (Crest of the Dead) just south of Bahía de los Muertos. Some camping along this road is accessible from Los Barriles to the south.

LORETO, BAJA CALIFORNIA SUR (LOH-RAY-TOE)
Population 7,200, Elevation sea level

Loreto is considered the oldest continuously occupied town on the Baja having been founded in 1697. This is theoretically true, however the town was virtually abandoned from the time of a major hurricane in 1829 until resettlement in the 1850's. The Museo de los Misiónes has exhibits explaining the history of the area and also of the missions throughout the Baja.

Today the town is part of a Fonatur development scheme like those in Cancún, Huatulco, Ixtapa, and Los Cabos (Cabo San Lucas and San José del Cabo). Most of the infrastructure was put in Nopoló, about 5 miles (8.2 km) south of Loreto. There you'll find an uncrowded but very nice golf course, a tennis center, the Loreto Inn, and a convention center. Even Bahía Escondido is part of the scheme, it is now supposed to be called Puerto Loreto. See the Puerto Escondido section below for more information.

Fishing and boating are popular activities in Loreto. You can arrange a trip in a panga or larger fishing cruiser. Just offshore from Loreto is Isla Carmen, the island has beaches and sheltered anchorages. Many experienced kayakers visit the island or you can arrange a panga for the trip.

Campground No. 1

VILLA DE LORETO RESORT
  Address: Antonio Mijares y Playa, Apdo. 132, Loreto, C.P. 23880 B.C.S., Mexico
  Telephone: (113) 5-05-86

  Price: Moderate

GPS Location: N 26° 00' 05.3", W 111° 20' 15.7"

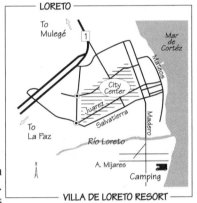

This is a cute little hotel on the waterfront in Loreto, it has some RV slots in the rear. Eventually the trailer park may disappear as more permanent structures are built in the area, meanwhile this is probably the nicest RV park in Loreto. You should be aware that this is a non-smoking destination, however.

There are about 11 sites with electricity, sewer, and water hookups and quite a bit of shade. The restrooms are modern and very spiffy, they have hot showers of course. There's also a coin-operated laundry in the building. The resort has a swimming pool out front overlooking the water. English is spoken but reservations are not accepted.

Zero your odometer at the Loreto turn-off from Mex. 1. Drive straight into town and take the turn to the right at 1.4 miles (2.3 km) onto Francisco Madero. You'll cross a dry arroyo and take the left fork just after it. At odometer 2.0 miles (3.2 km) turn left on Antonio Mijares and you'll see the resort on the right at odometer 2.1 miles (3.4 km).

Campground No. 2

LORETO SHORES VILLAS AND R.V. PARK
  Address: Apdo. 102, Loreto, C.P. 23880
  B.C.S., Mexico
  Telephone: (113) 5-06-29

  Price: Moderate

GPS Location: N 25° 59' 55.2", W 111° 20' 20.1"

LORETO SHORES
VILLAS AND R.V. PARK

This is the largest RV park in Loreto and a good place to stop for the night if you're traveling. It has plenty of room for big rigs on entry roads and inside the park. The spaces look a lot like those in the government parks, perhaps this was one of them. If so it has an unusually good waterfront location. Unfortunately the waterfront is now blocked by permanent structures. In fact, much of this campground has been used for permanents, the remaining free spaces seem to be managed as an afterthought.

There are about 30 pull-through spaces remaining here, all with electricity, sewer, water and patios. The restrooms are old and show it, but there are hot water showers. A few small trees have been planted but will have to grow to provide much shade. The campground is fenced in the rear but the beach side is open.

Zero your odometer at the Loreto turn-off from Mex. 1. Drive straight into town and take the turn to the right at 1.4 miles (2.3 km) onto Francisco Madero. You'll cross a dry arroyo and take the left fork just after it. At odometer 2.2 miles (3.5 km) turn left on Ildefonso Green, the RV park is directly ahead.

Campground No. 3

R.V. PARK EL MORO
  Address: Rosendo Robles No. 8, Loreto,
  C.P. 23880 B.C.S., Mexico
  Telephone: (113) 5-05-42
  Fax: (113) 5-07-88

  Price: Low

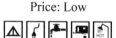

GPS Location: N 26° 00' 34.1", W 111° 20' 23.8"

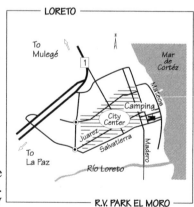

R.V. PARK EL MORO

The El Moro doesn't have a lot of extras in the way of facilities, just hookups and restrooms. It also has the lowest price of the Loreto RV parks.

There are 16 spaces, all are large back-in slots with 30-amp. electricity, sewer, and water. The restrooms are simple but clean and have hot water showers.

Zero your odometer at the Loreto turn-off from Mex. 1. Drive straight into and through town until you reach the waterfront malecón at 1.6 miles (2.6 km). Turn left and take the second left turn at odometer 1.7 miles (2.7 km). The RV park is on the left at odometer 1.8 miles (2.9 km).

Side Trips from Loreto

One of the most interesting missions on the Baja, **San Javier**, makes a good day trip if you have a vehicle with good ground clearance. The road heads west from Mex. 1 at Km. 118 about a mile south of the Loreto intersection. The road in to the mission and surrounding village is 21.5 miles (35.1 km) long, very scenic, and often in poor shape. Check in Loreto for information about the road condition when you visit. The mission was built in 1720 and is constructed of volcanic rock. December 3 is the day of the mission's patron saint, if you visit then you will have company in the form of many pilgrims. The week leading up to the saint's day is the small town's fiesta week.

Most people headed south follow Mex. 1, but if you have a suitable vehicle there is an alternate route. Near Km. 60 on Mex. 1, about 37 miles (60 km) north of Loreto, a graded road that is OK for pickups and other high-clearance vehicles heads west. There are actually two routes to Ciudad Insurgentes because the road splits after 11 miles (18 km). The much easier right fork leads through La Purisima and San Isidro oases. The total distance to Ciudad Insurgentes via this route is about 120 miles (193 km). The left fork also eventually reaches Ciudad Insurgentes, this time on a rougher road through Comondú. This route has a total distance from Mex. 1 to Ciudad Insurgentes of approximately 105 miles (169 km).

LOS BARRILES, BAJA CALIFORNIA SUR (LOES BAR-EEL-ACE)
Population 1,000, Elevation sea level

Los Barriles and nearby Buena Vista and La Ribera are enjoying a surge of popularity as development overtakes the campgrounds farther south near Cabo. This is an excellent area for windsurfing, winds off the mountains behind the town are frequent. You'll find a number of restaurants, some small hotels, trailer parks, an airstrip, and a few shops in Los Barriles. Fishing is quite good because deep water is just offshore, campers keep their car-top boats on the beach but often need assistance from trucks owned by the campgrounds in getting them launched.

Campground No. 1

MARTIN VERDUGO'S BEACH RESORT
  Address: Apdo. 17, C.P. 23501 Los Barriles,
  B.C.S., Mexico
  Telephone: (114) 1-00-54

Price: Moderate

GPS Location: N 23° 40' 56.7", W 109° 41' 56.5"

The largest of the Los Barriles campgrounds is a very popular place. Located on a beautiful beach there's a swimming pool and palapa bar overlooking the ocean. The resort also offers fishing expeditions on its own boats and a place to keep your own small boat on the beach.

The campground has 65 RV spaces with 20 and 30-amp. electricity, sewer, and water. The RV's seem a little crowded but plenty of big rigs find room. There are also 25 tent spaces with water and electric hookups. Restrooms are clean and modern, they have hot water showers. There is a coin-operated laundry, a library in the office, and of course the pool and palapa bar overlooking the beach. English is spoken and reservations are recommended. They require a $50 deposit.

Take the Los Barriles exit from Mex. 1 between La Paz and Cabo San Lucas near the Km. 110 marker. You'll reach a T in .3 miles (.5 km). Turn left and you'll see the RV park on the right in .2 miles (.3 km).

Campground No. 2

JUANITO'S GARDEN R.V. PARK
  Address: Apdo. 50, Los Barriles, C.P. 23501
  B.C.S., Mexico
  Telephone: (114) 1-00-24
  Fax: (114) 1-01-63

Price: Moderate

GPS Location: N 23° 40' 57.3", W 109° 42' 01.1"

The smaller Los Barriles RV park is slowly being converted to permanent structures, but continues to be an acceptable alternative for your stay.

The RV park has 20 open spaces remaining, all with 30-amp. electricity, sewer, and water. Restrooms are clean and modern and have hot water showers. There is a coin-operated laundry. A motel with the same management as the RV park is being built next door, it will have a swimming pool that can be used by guests at the RV park. The park also offers bonded rig storage. English is spoken and telephone reservations are recommended.

Take the Los Barriles exit from Mex. 1 between La Paz and Cabo San Lucas near the Km. 110 marker. You'll reach a T in .3 miles (.5 km). Turn left and you'll see the RV park on the left in .3 miles (.5 km).

Campground No. 3

CORRECAMINOS R.V. PARK
    Address: La Ribera, B.C.S., Mexico
        Price: Low

GPS Location: N 23° 35' 59.1", W 109° 35' 19.4"

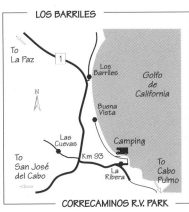

If you are looking for an out of the way, slow-moving, friendly place to spend some time this is it. Located near the quiet little town of La Ribera, Correcaminos R.V. Park might seem like a little piece of paradise. The people we met there certainly think so.

Correcaminos is nothing fancy. There are 19 spaces with electricity, sewer and water. The spaces aren't really market out, you can just see where someone else spent quite a bit of time before they moved on. If you don't need hookups there's lots more space, including an area near the beach. The bathrooms are rustic and have hot water showers. The wide beach is about a quarter-mile away along the sandy road that runs through the campground. Light boats can be launched across the sand.

To find the campground turn east on the unmarked paved road near Km. 93 south of Los Barriles. The excellent road runs 7.3 miles (11.8 km) to the small village of La Ribera. Drive through town, and at the T just after the pavement ends and down a hill turn left. You'll see the campground entrance on the right .2 miles (.3 km) after the turn.

Campground No. 4

RANCHO VERDE R.V. HAVEN
    Address: P.O. Box 1050, Eureka, MT 59917
        U.S.A. (Reservations)
    Telephone: (406) 889-3030 (U.S.)
    Fax: (406) 889-3033 (U.S.)

        Price: Moderate

GPS Location: N 23° 45' 45.8", W 109° 58' 45.7"

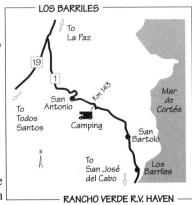

This is a brand-new campground located in the mountains west of Los Barriles. The green high country (1,700 feet) is a welcome change from flat desert and sandy seashore.

There are 29 widely separated back-in spaces. Each one has water and sewer hookups, there is no electricity. The restrooms are in a simple palapa-roof building but are extremely clean and have hot water for showers. This is ranch country and there are miles of trails for hiking, four-wheeling or horseback riding. Lots are for sale but you need not fear high pressure sales tactics. You may fall in love with the owner's open-air living area and RV shelter next to the campground. English is spoken and reservations are taken.

Rancho Verde is located in the mountains about 20 miles (33 km) west of Los Barriles. The entrance road is off Mex. 1 near Km. 143.

Side Trips from Los Barriles

From Los Barriles an unpaved road goes north up the coast to resorts at **Punta Pescadero** (9 miles (14.7 km)) and **El Cardonal** (14 miles (22.9 km)). There is a resort with RV parking at El Cardonal. Beyond there the road becomes much worse and is not recommended although its condition varies. It actually goes all the way north to where it meets a paved road from La Paz near **San Juan de los Planes**.

From near La Ribera a road heads south along the coast. It actually goes all the way to San José del Cabo, but heavy storms often cut it making the whole trip uncertain. There are plans to upgrade this road and pave it but last time we checked it was only paved and upgraded to a dead end about 8 miles (13.1 km) south of La Ribera. Small RVs and others use a different entrance that is actually in La Ribera to reach primitive campsites at **Cabo Pulmo** and other beaches but the road is really not suitable for RVs and should be scouted in a smaller vehicle. Campers with capable vehicles will find lots of good places to pitch a tent along this 70 mile (113 km) road and will be in no hurry to see it become a paved highway route.

About 17 miles (28 km) south of the Los Barriles cutoff on Mex. 1 a road goes east 2.5 miles (4.1 km) to the small but historic town of **Santiago**. Founded as a mission town in 1724 there is no trace of the mission today, but there is a small zoo.

LOS CABOS, BAJA CALIFORNIA SUR (LOES KAH-BOHS)
Population 20,000, Elevation sea level

For many campers headed down the peninsula for the first time Los Cabos (The Capes) is the end of the rainbow, the ultimate destination. While Los Cabos is a major resort and very popular destination for folks flying out from the states and Canada you will probably find that you've seen a fine selection of much more desirable stops during your trip south. The truth is that Los Cabos is hectic, over built, and oriented toward folks looking for a week or two of relief from their work-a-day lives back home.

Many old-timers decry the growth and avoid Los Cabos at all costs. That reaction to the Los Cabos area is probably a little extreme. Los Cabos has lots to offer and a good number of decent RV parks offer excellent accommodations. The number of RV parks in the Los Cabos area seems to be declining, however, as land values

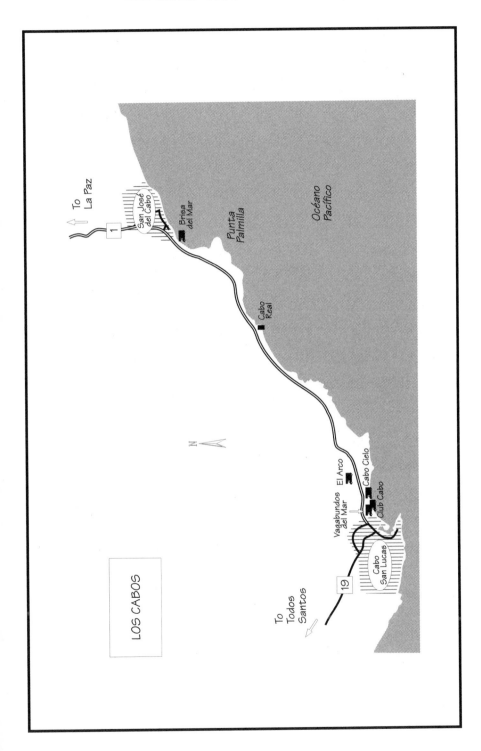

LOS CABOS

To La Paz

San José del Cabo

Brisa del Mar

Punta Palmilla

Cabo Real

Océano Pacífico

N

El Arco

Cabo Cielo

Vagabundos del Mar

Club Cabo

Cabo San Lucas

To Todos Santos

1

19

increase.

The Los Cabos area really covers two major towns: Cabo San Lucas and San José del Cabo which is located about 20 miles (33 km) east. San José del Cabo is the older town and is more relaxed and comfortable. Cabo San Lucas, on the other hand, is chock full of hotels, restaurants, shops, and activity. Most campgrounds are located just to the east of Cabo San Lucas.

Once you are settled in a good campground you'll be looking for something to do. Los Cabos may not be cheap but it does offer lots of activities. Deep-sea fishing is popular and good, check out a charter or panga rental at the huge marina in the center of Cabo San Lucas. Golf is popular in this area, there are at least six good courses here. If you are looking for a beach you will find several along the road between Cabo San Lucas and San José del Cabo. In the evening head for one of the many restaurants offering good food and music (often rock) in Cabo San Lucas.

Campground No. 1

EL ARCO R.V. PARK
    Address: Km. 5.5, Carr. Transp., Cabo San
    Lucas, B.C.S., Mexico
    Telephone: (114) 3-16-86
    Fax: (114) 3-39-86

Price: Moderate

GPS Location: N 22° 54' 20.5", W 109° 52' 34.1"

This is a large park located on a hillside overlooking Cabo San Lucas. Many permanents and the bar/restaurant have an outstanding view, but the sites available for travelers really don't have any view at all.

There are 90 camping slots, all have electricity, sewer, water, and patios. They are arranged around a semi-circular brick driveway or in a newer area farther up the hill. Some of them are pull-throughs. The restrooms are clean and have hot showers. There is a restaurant/bar, swimming pool, and a self-service laundry. English is spoken and reservations are recommended.

The campground is located just east of Cabo San Lucas with the entrance road on the north side of Mex. 1 at Km. 5.2. The kilometer markers have been moved a bit recently along this stretch of road so the address used by the campground does not agree with actual kilometer post location.

Campground No. 2

TRAILER PARK CABO CIELO
   Address: Carret. Transp. Km. 3.8, Cabo San
   Lucas, B.C.S., Mexico
   Telephone: (114) 3-07-21

Price: Low

GPS Location: N 22° 54' 09.4", W 109° 53' 11.2"

This is the simplest of the Cabo campgrounds
and is the least expensive.

The campground is a big sandy field with sites
along one edge and part of another. There are about 25 sites, most are back-in sites
with electricity, sewer, and water. There is a little shade at the sites. The restrooms
are basic but functional and have hot water showers. There's a palapa type lounge
area and a small store out front.

The campground is very near the Km. 4 marker on Mex. 1 east of Cabo San Lucas.
It is on the south side of the road.

Campground No. 3

VAGABUNDOS DEL MAR R.V. PARK
   Address: Apdo. 197, Cabo San Lucas,
   B.C.S., Mexico
   Telephone: (114) 3-02-90
   Fax: (114) 3-05-11

Price: Expensive

GPS Location: N 22° 54' 04.2", W 109° 53' 45.5"

The Vagabundos park probably has the nicest
facilities in Cabo. It has no view and is not on
the beach.

There are 85 spaces with 15 or 30-amp. electricity, sewer, water, and patios. The
roads are paved and the parking spaces are gravel. The restrooms are clean and
modern and have hot water showers. There's a swimming pool with a palapa bar and
restaurant, a laundry, vehicle washing facilities, and a fence all the way around.
English is spoken and reservations are recommended.

The campground is very near the Km. 3 marker on Mex. 1 east of Cabo San Lucas.
It is on the south side of the road.

Campground No. 4

CLUB CABO MOTEL AND CAMP RESORT
  Address: Apdo. 463, Cabo San Lucas,
  B.C.S, Mexico
  Telephone: (114) 3-33-48
  Fax: (114) 3-33-48

Price: Expensive

GPS Location: N 22° 54' 00.8", W 109° 53' 41.8"

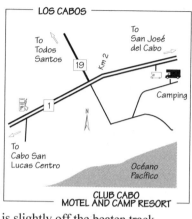

This campground is different than the others in Cabo. It seems more European than Mexican. It is a combination motel and campground and is slightly off the beaten track.

There are 15 campsites, most have electricity, sewer, and water. These are all back-in sites. There isn't room for really big rigs, 24 feet is about the maximum length motorhome that can easily enter and park. The bathroom and shower building is rustic but has a flush toilet, the shower has very low pressure but is plenty hot. There is a very nice pool and jacuzzi, coin-operated laundry, hammock lounge area with color TV, barbecue, and kitchen clean-up station. There's also a shuttle to town. English (and Dutch) are spoken and reservations are recommended.

The Club Cabo is located right next to the Vagabundos campground, behind the San Vicente. To get to it you must take a round-about route. Start from Mex. 1 about two miles (3 km) east of downtown Cabo San Lucas where Mex. 19 heads north. Go south from this intersection for .3 miles (.5 km) until it dead-ends. Turn left and drive .2 miles (.3 km) to a Y, the Villa de Palmas is right, go left for Club Cabo. You are now on a small winding road, in .6 mile (1 km) you'll see the Club Cabo on the left.

Campground No. 5

BRISA DEL MAR R.V. RESORT
  Address: Carret. Transp. Km 28 (Apdo. 45),
  San José del Cabo, B.C.S., Mexico
  Telephone: (114) 2-28-28
  Fax: (114) 2-28-28

Price: Front row - Very expensive,
    Otherwise - Expensive

GPS Location: N 23° 02' 11.8", W 109° 42' 27.1"

The Brisa del Mar is the only beachfront campground left in the Cape region. This is a large crowded park with decent facilities and is closer to San José del Cabo than to Cabo San Lucas.

There are about 110 sites at this campground, the ones along the beach are pull-in or back-in, the others are mostly pull-throughs. All have electricity and water, the beach sites don't have sewer. The sites back from the beach also have patios and some shade. Restrooms are OK but not outstanding, they have hot water showers. There is a bar and restaurant, a pool, and a laundry. There are also some game areas and equipment rentals. English is spoken and reservations are accepted and advised during the winter.

You'll see the campground just south of Mex. 1 near the Km. 30 marker just west of San José del Cabo. Access heading east is easy, just turn in. If you are heading west on this divided highway you'll have to go another .2 miles west (.3 km) to a returno and come back to get into the park. There is plenty of room at the turn-around for big rigs.

Other Camping Possibilities

There is apparently one other campground in Cabo San Lucas that we have not visited. It is El Faro Viejo Trailer Park and is located in the older north part of town at Av. Matamoros and Calle Mijares.

MULEGÉ, BAJA CALIFORNIA SUR (MOO-LAY-HAY)
Population 6,000, Elevation sea level

Situated near the mouth of the palm and mangrove-lined Río Santa Rosalía, Mulegé is a welcome tropical paradise after the long drive across desert country to the north. In many ways Mulegé may remind you of San Ignacio, both have a definite desert oasis ambiance. Mulegé is a popular RVer destination, many permanents make their seasonal home here, there are two decent RV parks, and the beaches and coves of the Bahía Concepción begin only 12 miles (19.6 km) to the south.

Fishing, diving, and kayaking are all popular here. Yellowtail are thick during the winter and summer anglers go offshore for deep water fish. The nearby Santa Inés Islands are popular diving destinations, dive shops in Mulegé offer trips to the islands and other sites. Kayakers love the Bahía Concepción and coastline north and south.

Sights in Mulegé itself are limited. The Misión Santa Rosalía is located about 2 miles (3.3 km) upstream from the bridge on the right bank (facing downstream). It is usually locked except during services but offers excellent views of the town and river. Mulegé is also known for its prison. Now closed the prison building houses a museum and you can take a look at the cells.

The level of services in Mulegé is surprisingly uneven. There are quite a few good restaurants and some small grocery shops but no banks or cash machines. Telmex street-side booths hadn't yet arrived at the time of our last visit. A few miles south of town is one of the only self-service Pemexes we've found in Mexico, this one has lots of room for big rigs and is an excellent place to fill up.

Campground No. 1

VILLA MARIA ISABEL RECREATIONAL PARK
Address: Apdo. 5, Mulegé, C.P. 23900
B.C.S., Mexico
Telephone and Fax: (115) 3-02-46

Price: Moderate

GPS Location: N 26° 53' 50.7", W 111° 57' 51.4"

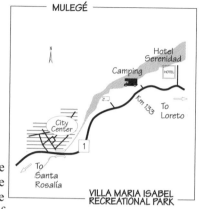

This is the best place to stay if you want to be in an actual R.V. park with hookups in the Mulegé area. It sits on the south shore of the Mulegé river. Although there are a lot of permanents here there also is a special grass-covered area set aside for travelers. There is a very popular little bakery, a great swimming pool, and a new laundromat.

The campground has 25 pull-through spaces with 30-amp. electricity, sewer, and water. Parking is on grass and the slots will accommodate larger rigs. There is also an area for tent campers. The restrooms are modern and spic-and-span with hot water showers. The swimming pool is a big attraction, especially during hot summer weather and the bakery draws people from well outside the campground. There is a boat ramp and a dry long-term storage area.

The campground is 1.3 miles (2.1 km) east of the Mulegé bridge off Mex. 1.

Campground No. 2

THE ORCHARD R.V. PARK
Address: Apdo. 24, Mulegé, B.C.S. Mexico
Telephone: (115) 3-01-09

Price: Expensive

GPS Location: N 26° 53' 41.5", W 111° 58' 25.8"

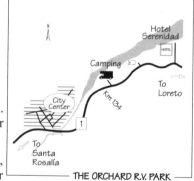

The Orchard is the second Mulegé trailer park. It is an attractive park set under date palms near the Mulegé River.

There are now about 30 spaces with electricity, sewer, and water with parking on gravel or packed dirt. The campground is gradually filling with attractive permanent-type units. Restrooms are modern but could be cleaner, they have hot water showers. Caravans often use this campground so it is likely to be overcrowded.

The Orchard is located .5 miles (.8 km) east of the Mulegé bridge off Mex. 1.

Other Camping Possibilities

From near the Km 156 marker about 12 miles (20 km) north of Mulegé it is possible to follow a road east to the coast at **Punta Chivato** where there is a hotel and an oceanside RV park with no hookups and little in the way of facilities. The distance in to the Punta is 13 miles (21 km).

PUERTO ESCONDIDO, BAJA CALIFORNIA SUR
(PWER-TOE ESS-KOHN-DEE-DOE)
Population none, Elevation sea level.

Long popular as a camping and yachting destination, Puerto Escondido is now a part of the Fonatur plan to turn the Loreto area into a world-class resort. You'll be amazed at the paved but deteriorating boulevards, quay, and abandoned half-built hotel sitting next to this beautiful hurricane hole. Yachts are thick offshore but campers are nowhere to be seen. We've had reports of harassment of free-campers in this area by officials, perhaps they would like to see more campers in the unattractive area set aside for transients at the Tripui R.V. Park.

Campground

TRIPUI R.V. PARK AND RESORT
Address: Apdo. 100, Loreto, C.P. 23880
B.C.S. , Mexico
Telephone: (113) 3-08-18
Fax: (113) 3-08-28

Price: Moderate

GPS Location: N 25° 48' 23.7", W 111° 19' 07.9"

This RV park has lots of permanents and OK facilities, unfortunately traveling rigs are relegated to a barren gravel parking lot. Still, full hookup campgrounds are scarce in this area so the Trupui is well-used.

There are 31 back-in spaces in a fenced gravel lot with 30 and 50-amp. electricity, sewer, and water. Cement curbs separate the sites. The sites are short but no problem for big rigs since you can project far into the central area without really getting in anyone's way. The restrooms are older but have hot showers and are located in what appears to be a prefabricated plywood building. The remainder of the park is of similar construction and includes a small store, a gift shop, and a laundry as well as a nice pool area and a restaurant.

Take the Puerto Escondido cutoff from Mex. 1 near Km. 94 about 16 miles (26 km) south of Loreto. Drive .6 miles (1 km) on the paved road and you'll see the campground on the right. You'll first pass the transient camping area and then see the sign for the office. Big rigs may want to pull into the camping area if there appears to be room and then walk over to sign in.

Other Camping Possibilities

There are quite a few alternate campsites near Puerto Escondido for folks willing to brave some rough roads or do without hookups. El Juncalito offers oceanside camping some 2 miles (3 km) north of Puerto Escondido near the Km. 97 marker. To the south you might try the beach near Ensenada Blanca near Ligui. The access road is near the Km. 84 marker and the road heads east for 3 miles (5 km) passing through the village of Ensenada Blanca at about the two-mile mark.

SAN IGNACIO, BAJA CALIFORNIA SUR (SAHN EEG-NAH-CYOH)
Population 3,000, Elevation 510 ft (155 m)

San Ignacio is a date-palm oasis built around lagoons formed by damning a river which emerges here. The town is located just south of Mex. 1 near the 74 Km. marker. The road into town is paved and big rigs should have no problems since they can drive around the main square to turn around. The main square is also the location of the mission church of San Ignacio, one of the easiest to find and most impressive mission churches on the Baja. This one is built of lava rock and has four foot thick walls. From San Ignacio it is possible to take a guided tour to see rock paintings in the surrounding hills. It is also possible to follow the thirty mile long unpaved road to Laguna San Ignacio to see gray whales. Tours to do this are also available in San Ignacio. Services available in this small town include a bank, Telmex phones, and a Pemex on Mex. 1.

Campground

R.V. PARK EL PADRINO
   Address: San Ignacio, B.C.S., Mexico
   Telephone: (115) 4-00-89

        Price: Low

GPS Location: N 27° 17' 06.2", W 112° 54' 01.2"

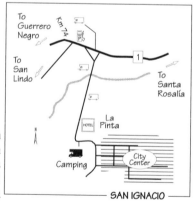

The El Padrino is the preferred trailer park in San Ignacio. It is the only reliable place with full hookups and has the best facilities. It is also the closest to town, you can easily stroll in to the zócalo or over to the nearby La Pinta Hotel for dinner.

There are about 15 back-in spaces with electric and water and the campground has a dump station. The restrooms have flush toilets but are not very nice, they have cold water showers. A centrally located restaurant also serves as an office. The campground offers gray whale watching tours to San Ignacio Lagoon which is about two hours away.

Next year may see major changes at El Padrino. They recently purchased a nearby parcel of land in a palm grove next to the river at a place where there is a small lake. They have big plans.

Take the San Ignacio cutoff near the Pemex. The campground is just past the La Pinta, 1.3 miles (2.1 km) from the cutoff from Mex. 1, at a 90° turn in the road.

Other Camping Possibilities

For a campground with little in the way of amenities try the Trailer Park Martin Quezada Ruiz. This is a grass-covered clearing in the trees with a pit toilet and dribbling cold water shower. The price is right, it is in our inexpensive category. There is room for a rig of any size, tent camping is pleasant. To find Martin's zero your odometer at the exit from Mex. 1 and head toward town. The campground entrance is on the left at 1.1 miles (1.8 km). If no one is around don't worry, someone will be around to collect.

There is a trailer park, sometimes called the San Ignacio Trailer Park, located behind the Pemex at the San Ignacio junction. This is one of the old government trailer parks, there are now about 20 spaces. Last time we stopped there was no one around and no working hookups but this could easily change at any time. Even if it is closed this would be a place to spend the night if you don't need hookups.

Last time we were in San Ignacio (spring 1997) there was a new campground under construction. Called La Muralla, it is located near the intersection of the cutoff to San Ignacio from Mex. 1, just before the road crosses the lagoon. The manager promises electricity, water, and sewer hookups with showers and even a mini-mart. Time will tell.

Side Trips from San Ignacio

The **Laguna San Ignacio** is one of three places along the west coast of the peninsula where gray whales calve from January to March of each winter, there is a 38 mile (61 km) road to the lagoon from San Ignacio. This road is not great but smaller RVs can usually negotiate it. Once at the lagoon you can probably find a boat and guide at one of the fish camps. It is also possible to arrange trips from San Ignacio, ask at the El Padrino RV Park.

The town **San Francisco de la Sierra** serves as the headquarters for excursions to view rock paintings in the area. Guides must be used to visit the rock painting caves. The easiest to reach is **Cueva del Ratón**, you reach it about a mile before entering town but must go on into town to get a guide before visiting. You can also arrange day trips from San Ignacio to see Cueva del Ratón. Longer mule trips that last several days can also be arranged in San Francisco de la Sierra. The town is reached by driving east on a cutoff that leaves Mex. 1 about 28 miles (46 km) north of San Ignacio. This road is suitable for pickups and sturdy vans and is about 22 miles (36 km) long.

SANTA ROSALÍA, BAJA CALIFORNIA SUR (SAHN-TAH ROH-SAH-LEE-AH)
Population 15,000, Elevation sea level

Don't pass through Santa Rosalía without stopping. This company mining town is unlike any other town on the Baja. Located at the point where Mex. 1 finally reaches the Gulf of California, Santa Rosalía was founded in the 1870's by a French mining company which operated here until the 1950's. Today the mining in Santa Rosalía is finished. Now the town is a fishing and ferry port, it serves as a hub for the surrounding area. The ferries run from here to Guaymas on Mexico's west coast.

Much of the town is constructed of wood imported from the Pacific Northwest, the building designs are French colonial. Santa Rosalía's church is unique, it was designed by A.G. Eiffel who also designed the tower in Paris. It was prefabricated in France and shipped by boat around Cape Horn. The town also has a well-known bakery that bakes French-style baguettes.

EIFFEL'S CHURCH IN SANTA ROSALÍA

Campground No. 1

LAS PALMAS R.V. PARK
  Address: Apdo. 123, Santa Rosalía, B.C.S.,
  Mexico
  Telephone: (115) 2-20-70

Price: Low

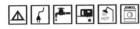

GPS Location: N 27° 18' 59.3", W 112° 14' 46.0"

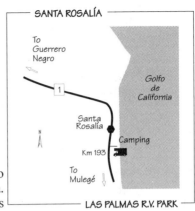

The Las Palmas is the most convenient place to stay if you want to be close to Santa Rosalía. It's a well-done full-hookup facility, but suffers from being away from the water.

There are 30 grassy spaces separated by concrete curbs arranged around the edge of the campground. All have electricity, sewer, and water. The restrooms are well-maintained and modern, they have hot water showers. There is a coin-operated laundry. English is spoken.

The Las Palmas is just off Mex. 1 about 2 miles (3.2 km) south of Santa Rosalía on the east side of the highway.

Campground No. 2

R.V. PARK SAN LUCAS COVE
  Address: Apdo 50, Santa Rosalía, B.C.S.,
  Mexico

Price: Low

GPS Location: N 27° 13' 08.5", W 112° 13' 15.4"

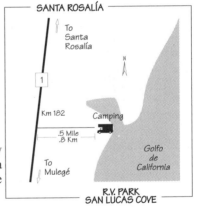

This is a waterfront campground that may remind you of those farther south on Bahía Concepción. It is not quite as scenic as those but has a similar ambiance.

There are about 20 parking sites along the beach and at least 40 more on a large hard-packed sandy area behind. The campground now has flush toilets and a hot water shower as well as a dump station, so it is possible to make an extended visit. Folks either pull their boats up on the beach or anchor them out front.

The campground entrance is just south of the Km. 182 mark south of Santa Rosalía. This is about 8 miles (13.1 km) south of Santa Rosalía. The road in to the campground is packed sand and is about .5 miles (.8 km) long. Big rigs will have no problems negotiating it.

TODOS SANTOS, BAJA CALIFORNIA SUR (TOE-DOES SAHN-TOES)
Population 3,000, Elevation 100 ft (30 m)

Located on Mex. 19 about 50 miles (81 km) north of Cabo San Lucas, Todos Santos is the Baja's art colony. This is an old mission and sugar cane town but today it is better known for the many artists who have arrived in search of a simple small-town ambiance. There are several galleries and artist's studios you can visit, the best place to get information is a bookstore called El Tecolote. The town is only a mile or so from the coast, there are decent beaches near town but the one at the San Pedrito R.V. Park is one of the best in the area.

Campground

SAN PEDRITO R.V. PARK
  Address: Apdo. 15, Todos Santos, B.C.S.,
   Mexico
  Telephone: (112) 2-45-20
  Fax: (112) 3-46-43

   Price: Moderate

GPS Location: N 23° 22' 08.7", W 110° 12' 04.2"

San Pedrito is located on a beautiful beach some 4 miles (6.5 km) south of Todos Santos. There's a sandy but decent road leading the 1.8 miles (2.9 km) from Mex. 19 out to the campground.

The campground has 71 pull-through spaces with electricity, sewer, and water. A new transformer has just been installed and 30-amp. circuits are planned for the summer of 1997. Each site now has a rock-work patio. This campground is built on sand and caution must be exercised to avoid getting stuck, the campground and sites are now pretty safe but exercise caution about straying off the beaten path. There is an area for tent or dry camping near the beach. Restrooms are basic but functional, they have hot showers. San Pedrito has a restaurant/bar with satellite TV, a pool, and a laundry. There are even a few cabañas for rent. English is spoken and reservations are accepted.

The cutoff for the campground is near the Km 59 marker about 4 miles (6.5 km) south of Todos Santos. It is well marked with a large sign. The sandy road to the campground has a Y at 1.4 miles (2.3 km), go left. You'll reach the campground gate at 1.7 miles (2.7 km).

Other Camping Possibilities

About 3 miles (5 km) south of the entrance to San Pedrito R.V. Park there is another road that leads toward the coast. It leads to one of the early government-built RV parks. This one is open but has no hookups in operation. Sometimes toilets and cold showers are available. Many people camp in the vicinity but not necessarily inside the RV park, they generally pay a small fee to do so.

Side Trips from Todos Santos

The central **Sierra de la Laguna** are most easily entered from near Todos Santos. These granite mountains have pine forests and a large flat meadow at 5,600 feet known as **La Laguna** that is a popular hiking and tent camping destination. These mountains are unlike others on the peninsula in that the eastern slopes are the most gradual with the western ones being much steeper. Unfortunately, access from the east is confusing and the trails hard to follow, unless you plan to use a guide the western access near Todos Santos is preferable.

There are three trails that cross the area, the northern-most which follows the Cañón San Dionisio is the most popular and the only one passing through La Laguna. Plan on at least two days for this hike, three would be better. You will need detailed topographical maps and warm clothes since the nights will be cold at high altitudes.

VIZCAÍNO JUNCTION, BAJA CALIFORNIA SUR (BIS-KAW-EEN-OH)

This junction is near the Km. 144 marker of Mex. 1 about 43 miles (71 km) southeast of Guerrero Negro and the border between North and South Baja. There's little at the junction except the Motel Kadekaman and a Pemex station. If you follow the intersecting road toward the west you will eventually reach the ocean at Bahía Tortugas and Punta Eugenia. The distance is about 111 miles (181 km) to Bahía Tortugas. This is a good road but it is only paved for about 22 miles (36 km), the remainder is gravel. Bahía Tortugas has a Pemex and there are free-camping possibilities along the coast.

Campground

MOTEL KADEKAMAN
   Address: Carretera Transp. Km. 143,
   Vizcaíno, B.C.S., Mexico
   Telephone: (212) 4-03-01

Price: Low

GPS Location: N 27° 38' 44.8", W 113° 23' 04.1"

VIZCAÍNO JUNCTION

If you find yourself on the road east of Guerrero Negro when night falls you have no problem, the Motel Kadekaman makes a convenient place to pull off the road and spend the night with electricity and water hookups.

This is a very small Motel with five RV sites next door. There will soon be 20 sites, 15 more are under construction (Spring 97). Electricity and water are available to all sites. The motel has no restroom facilities set aside for RVers but will put a room with hot shower at your disposal if you need it. There is also a small restaurant offering home-cooked meals.

The campground is located near the Km. 144 marker on Mex. 1 in the town of Vizcaíno. It is .4 miles (.6 km) east of the Pemex station.

Side Trips from the Vizcaíno Junction

The Vizcaíno Desert fills a huge sparsely-populated peninsula south of the Guerrero Negro lagoon. Long roads of varying quality cross it to reach the coast which has several decent sized towns including **Bahía Tortugas** and **Bahía Asunción**. Both towns can be reached by small RVs but the roads are long and rough. From the Vizcaíno Junction it is about 110 miles (180 km) to Bahía Tortugas and about 85 miles (139 km) to Bahía Asunción. The coast near both towns offers primitive camping opportunities and there is even an access road to the fabled beachcombing at **Malarrimo Beach**. Any excursions off the two main roads requires suitable vehicles (often 4-wheel-drive) and a caravan of several vehicles would be a safer way of visiting this remote area.

INDEX

Acamaya Reef Trailer Park, 299
Acapulco, 24, 123
Acapulco Trailer Park, 123
Acapulco West KOA, 126
Acosta Rancho Trailer RV Park, 89
Agua Azul, 270
Agua Caliente Parque Acuatico, 184
Agua Dulce, 237
Aguamarina RV Park, 379
Agua Prieta, 73
Aguascalientes, 28, 163
Air conditioners, 33
Alameda Trailer Park, 114
Álamos, 29, 87
Altata, 97
Angangueo, 190
Ants, 45
Arareco Lake Campground, 170
Árbol de Tule, 259
Archeological sites, 168, 171, 190, 194,
    195, 209, 239, 243, 248, 259, 260,
    268, 284, 289, 290, 295, 304, 307
Arriaga, 257
Auto Hotel El Parador, 257
Azteca Parador Hotel, 213

Bacalar, 289
Bahía Concepción, 18, 369
Bahía de Los Ángeles, 18, 339
Bahía de los Muertos, 384
Bahía Escondida Hotel and Resort, 203
Bahía Kino, 29, 90
Bahía Magdalena, 376
Bahía San Francisquito, 341, 379
Bahías de Huatulco, 24, 261
Bahía Tordillo, 371
Bahía Trailer Court, 100
Bajamar R.V. Park, 325

Baja Peninsula Itinerary, 17
Baja Seasons Beach Resort, Villas &
    RVs, 347
Balankanche Caves, 23, 290
Balneario Atonaltzin, 274
Balneario El Palmar, 360
Balneario Mocambo, 246
Balneario San José de Agua Tibia, 206
Balneario Santa Isabel, 176
Basaseachic Falls National Park, 170
Batopilas, 170
Benito Juárez Trailer Park, 377
Boca Beach, 135
Boca de Iguanas, 134
Boca Paila Road, 298
Bonampak (trailer park), 24
Bonanza Xpu-Ha Campground, 301
Breakdowns, 57
Bribes, 38
Brisa del Mar R.V. Resort, 394
Bucerías, 140
Budget, 31
Bugamville Trailer Park, 188
Bungalows and Trailer Park Playa
    Escondida, 112
Bungalows, Trailer Park, Y
    Campamento El Pequeño Paraiso,
    147
Buses, 48

Cabañas Paa Mul, 23, 298
Cabañas y Balneario Erendira, 189
Cabo Pulmo, 390
Cabo San Lucas, 19
Camargo, 74
Campeche, 22, 283
Campestre Altamira, 21, 245
Campestre La Pila Balneario and

Trailer Park, 375
Camp Gecko, 340
Campgrounds, 32
Camping Los Cabañas, 130
Camping Sacbe, 22, 306
Campo Mexico Motel, 178
Campo Playa R.V. Park, 346
Cancún, 23, 284
Caravans, 34
Carnival, 108
Casa Blanca RV Park, 382
Cash, 35
Cash machines, 35
Cataviña, 341
Cataviña Trailer Park, 341
Catemaco, 22, 237
Caverna del Seri Trailer Park, 90
Celestún, 22, 295
Cenote Azul, 23, 289
Cenote Azul Trailer Park, 23, 287
Centro Deportivo (Chihuahua), 165
Centro Deportivo Ojocaliente, 164
Chamela Hotel, 137
Chapala, 28
Chetumal, 286
Chichén Itzá, 22, 289
Chihuahua, 164
Chihuahua-Pacific Railroad, 25, 29,
    105, 164
Children, 35
Christmas, 44
Chunyaxché archeological site, 304
Churches, 87, 90, 179, 186, 193, 201,
    204, 212, 213, 215, 216, 229, 258, 400
Cielito Lindo Motel and R.V. Park, 358
City View R.V. Park, 383
Ciudad Acuña, 74
Ciudad Constitución, 19, 374
Ciudad de Dolores Hidalgo, 27
Ciudad de México, 191
Ciudad Juárez, 71, 74
Ciudad Miguel Alemán, 74
Ciudad Valles, 166
Ciudad Victoria, 20, 239
Club Cabo Motel and Camp Resort, 394
Club de Pesca R.V. Park, 324

Cobá archeological site, 304
Colinas Resort Hotel and Trailer Park,
    103
Colonial Mexico Tour, 26
Computers, 33
Condo Suites and R.V. Park Playa
    Bonita, 328
Copper Canyon, 25, 29, 105,164, 168,
    170
Corona Beach Park, 351
Correcaminos R.V. Park, 389
Cosalá, 97
Costa Esmeralda, 21
Cozumel, 303
Credit cards, 35
Creel, 168
Cuernavaca, 27, 171
Cueva del Ratón, 399
Culiacán, 95

Dainzú archeological site, 260
Debit cards, 35
Delia's Trailer Park, 152
Diamonte Acapulco RV Park, 128
Distance Table, 86, 122, 161, 236, 256,
    282, 312, 338, 368
Divisadero, 170
Doctors, 44
Dolisa Motel & Trailer Park, 87
Don Pepe, 356
Down the West Coast tour, 28
Drinking water, 36
Driving in Mexico, 37
Durango, 178
Dzibilchaltún Ruins, 295

Edzná archeological site, 22, 284
Eiffel's church, 19
Ejido Uruapan, 360
El Arco, 378
El Arco R.V. Park, 392
El Bañito Restaurant-Bar, 167
El Cactus Trailer Park, 93
El Caracol Bungalows & Trailer Park,
    147
El Caracol RV Resort and Ranch, 88

El Cardonal, 390
El Cardón R.V. Park, 382
El Chico National Park, 207
El Dorado Ranch, 330
Electrical service, 32
El Faro Beach Motel and Trailer Park, 350
El Faro Beach R.V. Park, 331
El Faro Viejo Trailer Park, 395
El Fuerte, 104
El Jardin Motel and Trailer Park, 241
El Marmól, 343
El Mesquite, 215
El Pabellón, 18, 358
El Padrino, 18
El Paraiso de los Acampadores Trailer Park, 174
El Pozo Trailer Park, 209
El Requesón, 373
El Rosario (B.N.), 19, 343
El Rosario (Mich.), 188, 190
El Sasabe, 73
El Tajín archeological site, 21, 243
El Tecuán, 137
Embarcadero Laumase, 228
Emerald Coast, 242
Ensenada, 18, 345
Escárcega, 23
Estero Beach, 349
Estero Beach Hotel/Resort, 18, 349

Fidel Velazquez Hotel and Balneario, 221
Fiestas, 44, 90, 105, 108, 114, 163, 179, 201, 258, 343
Fishing, 90, 102, 115, 140
Flamingo Hotel, 27, 212
Flamingos, 22
Flamingo Trailer Park, 151
FONATUR, 129
Free camping, 40

Gas stations, 40
Golf, 19, 93
Golfo de Santa Clara, 313
Gómez Palacio, 225

GPS (Global Positioning System), 79
Grand Coastal Tour, 20
Gray whales, 18, 367, 376, 378, 399
Green Angels, 43
Groceries, 43
Guadalajara, 28, 179
Guanajuato, 27, 186
Guaymas, 25, 29, 97
Guerrero Negro, 18, 376
Guillermo's Hotel and RV Park, 340
Gulf of California, 18

Hacienda Santa Veronica, 362
Hacienda Tetakawi R.V. Trailer Park, 100
Hacienda Trailer Park, 181
Hermosillo, 29
Hogar Infantil, 277
Holidays, 44
Home schooling, 35
Hotel and R.V. Park Granada del Mar, 318
Hotel and Trailer Park La Cabaña, 291
Hotel Bonampak Trailer Park, 272
Hotel, Búngalows y Trailer Park "Playa Dorada", 136
Hotel Calli, 275
Hotel Cuatro Caminos, 211
Hotel El Cangrejo Moro and RV Park, 102
Hotel Hacienda del Bosque, 230
Hotel Imperial del Norte, 214
Hotel Joker, 348
Hotel Los Tres Ríos, 96
Hotel Medrano, 28, 163
Hotel Meson Tarasco, 205
Hotel Nueva Castilla, 203
Hotel Playa de Cortés Trailer Park, 29, 98
Hotel Playa Paraiso del Tajín, 243
Hotel Valles, 167
Hotel Versalles, 176
Hotel Villa Jardín, 225
Howler monkeys, 24

IMSS Centro Vacacional La Trinidad,

222
IMSS Centro Vacacional Malintzi, 223
IMSS Centro Vacacional Oaxtepec, 177
Indians, 90, 105, 114, 166, 218
Insects, 45
Insurance, 64
Isla Aguada, 22, 291
Isla Contoy, 286
Isla de Piedra, 113
Isla Janitzio, 209
Isla Mujeres, 23, 286
Islandia Marina Trailer Park and
    Bungalows, 95
Ixtaccíhuatl volcano, 27
Ixtapa, 129
Izamal, 290

Juanito's Garden R.V. Park, 388

Kabah archeological site, 22
Kampamento KOA, 219
Kampamento Los Ayala Beach, 148
Key to Symbols, 78
Kino Bay, 90
Kino Bay R.V. Park, 92
KOA, 126, 155, 203, 313, 353
Koala Bungalows and Trailer Park, 220
Kohunlich archeological site, 289

La Aduana, 90
La Bufadora, 18
La Ceiba Trailer Park, 237
La Choca Fairgrounds, 250
Lago Dorado Trailer Park, 216
Laguna Bacalar, 289
Laguna Hanson, 362
Laguna San Ignacio, 399
Lagunas de Montebello 273
Laguna Verde, 21
La Hacienda Hotel and Trailer Park, 276
La Jolla Beach Camp, 352
La Jolla R.V. Park, 327
Lake Guerrero, 241
La Laguna, 403
La Marmota Trailer Park, 131
Lambityeco archeological site, 260

La Muralla, 399
La Paz, 19, 379
La Paz Trailer Park, 381
La Peñita Trailer Park, 153
La Pesca, 242
La Posta Trailer Park, 109
Las Estacas, 175
La Siesta Hotel, 217
Las Palmas Midway Inn, 191
Las Palmas R.V. Park, 401
Las Palmas Trailer Park, 111
Las Playitas Trailer Park, 99
Laundry, 45
La Venta Museum, 22, 248
La Vista Bahía Condominium and
    Trailer Park, 144
Lázaro Cárdenas, 138
Lerdo, 225
Lo de Marcos, 140
Lodge at Creel R.V. Park, 169
Loewen's R.V. Park, 166
Loltún Caves, 22, 307
Loreto, 384
Loreto Shores Villas and R.V. Park, 386
Los Alzati archeological site, 190
Los Azufres National Park, 188
Los Barriles, 387
Los Cabos, 390
Los Leones Hotel, Restaurant, and
    Trailer Park, 24, 270
Los Mochis, 19, 25, 29, 101
Los Mochis Copper Canyon R.V. Park,
    104
Los Tamarindos Hotel and Trailer Park,
    264
Las Yácatas archeological site, 209

Magdalena, 105
Mail, 46
Malaria, 45
Malarrimo R.V. Park, 18, 377
Malibu Beach RV Park, 360
Manfred's RV Trailer Park, 375
Manzanillo, 25, 29, 131
Map Legend 77
Maps, 46

Maravilla Trailer Park, 113
Marcos Trailer Park, 329
Mar Rosa Trailer Park, 111
Martin Verdugo's Beach Resort, 388
Matamoros, 73, 74
Matehuala, 26, 190
Mayabell Campground, 24, 269
Mazatlán, 25, 29, 106
Medical insurance, 44
Melaque, 25
Meling Rancho, 359
Mérida, 22, 292
Mexicali, 69
Mexico City, 27, 178, 191
Mike's Sky Rancho, 349
Missions (Baja), 227, 343, 359, 376,
    378, 384, 387, 395, 398
Mitla archeological site, 259
Mona Lisa R.V. Park, 350
Monarch Butterflies, 188, 190
Monte Albán archeological site, 24, 259
Monterrey, 26, 201
Mordida, 38
Morelia, 28, 204
Morelos Valley, 27
Morrill Trailer Park, 187
Motel del Bosque, 28, 230
Motel Kadekaman, 403
Motel Kino, 106
Motel Pátzcuaro, 208
Motel Pie de la Sierra, 227
Motel Sinai R.V. Park, 344
Motel y Trailer Park Villa del Charro,
    165
Mulegé, 19, 395
Municipal Markets, 108
Museums, 87, 90, 96, 102, 108, 164,
    166, 171, 179, 186, 193, 201, 205,
    212, 215, 218, 226, 229, 239, 245,
    248, 258, 265, 283, 286, 379, 384

Naco, 73
Nautla, 21
Navojoa, 114
Nogales, 19, 25, 71
Nuevo Ciudad Guerrero, 74

Nuevo Laredo, 26, 72
Nuevo Motel del Golfo, 313

Oasis Beach Resort, 354
Oasis RV Campground, 295
Oasis R.V. Park, 383
Oasis Trailer Park, 150
Oaxaca, 24, 257
Oaxaca Trailer Park, 258
Ojinaga, 74
Old Mill Trailer Park, 18, 357

Paa Mul, 23
Pachuca, 206
Palenque, 23, 267
Palenque archeological site, 268
Pal Lake Chapala RV Park, 185
Palmar R.V. Park, 321
Palmas de Cortes, 267
Palmera Trailer Park, 263
Palomas, 73
Papantla, 21, 243
Paracutín, 228
Parador Bella Vista Trailer Park, 94
Paraíso del Pescador Trailer Park and
    Bungalows, 150
Paraiso Miramar RV-Trailer Park, 153
Parque Acuatico Chimulco, 182
Parque El Ocotal, 224
Parque Nacional Constitución, 349
Parque Sierra Morelos, 224
Pátzcuaro, 28. 207
Pedro Antonio de los Santos, 168
Pepe's RV Park, 27, 193
Pérula Trailer Park, 136
Pets, 65
Piedras Negras, 74
Pionero R.V. 314
Playa Amor RV Park, 154
Playa Armenta, 374
Playa Azul, 24, 137
Playa Azul (Catemaco), 238
Playa Azul Hotel, 138
Playa Bonita R.V. Park, 320
Playa Buenaventura, 372
Playa Chemuyil, 301

Playa de Laura, 326
Playa del Burro, 372
Playa del Carmen, 296
Playa de Oro R.V. Park, 318
Playa El Coyote, 372
Playa Elegante R.V. Park, 315
Playa el Tambor, 97
Playa La Perla, 374
Playa Las Arenitas, 97
Playas Las Glorias, 102
Playa Las Lupitas, 117
Playa Los Cocos, 371
Playa Miramar R.V. Park, 320
Playa Santispac, 371
Playa Suave, 126
Playa Xcacel, 302
Point South Mazatlán Trailer Park, 110
Popocatépetl volcano, 27
Posada Concepción, 371
Posada Don Diego T.P., 356
Posada Santa Gemma Trailer Park, 94
Poza Rica, 21
Prescription medicine, 44
Pretty Sunset Trailer Park, 146
Progresso, 22, 296
Propane, 48
Puebla, 27, 210
Puertecitos, 331
Puerto Angel, 24, 263
Puerto Escondido (Oax.), 24, 265
Puerto Escondido (B.C.S.)
Puerto Escondido Trailer Park, 265
Puerto López Mateos, 376
Puerto Morelos, 298
Puerto Peñasco, 315
Puerto San Carlos, 376
Puerto Vallarta, 25, 29, 138
Puerto Vallarta KOA, 155
Punta Arena, 369
Punta Baja, 345
Punta Banda, 351
Punta Chivato, 397
Punta San Carlos, 345
Punta Vista R.V. Park, 105
Puuc Route, 307

Querétaro, 27, 211
Quinta Dora Trailer Park, 125
Quintana Roo Coast, 296

Rainbow RV Campground, 294
Rancho Hermanos Graham, 22, 249
Rancho Las Lupitas Trailer Park
Rancho Los Angeles
Rancho Ojai R. V. Park, 361
Rancho San Nicholás, 24, 272
Rancho Sordo Mudo, 347
Rancho Verde R.V. Haven, 389
Real de Catorce, 26, 191
Real de los Álamos RV Park, 88
Reserva Mariposa Monarca, 190
Reservations, 49
Reynosa, 20, 73, 74
Rincón de Guayabitos, 140
Río Bec archeological sites, 289
Río Fuerte Trailer Park, 103
Río Lagartos National Park, 291
Roads, 84, 120, 158, 234, 253, 280, 309,
    334, 366,
Rocky Point R.V. and Golf Resort, 321
Rosa Isabel Trailer Park, 259
Rosarito, 353
Rosarito KOA, 353
Ruben's R.V. Trailer Park, 328
R.V. Park and Bungalows Calderitas,
    288
R.V. Park Campo San Felipe, 326
R.V. Park El Moro, 386
R.V. Park El Padrino, 398
R.V. Park Mar del Sol, 324
R.V. Park San Lucas Cove, 401

Saguaro R.V. Park, 93
Saltillo, 26, 213
Salto de Exipantla, 239
Samula Trailer Park, 283
Sanborn's, 20
San Andrés Tuxtla, 239
San Bartolo Trailer Park, 112
San Blas, 29, 140
San Carlos, 25, 29, 97
San Cristóbal de las Casas, 24, 271

San Felipe, 322
San Felipe Marina Resort RV Park, 322
San Francisco de la Sierra, 399
San Ignacio, 18, 19, 398
San Ignacio Trailer Park, 399
San Jose del Tajo Trailer Park, 182
San Juan de los Planes, 384, 390
San Luis Potosí, 26, 214
San Luis Río Colorado, 70
San Miguel de Allende, 26, 216
San Pedrito R.V. Park, 19, 402
San Quintín, 18, 355
San Rafael R.V. Park, 317
Santa Ana, 105
Santa Clara del Cobre, 209
Santa Rosalía, 400
Santa Teresa Trailer Park, 275
Santiago Tuxtla, 239
Santo Tomás, 359
Saro Trailer Park, 94
Sayulita, 140, 145
Scammon's Lagoon, 18, 378
Sea of Cortez, 19
Security, 49
Semana Santa, 44
Servicio Morelos Trailer Park, 231
Showers, 32
Sian Ka'an Biosphere Reserve, 304
Sierra de la Laguna, 19, 403
Sierra San Pedro Martir National Park, 348, 359
Sonoyta, 70
Spanish language, 50
Stardust Inn, 290
Sumidero Canyon, 276
Sunrise Executive R.V. Park, 319

Tacho's Trailer Park, 142
Talavera, 27
Tamasopo Waterfall, 168
Tamazulapán, 273
Tampico, 20, 21, 245
Taxco, 27, 177
Teacapán, 115
Tecate, 69, 361
Tecolote beach, 384

Tecomán, 25
Tehuantepec, 24, 274
Telephones, 50
Temporary vehicle importation permit, 63
Tenacatita beach, 137
Teotihuacán archeological site, 194
Tepic, 218
Tepotzotlán, 27
Tepozteco Pyramid, 171
Tequisquiapan, 220
Termas del Rey, 221
The Orchard R.V. Park, 396
Ticul, 307
Tijuana, 18, 68
Tlaquepaque, 179
Tlaxcala, 222
Todos Santos, 19, 402
Toilet tissue, 32
Toll roads, 25, 52, 84
Toluca, 223
Tonalá, 179
Topolobampo, 19
Torreón, 225
Totonaka Trailer Park and Apartamentos, 101
Tourist cards, 61
T.P. El Dorado, 151
Trailer Park Bucerías, 143
Trailer Park Cabo Cielo, 393
Trailer Park Camping Manati Xpu-Ha, 300
Trailer Park Cuernavaca Diamonte, 171
Trailer Park El Coloso, 127
Trailer Park Kunkak, 92
Trailer Park La Joyita, 226
Trailer Park La Playa, 133
Trailer Park La Roca, 129
Trailer Park Las Americas, 210
Trailer Park Los Cocos, 155
Trailer Park Los Mangos, 261
Trailer Park Los Pinos, 218
Trailer Park Martin Quezada Ruiz, 399
Trailer Park Mecoloco, 23, 285
Trailer Park No. 1, 151
Trailer Park Oregon, 116

Trailer Park Piedra Blanca, 145
Trailer Park Puerto Vallarta, 143
Trailer Park Quinta Alicia, 242
Trailer Park Senorial, 319
Trailer Park "Sin Nombre", 327
Trailer Park Trópico Cabañas, 148
Trailer Park Villanueva, 150
Trancones, 131
Tres Zapotes, 239
Tripui R.V. Park and Resort, 397
Tropic of Cancer, 21
Tula archeological site, 195
Tulúm archeological site, 304
Tuxpan, 21
Tuxtla Gutiérrez, 24, 276
Tzintzuntzan, 209

Urique, 170
Uruapan, 226
Uxmal, 22, 304

Vagabundos del Mar R.V. Park, 393
Valladolid, 23, 290
Valle de Bravo, 27, 228
Valle de los Hongos, 170
Vehicle preparation, 57
Veracruz, 21, 246
Victoria Trailer Park, 20, 241
Victor's R.V. Park, 325
Villa Corona, 28
Villa de Loreto Resort, 385
Villahermosa, 22, 248
Villa Maria Isabel Recreational Park,
    396
Villa Polinesia, 135
Villarino Campamento Turistico, 352
Villa Vitta Hotel and RV Park, 339
Vista del Mar, 329
Vizcaíno Junction, 403
Voladores, 21, 244

Water, 36
Weather, 59, 120, 157, 234, 280, 309,
    333

Xcalak Peninsula, 289

Xcaret, 304
Xel-Ha, 303
Xochicalco archeological site, 171

Yagul archeological site, 260

Zacatecas, 28, 229
Zihuatanejo, 129
Zipolite Beach, 264
Zona Arqueológica El Consuelo, 168
Zone of Silence, 226

ABOUT THE AUTHORS

Five years ago Terri and Mike Church put their careers on hold and set out to do some traveling. There was no way to stretch their budget to cover hotels and restaurants for anything like the length of time they wanted to be on the road. On the other hand living out of a backpack wasn't a particularly attractive idea either. RV's turned out to be the perfect compromise.

In their time on the road the Churches have toured the continental U.S., Europe, Alaska, and Mexico in one type of RV or another. During the course of their travels they began to notice that few guidebooks were available with the essential day-to-day information that camping travelers need when they are in unfamiliar surroundings. *The Traveler's Guide to European Camping, The Traveler's Guide to Mexican Camping,* and the soon to come *Traveler's Guide to Alaskan Camping* (actual title not yet final) are designed to be the guidebooks that the authors tried to find when they first traveled to these places.

Terri and Mike now have a base of operations in the Seattle, Washington area but they continue to spend at least nine months of each year traveling. The entire Europe book and most of the Mexico book were written and formatted using laptop computers while on the road.

NOTES

ORDER FORM

To order complete the following and send to:

Rolling Homes Press
P.O. Box 2099
Kirkland, WA 98083-2099

Name_____

Address_____

City_____ State_____ Zip_____

Send me:

☐ Traveler's Guide To Mexican Camping
☐ Traveler's Guide To European Camping
☐ Traveler's Guide To Alaskan Camping (Actual title
         not yet final - available in Spring 1998)

Payment $19.95 Plus $4.00 Shippin

_____X $23.95=____

Quantity   Amou

☐ Check   ☐ MC

Charge Card No._____

Authorized Signature_____

Authorized Charge Amount_____

Exp. Date_____

To order by phone call toll free in the U.
or outside the U.S. call (425) 8
Have your MC or VISA r

U.S. dollars or MC/VISA only for non-U.S. orders